BIRMINGHAM

THE WORKSHOP OF THE WORLD

BIRMINGHAM

THE WORKSHOP OF THE WORLD

Edited by

Carl Chinn and Malcolm Dick

LIVERPOOL UNIVERSITY PRESS

First published 2016 by
Liverpool University Press
4 Cambridge Street
Liverpool
L69 7ZU

British Library Cataloguing-in-Publication data
A British Library CIP record is available

978-1-78138-247-9 paperback
978-1-78138-246-2 cased
978-1-78138-245-5 slipcase

Front cover image: The Bullring, Birmingham (Pete Tripp/Getty Images)

Back cover image: The Lunar men and the Library of Birmingham on Broad Street. Copyright Elaine Mitchell.

Front endpaper: *The East Prospect of Birmingham, in the County of Warwick*, 1753. Samuel and Nathaniel Buck.
Reproduced with the permission of the Library of Birmingham. 13996

Back endpaper: *The South West Prospect of Birmingham, in the County of Warwick*, 1751. Samuel and Nathaniel Buck.
Reproduced with the permission of the Library of Birmingham. 97572

Typeset by Carnegie Book Production, Lancaster
Printed and bound by Gomer Press, Llandysul, Wales

*This book is dedicated to Dr Chris Upton (1953–2015):
historian, writer, teacher and colleague*

Contents

Acknowledgements

The editors wish to thank many individuals and organizations for their support for and contributions to *Birmingham: The Workshop of the World*. First, Birmingham City Council, the University of Birmingham and Mike Gibbs of History West Midlands Ltd contributed financially to the costs of production. The book would not have been possible without their sponsorship. Secondly, the commissioned authors enthusiastically agreed to contribute, submitted their manuscripts on time and responded positively to requests for changes, cuts or additions to their text. The chapters in this volume draw attention to recent work on Birmingham's history and select in a limited number of words from a substantial quantity of published and unpublished material. At the same time the authors were tasked with presenting the history of Birmingham in an accessible and interesting form. We think they have achieved these varied tasks and, in so doing, contributed to the most substantial, scholarly, illuminating and visually attractive one-volume history of Birmingham to date. Inevitably, a number of aspects of Birmingham's past have not been explored directly, as the Introduction makes clear. Nevertheless the editors and contributors have learned from many historians and archaeologists, living and dead, who have studied the history of a unique global city and helped to shape the writing of *Birmingham: The Workshop of the World*.

This book also depends for its appeal upon the quality of its illustrations. These have had to be chosen, evaluated, digitized, supplied and captioned. Picture research and editing require an understanding of history, sensitivity to design, knowledge of copyright legislation, technical abilities, imagination, accuracy, persistence, inventiveness and tact. Elaine Mitchell has fulfilled these requirements admirably; the attractiveness of this publication and the editorial relevance of the images are to her credit.

We are extremely grateful to several institutions for supplying images to illuminate the chapters. In Birmingham these include Assay Office Birmingham (Marion Wilson, Craig O'Donnell and Alexandre Parré); The Barber Institute of Fine Arts (Sarah Beattie); Birmingham City University (Benjamin Goodwin); The Birmingham Civic Society; Birmingham Museums Trust (Domniki Papadimitriou); The Birmingham Gun Barrel Proof House; The Library of Birmingham (Corinna Rayner and her staff); Marketing Birmingham; Newman University, Birmingham

(Ian Cawood, Christine Porter and Chris Wormwell); Royal Birmingham Society of Artists (Natalie Osborne); and University Hospitals Birmingham NHS Foundation Trust. At the University of Birmingham, images were provided by the Cadbury Research Library, Special Collections (Susan Worrall, Martin Killeen and Helen Fisher); Classics, Ancient History and Archaeology; College of Medical and Dental Sciences; Library Services (Steve Leigh); Research and Cultural Collections (Clare Mullett and Susan Franklin); and the Press Office. Pictures have also been obtained from the following organizations outside Birmingham: Balfour Beatty, Bridgeman Images, Cambridge University Library, The Ironbridge Gorge Museum Trust, Library of Congress, Mary Evans Picture Library, The National Archives, Oxford and Wessex Archaeology, Victoria and Albert Museum and Wellcome Library.

Individuals have also supplied photographs, prints and postcards or helped to secure permission to use them, including Shirley Baer, Alistair Carew-Cox, Fay Crofts, Karen Daw, Nigel Dodds, Mary Harding, Yvonne Jones, Stephanie Ratkai, Rob Sutton and Keith Wadsworth. Carl Chinn thanks Caitlin Chandra, Des E. Gershon, Roger Gwynn, Barbara Malla and Maureen Smojkis for personal images which he used in his chapter; Duncan Probert expertly produced maps for two chapters written by Stephen Bassett and Richard Holt and Richard Cust and Ann Hughes. Jenni Dixon and Averil Maskew provided their expertise in digitally enhancing a selection of images.

The editorial, design and production teams at Liverpool University Press have ensured that *Birmingham: The Workshop of the World* proceeded effectively from conception to birth. Alison Welsby, Editorial Director at LUP, has been a sensitive, supportive, efficient and highly professional editor. Without her belief in the book and her skills and expertise in translating a concept from commissioning to reader, the book would not exist.

We have dedicated this book to Chris Upton, who was commissioned to write the chapter on leisure in Birmingham. Tragically, he died before he could contribute to the book. We are grateful to Fiona Tait, Chris's wife, for giving her permission to dedicate *Birmingham: The Workshop of the World* to him.

Introduction

CARL CHINN and MALCOLM DICK

Trade has been the core of Birmingham's economic life since the granting of the market charter in 1166. This nineteenth-century image of the Market Hall, Worcester Street, draws attention to a building which housed many of the town's retail activities. From *Views in Birmingham and its Vicinity* by Charles Radclyffe, Birmingham, Knott Hawker & Coburn, c.1840. Courtesy of Newman University Library

The occasion for *Birmingham: The Workshop of the World* is the 850th anniversary in 2016 of the granting of a market charter by King Henry II to the lord of the manor, Peter de Birmingham, in 1166.[1] This event brought traders, entrepreneurs and workers into the town and marked the birth of modern Birmingham as a commercial and manufacturing centre. The justification for this publication is, however, the vast amount of investigation that has been conducted into the history of the city since the last academic study on the history of Birmingham, published between 1952 and 1974. The three volumes of the *Oxford University Press History of Birmingham*, commissioned by the City of Birmingham and written by Conrad Gill, Asa Briggs, Anthony Sutcliffe and Roger Smith,[2] were landmarks in local and national urban history, but the effervescence of archaeological and historical research during the last sixty years and the new perspectives of historians have rendered their approaches and findings, at least in part, incomplete and outdated. Their focus on a top-down narrative – the activities of local governments, major industries and important men – inevitably created a partial picture of Birmingham's diverse history and culture. Since the publication of those volumes, the demise of much heavy manufacturing has altered the local economy, the environment of both the central and suburban city has been dramatically transformed, and ethnic and religious change has shaped a new demographic landscape. The absence of major academic studies of Birmingham's history since these magisterial studies is surprising, given the complexity and significance of the changes that have taken place in the city. Gordon Cherry's survey of the landscape of Birmingham is one exception to this neglect.[3]

Birmingham: The Workshop of the World is the first substantial single-volume publication to present recent research into the prehistoric, medieval and modern

A sterling silver rattle with whistle, six bells, teething coral and swivel suspension ring made by George Unite and dated 1837. Birmingham industry was served by global trading links, in this case imported silver and coral.
By permission of Assay Office Birmingham

history of Birmingham. Some of this research is located in academic publications which are not easily accessible by the general reader, but a lot has not been published at all. The book moves beyond traditional political and economic perspectives and addresses education, the visual arts, medicine and print culture: areas, like politics and manufacturing, in which Birmingham people had a significant national as well as a local reputation. The history of Birmingham, moreover, cannot only be told by repeating traditional perspectives. Women and migrants have also influenced Birmingham's past. Birmingham has been a global city for centuries and working-class men, women and children have shaped and been shaped by the town.

Despite the newness of many of its findings, the book stands on the shoulders of previous historians. Individual authors in their chapters chart their antecedents explicitly, but it is appropriate in this Introduction to draw attention to changing emphases in the published general histories of the town over the past few decades. Writers have focused on three main areas: first, that Birmingham's emergence as a major city ought to be seen as evolutionary rather than revolutionary; secondly, that Birmingham's past needs to be interpreted in a more democratic and egalitarian way so that the contribution of all of its people is understood and appreciated; and thirdly, that, contrary to popular perceptions and the beliefs of most historians, Birmingham did have a history before its first documented mention in Domesday Book of 1086.

For generations it was presumed that Birmingham was thrust forward as a major settlement by the firing of the Industrial Revolution. Although acknowledging that the seventeenth century brought rapid growth and new enterprise to Birmingham, Conrad Gill's work focused largely on the town from 'the age of steam'. Moreover, he paid little attention to medieval Birmingham. He saw it as a village which evolved slowly from the granting of the 1166 market charter. In this mainly agricultural village there were a small number of merchants and manufacturing was of little importance.[4] This interpretation was challenged successfully by Richard Holt in 1985.[5] Though Birmingham's early years are poorly documented and the available sources are scattered, Holt showed that rapid economic growth was experienced after the coming of the market. The town changed swiftly from a small agricultural village into a prosperous manufacturing and market town. In the 1980s Victor Skipp drew attention to the outer areas of the city as well as the nucleus of the market town. Drawing on his research into local medieval manors, Skipp shied away from an over-centralist approach, although the story of Birmingham itself remained the thread with which he wove his history. His concentration was on Yardley and Sheldon and he had less material on Aston, Erdington, King's Norton and Harborne.[6]

The lack of information and analysis of the changing economy and experience of work on the part of Gill and Briggs was substantially rectified by Eric Hopkins. In two books, he explored the development of Birmingham since the second half of the eighteenth century and questioned existing interpretations of business and manufacturing which were contained in the *Victoria County History*. Birmingham's development during the Industrial Revolution of the late eighteenth and early nineteenth centuries was not marked by major technological innovations as in, for example, the cotton industry in north-west England. Instead, Birmingham became 'the first manufacturing town in the world' because of its varied industrial base, including a wealth of small firms, not always dependent upon technological innovation, and its ability to meet demand from domestic and overseas markets.[7]

In the 1990s Chris Upton wrote a general history of Birmingham for a wide audience which brought much recent research to the fore. He looked at Birmingham's beginnings before the market charter of 1166 by considering the archaeological and landscape evidence for human settlement before Domesday Book. Although taking a chronological approach, he covered themes that had traditionally been ignored by most local historians such as music, libraries and schools, and avoided attending only to the political and manufacturing history. Upton's book, however, focused mainly on central Birmingham and had less to say on the districts that joined the city from 1838 onwards.[8]

From the 1990s Carl Chinn, who also wrote for a wide audience, provided a different focus on Birmingham's history. Deeply affected by his researches into working-class life, manufacturing and ethnic minorities, he told Birmingham's history through the work of its people and emphasized the contribution made by all, whatever their class, ethnicity or gender.[9] Although his approach differed from previous historians, especially Gill and Briggs, who stressed the significance of major figures such as Matthew Boulton and Joseph Chamberlain, the two approaches were complementary. Briggs's work, for instance, focused on the civic gospel, the workings of local government and municipal socialism between 1865 and 1938, which provided the political framework within which people lived their lives.[10] Sutcliffe and Smith also pursued a top-down approach. Despite this focus, their book provided valuable information about the impact of the Second World War, post-war redevelopment and immigration from the New Commonwealth. In another publication, Chinn looked at the history of Birmingham through its place names. Influenced by the writings of Margaret Gelling, one of the foremost place-name authorities in Britain, Chinn examined the meaning of local place names, their recorded references and their development to the present day.[11] This approach built upon Skipp's desire to draw attention to the histories of Birmingham's districts as well as its central core.

Birmingham: The Workshop of the World builds upon these studies and brings specialist research in an accessible form to a general audience. In the first substantial chapter, Carl Chinn provides a changing picture of Birmingham's diverse peoples from earliest times until the present and provides the frame – that history is about people – within which the rest of the book is placed. Since the 1990s new research has been pursued into the history of Birmingham's prehistoric, Roman and medieval pasts. Michael Hodder's survey of prehistoric and Roman Birmingham presents and examines the substantial discoveries by archaeologists, which enable us to appreciate a past which was unknown to historians before 2000. Steven Bassett has investigated local Anglo-Saxon history. Before 1086 Birmingham itself (as opposed to its surrounding areas) had no recorded Anglo-Saxon history nor, indeed, have any examples of Anglo-Saxon archaeological finds been uncovered. Based on extensive research over twenty years, Bassett and Richard Holt explore the evolution of Birmingham from an insignificant village to a market town after 1166.[12] The town in the sixteenth and seventeenth centuries has been barely explored, but Richard Cust and Ann Hughes, in a chapter that contains much new research, provide an insight into a largely unknown period when Birmingham was beginning to expand economically and demographically.

For the post-1700 period, the book looks at several themes. Malcolm Dick surveys the history of the 'city of a thousand trades' up to 1945, by looking at how local writers and visitors have represented the changing economy of the town and how the town has been shaped by commerce, technology, war and the experience of work. Roger Ward combines the evolution of the town and city's local government with the interplay of national politics and local protest before the Second World War. The description of Birmingham as the 'best-governed city in the world' by the United States' journalist Julian Ralph was only one aspect of a complex political history. Ruth Watt considers both elite and popular instruction and the impact of educational ideas. Her chapter covers the education of boys and girls in schools and male and female students in institutions of higher education and notes how changing agendas have required the telling of new educational stories. Since the eighteenth century, art and design have been important features of the changing experience of Birmingham, though they are almost always excluded from conventional histories. Sally Hoban explores both men and women in painting, sculpture, architecture, education and design. The history of health and medicine is a relatively new area of research into Birmingham's history. Moving beyond the importance of medical pioneers and institutions, Jonathan Reinarz covers the changing history of healthcare, public health and medical personnel to provide a social and cultural history of the subject. Birmingham has been a particularly important national centre of printing and print culture since the eighteenth century. Caroline Archer-Parré

Dudley Street was a thoroughfare in nineteenth-century Birmingham. The presence of a Pickford's van is a reminder of a local business venture and the buildings reveal the variety of commercial activities. The buildings were due to be demolished when the image was made. From *The Buildings of Birmingham, Past and Present* by Thomas Underwood, Birmingham, 1866.
Private Collection

Arts and Crafts ceramic friezes on the façade of the Aston Webb buildings of the University of Birmingham, by Robert Anning Bell (1863–1933). These images celebrate the world of work. The university was a civic as well as an academic institution. It was created by local businessmen and provided opportunities for learning for local women and men.
© The University of Birmingham Research and Cultural Collections

gives due attention to great figures of typography such as John Baskerville, but she also looks at the diverse history of printing, bookselling, kinds of printing and printing education. Matt Cole considers the history of Birmingham since 1945 by focusing on the interplay between regeneration, redevelopment and economic change. Finally, Carl Chinn reviews very recent history and projects Birmingham's experience 'Forward into the Future'.

Birmingham's people, including its civic leaders, have attempted to reinvent the city during its history, but since 1945 the process of urban transformation

DUDLEY STREET.

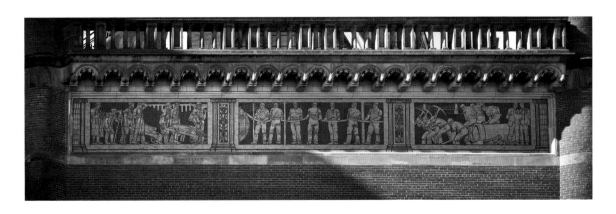

has proceeded particularly rapidly. The changes of all kinds that were altering Birmingham – and not only its landscape – while this book was being researched, written and published will provide new opportunities for investigation for future historians. The importance of Birmingham as a place of opportunities is the reason why the editors chose 'workshop of the world' as this book's subtitle. The label implies more than Birmingham's global economic significance: it identifies the town as a workshop for initiating, testing and implementing political, educational, medical and cultural ideas and practices throughout its history.

The editors are conscious that this book could have been shaped in other ways. The changing built environment of Birmingham has not been covered as a discrete entity but is explored within individual chapters. We could have looked distinctly at women's history, social class and religion after 1700, when the quantity of surviving records improves noticeably compared to earlier periods, but we reasoned that these areas of life were properly considered within other chapters which covered the shaping and impact of political, economic, social and cultural experiences. One area that we were unable to include was the history of leisure. It is important to appreciate the significance of sport, music and popular entertainment in shaping local life and Dr Chris Upton, Reader in Public History at Newman University, was commissioned to write a history of leisure for this book. Very sadly, at the end of 2015, Chris died following a brave battle with cancer before he could complete his chapter. This book is dedicated to his memory.

Birmingham's Frankfurt Christmas market and craft fair. Birmingham's commercial and cultural connections with the wider world are celebrated in the annual Frankfurt Fair, which is held in the historic centre of civic Birmingham just before Christmas.
Courtesy of Marketing Birmingham

Notes

1 See Bassett and Holt in this volume.

2 C. Gill, *History of Birmingham vol. I, Manor and Borough to 1865* (London and New York, 1952); A. Briggs, *History of Birmingham vol. II, Borough and City, 1865–1938* (London and New York, 1952); A. Sutcliffe and R. Smith, *History of Birmingham vol. III, Birmingham 1939–1970* (Oxford, 1974).

3 G. Cherry, *Birmingham: A Study in Geography, History and Planning* (Chichester, 1994). See also M. Hodder, *Birmingham: The Hidden History* (Stroud, 2004) and C. Patrick and S. Ratkai, *The Bull Ring Uncovered: Excavations at Edgbaston Street, Moor Street, Park Street and The Row, Birmingham, 1997–2001* (Oxford, 2009).

4 Gill, *Manor and Borough*.

5 R. Holt, *The Early History of the Town of Birmingham, 1166 to 1600* (Oxford, 1985).

6 V. Skipp, *History of Greater Birmingham down to 1830* (Birmingham, 1980); see also V. Skipp, *The Making of Victorian Birmingham* (Birmingham, 1983).

7 E. Hopkins, *Birmingham: The First Manufacturing Town in the World, 1760–1840* (London, 1989), republished as *The Rise of the Manufacturing Town: Birmingham and the Industrial Revolution* (Stroud, 1998); E. Hopkins, *Birmingham: The Making of the Second City* (Stroud, 2001); the relevant chapters in the *Victoria County History* are D.E.C. Eversley, 'Economic and social history: industry and trade, 1500–1880', and B.M.D. Smith, 'Economic and social history: industry and trade, 1880–1960', in W.B. Stephens (ed.), *A History of the County of Warwick. Volume VII: The City of Birmingham*, Victoria County History (London, 1964), 81–208, http://www.british-history.ac.uk/vch/warks/vol7/ (accessed 31 December 2015).

8 C. Upton, *A History of Birmingham* (Chichester, 1993).

9 C. Chinn, *Birmingham: The Great Working City* (Birmingham, 1994).

10 Briggs, *Borough and City*.

11 C. Chinn, *One Thousand Years of Brum* (Birmingham, 1999).

12 S. Bassett, 'Anglo-Saxon Birmingham', *Midland History*, 25 (2000): 1–27.

CHAPTER ONE

The Peoples of Birmingham

CARL CHINN

With its high-rise towers, wide American-style roadways and underpasses, and futuristic shopping malls, Birmingham is a contemporary city from which the past seems to have been banished and where each generation knocks down the buildings put up by its predecessors. A city of change, adaptation and inventiveness, its modernity is heightened by a belief that Birmingham emerged suddenly almost from nothing as a creation of the Industrial Revolution. Yet Birmingham is not a phenomenon of the modern world only; instead it has deep roots. Still, while we know that people have lived within its bounds for thousands of years, they are anonymous before the tumultuous Dark Ages. Then, around the time of the Staffordshire Hoard, the first name appears: *Beorma*, whose folk founded the settlement named after him. His name is all that we know of him and it suggests that he and his group were immigrants: Angles, a Germanic people, moving westwards from their original conquests in eastern England.

Although it is likely that they intermingled with the existing British population, the Anglo-Saxon takeover changed the language and the great majority of place names, some of which remember men from the early Middle Ages.[1] Machitone, recalled in Mackadown Lane in Sheldon, was Macca's farm; Honesworde, Handsworth, was the enclosure (worth) around the homestead of Hun; and Egbaldestone, Edgbaston, meant Ecgbald's farm.[2] Victor Skipp's pioneering investigation of Yardley draws attention to two other Anglo-Saxon men: Leomann, after whom a way was named, and Mund, brought to mind in Moundsley in King's Norton; while several others are recorded as holding or having held manors in Domesday Book of 1086. They are Godmund of Aston, Stannechetel of Witton, Alnoth of Mackadown, Aelfwold of Northfield (remembered in Alwold Road),

A view looking up Moat Lane towards St Martin's in the Bull Ring during the inter-war years. On the left is Smithfield, the wholesale fruit and vegetable market, which stood on the site of the manor house of the lords of Birmingham. Later known as the Moat House, it was cleared and its moat filled in for an open market for the sale of beasts, hay and straw that opened in 1817. Part of this area was then built upon in 1884 for the Smithfield Covered Vegetable Market, which was soon extended to include the former pig market, and in 1903 it was renamed the Wholesale Fruit and Vegetable Market. This building was knocked down for the new Wholesale Markets in the early 1970s and in 2015 plans were revealed to demolish these markets and move them to Witton.
BirminghamLives Archive

Wibert of Selly (recalled in Wibert Close, Selly Oak), and Tumi and Elwe of Weoley.[3]

Given the lack of Scandinavian settlement in the Birmingham district, the Norman Conquest of 1066 and its aftermath brought the first significant influx of new peoples since the coming of the Anglo-Saxons. They were knights and men-at-arms, and perhaps their families, who had supported Duke William, and who came from Normandy, Brittany, Flanders and elsewhere in northern France. Among them may have been a number of lords mentioned in Domesday Book: Richard of Birmingham, Peter of Erdington, Robert of Weoley, Drew of Edgbaston, and Drogo of Handsworth and Perry.[4] Their overlord was Ansculf from Picguiny on the River Somme, who was given the barony of Dudley, to which Birmingham then belonged, in about 1070. This lordship passed to the Paganells by 1095. Hailing from Moustier-Herbert in France, they are brought to mind in Paganel Road in Weoley Castle.[5]

But the story both of Birmingham's emergence as a great city and of its people really begins in 1166, a century after the Battle of Hastings, when the lord of the manor, Peter de Bermingham, obtained a royal charter to hold a weekly market at his 'castle'. Thereafter Birmingham grew strongly as a manufacturing and commercial centre, and it was these firm foundations that enabled its 'take off' in the age of industrialization and urbanization. Yet there is something unusual about Birmingham's growth and success, for unlike most great centres of population it was not facilitated by providential physical or geographical features. Landlocked in the middle of England, it could not reach out to the markets of the world through a port; and distant from major rivers such as the Avon and the Severn, it was not connected to those markets by a navigable waterway. Nor is Birmingham a defensive site such as Dudley or Warwick, while below its ground there were none of the deposits of coal, iron ore, fire clay or limestone that were so essential for the Industrial Revolution.

For its expansion into an important city, Birmingham relied almost entirely upon the talents of its people and upon the relationships they formed. So who were these people and where did they come from and, in the succeeding centuries, who were those who followed them and whence did they move?[6] Because it includes surnames, a detailed analysis of the origins of the people of Birmingham a few generations after its foundation as a town is enabled by the borough rental of 1296, discovered by George Demidowicz. Over 300 individuals were recorded, most with a forename and surname, of which latter 160 are unique. Demidowicz noted that the three surnames of Jones, Prys and Brangwayn, meaning fair raven in Welsh, would seem to indicate immigration from Wales; and that of John de Parys implied that he was French. Other surnames arising from first names point to ethnic ancestry: the Old English of Edrich, Edwyn and Aldich; the Old Norse of Asketel and Anketel; and the Norman French of Gerard. However, with 40 per cent of the total, the most numerous last names relate to a place and are usually preceded by 'de' (of) or, more rarely, 'atte' (at).[7]

Importantly, this rental was recorded in the midst of a period when surnames were adopted by people other than barons and knights – a trend especially noticeable among merchants, craftsmen and burgesses in general.[8] Moreover, last names connected to places have been interpreted as direct evidence of immigration into medieval towns because the incomers were identified by the location from where they came. Of this type of surname in the rental, 60 per cent can be associated with a specific place, with two-thirds of them within a ten-mile radius of Birmingham. They included districts now within the city such as Aston, Deritend, Erdington, Bordesley, Duddeston, Edgbaston, Selly, King's Norton, Moseley, Billesley and Greet. Other surnames within that circle were Coventry, Hampton, Packwood and Studley in Warwickshire, and Cofton in Worcestershire. But the most numerous surnames related to parts of Worcestershire and Staffordshire in the modern Black Country, such as Barr, Bilston, Dudley, Halesowen, Oldbury, Rowley, Smethwick, Walsall and Wednesfield. The evidence indicates that Birmingham looked to its immediate hinterland for its people and its economic bonds and emphasizes that then, as today, there was a particularly strong bond to the west. Other names related to localities were likely to have come from within the manor of Birmingham, which included a large rural district. Two that are identifiable are Ladywell (recalled in Ladywell Walk) and Wynesdon (Winson Green). Their inclusion, and others yet to be recognized, would significantly boost the number of surnames from the ten-mile sphere, and as Demidowicz highlights, 'confirm that most immigrants arrived from places closest to the town'.[9]

Demidowicz also found the 1344–45 borough rental, compiled at the end of a particularly formative time for the adoption of surnames.[10] The Birmingham document contains about 290 personal names, of which 170 are unique. In all, 35 per

cent have a 'de' prefix. Of these, 58 per cent represented new place names. Among them were several areas of modern Birmingham: Bartley (Green), Handsworth, Spark(brook), Nechells, Saltley, Witton and Shard (End). To them can be added Coleshill, Curdworth, Elmdon, Hinkley and Middleton in Warwickshire. Only a few place names were connected to more distant places, such as Shutteford in Oxfordshire and Burkeby, near Hay-on-Wye. Demidowicz reflected that 'in an earlier period of vigorous immigration, it would be tempting to consider such names as indicating newcomers'. Despite his caution, he concluded that 'many of the people bearing these names arrived in the fifty years between the rentals, for how else would they have gained them?'[11]

Importantly, the two borough rentals included a few women. In 1296 appear Felic[ia] the Tipper, Isabell[a] the Sonster (perhaps songster), Julia the Whitemaiden, Marg[eria] of Ham[p]ton, Isold[a] of Moseley, Cristina of Edgbaston and Crist[ina] in the Dale, the modern Dale End, who is mentioned several times. As for the 1344–45 document, it named Felic[ia] Barre, Marg[ereta] Micel (meaning a large amount), Agneta the Bailiff and Cristina[a] the Muleward (perhaps the later Millward and meaning miller).[12]

It is evident that Birmingham was continuing to pull in newcomers from its immediate hinterland. By contrast, the agricultural parish of Yardley did not attract outsiders, as demonstrated by Skipp's study of the 1272 Lay Subsidy Rolls.[13] Indeed this parish in the Forest of Arden was more likely to send people to Birmingham,

Much of Yardley remained agricultural until the housing developments of the inter-war years, which followed its incorporation by Birmingham in 1911. This photograph of three horses led by a boy pulling an iron-framed plough and guided by an older man highlights the continuity of older ways close to the ever-changing city. It was taken at Field House farm, Stechford, on an autumn day in the 1890s by George Wilkes, a Yardley man. Many of his impressive and evocative photographs were given to Birmingham Museum and Art Gallery in 1957. However, this particular photograph is from a collection acquired by the late Phil Waldren and handed to the BirminghamLives Archive.
BirminghamLives Archive

as exemplified by Richard Smallbrook, one of the most successful men in the Tudor town. By the 1550s he had substantial property holdings in both Yardley and Birmingham, as well as elsewhere, and he became one of the first governors of King Edward's School in 1552. William Colmore the elder and William Colmore the younger were two others of that select body, and their family also originated in the Forest, from Solihull. Involved both in commerce and buying land, they became the most powerful and wealthy family locally, and branches of the Colmores remained in the city until the twentieth century.[14] Two other families connected to the town also maintained long connections with it: they were the Holtes, who gained the manor of Aston in 1366 and who lived there until the late eighteenth century; and the Middlemores, lords of Hawksley, Hazelwell and Edgbaston, who had a strong presence until the early twentieth century.[15]

After the fourteenth century there are no sources yet available relating to migration until the settlement certificates of 1686–1726. Arising from the 1662 Poor Relief Act (the Settlement Act), these were only issued to the poor and less well off when they left the parish to which they belonged. Some parishes gave certificates conscientiously and regularly, while others did not. Consequently, W.H.B. Court advised that it would be 'unwise to suppose that all of those who came to Birmingham carried certificates and that here we have a total figure of those entering the town'. Yet, though 'not an ideal sample of the mass of comers-in', he argued that the certificates did illustrate movement into the town over forty-one years.

Altogether, 695 certificates give the name and parish of origin of the newcomer. An analysis of their distribution by counties makes clear the ongoing dominance of local migrants, with 77.5 per cent coming from the surrounding counties of Warwickshire, Staffordshire and Worcestershire. As in the past, people tended to have moved from places that were closer to Birmingham. Indeed over thirty of those from Warwickshire hailed from the parish of Aston, Birmingham's neighbour on the north, north-east and south-east. Interestingly, a strong bond with Shropshire further west was made evident by 43 incomers. By contrast only 35 people had moved from the east midlands, while there were almost as many migrants, 30, from the three northern counties of Lancashire, Cheshire and Yorkshire. Middlesex, London and Surrey provided another 22.

Until 1692, no person was recorded from anywhere but the four main counties, but among the later certificates were immigrants from Montgomery, Monmouth, Denbigh, Radnor and Flint in Wales. There were also two from Scotland and one from Ireland. Court felt that 'although there may be something accidental here it is probable that with the lapse of years, Birmingham actually was recruiting from a wider area'. That this would be a slow development was to be expected given that long-distance travel was made formidable by both a lack of transport and 'the network of personal acquaintance and experience upon which the whole process of immigration depended'. Based on his findings, Court asserted that the 'seventeenth century began to dig the channels along which, for a long time to come, the human resources of the surrounding country flowed into Birmingham'. In fact, those channels had been dug in the later Middle Ages but the evidence for succeeding generations reinforces his assertion that the migrants between 1686 and 1726 'pretty certainly followed lines very similar to those taken by the migrants of a century or more later'.[16]

R.A.S. Pelham also discussed the settlement certificates, dividing the migrants into three zones. The inner encompassed Birmingham's boundary as it was in 1937; the middle included newcomers from the remaining parts of Warwickshire, Worcestershire and Staffordshire; and the outer related to those from further away.[17] Alan Parton adopted Pelham's methodology in his examination of a second set of Poor Law settlement certificates from 1726 to 1757. This was a period of remarkable growth for Birmingham when it was on the cusp of the Industrial Revolution, with its population burgeoning from about 23,000 in 1731 to over 42,000 in 1778. Parton's findings supported Court's belief that Birmingham had begun to draw in people from a greater area. Migrants from the inner zone had made up almost 46 per cent of the total from 1686–97, but between 1698 and 1726 that figure dropped to 26.1 per cent and then to 18.9 per cent for 1727–57. This fall was matched by a rise in those coming to Birmingham from the middle zone, from 47 per cent to almost 51 per cent and finally to 60 per cent. Parton observed that these figures reinforced the notion that Birmingham 'was increasingly becoming the centre of the West Midlands region'.

By mapping the migrants from the middle zone Parton also recognized the effect of 'distance-decay', whereby the interaction was less between Birmingham and places

Celebrations at the Gate Inn, Studley Street, Sparkbrook, in 1910 for the coronation of King George V; my Granddad Chinn is sitting on the kerb to the right of the woman with the large hat. Studley Street had a high proportion of people who had been born in Birmingham or nearby and my own family exemplified the preponderance of local migrants among poorer Brummies.
BirminghamLives Archive

that were further away. In particular, the majority of moves were up to fifteen miles from the town with 'a directional bias towards the north-west; that is including the Black Country settlements towards Walsall and Wolverhampton'. Parton deduced that 'this pattern may well be related to Birmingham's trade and commercial relationships with this area reflecting linkages within the coal-producing, metal-making and metal-using districts'. Beyond fifteen miles, the scatter of contributing settlements was more haphazard with no clear patterns of movement emerging. And although the number of people settling in Birmingham from the outer zone also grew, there was a clear concentration from districts fringing the middle zone. Few migrants came from distances beyond sixty miles from Birmingham, with the exception of London, which, because of its size, contributed a large number of people.[18]

Birmingham's population rose dramatically as it developed into a major manufacturing town. By the first census of 1801 it numbered 60,822 for the area covered by the ancient parish alone. Thirty years later, that population had almost doubled to 110,914. Much of this massive increase was the result of migration and not natural increase, and it seems that incomers from the town's hinterland remained in the majority.[19] However, there is no detailed investigation of that movement although, through the 1881 Census, Carl Chinn compared the origins of the inhabitants of three streets reflecting different strata of the working class in West Sparkbrook. Studley Street was the poorest and while 45 per cent of its people were born in Birmingham, a mere 12.5 per cent were from outside the region. By contrast, Saint Paul's Road, the highest status, only had 31.5 per cent Birmingham born, with 27 per cent from outside. One explanation for this stark difference is that as a centre of multiform industry, Birmingham drew in skilled men from all over the country and with their better pay they would be more likely to live in roads of higher status.[20]

An in-depth approach was taken by Margaret Jager in her research into migratory patterns in the Jewellery Quarter. She related this to Anderson's work on Preston through the 1851 Census – the first that required details of the birthplace of individuals by county and town or parish.[21] Jager picked 17 streets that reflected class distinctions and strata within a class and included all their residents. Even accounting for the probability of errors, incorrect census information, omissions and shortfalls, her results were suggestive. She found that a very high percentage had been born in Birmingham and that most migration was from a short distance, while there was 'a consistent decrease in strength of migratory flow with an increase in distance from Birmingham'. As in the past, the strongest bond was with 'the densely populated and highly industrialised Black Country which had a large pool of potential migrants with trade experiences and skills that would have been easily transferable to Birmingham trades and industries'. E.G. Ravenstein was the pioneer of the study of migration in 1885, and in partial support of one his 'laws' that 'families rarely migrate', Jager noticed that households without children showed the strongest flows at the longer distances. Although Birmingham's size meant that it offered more scope for movement within its own bounds than did Preston, in

her view the high number of locally born people may have been an indicator that Birmingham was eminently capable of retaining its native inhabitants.[22]

Overall, most of the migrants appeared to have come from the area immediately surrounding Birmingham and there was evidence of both single and multiple step migration. My own family provides an example of these phenomena. The Chinn side goes back to 1619, to Rowington in the Forest of Arden. That was within Pelham's middle zone, but by the early nineteenth century the family was in King's Norton in his inner zone – as was Sparkbrook where my widowed great, great grandmother and her children settled in the 1870s. By contrast, the Derricks, the most distant ancestors of my father's mother, were from Ireland but were living in Bilston in the Black Country in 1841 and forty years later were also in Sparkbrook. Similarly, the Perrys, the family of my mother's father, were from the Black Country, in their case from Dudley, and moved to Highgate, next to Sparkbrook, in the 1870s. As for my mother's maternal grandparents, they arrived in the city in 1915, making their home in Whitehouse Street, Aston where they had relatives; the Woods came from Tewkesbury, but had working associations with Birmingham, while the Kendalls were from Worcester, in Pelham's outer zone but at the furthest edge of Birmingham's orbit.[23]

All sides of my family lived in badly built and insanitary back-to-backs, as did almost 200,000 other Brummies by 1918. Helen Butcher, née Smith, knew only too well the hardships of poverty and bad housing. Born in 1917, she lived in the Big Yard in Sheepcote Street, near the junction with Broad Street, in an 'attic-high' back-to-back. This had a single ground-floor room, bedroom, attic and cellar. Outside in the shared yard was a single water tap for nine families, communal toilets, the 'miskins' (dustbins) and the 'brewhouse', washhouse. Butcher recalled that when 'the suff [drain] in the yard was blocked the water would seep into our cellar. Soon the damp would rise up the walls and the snails would follow with the "black bats" [beetles], so food was kept in a cupboard which hung in the living room.' As in all back-to-backs 'everything happened in our ground floor living room: cooking, eating, washing'.[24]

Like the majority of poorer Brummies, Butcher and my family spoke with a strong accent and used dialect words that originated in the later Middle Ages, some of which were familiar to Shakespeare, for like Butcher, he also mentioned the brewhouse and the suff.[25] The pronunciation 'mon' for 'man' also provided a powerful connection with the past. In the Anglo-Saxon period, Mercians turned 'a' into 'o' before a nasal consonant such as 'n', 'm' and 'ng'. Thus they would have said mon for man, hond for hand and lond for land.[26] This pronunciation was written down in a legal document relating to Little Bromwich from the reign of Edward III (1330–77), which referred to 'Warnereslond', Warner's land. Remarkably this linguistic feature has survived strongly into the twenty-first century in Birmingham and the Black Country, with the use of mom as the diminutive for mother instead of mam or mum.[27]

As for the word 'miskin', it derives from the Old English word 'mixen', meaning dung and later dung heap. In the communal yards of back-to-back housing, the miskin was an old-style ash pit surrounded by brick walls.[28] In the 1920s Percy Shurmer, a champion of Birmingham's poor and later Labour MP for Sparkbrook, campaigned for improvements in back-to-back yards, and sometimes, to force both landlords and the council into action, he and his supporters knocked down crumbling communal brewhouses and the decrepit miskin walls over which rubbish overflowed. They were replaced by dustbins, which then were called miskins, while Shurmer himself was hailed as 'the Miskin King'.[29]

The importance of local migration to Birmingham remained a constant from the later Middle Ages until at least the early twentieth century; indeed, in 1951 71 per cent of the city's people had been born in Warwickshire (including Birmingham).[30] By then, nevertheless, the appeal of Birmingham to migrants from distant parts of England had become more pronounced, and this trend was increasingly apparent from the early nineteenth century. Joseph Gillott was one of those long-distance migrants. Leaving Sheffield in about 1822, he soon found a job in Birmingham and then set up as a small gaffer in the light steel toy trade whence he moved into making steel pens. Helped by his wife, Maria Mitchell, Gillott was spectacularly successful. His pens sold across the world and he became so wealthy that he owned much of Rotton Park, an estate near London, and a wonderful collection of paintings by Turner and others.[31]

Gillott was a rarity, having made his fortune from little, although the input of his wife should not be overlooked.[32] Unlike him, the great majority of those who prospered during and after the Industrial Revolution started with some capital or else with influential connections. Among them was Charles Geach, a Cornishman who became a senior figure in the Bank of England in Birmingham, then a leading promoter of the Birmingham and Midland Bank and later a wealthy industrialist and MP.[33] Another was Richard Tipper Cadbury, a Quaker from Exeter. In 1794, after serving his apprenticeship as a draper, he and a friend opened a shop in Bull Street. They had the goodwill of a Mr Phillips of London who wrote to the powerful manufacturer Matthew Boulton to introduce them to his notice and patronage. It was Cadbury's son, John, who began making cocoa and chocolate and his two grandsons, Richard and George, who built up the chocolate-making business in Bournville into a global concern.[34]

Londoners also played a vital role in Birmingham and three in particular helped to transform Birmingham into the 'best-governed city in the world'. They were the nonconformist preacher George Dawson and Congregationalist minister Robert Dale, through their belief in a civic gospel; and Joseph Chamberlain, a Unitarian, who as a dynamic mayor pushed through a radical programme of municipal socialism. Indeed, relative to their small numbers, Unitarians and Quakers had

An atmospheric photograph looking down Broad Street in August 1952. On the right, and just past the car, is the Crown pub on the corner of King Edward's Place and behind it is the elegantly designed Unitarian Church of the Messiah. For a few decades in the later nineteenth century this was arguably the most important place of worship in Birmingham because of its association with influential families such as the Chamberlains, Byngs, Kenricks and Martineaus and because it was the centre of the local women's movement.
BirminghamLives Archive

a disproportionately important economic and political effect upon Birmingham. Unitarian families like the Byngs, Kenricks and Martineaus were particularly active on the council, while Helen Plant emphasized that during the 1870s and 1880s women's rights organizations in Birmingham were dominated by those connected with the city's leading Unitarian chapel, the Church of the Messiah. Its minister, Henry Crosskey, preached a 'feminist gospel' and his wife, Hannah, was a prominent member of the local Women's Liberal Federation along with Caroline and Mary Kenrick, Hannah Crosskey and Catherine Osler.[35] A prominent advocate of women's rights, Osler was secretary and then president of the Birmingham Women's Suffrage Society, and through her position strove to reach out to working-class women and understand their problems.[36]

Nineteenth-century writers increasingly emphasized the importance of nonconformist migrants to the development of Birmingham in the later seventeenth century and their positive effect on the town's rapid growth thereafter. They asserted that the town was a magnet because of its absence of guilds and their restrictions and, as the council eagerly proclaimed in 1938, because it had been a refuge for 'relatively large numbers of educated and religious minded people, chafing under restrictions imposed on their religious opinions elsewhere'. These immigrants had 'contributed to the furtherance of that particular type of individualism which to this day is considered to characterize much of the industrial life of the city'. As emphasized in the *Victoria County History* in 1964, 'such an assessment appears to be purely deductive, and has yet to be sustained by material evidence'.[37] It remains so.

The Welsh Presbyterian church (Welsh Calvinistic Methodists) in Suffolk Street in 1957. This building was opened in 1898 to replace the chapel in Granville Street, where the congregation had worshipped since 1849. The demolition of the Suffolk Street chapel and another Welsh chapel led to the Bethel Presbyterian Church of Wales which was opened in 1968 on Holloway Head.
BirminghamLives Archive

Pelham's research into the growth of settlement and industry in Birmingham provided no evidence for a perceptible increase in its population immediately before 1680, by which time the most stringent laws against nonconformists had been relaxed, while they accounted for a negligible proportion of the total population of Birmingham.[38] Moreover, as the chapter by Richard Cust and Ann Hughes reveals, although the town was viewed as a refuge for Puritan ministers, from the later seventeenth century it was also beset by serious and deep religious divisions. The Presbyterians, later to become Unitarians, were small in number but prosperous and influential, and their beliefs, attitudes and wealth aroused the anger of the Anglican elite, such as the Holtes, as well as that of the Anglican poor. That anger erupted into riots in 1715 but it did not disappear. Resentment towards the Unitarians again resulted in violence in 1791 during the Church and King riots.[39]

One nonconformist family, the Quaker Lloyds of Dolobran in Montgomeryshire, arrived in Birmingham in the later seventeenth century and made a significant impression through manufacturing and banking; but it was the marriage of Elizabeth Lloyd to the wealthy local Quaker, John Pemberton, that led to the move and not a desire to seek refuge.[40] The Kenricks from Denbighshire also made their mark as cast iron manufacturers in West Bromwich and local politicians in Birmingham. The Welsh were as influential culturally. Edward Burne-Jones, the celebrated stained glass artist, had Welsh ancestors, as did John Henry Langford. A self-taught working man who strove for the improvement of the working class, Langford became a journalist, compiler of histories of Birmingham, and campaigner for free parks and free libraries. Growing up, though, he had known hard times, as did many of the Welsh in Birmingham.[41] Indeed, in 1824 their difficult situation induced several wealthy men connected to Wales to start a Saint David's Society to help the estimated 5,000–7,000 Welsh labouring families residing within fourteen miles of Birmingham.[42]

The bond between Birmingham and Wales had been forged in the later Middle Ages, when Welsh drovers from Brecon and Radnorshire brought cattle to Birmingham. Richard Holt believed that this trade must have been well established by the sixteenth century when one end of the cattle market in High Street was called the Welsh Market.[43] Migrants from those counties and elsewhere continued to move to Birmingham into the twentieth century, but from the 1920s, as Brinley Thomas emphasized, South Welsh were to the fore in migration to the midlands.[44] Leslie John Jones from the Rhondda was one of them. Aged 16 in 1937, he left rather than be condemned to a life of dire poverty through the closure of the coal mines. He joined his two older brothers in Small Heath and quickly found well-paid work in a variety of factories, as did most Welsh newcomers.[45] A conspicuous number were teachers and they maintained a strong presence in Birmingham schools into the later twentieth century. Although the South Welsh were not gathered in one area, they were noticeable in Tyseley, where some were employed at the large Great Western Railway Loco depot. Their presence was reinforced after the Second World War when Arthur Lloyd, a director of the local Bakelite factory, recruited 200 men from his home area of the Rhondda Valley.[46]

Women workers in front of a priming shed at the ammunition works of George Kynoch in Witton in the late 1880s or early 1890s. In the middle is Mrs McNab. She had joined the company in 1862 as a 12-year-old and was one of its first thirteen employees of one man and twelve young women. From 1872 until she retired in 1902 she was in charge of the percussion cap department, operating it with efficiency and dedication. As such, she was crucial to Kynoch's gaining a world-wide reputation for its caps with output reaching an annual peak of 449 million caps a year in the 1880s.
BirminghamLives Archive

In 1951 there were twelve counties in England and Wales which were of primary importance for sending people to Birmingham. Six of them were in the Principality and, in total, 25,000 people were Welsh born.[47] This was less than the Irish, but greater than the Scots. Yet despite their small numbers, the Scots had a significant impact upon Birmingham, not least through two celebrated inventors and engineers associated with Matthew Boulton: James Watt from Greenock, and William Murdock from Cumnock.[48] Another influential figure was George Kynoch. A bank clerk from Peterhead in Aberdeenshire, after moving to Birmingham he eventually took over an ammunition company and oversaw its rapid expansion at Witton. As president of Aston Villa from 1887, Kynoch knew another Scotsman, William McGregor. A draper and committee member of Aston Villa, it was through his vision and planning that the English Football League was organized in 1888.[49]

In spite of such influential Scots, their numbers were small until the inter-war years when the heavy industries of central Scotland were hit hard by the Depression. One of those who left was Bill Henry from Lanarkshire. After losing his pit job, he was unable get work in the steel plants of Motherwell, which were believed to hire only Protestants and not Roman Catholics like him. As a result, he hitched a lift to Birmingham where he had a cousin in Small Heath. Henry became a blacksmith's striker at BSA, where he met his wife, Cath Shields, also from Lanarkshire. A single woman, she had been directed to work at the company early in the Second World War. Another Roman Catholic, she too had experienced religious discrimination in Scotland and its absence in Birmingham impressed her so much that she felt 'more fond of Birmingham than youse. Youse took everything for granted.'[50]

Jones felt that local people feared that the Welsh would work for less money and so there was 'a little mistrust of the new inhabitants'. He added that the Scots and Irish who followed the Welsh influx had the same experiences and that 'with others to contend with, the Welsh were more acceptable'.[51] This migration of the

Irish noted by Jones was the second to Birmingham, the first having begun in the mid-1820s when deteriorating economic conditions devastated much of rural Ireland.[52] The Irish population then peaked at 11,322 in 1861, which was 3.8 per cent of the population. Both figures dropped in the following years and the Irish never formed as large a proportion as they did in Liverpool, Manchester and Glasgow; yet they did constitute the largest ethnic minority in nineteenth-century Birmingham and had a considerable impact on local affairs.

Most of the pioneers came from Connacht, in the west of Ireland, and were spalpeens, seasonal agricultural labourers. Arriving annually in Liverpool from Dublin or Sligo Town, they headed south via Manchester and the Potteries to Birmingham, where many of them rented a bed in lodging houses in the poorest streets. Soon an increasing number stayed throughout the year and were joined by others intent on permanent settlement. The 1851 Census provides snatches of evidence about some of them, such as John Noon. A blacksmith aged 40, he was living at 24 Smallbrook Street with his wife, Jane, and two cousins. All were from Roscommon. Three other Noon cousins aged between 15 and 28 lodged at the house. They were born in Birmingham, signifying that members of the family had moved from Roscommon sometime in the early 1820s.[53]

By 1851 the Irish in Birmingham had increased dramatically because of the Famine. Most lived in the older, overcrowded and central localities of the town, although there was no distinctive 'Little Ireland' as Engels described in Manchester.[54] Still, certain streets did stand out as having a strong Irish presence and here people from Roscommon, Mayo, Galway and Sligo made up the great majority. However, only in Henrietta Street did the enumerator note the parish of birth of a significant number of Irish migrants. This provides vital information on the importance of chain migration. Of the 70 who came from Roscommon, the most numerous were from Elphin, Tulsk, Kilkeeven, Oran and Rathcarn. County, township and kinship networks were essential in the emergence of the Irish community in Birmingham, as Chinn's researches revealed, but so too were occupational linkages.[55]

However they had been pulled to Birmingham, the Irish faced religious and racial discrimination and were blamed unfairly for their insanitary living conditions.[56] Patsy Davies made it clear that they also shared the general experience of the Irish in England in that they were more likely than the indigenous population to be victimized by the police and imprisoned. This was highlighted in the Murphy Riots of 1867 when an English mob attacked the Irish and sacked their homes in Park Street.[57] Yet at a time when Birmingham's population was expanding rapidly and new buildings were essential for work and homes, English builders relied overwhelmingly on the hard work and skills of Irish labourers because the English poor preferred factory work.[58]

Park Street, a few days after the Murphy Riots of 1867. On the right is W. Broughton, stables and cartmaker, and next door is the Old Phoenix Inn. Six years before, the Census had recorded 79 Irish households in the street, and overwhelmingly they lived between the Phoenix and Bordesley Street. The Irish presence in this part of the street had been noticeable since the mid-1820s when agricultural labourers, mostly from Mayo and Galway, had begun to settle there.
BirminghamLives Archive

A sing-a-long at the Benyon Arms, Hockley, in the 1950s, with players of the famous Shamrock Rovers and their friends and families. Manager Ned Grogan is sitting on the left of the piano. The team played in green and white hoops and was highly successful in amateur football locally. But Shamrock Rovers was not only a football team but also a social club for the wives, girlfriends and children of the players, most of whom were Irish, and each Saturday night all the adults congregated at the Benyon which was the club's headquarters.
BirminghamLives Archive

As the Irish-born population declined from 1861, their children also moved into manufacturing, a phenomenon noted by John Denvir in 1892. He also felt that there were few other places where the Irish were more intermixed and intermarried into the general population than in Birmingham.[59] Chinn's research supported these views, although the ongoing importance of Irish cultural and political organizations was emphasized by James Moran in his work, which not only studied the Irish in Birmingham but also examined how events in the city influenced leading Irish political figures and dramatists.[60] In turn, Irish figures made a significant political and civic impact on Birmingham, including the Revd Thomas M. McDonnell of St Peter's Catholic church in Broad Street, who was the first Irish priest in the town and the only Catholic on the council of the Birmingham Political Union.[61] Another was John Frederick Feeney from Sligo. He came to Birmingham in 1835 as a journalist on a radical newspaper and later bought the weekly *Birmingham Journal*. In 1857 he started the *Birmingham Daily Post* with John Jaffray, a Scot from Stirling who had arrived in 1844. Jaffray and Feeney's son, John, established the *Birmingham Daily Mail* in 1870 and nineteen years later they set up the Birmingham Mail Christmas Tree charity to raise funds for 'toys and cash to brighten the lives of poor children in hospital'. John Feeney was also an outstanding benefactor to Birmingham's Art Gallery, the University of Birmingham, and to various hospitals and good causes.[62]

Later in the nineteenth century, the Byrne brothers and their rubber works in Aston were crucial to the development of Fort Dunlop in Birmingham, while in 1899 Charles Haughton Rafter left the Royal Irish Constabulary to become chief constable of the city. A Belfast man, he recruited a significant number of Irish Catholic men from Mayo especially. Knighted in 1927, Rafter was concerned deeply for the welfare of children, pre-empting national legislation by insisting that juveniles should not appear in courts intermixed with adults. Praised for cleaning up the 'black spots of

Birmingham and cracking down on the peaky blinder gangs', he died in office in 1935. His successor was his deputy, Cecil C.H. Moriarty from Dublin. Capped for Ireland at rugby, he was regarded highly as 'a professor of his profession' for his books on police law and procedure.[63]

Rafter's death coincided with the revival of immigration from Ireland, as revealed by Chinn's work. Birmingham was recovering from the Depression as the government invested in rearmament. The Second World War accelerated this phenomenon because of the city's importance as a munitions centre. This pulled in more Irishmen to the munitions factories as well as Irishwomen to nurse in hospitals.[64] So short was the labour supply in Birmingham that ICI and Austin sent representatives to the Republic of Ireland to sign up employees, while Birmingham City Transport Department set up an office in Dublin in 1942 to recruit conductresses.[65] According to Moran, they were joined by many men who found jobs 'in some of the less pleasant manufacturing industries' and in the building sectors, and by increasing numbers of women who came for work as nurses and factory assistants.[66]

By 1951 the Irish in Birmingham numbered 36,000 and a decade later they reached their highest figure at just under 59,000.[67] This was 5.31 per cent of the city's population, a proportion that could be increased greatly by taking account of their children. Once again people from the West of Ireland were numerous. Tending to settle in south Birmingham, especially in Sparkbrook, Balsall Heath and Sparkhill, they included Seamus Dunleavey. Belonging to an impoverished family in Charlestown, Mayo, in the late 1950s he moved first to Liverpool and then to Birmingham, where work was easier to find. He and his brother, Mickey, took lodgings in Balsall Heath and then in Perry Barr and Saltley before finding digs in Sparkhill. Making a living from wrestling, they pooled their savings and bought a house in Wilton Road with five bedrooms and a big attic, 'taking in Irish immigrant tenants'.[68] Dubliners were also well represented among the Irish who came to Birmingham. They were noticeable in the north, particularly in Aston and Hockley, and were more likely to work in factories. Molly and Mick Kelly were among their pioneers, coming to Birmingham in 1940. They rented a house in South Road, Hockley, which became a 'half-way house' for Molly's brothers as they arrived, while there was always a room for anyone else from Ireland who needed a bed and board for a few weeks until they found work and lodgings.[69]

In 2015 parts of Digbeth and Deritend were known as the Irish Quarter; nearby, until the later 1940s, was an Italian Quarter, focused on Bartholomew Street and Duddeston Row. Although Chinn noted Italian street musicians from at least 1841, most were youths tied to a *padrone* and they did not stay in the city. Consequently, the settled Italian community did not emerge until the 1880s with a striking chain migration by families like the Tavoliers and Boves from Picinisco, Atina, Gallinaro and Carnello, then in the region of Naples, close to the larger town of Sora. Speakers of the Noblidani dialect, many of them arrived in Bristol and busked their way to Birmingham playing mandolins and organs.[70] Baptismal and marriage certificates from families like the Volantes, still resident in Birmingham, point to a Giuseppe

Delicata as the first link in the chain. From the early 1880s he and his family were the point of reception for newcomers connected to them by communal and kinship loyalties. But he was also a *padrone*, recruiting organ grinders to play in the streets for low wages.[71] Recognized in the local newspapers as the head of the local Italians, in 1886 Delicata was involved in a successful defence of the main yard of Italians in Bartholomew Street, where up to thirty men and women lived, after it was attacked by local English roughs.[72] Doreen Hopwood and Margaret Dilloway explained that this street drew in Italians because of the availability of cheap-rental back-to-back housing; its proximity to the Bull Ring, which gave the opportunity to earn money by playing barrel organs to shoppers; and the closeness of St Michael's Roman Catholic church on Moor Street, which came to be regarded as the Italians' church.[73]

Between 1891 and 1914 the profile of the Italians in Birmingham changed from a preponderance of young men living in lodging houses to family households.[74] Intermarriage with English and Irish descent families also increased, encouraged by the smallness of the Italian community and the mixing of second-generation Italians with second- and third-generation Irish Brummies and English Catholics at St Michael's school.[75] By 1915 it was estimated that there were between six and seven hundred members of 'the Italian colony' in Birmingham, some of whom were probably English-born children.[76] A significant proportion of the adult Italians

Tavolier's sweet shop at 39 Duddeston Row in the 1920s. Antonio Tavolier is on the right and his wife, Antonia, née Bove, is on the left. Antonio had been born in 1863 in the commune of Atina close to the town of Sora. Both played a crucial role in the chain migration from their village to Birmingham.
BirminghamLives Archive

were self-employed as shopkeepers, lodging-house keepers and musicians, and although organ grinders remained, their numbers had declined noticeably. Italians also operated terrazzo flooring businesses and along with a few families from Friuli in northern Italy, who gathered at the Camp Hill end of Bradford Street, they were responsible for the imposing entrances to many municipal and public buildings. Despite the variety of jobs undertaken by Italians, Hopwood and Dilloway emphasized that ice-cream making and its allied trades were the main sources of work from the 1890s to 1920s.[77] Indeed a number of families continued to be involved for much longer.[78]

By the 1920s there was a thriving Anglo-Italian Society in Birmingham, but during the Second World War Italians were registered as 'enemy aliens'. Under the Emergency Powers Act, 52 men from the city were interned on the Isle of Man, and four of them were among a large number of Italians and Germans sent to Canada on the *Arandora Star*. They were killed when it was sunk by the enemy and since 2015 they have been commemorated by a plaque in St Michael's church and another at Eastside City Park. This latter is accompanied by a storyboard telling some of the story of the people of Birmingham's Italian Quarter, which disappeared in the post-war redevelopment of Birmingham and the scattering of its families.[79]

The Jews of Birmingham were another small community. The first of them appeared in the mid-eighteenth century and they included merchants and manufacturers.[80] In addition to the more prosperous Jews, in 1781 William Hutton noted that there was a small synagogue in the Froggery, a very poor locality which seems to have been the base for Jewish hawkers. Hutton's language about these people is infused with prejudice, with condemnations such as 'the honesty of a Jew is seldom

Harry Cohen outside his tailor's shop with his pal, Barney Sharp, who had a boarding house in Hurst Street catering for theatrical people and whose family were bakers. Harry's shop was at 53 Inge Street, on the corner across from the Hippodrome theatre, and he did a lot of tailoring for stars who appeared there, such as Ken Dodd, Morecambe and Wise, Tom Jones and the Beatles.
BirminghamLives Archive

pleaded but by the Jew himself'.[81] As Malcolm Dick noted, this loaded language presented Jewish pedlars as outsiders who offered little to the town. Yet Hutton's anthropology of otherness did give a picture of a community that engaged in trade and had religious and organizational identity. And in highlighting the biography of Samuel Harris, a later Jewish pedlar, Dick provided a vital personal dimension to set alongside Hutton's sweeping account. Born in Poland, Harris arrived in England in 1821 and walked to Birmingham, where he stayed some months before moving on. Throughout his travelling he received aid from local Jews when falling upon bad times.[82]

Thirty years later there were only about 700 Jews in Birmingham, but by 1901 their numbers had increased to 3,200. Most of this growth was because of migration. One newcomer in 1855 was Moritz Stern, a clerk from Munich. He did not know many Jews in Birmingham but became friends with his 'co-religionist' from Germany, Mr Hirsch, who was involved in the wholesale tobacco trade. In 1864 he and Stern became partners in an export business. After his marriage, Stern and his family eventually moved to Richmond Hill in Edgbaston, where they faced the full force of 'snobbism and anti-semitism', which he had not felt before in Birmingham.[83] Despite this, other prosperous German Jews relocated to Edgbaston and until the early twentieth century they remained separate from the poorer Yiddish-speaking Ashkenazi Jews who had become evident by 1851.[84]

According to Aubrey Newman, these latter mostly made slippers, boots, caps and cigars, while some were glaziers and hawkers.[85] Their numbers increased dramatically from the 1880s because of the pogroms in the Russian Empire. Many of them were tailors, as were Ray Rosen's paternal grandparents.[86] They came from Warsaw, where they had been prosperous, but after they fled they lost everything and settled in Ellis Street, close to the Singers Hill synagogue, in about 1910. Very hard pushed to make a living, Rosen's grandfather 'had his workshop in the front of the house, they lived in the back, and they slept in the bedroom on top'.[87] Both sides of his family 'lived in this ghetto community' of Ellis Street. Close by was another in Hurst Street, where there were also a number of Jewish shopkeepers and a synagogue. Running off it was Inge Street, known as 'Little Jerusalem' because of the high number of Jewish families living there until the late 1930s.[88]

By then the sons and daughters of the immigrants had begun to prosper and move out, especially to Varna Road in Edgbaston because of its proximity to the old Jewish quarters; while the distinctions with the German-descent families were breaking down. During the Second World War, all Birmingham's Jews came together to support those fleeing Nazi Germany. A Birmingham Jewish Refugee Club was set up in 1939 and Bernard and Hanna Simmons made their home in Duchess Road, Edgbaston 'a haven for the newcomers'.[89] Another prominent figure speaking out against the persecution of Germany's Jews was Oscar Deutsch. The son of Hungarian Jews, he was president of the Birmingham Hebrew Congregation and the greatest name in the British cinema industry through his Odeon chain of cinemas.[90] After the war, and boosted by refugees who stayed, Birmingham's Jewish population peaked at about 6,000. Since then it has declined dramatically

because of emigration to Israel and the more densely populated Jewish centres of Manchester and London.[91]

Lawrence Levy came to Birmingham as a school teacher at the Hebrew School in 1870 and later became a well-known athlete and weightlifting champion. He recalled how Jewish children used to be 'chased by Christians to the very doors of the school room' and that verbal and physical abuse was common.[92] Such persecution was also familiar to Romanies, the most marginalized community in nineteenth-century Birmingham. Even more than other ethnic minorities, they have been ignored until the recent research of Ted Rudge. Romanies settled at times in various places within Nechells and Duddeston especially, but the most populous group made the Black Patch their winter base from the 1860s. This was an inhospitable and desolate spot on the borders of Birmingham, Handsworth and Smethwick, upon which the waste from nearby furnaces had been dumped and through which the Hockley Brook flowed. The Romanies were led by their king Esau Smith, who administered justice. He and his wife Sentinia (Henty) had been born in Weedon, Northamptonshire and the main families with them were the Smiths, Badgers, Davises, Claytons and Loveridges. Rudge recognized that their day-to-day existence must have been a struggle, with cooking on open fires, water only from the brook, and very basic sanitary arrangements using a shovel.

These families got by through the men dealing in horses and labouring and the women hawking pegs and *durkerin*, fortune telling; but after Esau died aged 92, his people suffered trials and tribulations. In July 1905 they were evicted by a large force of policemen who destroyed the camp and made most of the Romanies homeless. Esau's wife, Queen Henty, was allowed to stay on with a few of the Smiths, but they were pushed out when she died in January 1907. A week later, a funeral pyre was made of her *vardo* (caravan) and possessions, and soon after what was left

Esau Smith, at the head of the horse on the right, king of the Black Patch Romanies, and his queen, Henty, standing at the back on the left in a white pinny and headscarf, with other Romanies at the Black Patch in 1898. Notice the clean white pinnies of the women and girls, emphasizing the attempts made to stay clean in the most challenging of living conditions. Photographs such as this are vital in countering the contemporary negative perceptions of the Black Patch Romanies. In reality they were not lazy or criminal but rather were hard-working and respectable folk who faced severe discrimination because of who they were.
BirminghamLives Archive

of the Black Patch was laid out as a park. The evicted Romanies tended to move into Winson Green Road and many of their descendants remain in Birmingham.[93] Charlie Chaplin was one of those believed to have been born on the Black Patch and in the summer of 2015, his son, Michael, unveiled a memorial to the evicted Romany families.[94]

During their time on the Black Patch, the Romanies were often subjected to racial prejudice and their descendants continued to be insulted for who they were.[95] The Yemenis suffered similar problems. Mohammed Siddique Seddon stated that the forerunners of that community arrived in the later 1920s, when Yemeni lascars, merchant seamen who had settled in ports like Cardiff, were beset by a loss of unskilled work, racial prejudice and legal restrictions. In response, some moved to industrial areas such as Birmingham, where they gathered in Balsall Heath. In 1941 they were joined by Shaikh Muhammad Qassim al'Alawi. Raised in a village, he had received a rudimentary education and was a goatherd before joining the Merchant Navy in 1925. He sailed to Cardiff, which became his base for further journeys, but when he came to Birmingham he stayed and established the city's first *zawiya*, or prayer centre, in Edward Road. In effect this was Birmingham's first mosque. Acknowledged as the leader of the community, al'Alawi died in 1999.[96]

By 1952 there were about 400 Yemenis in Birmingham, the great majority from the former British colony of Aden, which became South Yemen from 1967. Their

Irish Travellers in Ingleby Street, Ladywood in 1967 – like the Romanies they suffered severe prejudice. It is believed that Irish Travellers have been migrating to England from at least the early nineteenth century, although no specific research has been carried out on either their lives in Birmingham or their contribution to the city.
BirminghamLives Archive

A Yemeni man walking up Edward Road past the New Moseley Arms, near the junction of Tindal Street, Balsall Heath, in 1970, photographed by the photojournalist Des E. Gershon. He was so captivated with the mix in this inner-city area between the old white working-class population and the Caribbean and South Asian newcomers, all of whom were living in an almost derelict area, that he decided to capture a series of images that depicted the area as he saw it. In a little over an hour he recorded over 200 images in black and white. Later a long sequence of stills was run on one of the evening news programmes of the Midlands television company, ATV. Gershon's photographs are a vital insight into Balsall Heath and a changing Birmingham and as such they make a major contribution to the city's history.
© Des E. Gershon Image Archives

numbers grew steadily during the 1950s and 1960s and the man recalled as the main figure in helping emigrants was a government official named Zindane, who belonged to a wealthy and respected family.[97] Most of the newcomers were young men coming to work in dirty and hard factory jobs, as did Mohamed Mockble in 1955. He was employed at the Chrysler factory in Small Heath, but after he had saved enough money he bought a small general store on Stoney Lane, Sparkhill. He married an Irishwoman, but from the 1970s other men were joined by their wives whom they had married on visits home. This pattern of settlement was also reflected among the North Yemenis, whom Badr Ud-Din Dahya explained had begun to move to Birmingham in growing numbers from the 1950s and were from one province. Indeed he asserted that they made up two-thirds of the 1,200 Yemenis in Birmingham by 1965.[98] Today, according to Seddon, the Yemeni community in Birmingham is the biggest in Britain and its size has begun to draw them out of their previous invisibility.[99]

In the 2011 Census almost 11,000 people identified themselves as Arabs, among whom the Yemenis formed the largest proportion. The Chinese population was given at slightly more, at just under 13,000. They first came to notice in September 1917 when an alarmist headline in Birmingham's *Evening Despatch* declared 'Chinese Invasion of Birmingham'. Hundreds of Chinese men had supposedly come to the city to work in the munitions factories and were undercutting the wages of Englishmen and marrying English girls. A sympathetic trade union leader rebuffed the claims, stating that there were no more than 250 of them and they were doing heavy and dirty work in the metal trade for which Englishmen could not be obtained. With the end of the First World War, these Chinese workers drifted away, probably back to ports.[100] Consequently, the foundations of the modern Chinese community in Birmingham were laid in the 1950s by Cantonese and Hakka speakers, many of whom were from farming communities such as Yuen Long in the New Territories of Hong Kong. In Birmingham they were unable to find work in their previous occupations and so they opened restaurants and takeaways. Working as teams of husbands and wives or brothers, they then began to employ staff from their villages in a chain migration similar to that of the Italians. Competition led to many families moving out of the city centre to open suburban takeaways. With unpaid family labour and living directly above the shops, their running costs were two-thirds those of restaurants.

Despite the dispersal of the Chinese community, since the late 1980s a vibrant Chinatown has emerged in the city centre. During this decade more people from Hong Kong began to arrive, fearful of the Chinese takeover in 1997. Since then there has been a sharp rise in the number of Mandarin speakers from mainland China, who now outnumber the Hong Kong Chinese. The Malaysian-Chinese are also prominent in Birmingham. English is their first language, many are from middle-class backgrounds and most are qualified professionals, running their own businesses. By contrast, the Chinese from Vietnam have faced a variety of difficulties. Forced from their country by the Sino-Vietnamese border war of 1979, initially they settled in Sparkbrook, especially in Braithwaite Road, which was nicknamed 'Chinese Street' – Tang Yahn Gaai. This migration was the catalyst for the establishment of the Chinese Community Centre, which provided advice and advocacy services to the non-English speaking newcomers and which continues to work for the benefit of Birmingham's Chinese.[101]

The expansion of the Yemeni and Chinese communities was part of a wider migration to Birmingham from across the world after the Second World War.

Mr Phoo (right), Mr See and Madge Wills with some of the decorations they had made for the celebrations for the coronation of Queen Elizabeth II in 1953. The two men were wholesale traders and Mr Phoo had several businesses around Birmingham.
BirminghamLives Archive

Boleslaw (Barry) Smojkis, his wife, June, and two of their children, Caroline and Susan, at a Coronation Day party in 1953; they then lived on Needham Street in Nechells. Their daughter, Maureen, wrote that 'because Our Mom was a Brummie us kids, all eight of us, never learnt much Polish and we didn't go to the Polish Club but we did eat Polish food and Dad took Our Mom and six of us to Poland by train and boat in 1971 to meet his family. In later life I have tried to learn the language and I have taken my son to visit Poland. All the family is influenced by our Polishness in some way. We do go to the Polish Club now and I have learnt a lot about the Poles, their difficulties, their resilience, and their independence.'
By permission of Maureen Smojkis

It included some Polish men who had fought with the British but who had become stateless after the redrawing of national boundaries in Europe. Regarding themselves as political exiles, many originated from the Kresy region in eastern Poland which was taken over by the Soviet Union. They and their families never exceeded 3,000 and included academics, teachers and doctors as well as workers. Nevertheless, most had to take unskilled work or retrain, and even then many Poles found it difficult to find employment because of concerns that they might take jobs from British workers. Consequently they were mostly directed to work in mines, foundries and factories.[102]

One of these Poles was Boleslaw (Barry) Smojkis. He was 14 in 1941 when he was taken by the Nazis to a slave labour camp. After his liberation he joined the Polish army and was stationed in Italy until he was demobbed, when he went to work in Leek. He came to Birmingham in 1947, labouring in a factory until he picked up more English. Smojkis later worked in foundries and steelworks and recalled that he did not find it difficult to find work because the Poles became known as reliable and hard workers. His first lodgings were in Alum Rock, sharing a room with five other Poles. Eventually he moved to lodge with an English family and from there married his English wife from Nechells in 1950.[103] By then, the Polish Catholic community was focused on St Michael's church under the leadership of Father Krause. He called the first meeting of the Polish Circle and allowed the organization the use of rooms adjacent to the church – which also had a little shop that sold Polish food and a delivery van that went round to Handsworth, Sparkhill, Small Heath and Erdington where Poles lived. Then in 1962 the Polish Millennium House in Digbeth was opened. This became a major centre for Poles locally, providing a variety of clubs and groups as well as Polish classes for children.[104] It has gained an added importance since 2004, when large numbers of young Poles began to arrive in Birmingham following the accession of Poland to the European Union.

The post-war Poles did not gather noticeably in a specific area and nor did Birmingham's much smaller Ukrainian community. It also emerged soon after 1945 with former soldiers who were against the communist rule of their country and it gained unity through a local branch of the Union of Ukrainians in Great Britain (SUB), based at St Anne's Roman Catholic church in Alcester Street.[105] The small Serbian community arrived for the same political reasons, and since 1968 its members have had as their focus the Church of the Holy Prince Lazar in Bournville.[106] Like the Serbs, Ukrainians and Poles, the Greek Cypriots of Birmingham were also scattered, although the Midlands Greek Cypriot Association now meets in Erdington, where there is also a church.[107] The roots of the community began in the late 1930s, with travelling men who sold lace made by their wives in the villages around Paphos. Two decades later some of them settled with their wives and families, as did men from the villages of Mazotos and Aradippou in Larnaca province. They worked in the Burlington restaurant, just off New Street, and other dining places and beat a path for others. In the words of Bambous Charalambous, 'if one person from one village comes then he brings his relatives and his friends and one brings another'.[108]

Through hard work and pooling their savings, a few men would buy a house and either live together or take in lodgers to raise the money to start a business and then bring their families over. Many took over fish and chip shops, with Barbara Malla recalling that 'they worked from early morning, preparing the food, peeling potatoes and constantly cleaning and serving. They had a two hour break in the afternoon during which they cut up the newspapers in half for wrappings and put the potatoes one by one on a little machine with squares cut out, pulled a handle and produced chips.'[109]

The 2011 Census recorded just over 9,000 people born in Poland, while less than a thousand classified themselves ethnically as Greek Cypriots. By contrast those born in Jamaica numbered a little over 15,000, with almost 5,000 from elsewhere in the Caribbean; while a total of almost 48,000 identified themselves as Black or Black British Caribbean. This significant population emerged in the immediate aftermath of the Second World War, yet they were not the first West Indians to have lived in Birmingham. From the 1870s Benjamin Rowe, who is thought to have come from St Elizabeth, Jamaica, had lived with his English wife around Latimer Street. Like many working-class people, he came to attention only because he was arrested and mentioned in the press as 'a man of colour'.[110] However, one black immigrant who did draw positive notice was the Revd Peter Stanford, a former American slave who became Birmingham's first black preacher at Hope Street Baptist church from 1889 to 1895.[111]

Still, black people remained few and the arrival of almost 500 Jamaicans on the SS *Empire Windrush* in June 1948 is regarded by many as signalling the beginnings of this large-scale migration. In effect, however, it had started with the 5,000 West Indian men who served with the RAF during the Second World War. Some stayed behind after they were demobbed, while others went back to the Caribbean but quickly returned to Britain, such as Prince 'Jake' Jacobs. A well-educated and skilled man, he left Trinidad in 1947, but he found that in Birmingham 'there was a lot of work but for a black man you couldn't get a job unless you were willing to sweep the floor or do the lowest of the low. Then you couldn't get a job no matter how well educated you were.' Eventually, and helped by the Royal Air Force Association, he did manage to gain good employment.[112]

At first, Jacobs lived in the Causeway Green Hostel in Oldbury, one of a number of wartime hostels where West Indian men were directed to stay. He remembered that there was always trouble there, especially with the Poles. Kevin Searle's research into a 'riot' there in 1948 showed how the post-war government attempted to limit 'the numbers of black workers in the hostels, keep them apart from others and blame them for attacks instigated by others'. This foreshadowed 'a more fully fledged "commonsense" racism that posited the numbers of black workers as the problem, rather than any lack of social provision'.[113] The biased press reporting of the 'riot' at Causeway Green blamed the outnumbered Jamaicans and declared that afterwards they had been told to leave.

Although men and women from Barbados and other islands also moved to Birmingham, Simon Taylor demonstrated that 'Birmingham was to become the English capital of Jamaica'. About one-quarter of all Jamaicans settled in the West Midlands, where they outnumbered the smaller islanders by four to one. With its skilled and

Chris Malla and his wife, Christafora, in their white coats outside their fish and chip shop on the Stratford Road in the 1960s. They are with various family members. Barbara Malla is married to the Mallas' oldest son, Mike, and she told me that the suitcase is significant as 'nearly all the people you have written about in your tales, Carl, have carried their lives in a suitcase of some description'. Her father-in-law, Chris Malla, left his village of Mazotos in the province of Larnaca in Cyprus just after the Second World War.
By permission of Barbara Malla

Andy Hamilton and the Blue Notes in the 1950s, with Hamilton on the saxophone. Rudi Williams is on bass, Lloyd Grant on vocals, and Eddie Hopkins on drums. Hamilton believed that there was no colour in music, a belief emphasized by Eddie's involvement when few white musicians played in black bands. On trumpet was Clem David, known as Scotty. He lived in lodgings run by my Aunt Vi, my Dad's oldest sister, at a large, old Victorian house in Trafalgar Road, Moseley. She had married my Uncle Johnny Brown in 1956, not long after he had arrived from Kingston, Jamaica. The pianist was Ron Daley, a former driver in the RAF in the Second World War. After going back to Jamaica he missed the hustle and bustle of the big cities of England and soon returned to settle in West Bromwich.
BirminghamLives Archive

semi-skilled work in engineering, the city continued to have a pull for Jamaicans.[114] Among them was the jazz musician Andy Hamilton, MBE, who moved there in 1949 and worked in a factory. In the early 1950s, he teamed up with another Jamaican, ex-RAF man Ron Daley, to start the famed band Andy Hamilton and the Blue Notes, and through his music he countered racism – even after he was attacked by fascist thugs who knocked out his front teeth.[115]

By the middle of the 1950s the number of West Indian immigrants was rising. As late as 1953 only 3,000 had made the journey to Birmingham, but economic problems in Jamaica, especially, and the imposition of new immigration restrictions by the USA pushed up emigration from Jamaica alone to almost 18,000 just two years later.[116] Skilled women like Esme Lancaster were numerous among them. She was 33 when she came to 'the land of money … from the land of poverty that was what we had supposed, but soon our hearts with sorrow were filled as we wandered along each day, trying to find somewhere to live and to make our new abode'. Although she was a social worker, Lancaster could only rent inferior housing that left her crying at the conditions, while she found the churches unwelcoming.[117] This was to lead her and others to form black-led churches.[118]

Jake Jacobs experienced similar housing problems, recalling signs on rented accommodation warning 'No blacks, no dogs, no Irish'.[119] A colour bar in housing by private landlords in certain districts had quickly arisen. Reinforced by a council housing policy based on years of residence, this ensured that West Indian immigrants tended to move into privately rented accommodation in large Victorian houses in the middle ring, from which the upper middle class had moved and which had been converted into lodging houses. This was particularly noticeable in parts of

A mother and her children walking along the Stratford Road towards the junction with Highgate Road and Walford Road in 1967. On the right and behind them is the local Baptist church on the corner with Palmerston Road. This led to that part of Sparkbrook which had been a middle-class area before the Second World War; however, by the late 1940s the prosperous families had moved out and their large Victorian homes had been turned into lodging houses. This was where many Irish and West Indian men and women settled, along with South Asian men, and it was the focus of the study by John Rex and Robert Moore. BirminghamLives Archive

Handsworth, Small Heath, Sparkbrook, Rotton Park, Birchfield and the borders of Balsall Heath and Moseley.[120] Indeed, as early as December 1949 Balsall Heath was declared to be 'Birmingham's Harlem'.[121]

There was also a colour bar in employment, against which Henry Gunter campaigned. Well-qualified as an accountant, after moving to Birmingham in 1949 he could only find factory work. Active in the Afro-Caribbean organization and the Labour movement, he was elected the first black member of his union branch and the first black delegate to the Trades Council. He and Arthur Leigh then founded the Birmingham branch of the Caribbean Labour Congress in 1951. Two years later Gunter wrote a powerful article on the 'colour bar' in the city, whereby black people were excluded from hotels, dances, social clubs and jobs with Birmingham's public transport system – against which he led a successful fight in 1954. An inspirational figure, Gunter became a correspondent for the *West Indian Gazette*, and although he left Birmingham, he later returned in 1985.[122]

Because of the problems and discrimination faced by West Indians regarding housing, work, politics, policing and media attitudes, Peter Edmead pronounced that the 1950s was 'the divisive decade' which set the tone for the experiences of West Indians who arrived in the 1960s.[123] There is much to justify his assessment. Taylor's research revealed that landlord discrimination continued and that this and other factors encouraged West Indians to save to buy their own house. By the end of the 1960s it was estimated that 40 per cent of black migrants in Birmingham

This evocative photo of three Sikhs in conversation was taken by the late Edwin (Stan) Millington (1909–72). Stan was a most talented photographer whose pictures are a compelling record of a changing city. This one is particularly important as few photographs were taken of ethnic minorities by newspapers or local government bodies in the 1950s and 60s, and even fewer were taken of people in relaxed settings. BirminghamLives Archive were owner-occupiers – overwhelmingly living in tunnel-backed houses in the middle ring. Henry Brotherson of St Kitt's typified them. In 1955 he and his brother and sister rented rooms in Cattels Grove, Nechells from a Pakistani landlord. Two years later, his wife joined him to work as a nurse at the Accident Hospital. They rented rooms in Saltley and by the late 1950s had bought their own home, where their children joined them.[124] Brotherson acknowledged that he had shared all the problems that black people had endured but he was never embittered. Yet despite their manifold positive contributions, discrimination continued to beset African Caribbean communities in the city throughout the 1960s, 70s and 80s, particularly with regard to schooling, employment, policing and media coverage.[125]

In June 1948 Percy Shurmer spoke in the House of Commons about the problems faced by both West Indian and African students and workers seeking accommodation

in Birmingham.[126] Despite this early mention of Africans and their ongoing presence, little attention was paid to them until Dick's work on refugees from the late twentieth century, which highlighted the Sudanese and Somalis.[127] However, in the immediate post-war period it seems that most Africans came from Nigeria and Ghana. Steve Ajao's father was among them. He left Lagos in Nigeria 'attracted by adverts to help get things going again in the mother country' and was about 18 when he arrived by sea, shortly after the war. After training as a tailor, he 'worked repairing bomb damaged railway tracks, and went on to work at Fisher and Ludlow on nights for 28 years. Dad was also known as a musician, being an excellent jazz drummer and he played with Andy Hamilton when they were both young men most weekends at dances and social clubs. He also taught himself to play guitar.'[128]

The 1948 British Nationality Act guaranteed free right of entry to British subjects and Commonwealth citizens and until 1961 it was mostly West Indians who took advantage of this legislation. However, a large number of Indians and Pakistanis also did so, with 3,000 of them living in Birmingham in 1951 and 10,000 a decade later.[129] They had been preceded by a few others, such as Dad Bhai, who had run one of three lodging houses for Asians in one of the poorest parts of Birmingham in the 1860s.[130] Thereafter a few students, doctors and lascars arrived and by 1939 R. Visram thought that there were about one hundred Indians in Birmingham.[131] The most prominent was Dr Dhani Prem, a general practitioner, who joined the Birmingham Indian Association and later became active in the Labour Party.[132] Another pioneer was Ram Singh Bhatra, a Sikh in the Auxiliary Fire Service, who met King George VI when he visited blitzed areas on 12 December 1940.[133]

Five years later, Visram calculated that the Indian population locally had reached a thousand, boosted by lascars working in the munitions factories. It continued to grow with former soldiers from the Indian army and then with Hindus and Sikhs from the Indian Punjab, especially from the villages close to the city of Jalandhar. One of the first in this chain migration was Dev Raj Sirpal, born in 1927 in Pasla. In 1954 he left behind his wife and four children and emigrated after meeting a man who talked about his big earnings in Britain. Arriving in Smethwick, he lodged in the house of a fellow villager. There was no heating; cooking was only in the evenings and in turns, as six or seven people shared a double bed in each room. Food was mostly masoor dal (red lentils cooked like a stew) with bread but 'we also had canned spinach, kidney beans and baked beans and we cooked chickens at weekends'. There was no refrigerator and cooking utensils as well as milk bottles were stored under the bed. Sirpal found work in a factory and by doing as much overtime as he could, for a 72-hour week in 'a routine, tiring and very tedious job', he earned £12.10s. Out of this he put £3 towards rent and food and made repayments for the loan he had taken out to pay for his flight – and yet he still managed to send money home to his family in India.

When the factory closed down, Sirpal was out of work for eight months but was supported by his fellow Punjabis, because 'it was the established custom that the house owners from India did not charge rent and expenses for food as a long as a person remained jobless'. After finding more work, he also sold clothes from

Not all Indians were from the Punjab or Gujarat, and among these others was Bimal Bhattacharjee, known as John, shown here with his friend, Martin, at work at the GPO. Born in 1933, the son of Hindu parents, Bhattacharjee grew up in poverty in Kolkata in West Bengal. After a time in the Merchant Navy, he moved to Birmingham, where he married Audrey Wynne. They moved to rooms in Golden Hillock Road and applied for a council house when their first son was born but were turned down. Bhattacharjee felt that this was because he was an Indian man with a white wife and so he saved hard to buy a house on St Benedict's Road in Small Heath. He told his granddaughter that his journey from Bengal to Birmingham was the 'greatest thing he could have possibly done' and that there was absolutely nothing he regretted about it.
By permission of Caitlin Chandra

door-to-door. Eventually he and a friend saved enough money to buy a house and Sirpal was able to send for his family in 1959. Three years later he contracted TB but after he recovered he opened his first shop on the Ladypool Road in Sparkbrook, selling the anoraks he made. His business was so successful that by 1980 he had a large factory in Constitution Hill where 70 workers operated 25 machines and manufactured a wide range of products.[134]

Many Sikhs and Hindus continued to live in all-male lodging houses and to send money back to their families until after the passage of the Commonwealth Immigrants Act of 1962. This encouraged them to bring over their wives and children to join them. The result was a rapid rise in what was then termed the 'New Commonwealth' population from 28,169 in 1961 to 49,870 in 1966, and this in turn precipitated a move towards home ownership.[135] Their numbers were further increased from the late 1960s by those of Punjabi descent from Kenya, Uganda and Tanzania, along with Hindus and Muslims originally from Gujarat. They included the Gosai family. Its head, Rajbharthi, was 14 when he left his village of Modpur for Dar-es-Salaam, but with hard work he was able to open a restaurant. The family left in 1972 and settled in Leicester where his sons worked as machine operators. With his savings, Rajbharthi came to Sparkbrook four years later, opening a shop on the Ladypool Road selling Indian sweets and vegetable savouries. Other Gujaratis established themselves as leather traders, pharmacists, newsagents and retailers of Indian clothing, especially on the Soho Road in Handsworth.[136]

Dahya's work on British Pakistanis in 1974 remarked that while most immigrant groups had initially resided in Balsall Heath and then Sparkbrook, by 1956 they had 'already sorted themselves out on the basis of national origins and ethnicity'. Pakistanis had begun to settle in Moseley, Sparkbrook, Small Heath and Aston, Jat Sikhs in Sparkbrook and Smethwick, and Ramgarhia Sikhs in and around Balsall Heath.[137] Some adjustment to that picture is needed, for Sikhs also settled strongly in Handsworth, while it is important to note that the Pakistanis who made Aston their home were from what was then East Pakistan and would become Bangladesh. It is also vital not to assume that Hindus, Muslims and Sikhs made up homogeneous social groups.[138]

In her study of Asian minorities in Birmingham, Sharla Kalpoe emphasized that while they might simplistically be denoted as Pakistani, Indian and Bengali minorities, they actually encompassed 'different identifications on various levels, rather than a solely (trans) national basis', thus identifying themselves religiously and linguistically as well. So, Sikh Asians exhibited strong ethno-national sentiments, while Gujaratis had a dual transnational loyalty because of their migrations from India and then East Africa, but also still identified themselves transregionally and linguistically with Gujarat. As for Kashmiri Mirpuris or Kashmiris, they demonstrated transregional identification in Pakistani transnationalism.[139]

In their seminal study of race, community and conflict in Sparkbrook in 1967, John Rex and Robert Moore observed that although Pakistanis were the smallest of the three major immigrant groups in the area, behind the Irish and West Indians, their presence and special influence was out of proportion to their numbers. This was because of the tightness of their community organization, the fact that they spoke a different set of languages, and their role as housing entrepreneurs through saving hard and buying lodging houses. Rex and Moore also discerned that the origins of the Pakistani immigrants made clear how world history impinged on a small section of England. Their sample consisted of 18 Azad Kashmiris from the Mirpur District, 18 from the Campbellpur District (now Attock District) of the North-West Frontier Province, and four from elsewhere in Pakistan. The links between Campbellpur and England had been forged by the British North West Frontier Army which had recruited its bearers, cooks, batmen and caterers from the area. As for Mirpur, it was like Yemen and also Syhlet, a place where British steamship companies had engaged cheap labour. Some of these Mirpuri seamen then jumped ship in England, especially between 1943 and 1949, and made their way to Birmingham.[140]

One of them was Choudhury Zaman Lal, whose remarkable life has been described by Dick. Born in the village of Kalyal, he became a lascar and settled in London in the 1930s before moving to Birmingham in the next decade. Although he only spoke Mirpuri, he met and married his Scottish wife, Margaret, and together they opened a drapery shop in Balsall Heath. It also became a community centre, as newcomers sought out help and advice. Quickly becoming a prominent personality in the local and national Pakistani communities, Lal led successful campaigns to establish an exclusive graveyard for Muslims and a slaughter house operated under Islamic teaching, while he was a leading figure in securing the land for the Central Mosque in Highgate in the 1970s.[141]

Like Lal, the early Pakistani immigrants were predominantly male; indeed in 1961 men outnumbered women by twelve to one. Among them was Fazal Karim, and in common with Lal and some others, he married an English woman, Mabel Norman. They set up their first home in Sampson Road, Sparkbrook, part of Rex and Moore's study area. Then in the early 1950s they moved to St Martin's Flats in Highgate, where Karim was the first Asian (Kashmiri) resident – although 'no-one believed he was Asian and were convinced he was Greek, which must have been more acceptable in those days I suppose'.[142] Lacking manufacturing skills, most Pakistani workers such as Karim were employed in factories as machinists and labourers. However, and by contrast to his experiences, Rex and Moore noted a pattern among Pakistanis of returning home and then re-emigrating. They also emphasized that each man came to England 'launched by his family, sheltered and sustained by relatives and co-villagers … who help him find to find a job so that he may be independent and able to send money home back to his family'.[143]

This photograph of a mixed-race couple in the 1950s is from the Dyche Collection at the Library of Birmingham. A self-taught photographer, Ernest Dyche (1887–1973) opened his first studio in 1910 in Bordesley, followed by a second in Balsall Heath – which became his main base. During the 1950s his theatre-based business declined and he and his son, Malcolm, then focused on photographing migrants who had arrived from Africa, the Caribbean and the Indian subcontinent and who wanted to send something to their families to show that they were doing well. The studio closed in the 1980s, but by then it had unintentionally recorded the emergence of multicultural Birmingham.
By permission of the Library of Birmingham, MS 2912 Dyche 0159

Such support was especially obvious among immigrants from Mirpur, whose numbers increased in the early 1960s following the building of the Mangla Dam. They arrived on work permits granted by the British government, which was seeking labour from across the Commonwealth, and which the Pakistani authorities tended to distribute to what were then poorer, rural localities. Many Mirpuris came from the *tehsil* (district) of Dadyal, where the social structure was similar to that of the other predominantly agricultural districts from which the peoples of Birmingham have been drawn: it was a place where the emotional and physical support of kin was valued and needed. This resulted in 'a chain linkage of family right across the region', while 'close neighbours tend to be called family'.[144]

Dahya stressed that most Pakistani immigrants clung to a 'myth of return', aiming to earn and save as much money as possible so as to eventually go back to their homeland.[145] This intention began to break down in the 1960s according to Makhdoom Chishti, when many began to believe that it would become more difficult to return because of higher living standards in Britain and political instability in Pakistan, among other factors.[146] Deciding to make Birmingham their permanent home, they sent for their families. Mariam Bi and her two-year old daughter joined her husband in 1967. They lived with her brother-in-law in Alum Rock, but she was shocked at how small the house was. There were beds everywhere in the house, even in the living room, with the men taking turns at sleeping because of their shift work. Her uncle showed her how to use the gas cooker and she started cooking traditional food, recalling that there were then no grocery shops locally which catered for the Pakistani community. Still 'I always liked living in Alum Rock everyone around here is from the same place as us back home, so we feel safe working and living here.'[147]

The trend to permanent settlement was boosted by the 1971 Immigration Act, after which more Pakistani men were joined by their families. As Rex and Sally

Tomlinson explained, while the south and south-east of the city centre had been the initial areas of South Asian settlement, an increasing number of Pakistanis were now making their homes in the north, in Handsworth and Soho wards;[148] but it is also important to be aware of the growing numbers of Mirpuri families in east Birmingham, especially in Small Heath, Saltley, Alum Rock and Washwood Heath, where they bought the older terraced housing sold by the white working class. Along with Sparkhill, these areas were also favoured destinations for Pakhtoons from the North-West Frontier Province of Pakistan. Most were from the Swat area or from the district surrounding Peshawar, and many of the men had close connections with the British army. Before arriving in Birmingham they had operated canteens and shops on military bases in Cyprus, Northern Ireland and elsewhere. Now they found work in factories, as did other Pakistani men who come from Gujar Khan and Rawalpindi in the Punjab. They gathered in the same neighbourhoods as the

Mirpuris and, like the Campbellpuris of Sparkhill, some of them bought businesses with the help of relatives and friends involved in savings committees. On a weekly or monthly basis, members deposited a sum with a holder and on a rotating basis one person collected the pool of cash.

The 2011 Census recorded 144,627 people who classed themselves as Asian or Asian British Pakistani. This was almost 13.5 per cent of the population and it compared to 6 per cent Asian or Asian British Indian and 3 per cent Asian or Asian British Bangladeshi – a third more than the Irish, a reversal of the situation a decade before. According to Kalpoe, the Bangladeshis in Birmingham exhibited both a transnational and transregional loyalty. Most came from the Sylhet region and called themselves Sylheti or Sylheti Bengali, all the more so when comparing themselves with other Bangladeshis; but because of their dominance in the city, their transregional identification was not so prevalent. Their large-scale movement began in the 1950s, again with lascars who had 'jumped ship'. As Aftab Rahman made clear, the 1962 Commonwealth Immigration Act then led to a specific regional migration from Sylhet as existing settlers worked to bring over friends and relatives.[149]

According to Yousuf Choudhury, work was the first priority of all these newcomers, while they aimed to spend as little as possible so as to send as much as possible back to their families. Finding low-paid employment in factories, they rented cheap dwellings in Spring Hill, Balsall Heath, Aston and Lozells, which were in the throes of the clearance of back-to-backs and redevelopment. Some of them formed informal savings groups and bought run-down terraced houses collectively or jointly. As for work, some men went into catering and since the 1970s the majority of Indian restaurants in Birmingham have been run by Bangladeshis from Sylhet. Others operated markets stalls, especially in the King's Hall Market in Corporation Street. But the majority became labourers, doing jobs that English people did not want. Some companies continued to operate a colour bar and even in those that did take on Asians 'it was not necessarily straightforward to get a job'. The prospects for Bangladeshi labourers deteriorated further from the late 1970s with the rapid and widespread decline in manufacturing in Birmingham. With less work and more mechanization in the remaining factories, they began to suffer high unemployment at a time when their older housing was deteriorating.

It was during this difficult period that Bangladeshi men began to bring over their wives and children. Until then, Rahman explained, most men thought that they would work in Birmingham for a few years and return to Bangladesh. This 'myth of return' was shared not only with Pakistanis but also with other immigrant communities such as the West Indians, most of whom had believed that they would only stay for five years. Still, the myth lasted longer among the Bangladeshis, resulting in delayed family reunification and permanent settlement. Rahman stated that this was because most of the men did not wish to bring their families to an un-Islamic country. But after Bangladesh's independence in 1971 and a widespread famine five years later, the ageing men were prompted to bring their families over even though it had become more difficult to do so because of the 1971 Immigration Act.[150]

This photo was taken by Roger Gwynn in Golden Hillock Road, Small Heath, in 1971. Left to right are Mohibur Rahman, unknown, Gyas Uddin Islam and Mukim Uddin. This is one of a number of photographs taken by Gwynn relating to the Bangladeshi community in Small Heath in the period 1969–71. It is a remarkable collection showing the emergence of a new community in Birmingham.
© Roger Gwynn

Badrun Pasha was one of the few Bangladeshi women in the city before then. She had arrived in England in 1963 to study law and, after marrying, moved to Small Heath in 1970. At first she was an immigration counsellor but then she worked in family and child services for Birmingham social services. Soon after arriving, she set up the Bangladesh Women's Association and later started a Bangla school. Taslima Akbar's mother was also a pioneering woman who had moved to Birmingham in the 1950s and who joined the Association at the start. She worked in a factory making pots and pans and her daughter found that interesting because 'it was the first time we saw her in western clothes. Usually she wore a sari but for work she wore a smock top and trousers.'[151]

One of the first Bangladeshi children in Birmingham was Gyas Uddin Islam, who was eight when he arrived in Aston with his mother and father, a former lascar, in 1964. They bought chickens from a relative who owned a shop nearby. The animals were slaughtered there or at home, so that the meat was halal. Islam spoke no English when he arrived and with no friends either at school 'there wasn't a day that I did not have an argument … They used to swear and call me black. When I told the teachers I did not get any justice.' His life was like a living war, with English, Irish and Jamaicans targeting him, but Islam fought back. Today he is a prosperous businessman in the grocery trade.[152]

The migration of West Indians, Indians and Pakistanis was correlated to low unemployment in Birmingham; by contrast that of Bangladeshis was connected with the rise of unemployment.[153] This phenomenon also applies to the people who have arrived in Birmingham since the 1980s. Dick's work on refugees who made their homes in Birmingham highlighted the experiences of Sudanese, Hutus from Burundi, ethnic Albanians, Bosnians, Afghans, Somalis, Iranians and Kurds.[154] Most of them have fled war and persecution, as with the Albanians from Kosovo. Gëzim Alpion estimated that since 1997, 4,000 have settled in Birmingham.[155] They tend to have a more cohesive identity compared to the Afghans. Their ethnic background, as Jahan Mahmood has emphasized, is complex; moreover they manifest a variety of reasons for leaving their country, including extreme poverty, war, political and ethnic persecution and imprisonment.[156] Comparable to the ethnic Albanians in size, the Somalis have both a strong identity and a distinct presence in Sparkbrook – where previous generations of newly arrived immigrants had also settled. Like their predecessors they have begun to establish self-help organizations, but because of a variety of barriers, as pointed out by Mohammed Aden, they constitute one of the most deprived and disadvantaged communities in Birmingham.[157]

Recognition of the need to record and understand the lives of the recent communities who have settled in Birmingham is in stark contrast to the lack of attention paid to nineteenth-century incomers and to the working class in general. Older histories of the city mostly focused on prominent political or manufacturing personalities. This 'top-down' approach continued well into the twentieth century, so that the voices of the common people were lost and what little was written about them comes through the prism of middle-class outlooks. A reaction to the 'great white men' attitude began nationally in the 1960s and 1970s, when some historians asserted the importance of 'history from the bottom up', a belief that also took hold of the popular imagination. In Birmingham from the early 1980s, this led to an outpouring of working-class life stories by women as well as men, which played a seminal role in changing attitudes.[158] This grassroots movement was matched by a growing awareness among librarians that the collections in both the city's Central Library and community libraries needed to be extended to make them more inclusive and democratic, while a few professional historians locally also embraced community history by encouraging people to pass on their life stories and by engaging in oral history projects. This growth in interest in the lives of supposedly ordinary people led to some important collections and websites including the Millennibrum Project, the BirminghamLives Archive and Connecting Histories,[159] while it also deeply influenced the 'Birmingham: its people, its history' gallery, opened at the city's museum in 2012. Increasingly the social importance of this more egalitarian history has been highlighted. As Birmingham is one of the most culturally and religiously diverse cities in the world, inclusive histories can play a vital role in enhancing understanding between communities and in ensuring that the many peoples of Birmingham feel that the city belongs to all of them.

Notes

1 See E.B. Gover, A. Mawer and F.M. Stenton in collaboration with F.T.S. Houghton, *The Place-Names of Warwickshire. English Place-Name Society: Volume 13* (Cambridge, 1936), 34–5; S. Bassett, 'Anglo-Saxon Birmingham', *Midland History*, 25 (2000), 8; and M. Gelling, *The West Midlands in the Early Middle Ages* (Leicester, London and New York, 1992), 61

2 V.H.T. Skipp, *Discovering Sheldon. A Brief History of a Birmingham Parish from Anglo-Saxon to Modern Times* (Birmingham, 1960), 9; D. Horovitz, *The Place Names of Staffordshire* (Brewood, 2005), 297; and Gover et al., *The Place-Names of Warwickshire*, 45.

3 V. Skipp, *Medieval Yardley. The Origin and Growth of a West Midland Community* (London and Chichester, 1970), 9–15; J. Plaister (ed.), *Domesday Book 23: Warwickshire including Birmingham* (Chichester, 1976), 241a and 243a; and F. and C. Thorn (eds) *Domesday Book 16: Worcestershire* (Chichester, 1982), 177a and b.

4 Plaister, *Domesday Book 23*; Thorn, *Domesday Book 16*; and J. Morris (ed.), *Domesday Book 24: Staffordshire* (Chichester, 1982), 250a and 250b.

5 J. Hemingway, *An Illustrated Chronicle of the Castle and Barony of Dudley 1070–1757* (Dudley, 2006), 11–15, 21.

6 This chapter focuses on the origins of the peoples of Birmingham, but there are other aspects of their lives that need to be researched in more detail. These include the lives of the disabled (see, for example, D. Barnsley, 'My life and times', *Carl Chinn's Brummagem Magazine* [October 2015], pp. 24–6), the mentally ill (see D. Hutchings, *Monyhull 1908–1998. A History of Caring* [Studley, 1998]) and gay, lesbian, bisexual and transgender people (see 'Gay Birmingham. Back to back', http://www.blgbt.org/sample-page/gay-birmingham-back-to-back; and D. Viney, 'Fred Barnes: music hall star', *Carl Chinn's Brummagem Magazine* [May 2012], 26–8).

7 G. Demidowicz, *Medieval Birmingham: The Borough Rentals of 1296 and 1344–45*, Dugdale Society Occasional Papers, 48 (Bristol, 2008), 17–18, 28.

8 G. Redmonds, T. King and D. Hey, *A Surnames, DNA, and Family History* (Oxford, 2011), 2–3.

9 Demidowicz, *Medieval Birmingham*, 35–49, 17.

10 Redmonds et al., *Surnames*, 3.

11 Demidowicz, *Medieval Birmingham*, 18.

12 Ibid., 35–49, 50–65.

13 Skipp, *Medieval Yardley*, 23–5.

14 C. Chinn, *The Streets of Brum. Part 5* (Studley, 2009), 45–66.

15 'Manors', in W.B. Stephens (ed.), *A History of the County of Warwick. Volume VII: The City of Birmingham*, Victoria County History (London, 1964), 58–72, http://www.british-history.ac.uk/vch/warks/vol7/ (accessed 31 December 2015); and W.P.W. Phillimore, *Some Account of the Family of Middlemore of Warwickshire and Worcestershire* (London, 1901).

16 W.H.B. Court, *The Rise of the Midland Industries: 1600–1838* (London, 1938), 8–50.

17 R.A.H. Pelham, 'The immigrant population of Birmingham 1686–1726', *Transactions of the Birmingham Archaeological Society*, 61 (1937), 45–82.

18 A. Parton, 'Poor-law settlement certificates and migration to and from Birmingham, 1726–1757', *Local Population Studies*, 38 (1987), 24–6.

19 A. Redford, *Labour Migration in England between 1800 and 1850* (Manchester, 1964), 183.

20 C. Chinn, 'The anatomy of a working class neighbourhood. West Sparkbrook. 1871–1914' (PhD thesis, University of Birmingham, 1986), 285–6.

21 M. Anderson, 'Urban migration in nineteenth century Lancashire: some insights into two competing hypotheses', *Annales de Démographie Historique* (1971), 13–26.

22 M. Jager, 'Migratory patterns in the Jewellery Quarter of Birmingham in the nineteenth century with particular reference to Anderson's study of Preston, 1851' (MA dissertation, University of Birmingham, 1998), 4–7, 12–13, 41–4.

23 C. Chinn, 'Becoming a Brummie: a family's move to Birmingham', *History West Midlands Podcast*, February 2015, http://www.historywm.com/podcast/becoming-a-brummie-a-sound-journey-of-a-familys-move-to-birmingham; C. Chinn, 'Black Country Irish', *Express and Star*, 14, 21 and 28 March 2009; C. Chinn, 'Granny Crenley and Granny Wood', *Express and Star*, 17 March 2011; and C. Chinn, 'Top Church Perrys', *Express and Star*, 22 October 2009.

24 H. Butcher, *The Treacle Stick. Ladywood, Aston & Erdington 1917–1942* (Birmingham, 1999), 1–2. For a working-class perspective from the 1860s, see W. Thorne, *My Life's Battles* (London, 1989), 13–15; and for the Edwardian period, see K. Dayus, *Her People* (London, 1982), 3–6. For a discussion of back-to-back housing and public health, see C. Chinn, *Homes for People: Council Housing and Urban Renewal in Birmingham 1849–1999* (Studley, 1999), 1–120; C. Upton, *Living Back to Back* (Andover, 2005); and T. Rudge and M. Joseph, *Birmingham: We Lived Back to Back – The Real Story* (Oxford, 2015). For a full list of working-class autobiographies, see C. Chinn, 'The people of Birmingham', in C. Chinn (ed.), *Birmingham: Bibliography of a City* (Birmingham, 2003), 254–8.

25 C. Chinn, *Brum and Brummies* (Studley, 2000), 5–6.

26 C. Chinn and S. Thorne, *Proper Brummie. A Dictionary of Birmingham Words and Phrases* (Studley, 2001), 16.

27 Chinn, *The Streets of Brum. Part 5*, 114.

28 Chinn and Thorne, *Proper Brummie*, 120.

29 C. Chinn, 'Shurmer, Percy Lionel Edward (1888–1959)', *Oxford Dictionary of National Biography* (Oxford, 2004) (hereafter *ODNB*), online edn, http://www.oxforddnb.com/view/article/105130 (accessed 1 December 2015).

30 A. Sutcliffe and R.R. Smith, *Birmingham, 1939–70. History of Birmingham. Vol. 3* (Birmingham, 1974), 202–3.

31 G.C. Boase, 'Gillott, Joseph (1799–1872)', rev. C. Chinn, *ODNB*, online edn, http://www.oxforddnb.com/view/article/10751 (accessed 14 September 2015).

32 Another self-made man who was also aided by his wife

and her money was Sir Josiah Mason: see G.C. Boase, 'Mason, Sir Josiah (1795–1881)', rev. E. Hopkins, *ODNB*, online edn, http://www.oxforddnb.com /view/article/18286 (accessed 14 September 2015).

33 S. Kinsey, 'Geach, Charles (1808–1854)', *ODNB*, online edn, http://www.oxforddnb.com/view/article/49133 (accessed 7 November 2015).

34 C. Chinn, *The Cadbury Story. A Short History* (Studley, 1998), 2.

35 H. Plant, '"Ye are all one in Christ Jesus": aspects of Unitarianism and feminism in Birmingham, c.1869–90', *Women's History Review*, 9.4 (2000), 721–42.

36 C.A. Osler, *Why Women Need the Vote* (London, 1910).

37 'Religious history: Protestant nonconformity', in Stephens (ed.), *A History of the County of Warwick: Volume VII*, 411–34.

38 R.A. Pelham, 'The growth of settlement and industry c.1100–c.1700', in *Birmingham and its Regional Setting* (Birmingham, 1950), 157.

39 For the Church and King riots, see J. Atherton, 'Rioting, dissent and the Church in late eighteenth century Britain: the Priestley Riots of 1791' (PhD thesis, University of Leicester, 2012).

40 S. Lloyd, *The Lloyds of Birmingham* (London, 1907), 5–14.

41 S. Roberts, *Dr J.A. Langford 1823–1903: A Self-Taught Working Man and the Sale of American Degrees in Victorian Britain* (Birmingham, 2014).

42 C. Chinn, *The Streets of Brum. Part 3* (Studley, 2006), 50–1.

43 R. Holt, *The Early History of the Town of Birmingham, 1166 to 1600*, Dugdale Society Occasional Papers, 30 (Oxford, 1985), 10.

44 See T. Lewis, 'Any road', in *Pictures of Small Heath, Sparkbrook and Further Afield 1902–1939* (Birmingham, 1979); and B. Thomas, 'The influx of labour into the Midlands 1920–37', *Economica*, NS, 5.20 (1938), 410–34.

45 L.J. Jones, *Three Times for a Jolly Welshman. An Autobiography of a Rhondda Exile* (Birmingham, 1984), 20–9. See also M. Rees, née Llewellyn, 'Working for victory', *Carl Chinn's Brummagem Magazine* (November 2010), 4–6.

46 C. Chinn, *Birmingham. The Great Working City* (Birmingham, 1991), 88.

47 Sutcliffe and Smith, *Birmingham, 1939–70*, 202–6.

48 For Watt, Murdock and also Matthew Boulton, see the 'Revolutionary Players' website at www.revolutionary-players.org.uk.

49 Chinn, *Birmingham*, 9 and 89–90; and D.H.L. Back, 'Kynoch, George (1834–1891)', *ODNB*, online edn, http://www.oxforddnb.com/view/article/48741 (accessed 1 December 2015). See also J. Lerwill, *The Aston Villa Chronicles, 1874–1900 (and after), Volume 1. From Nothing to the Top (1874–1900)* (Aston, 2009).

50 Chinn, *Birmingham*, 90.

51 Jones, *Three Times for a Jolly Welshman*, 23.

52 There were a very few Irish who came to Birmingham from the mid-seventeenth century; see J. McKenna, 'The Irish in Birmingham' (unpublished manuscript, Birmingham, 1991), 1–6; and Court, *The Rise of the Midland Industries*, 4.

53 C. Chinn, *Birmingham Irish. Making Our Mark* (Birmingham, 2003), 39–45.

54 F. Engels, *The Condition of the Working Class in England in 1844, with a Preface written in 1892* (London, 1892), 54–65.

55 C. Chinn, 'Sturdy Catholic emigrants', in R. Swift and S. Gilley (eds), *The Irish in Victorian Britain. The Local Dimension* (Dublin, 1999), 58–60, 64–6.

56 See, for example, *Journal of Thos. Augtn. Finigan, Missionary Birmingham Town Mission 1837–1838* (Birmingham, 2010); and Chinn, *Birmingham Irish*, 63–5.

57 P. Davis, 'Green ribbons: the Irish in Birmingham in the 1960s. A study of housing, work and policing' (MPhil thesis, University of Birmingham, 2003), 136–95.

58 Chinn, *Birmingham Irish*, 67.

59 J. Denvir, *The Irish in Britain from the Earliest Times to the Fall and Death of Parnell* (London, 1892), 415.

60 Chinn, *Birmingham Irish*, 79–80; J. Moran, *The Irish in Birmingham. A History* (Liverpool, 2010), 89–152.

61 J.F. Champ, 'Priesthood and politics in the nineteenth century: the turbulent career of Thomas McDonnell', *Biographical Studies, 1534–1829*, 18.3 (1987), 289–303.

62 A. McCulloch, *The Feeneys of the Birmingham Post* (Birmingham, 2004).

63 Chinn, *Birmingham Irish*, 30, 33, 94.

64 Ibid., 30, 33, 94, 96–138.

65 Ibid., 116; J. Clows, 'The Irish worker in English industry (with particular reference to the Birmingham district)', *British Association for the Advancement of Science* (Belfast meeting, 1952).

66 Moran, *Irish in Birmingham*, 164–5.

67 Sutcliffe and Smith, *Birmingham, 1939–70*, 207–8.

68 S. Dunleavy and S. Thompson, *Finally Meeting Princess Maud* (Studley, 2006), 100–1.

69 Chinn, *Birmingham*, 84–5; J. Rex and R. Moore, *Race, Community and Conflict: A Study of Sparkbrook* (London, 1967), 85

70 C. Chinn, 'We all come from round Sora: Italians in Birmingham', in O. Ashton, R. Fyson and S. Roberts (eds), *The Duty of Discontent. Essays in Honour of Dorothy Thompson* (London, 1995), 260–2.

71 Chinn, 'We all come', 255–9; 'Importing organ grinders', *Birmingham Daily Post*, 3 February 1891.

72 'Serious affray in Bartholomew Street', *Birmingham Daily Post*, 24 April 1886.

73 D. Hopwood and M. Dilloway, *Bella Brum. A History of Birmingham's Italian Community* (Birmingham, 1996), 2.

74 E. Divo, 'Irlandais et Italiens dans le quartier de Saint Bartholomew à Birmingham à la fin du XIXe siècle' (unpublished Mémoire de Mâitrise d'Histoire, Université de Franche-Comté, 1993), 63–5.

75 Chinn, *Birmingham*, 79–81.

76 'Italian demonstration in Birmingham', *Birmingham Daily Mail*, 2 June 1915, 3.

77 Hopwood and Dilloway, *Bella Brum*, passim.

78 See M.P. Ward, 'Italian Brummies. The Pagetts', *Carl Chinn's Brummagem Magazine* (March 2007), 16–18.

79 C. Chinn, 'Remembering Birmingham's Italians', *Birmingham Mail*, 27 June 2015.

80 Z. Josephs (ed.), *Birmingham Jewry 1749–1914* (Oldbury, 1980), 7.

81 W. Hutton, *An History of Birmingham* (Birmingham, 1783), 128.

82 M. Dick, 'Birmingham Anglo-Jewry c.1780 to c.1880: origins, experiences and representations', *Midland History*, 36.2 (2011), 196–201. Dick points out that the nineteenth-century population figures may be an underestimate, as many local Jews travelled outside Birmingham on business.

83 M. Stern, 'Wisdom and folly: reminiscences of an octogenarian. Part I' (unpublished typescript manuscript, 1917–20), 37–54, and 'Part II', 2, 25.

84 Chinn, *Birmingham*, 86.

85 A. Newman, 'A portrait of Birmingham Jewry in 1851', paper delivered to the 'Provincial Jewry in Victorian Britain' conference at University College London, convened by the Jewish Historical Society of Great Britain, 1975, JCR-UKhttp://www.jewishgen.org/JCR-uk/Community/Birmingham2.html (accessed 7 October 2015).

86 Z. Josephs, 'The tailors', in Z. Josephs (ed.), *Birmingham Jewry. More Aspects* (Oldbury, 1984), 35–45.

87 Chinn, *Birmingham*, 86–7.

88 C. Chinn, *Brum and Brummies 3* (Studley, 2002), 50.

89 Z. Josephs, *Survivors. Jewish Refugees in Birmingham, 1933–1945* (Exeter, 1988), 7.

90 A. Eyles, 'Deutsch, Oscar (1893–1941)', *ODNB*, online edn, http://www.oxforddnb.com/view/article/46878 (accessed 7 December 2015). Another leading figure in the entertainment sector was Leon Salberg, owner of the Alexandra theatre, who had been born in Warsaw; see Derek Salberg, *My Love Affair with the Theatre* (Luton, 1978), 8–56.

91 A. Chesses, 'A brief history of the Birmingham and West Midlands Jewish community', http://www.jewishbirmingham.org/history-of-the-community.html (accessed 7 October 2015).

92 E.L. Levy, *Birmingham Jewry, 1870, Then; And 1929, Now* (Birmingham, 1929), 52. See also D.M. Fahey (ed.), *E. Lawrence Levy and Muscular Judaism 1851–1932* (Lewiston, NY, and Lampeter, 2014).

93 T. Rudge, *Brumroamin. Birmingham and Midland Romany Gypsy and Traveller Culture* (Birmingham, 2003), 27–31, 50–4.

94 T. Rudge, 'Romanies, memorials and Charlie Chaplin', *Carl Chinn's Brummagem Magazine* (July 2015), 19–20.

95 Chinn, *Brum and Brummies 3*, 34.

96 M.S. Seddon, *The Last of the Lascars: Yemeni Muslims in Britain 1836–2012* (Markfield, 2013); see also F. Halliday, *Arabs in Exile: Yemeni Migrants in Urban Britain* (London and New York, 1992).

97 Chinn, *Birmingham*, 99.

98 B.U-D. Dahya, 'Yemenis in Britain: an Arab migrant community', *Race & Class*, 6 (January 1965), 181–5.

99 During the 1920s Birmingham also became home to some Europeans who arrived as individuals, such as Christian Kunzle, the confectioner and philanthropist from Davos in Switzerland, or as small family groups, like the Olgiatis from Poschiavo in Switzerland. See S. Roberts, 'Kunzle, Christian (1879–1954)', *ODNB*, online edn, http://

www.oxforddnb.com/view/article/104912 (accessed 7 December 2015), and Nora Angelina Olgiati, late Nora Davis, 'Little foreigner' (unpublished manuscript, 1982), BirminghamLives Archive MS 1902/6/7.

100 C. Chinn, 'Coins and munitions: Birmingham and the Chinese', *Birmingham Mail*, 13 September 2014.

101 Chinese Community Centre, Birmingham, 'Chinese lives in Birmingham', *Carl Chinn's Brummagem Magazine* (August 2014), 8–11. See also http://chineselivesinbirmingham.com/; and Chinn, *Birmingham*, 100. For the Vietnamese, see also Birmingham City Council, *The Vietnamese in Birmingham: A Community Profile* (Birmingham, 1997); and M. Dick, *Celebrating Sanctuary. Birmingham and the Refugee Experience 1750–2002* (Birmingham, 2002), 6–7.

102 Midlands Polish Community Association, *In War & Peace. Collected Memories of Birmingham's Poles* (Birmingham, 2011), 2–7. See also Chinn, *Birmingham*, 95–6. The Muntz family, whose members had a major impact on political and manufacturing affairs in Birmingham in the mid-nineteenth century, originally came from Minsk in Poland, although they later moved to France. See S. Timmins, 'Muntz, George Frederick (1794–1857)', rev. Matthew Lee, *ODNB*, online edn, http://www.oxforddnb.com/view/article/19551 (accessed 5 December 2015).

103 M. Smojkis, 'The Birmingham Polish community', *Carl Chinn's Brummagem Magazine* (November 2009), 24–5.

104 Midlands Polish Community Association, *In War & Peace*. See also M. Smojkis, 'Out of the shadows: exploring the lives of the Birmingham Polish' (MPhil thesis, University of Birmingham, 2013).

105 A. Rose, 'The Ukrainians of Birmingham: the beginnings', *Carl Chinn's Brummagem Magazine* (January 2016), 26–9.

106 Dick, *Celebrating Sanctuary*, 4.

107 www.midlandsgreek.org (accessed 5 December 2015).

108 Chinn, *Birmingham*, 95–6.

109 B. Malla, 'Greek Cypriot Brummies', *Carl Chinn's Brummagem Magazine* (July 2009), 14–17.

110 B. Francis, 'Benjamin Rowe. Birmingham c. 1873–unknown', in B. Willis-Brown and D. Callaghan (eds), *History Detectives. Black People in the West Midlands 1650–1918* (Birmingham, 2010), 26–7.

111 P. Walker, 'The Revd Peter Thomas Stanford (1860–1909): Birmingham's "coloured preacher"' (PhD thesis, University of Manchester, 2004), 17–68 and 167–95. Walker is minister at Highgate Baptist church, the successor to Stanford's church.

112 C. Chinn, 'From Trinidad to Birmingham: Prince Albert "Jake" Jacobs', *Carl Chinn's Brummagem Magazine* (December 2012), 8–10.

113 K. Searle, '"Mixing of the unmixables": the 1949 Causeway Green "riots" in Birmingham", *Race and Class*, 54.3 (2013), 44–64.

114 S. Taylor, *A Land of Dreams, A Study of Jewish and Afro-Caribbean Migrant Communities in England* (London, 1993), 106.

115 S. Bradley, 'From Errol Flynn's yacht to the Tower ballroom', *Birmingham Post*, 5 April 2012.

116 Taylor, *A Land of Dreams*, 100.

117 D. Price and R. Thiara (eds), *The Land of Money? Personal*

Accounts by Post-War Black Migrants to Birmingham (Birmingham, 1992).

118 See also B.A. Miles, *When the Church of God Arises. A History of the Development of the Church of God of Prophecy in the Midlands and More Widely Britain* (Studley, 2006).

119 Chinn, 'From Trinidad to Birmingham', 9.

120 Sutcliffe and Smith, *Birmingham, 1939–70*, 210–13.

121 'Man stabbed – police cast net', *Aberdeen Journal*, 19 December 1949.

122 F. Tait, 'Gunter, Henry Charles (1920–2007)', *ODNB*, online edn, http://www.oxforddnb.com/view/article/105624 (accessed 1 December 2015).

123 P.L. Edmead, *The Divisive Decade. A History of Caribbean Immigration to Birmingham in the 1930s* (Birmingham, 1999); see also Taylor, *A Land of Dreams*, 110–57.

124 H. Brotherson, *Why I Came to England and What I Discovered* (Birmingham, n.d.), 10–21.

125 For schooling, see I. Grosvenor, *Assimilating Identities. Racism and Educational Policy in Post 1945 Britain* (London, 1997); for policing, see D. Webb, *Policing the Rainbow* (Blackpool, 2004); and for the media, see S. Cushion, K. Moore and J. Jewell, *Media Representations of Black Young Men and Boys* (London, 2011).

126 Sutcliffe and Smith, *Birmingham, 1939–70*, 365.

127 Dick, *Celebrating Sanctuary*, 7–9.

128 S. Ajao, 'Jazz in Stour Street', *Carl Chinn's Brummagem Magazine* (October 2009), 16–17. In common with some other single men from Africa and the West Indies, Steve Ajao's father married an English woman; according to the 2011 Census, 3,223 people in Birmingham identified themselves as Mixed White and Black African, with another 24,720 stating that they were Mixed White and Black Caribbean. For the history of the first generation of black mixed-race families in Birmingham, see *Guess who Came to Dinner... The Stories of Black Mixed Race Families in Birmingham during the 1950s and 1960s* (Birmingham, c.2002); and for a mixed-race woman in late nineteenth-century Birmingham, see '"A life on stage": the amazing story of Esther Ann Johnson, www.connectinghistories.org.uk (accessed 5 December 2015).

129 Sutcliffe and Smith, *Birmingham, 1939–70*, 207–8.

130 I. Grosvenor, 'Never again will a single story be told as though it's the only one', in I. Grosvenor, R. McLean and S. Roberts, *Making Connections. Birmingham Black International History* (Birmingham, 2002), 25, 28.

131 R. Visram, *Ayahs, Lascars and Princes: Indians in Britain, 1700–1947* (London, 1986), 54–74, 191–2.

132 I. Grosvenor, 'Prem, Dhani Ram (1904–1979)', *ODNB*, online edn, http://www.oxforddnb.com/view/article/103441 (accessed 21 October 2015).

133 C. Chinn, *Brum Undaunted. Birmingham During the Blitz* (Birmingham, 2005), 122.

134 K. Bhushan (ed.), *Eternal Memories* (Birmingham, 2009).

135 P.N. Jones, 'Some aspects of the changing distribution of coloured immigrants in Birmingham, 1961–1966', *Transactions of the Institute of British Geographers*, 50 (1970), 199–220.

136 Chinn, *Birmingham*, 103.

137 B.U-D. Dahya, 'The nature of Pakistani ethnicity in industrial cities in Britain', in A. Cohen (ed.), *Urban Ethnicity* (London, 1974), 77–118.

138 R. Ballard (ed.), *Desh Pardesh. The South Asian Presence in Britain* (London, 1994); for the heterogeneity of the Muslim community in Birmingham, see D. Joly, *Britannia's Crescent: Making a Place for Muslims in British Society* (Aldershot, 1995), 28–9.

139 S. Kalpoe, 'Right to culture discourse in practice: a variety of Asian identities in Birmingham leads to a puzzle of rights' (MSc thesis, University of Utrecht, 2004), abstract, 2, 5.

140 Rex and Moore, *Race, Community and Conflict*, 115.

141 M. Dick, 'Choudhury Zaman Ali: a leader in his community', in M.A. Chishti, *Lok Virsa Cultural Voyage. Exploring the Muslim Heritage* (Studley, 2008), 38–40. Sufi Sahib, a former soldier in the British Indian Army, was another leading figure in the Pakistan community. See Pnina Werbner, 'Seekers on the path: different ways of being Sufi in Britain', in Jamal Malik and John Hinnells (eds), *Sufism in the West* (London, 2006), 127–41.

142 L. Karim, 'St Martin's Flats', *Carl Chinn's Brummagem Magazine* (May 2012), 4.

143 Rex and Moore, *Race, Community and Conflict*, 120.

144 Chinn, *Birmingham*, 101. See also J. Akhtar, *Destiny: Memories and Experiences of First Generation Pakistanis* (Birmingham, 1999).

145 Dahya, 'The nature of Pakistani ethnicity', 98–9.

146 M.A. Chishti, 'Pakistanis and Kashmiris. Pakistani community', in Chishti, *Lok Virsa*, 31.

147 'Ms Mariam Bi', www.mirpurtobirmingham.org (accessed 4 December 2015).

148 J. Rex and S. Tomlinson, *Colonial Immigrants in a British City: A Class Analysis* (London, 1979), 74–5.

149 A. Rahman, *Bangla Food Journeys* (Birmingham, 2012), 11.

150 Y. Choudhury and P. Drake, *From Bangladesh to Birmingham: The History of Bangladeshis in Birmingham* (Birmingham, 2001), 11, 14–34.

151 G. Limbrick, *Unlocked. Hidden Stories of the Lives of Birmingham Women 1900 to the Present Day* (Birmingham, 2014), 32–5.

152 Rahman, *Bangla Food Journeys*, 20–1. Not all of Birmingham's South Asian Muslims came from Bangladesh or Pakistan; some arrived from East Africa and were of Gujrati origin.

153 Bangladesh Council, *The Bangladeshis in Birmingham. Community Profile* (Birmingham 2001), 34.

154 Dick, *Celebrating Sanctuary*.

155 G. Alpion, 'The Albanian community', in Chishti, *Lok Virsa*, 14–15.

156 J. Mahmood, 'The Afghan community', in Chishti, *Lok Virsa*, 10.

157 M. Aden, 'The Somali community', in Chishti, *Lok Virsa*, 46.

158 For the Birmingham Black Oral History Project, see www.bbohp.org.uk. Its archive is held at the Cadbury Research Library at the University of Birmingham.

159 These three collections are held in the Library of Birmingham.

CHAPTER TWO

Before *Beorma*: Prehistoric and Roman Birmingham

MIKE HODDER

Birmingham's first historians, from William Hutton onwards, largely dismissed the prehistoric and Roman periods as little more than a footnote to documented history because of the absence of written records and the perceived scarcity of physical remains. Most assumed that much of the area remained wooded and sparsely populated until the Anglo-Saxon period (when we can first identify one of its inhabitants – *Beorma*, after whose people Birmingham is named).[1] Exceptionally, a few appreciated the contribution of structures and objects to an understanding of Birmingham's early history.[2]

Our knowledge of Birmingham before the Anglo-Saxon period is derived mainly from archaeological remains, consisting of features still visible above ground, excavated structures and objects, and chance discoveries, supplemented by pollen, seeds, beetles, soils and sediments which provide a vivid picture of the past landscape and people's exploitation and management of their environment. This information enables us to relate a narrative, inevitably with gaps, that runs from hunters and gatherers hundreds of thousands of years ago to Roman soldiers, farmers and potters.[3]

Much archaeological evidence comes from work undertaken as part of new developments and mostly required by Birmingham City Council as part of the planning process, including excavations by Alex Jones and colleagues from the former Birmingham Archaeology (University of Birmingham) at Metchley Roman fort in Edgbaston[4] and Longdales Road in King's Norton,[5] and by Oxford Wessex Archaeology on the line of the M6 Toll motorway in Sutton Coldfield,[6] together with many smaller but no less significant projects. Other research includes fieldwalking (systematic collection of objects from ploughed field surfaces) by

the Birmingham and Warwickshire Archaeological Society in the Green Belt east of Sutton Coldfield,[7] and the excavation and survey of burnt mounds by the late Lawrence Barfield and the present author, accompanied by experiments to test their function.[8]

Objects found by chance (i.e. other than in deliberate archaeological work) are restricted to easily recognized items, such as flint arrowheads, stone and bronze axes and Roman coins. Their exact findspots are not always precisely recorded, and in some cases the objects are known only from antiquarian accounts. Such accounts and historic maps may, however, provide information on features that have since disappeared.

Charred seeds and charcoal found on archaeological sites provide evidence of food and fuel, and pollen, seeds and parts of beetles survive in suitable conditions, particularly wet deposits, both on archaeological sites and in other locations such as the peat layers at Aldridge Road in Perry Barr.[9] Many species of beetle have distinct habitats and therefore indicate past environmental conditions, and the changing proportion of pollen of different trees or plants over time has been analysed in radiocarbon-dated deposits like that at Perry Barr.[10]

Much archaeological evidence is uncovered as part of work on new developments. Excavations in Park Street in the city centre were undertaken during the redevelopment of Birmingham's Bull Ring area during the late twentieth and early twenty-first centuries.
© Michael Hodder

Stone handaxes which date from the Palaeolithic period (up to about 9000 BC) were used, probably to chop meat, by people living in warm periods between or during glaciations.[11] The population of the country as a whole was sparse and mobile at this time, but hunting was apparently organized rather than opportunist, and uniform tool types over large areas demonstrate communication between groups.[12] Handaxes found in Erdington[13] and Saltley[14] were made from quartzite pebbles which have been sharpened at one end by chipping off pieces, but they are worn as a result of being moved, probably by the Anglian Glacier nearly half a million years ago.[15] A

This drawing in John Evans' *Ancient Stone Implements, Weapons and Ornaments of Great Britain*, published in 1897, shows how a Palaeolithic handaxe found in Saltley was made by skilfully chipping flakes from a pebble.
By permission of the Cadbury Research Library: Special Collections, University of Birmingham

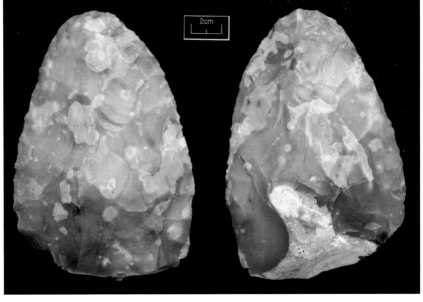

Scars show where flakes have been chipped from a Palaeolithic handaxe found in Sutton Coldfield to shape it and create a cutting edge. Part of the cortex, or white crust, has been left intact.
© University of Birmingham; Classics, Ancient History and Archaeology, photograph by Graham Norrie

carefully shaped flint handaxe found in Sutton Coldfield[16] dates to about 50,000 BC. Unlike the other two, it is unworn and therefore was potentially in its original location, raising the possibility that land surfaces from the distant past survive in Birmingham.

Woodland which developed when temperatures rose after the last glaciers melted was composed of birch and Scots pine, whose pollen was found in a soil layer dated to about 8900 BC at College Road near the River Tame in Perry Barr.[17] Organic clay that survived in two natural hollows under Victorian cellars near Banbury Street in the city centre was dated to about 8300 BC, early in the Mesolithic period (c. 9000–4000 BC), and contained, in addition to birch and pine pollen, two pieces of flint that had been chipped into shape by people living there. A layer of pine charcoal suggested that they used fire to create clearings to attract the grazing animals that they hunted and encourage the growth of fruit and nuts that they gathered, and that they were therefore managing their environment.[18] At about the same time as the Banbury Street deposits, lakeside timber platforms were built at Star Carr in Yorkshire by people hunting deer and other animals, and houses of this date have been found at several sites. Small communities of people exploited different areas seasonally, and there is widespread evidence for the use of fire to clear trees.[19]

An upper, later layer of soil at Banbury Street probably dating to between 6000 and 5000 BC contained alder, hazel, lime and birch pollen, and in Sutton Park peat covering pine stumps (the remnants of ancient woodland, similar to that at Banbury Street and College Road) contained pollen that shows that oak, elm, birch and lime were growing nearby.[20] The upper soil layer at College Road, dating to about 4400

These Mesolithic flint tools and manufacturing debris found in Sutton Park include scrapers with a serrated edge. They would have been held between thumb and fingers in use.
© Michael Hodder

BC, contained pollen of alder, lime, oak and elm, and pollen, seeds and other plant fragments in a peaty soil near a former stream in Sheldon showed that there was Scots pine, hazel and birch woodland there in about 4200 BC.[21]

Flint tools and debris from their manufacture which have been found near Bracebridge Pool in Sutton Park and near Manorial Wood north of Sutton Coldfield[22] were made and used by people living in predominantly deciduous woodland between about 6000 and 4000 BC (the late Mesolithic period). They include scrapers and cores resulting from the production of flakes, some of which were shaped into tiny pieces and set in a haft of wood, bone or antler. The flints are often found near streams providing fish, wildfowl and rushes. Most of the Mesolithic flints found in the West Midlands date to the later part of the period, when communities may have been more settled.[23]

Altering the land: herdsmen and ploughmen (c. 4000 BC–AD 43)

Birmingham's first farmers

Fieldwalking in the rural area east of Sutton Coldfield located several worked flints dating to the Neolithic period (c. 4000–2500 BC), some of which were made from black flint mined in southern and eastern England.[24] Other objects from this period found in Birmingham, by chance rather than deliberate search, include axes made of flint and other stones from various parts of the country, chipped to shape and then ground to a smooth finish, which would have been hafted and used to fell trees, and flint arrowheads used for hunting or warfare.[25] No houses of this date, nor any burial or ceremonial monuments known elsewhere,[26] have been found in Birmingham, but a pit dug next to Griffins Brook in Bournville in about 2700 BC contained 28 pieces of pottery, from five different vessels, of a type known as 'Grooved Ware', which has been found at settlements and monuments throughout Britain. Charcoal in the pit was mainly oak and ash.[27] Pollen from a layer of peat

Fieldwalking in Sutton Coldfield retrieved these Neolithic flints. On the right is a 'core' showing scarring where flakes have been broken off to make into other tools.
© Michael Hodder

next to the River Tame at Aldridge Road, Perry Barr, also dates to about 2700 BC and shows that the surroundings were predominantly woodland of alder, lime, hazel, oak and Scots pine.[28] People were probably farming in Birmingham at this time, possibly alongside hunting and gathering,[29] but there is no evidence for their impact on the environment until the Bronze Age.[30]

A fall in the percentage of lime pollen in the peat at Aldridge Road about 2100 BC, in the early Bronze Age, is probably the result of people clearing woodland to grow crops and graze animals. It is accompanied by pollen of ribwort plantain, which grows in clearings. A rise in heather and bracken indicates the development of heathland, which is a manmade landscape that results from woodland clearance followed by grazing, preventing regrowth of trees, and leaching (percolation of nutrients), resulting in acidic soils. Birmingham's heaths (most of which now survive only as place names) may have originated at this time. In about 1500 BC, during the middle Bronze Age, there is a further decline in lime and alder pollen at Aldridge Road. Oak almost disappears and there is an increase in grasses and sedges. This indicates substantial clearance of woodland and coincides with the earliest dates for burnt mounds.

The burnt mound period

Forty burnt mounds have been found in Birmingham.[31] They are usually oval, up to 20 metres across, and are composed of heat-shattered stones and charcoal (resulting from incomplete combustion of wood used as fuel). A few survive as upstanding mounds, others are visible as distinctive layers in stream banks or as burnt stone and charcoal on ploughed field surfaces, and some have been identified from antiquarian accounts.[32] Radiocarbon dates from charcoal and wood from excavated sites and stream banks show that Birmingham's burnt mounds were in use between 1500 and 1000 BC.[33] Burnt mounds occur in large numbers in other parts of Britain and Ireland and they have been interpreted as the remains of cooking (in water boiled with heated stones), sweat or sauna-type bathing (in steam produced by pouring water on heated stones) or woodworking, leatherworking, textile processing and brewing. Some of these possible uses have been tested by experiments.[34]

The burnt mound excavated at Cob Lane in Bournville[35] was dated to about 1370 BC, and charcoal showed that stems or branches were used as fuel, predominantly from alder trees that grew in damp conditions alongside the nearby stream. Under the burnt mound, a layer of silty clay overlay mud

One of a number of burnt mounds found in Birmingham, this example at Cob Lane in Bournville lies next to Griffins Brook. The archaeologist is on the surface of the mound which slopes down into a former stream course on each side.
© Michael Hodder

containing branches and trunks of alder trees and many hazelnut shells, one of which was radiocarbon-dated to about 1400 BC. It contained species of beetles which live on oak, ash and lime trees, but the woodland canopy was sufficiently open for hazel to bear nuts. There were also open-grassland beetle species and dung beetles, which showed that animals grazed nearby. The radiocarbon date is virtually identical to that of the burnt mound, showing that this is the landscape in which the burnt mound was used and that the silty clay accumulated, probably all at once, very shortly before the mound was established. Tree trunks and branches in the former stream bed suggest woodland clearance and subsequent soil erosion, resulting in the silty clay which blocked former stream channels and created a floodplain.

In addition to keeping animals, people using the burnt mounds grew crops: pollen of cereals and of corn cockle (a weed of cereal fields), which appears in the peat at Aldridge Road at about 1000 BC, is the earliest evidence for local arable cultivation.[36] The beginning of the burnt mound period in Birmingham corresponds with the establishment of settlements and field systems elsewhere in the country, which suggests increased population and intensification of land use. The end corresponds with the abandonment of some settlements, the replacement of field systems with ditched boundaries and the construction of hilltop fortifications. This indicates pressure on land, insecurity and conflict.[37]

An organized landscape
Excavations near Langley Mill Farm on the M6 Toll motorway route in Sutton Coldfield revealed a farmstead consisting of circular houses inside a ditched enclosure linked to another, smaller enclosure containing a single house.[38] The sites are dated by radiocarbon to about 300 BC, in the middle of the Iron Age (c. 700 BC–AD 43). Charred grains of wheat and barley, chaff (waste from crop processing) and seeds from weeds of arable fields show that cereals were grown. The enclosures might have been located between arable fields and open grazing land: they lie on the edge of what was unenclosed common land in the eighteenth century, mainly heathland used for rough grazing.[39] This pattern of land use may have begun in the Iron Age.

Farms in ditched enclosures are characteristic of the Iron Age landscape of the West Midlands and other parts of the country. Their numbers suggest that the land was extensively used but in some areas there may have been a greater concentration on stock-rearing.[40] Iron Age pottery found in Selly Park and King's Norton may indicate the locations of other farmsteads of this period.[41] An undated ditch found at Broadmeadow Close in King's Norton[42] and two joined rectangular enclosures visible as cropmarks (different vegetation growth over buried archaeological remains) on an aerial photograph at Spreading Tree Hill in Sutton Coldfield[43] are likely to be of Iron Age or Roman date.

The Iron Age farm at Langley Mill Farm was probably occupied through the late Iron Age, because it is adjoined by enclosures of Roman date. On the other side of Birmingham, excavations at Walkers Heath revealed three converging and

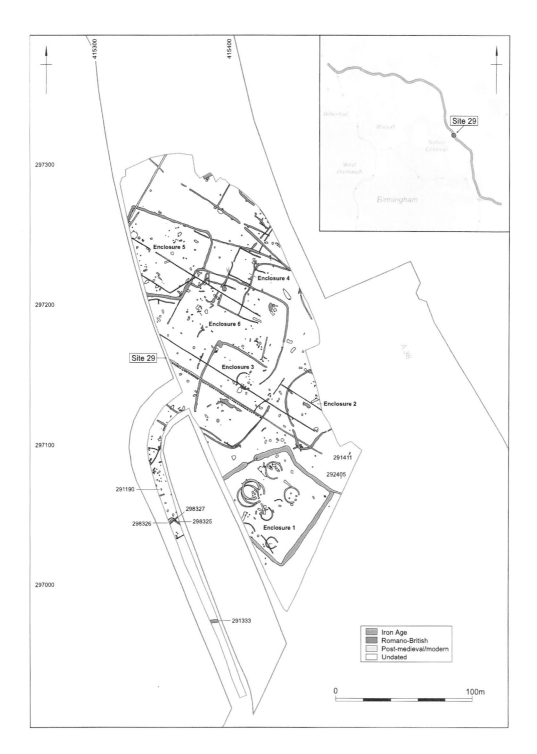

successive gullies of late Iron Age date which were probably field boundaries. They contained pottery dating to the early first century AD, together with charred wheat and barley and some possible burnt daub, which suggests there was a dwelling nearby.[44]

Roman Birmingham: soldiers, farmers and potters (AD 43–410)

First to early second centuries AD

The Roman fort at Metchley[45] was initially built between the late 40s and late 50s AD, on a site now occupied by the campus of the University of Birmingham and Queen Elizabeth Hospital. It probably housed a garrison of about 1,000 auxiliary soldiers, which may have included cavalry. The fort covered about four hectares and was square in plan, with rounded corners. Its defences consisted of a turf rampart with a timber fence on top of it, corner towers and gatehouses, and two ditches outside. The fort contained timber buildings including the headquarters, the commanding officer's house, barrack blocks and granaries. It was later enlarged with annexes on all four sides. A short-lived civilian settlement (*vicus*), which developed to provide goods and services to the garrison, consisted of scattered timber buildings based around a road leading out of the west gate of the fort.

The fort was established as part of the Roman conquest of the West Midlands. It may have been deliberately located at or close to the boundaries between the Iron Age tribes identified in Roman sources – the *Cornovii*, *Corieltauvi* and *Dobunni* – although the extent of their territories is not known. The fort was built in a landscape

The banks in the centre, on a grassed area around the University's Medical School, mark different periods of the defences of Metchley Roman fort. The fort extended from the curving banks in the foreground, beyond the car park in the centre and on to what is now the University of Birmingham's campus.
© Balfour Beatty plc

This reconstruction of the western gate of Metchley Roman fort shows its timber defences. Excavation of the site located the holes left by the posts of the gateway and the timber tower.
© Nigel Dodds, reproduced by permission

Excavations at Metchley Roman fort in 1969, with the university clock tower in the distance. The shallow trenches contained ground beams of timber buildings.
© University of Birmingham, photograph by Phyllis Nicklin, 1969

The interior of Metchley Roman fort reconstructed in a drawing that shows the barracks in the foreground and the *principia* or headquarters behind. Excavations revealed the ground plans of these buildings and pottery shown on the right in the drawing.
By permission of University Hospitals Birmingham NHS Foundation Trust

of farms and fields like those excavated at Walkers Heath and its construction had a substantial impact on the environment, taking up land and drawing on other resources that were already being used by the local population. Large numbers of timber trees were needed for the defences and the buildings inside the fort. Stripping turf for the rampart may have resulted in soil erosion which has been detected in excavation to the west of the fort,[46] and removed opportunities for pasture. Once the garrison was established, men and horses needed feeding. Charred wheat and barley probably came from cereals grown locally, but other foodstuffs arrived from further afield, such as olive oil contained in *amphorae* (large globular pottery vessels with handles for lifting them) from southern Spain. Other pottery vessels used at the fort were made in the Severn Valley and the Malverns, but some were from continental Europe. Ovens and hearths used wood for fuel, which was obtained locally. Coal found in Roman features at Metchley[47] probably came from the Black Country where it would have been extracted by shallow excavation.

Soldiers stationed at Metchley, as well as some of the commodities reaching them, moved along the network of military roads that was imposed on the existing landscape to link forts and that subsequently served towns and other settlements. A well-preserved stretch of Ryknield or Icknield Street which ran between Metchley and Wall in Staffordshire survives in Sutton Park, and some modern roads follow the lines of Roman roads, such as parts of Pershore Road in south Birmingham and Wellhead Lane in Perry Barr. In addition to the roads, many other trackways would have been used. For example, a route along the sandstone ridge which later became a medieval road running north from Birmingham to Sutton Coldfield and Lichfield was probably used to transport pottery made at the Sherifoot Lane kiln.[48]

The fort was modified during the 60s AD to store goods and livestock requisitioned for the army which was then campaigning in Wales and northern England.[49] Fenced enclosures were built inside, and converging fences which led into its west gate formed part of a group of enclosures outside. This layout is likely to have been designed to control livestock, an interpretation which is supported by dung beetles and beetles of grazed land in the infill of the ditches.[50]

Permanent garrisons were established in northern England and Wales following further campaigns in the 70s and 80s.[51] At Metchley, a smaller fort was built inside

A view along the well-preserved Roman road in Sutton Park which is visible as a turf-covered bank beyond the modern track. The scale is one metre long.
© Michael Hodder

The Roman road in Sutton Park consists of a bank of gravel dug from pits alongside it. The scale is one metre long.
© Michael Hodder

the earlier defences in the 70s AD, with granaries inside and enclosures outside. It had a turf rampart, implying loss of more grazing land, and the turves contained pollen of woodland, heath and grassland.[52] Pollen from the infill of a ditch showed that willow and hawthorn scrub, which was resistant to grazing, developed following the fort's abandonment. This was replaced by woodland containing hazel, ash, birch and oak, which may have been managed partly as coppice and partly as wood pasture for grazing animals.[53] Pottery shows the site was occupied until the end of the second century, but not necessarily as a military post. Modifications to the former western entrance of the fort were probably related to livestock management.

Roman pottery dating from the first to third centuries, together with daub and charcoal, was found at Parson's Hill, King's Norton, on gravel surfaces which may include part of Ryknield Street.[54] Excavations nearby revealed a ditch that contained first- to second-century pottery and charred seeds of weeds that occur on cultivated land.[55] The ditch could have formed one side of a settlement enclosure. Small amounts of Roman pottery, including types of first- to second-century date, were found 100 metres west of the probable line of a Roman road in Northfield, together with a possible circular house and part of a quern.[56] Some Roman pottery of the same date found in excavations at the Saracen's Head, King's Norton,[57] suggests a nearby settlement. A relatively small quantity of pottery of late first- to early second-century date was found at Langley Mill Farm and Longdales Road.

Second to third centuries AD

By the early second century there was no longer a military garrison at Metchley, but agriculture and the exploitation of resources such as woodland may have been managed as part of a 'resource-procurement zone', to supply the army to the north and west.[58] The archaeological evidence at Langley Mill Farm in Sutton Coldfield in north Birmingham and Longdales Road in King's Norton in the south suggests that both these sites specialized in livestock, replacing the mixed farming practised in the Iron Age.

Acid soils have resulted in poor survival of animal bone, but livestock management, whether as cattle ranches, sheep runs or horse studs, is implied by the ditched enclosures, converging ditches to funnel animals and roadside plots at Longdales Road, and the ditched enclosures at Langley Mill Farm. Extensive areas of grassland, heathland and wood pasture for grazing, and possibly hay meadows, would be required to feed the stock and this would have resulted in a low density of settlements. A podzol (a soil low in nutrients and characteristic of heathland) under the Roman Ryknield Street in Sutton Park[59] suggests the presence of heathland when the road was constructed in the mid-first century AD, as do impressions of bracken found in the fired-clay dome of the oven of the second-century pottery kiln at Sherifoot Lane.[60]

Pottery and radiocarbon dating showed that the Roman features adjacent to the Iron Age farmstead at Langley Mill Farm[61] mainly dated from the middle of the second to the early third century. At least five large rectilinear ditched enclosures were constructed and there were also probable ditched droveways, suggesting that this site concentrated on stock-rearing. The enclosures continued beyond the excavated area and cropmarks suggest further enclosures nearby. There was also a small timber building which was possibly a stockman's hut, but the main dwelling in the Roman period must have been outside the area excavated. The small quantity of charred grain found in Roman features on the site does not contain processing waste, in contrast to that from Iron Age features, therefore the rotary querns found on this site were used to mill grain that was grown and processed elsewhere.

Excavations at Langley Mill Farm on the line of the M6 Toll motorway uncovered a Roman quernstone used to mill grain.
© Michael Hodder

Excavations at Longdales Road[62] revealed a group of features that were in use from around AD 120 and into the later third century AD and are interpreted as an elaborate livestock management system, possibly functioning as a collecting point for livestock from the surrounding countryside to take live animals or their products south along Ryknield Street to market at Alcester. A double-ditched enclosure subdivided into probable stock pens and containing a circular house and stone surface lay within a ditched compound whose entrances had converging ditches. The enclosure and compound adjoined a series of plots that were laid out at right angles to Ryknield Street, bounded by ditches with metalled roads alongside, and contained a ditched enclosure and two circular houses. The original extent of the roadside layout is indicated by field boundaries marked on historic Ordnance Survey maps to the north and south of the excavated area, some of which still survive. They show that a frontage of approximately 500 metres along Ryknield Street was occupied by at least 16 plots, each 28 metres or 35 metres wide.

Small but locally significant concentrations of Roman pottery, mainly second to third century in date, found in fieldwalking at Over Green and Wiggins Hill in Sutton Coldfield probably indicate the location of settlements. They contrast with the extensive distribution of small quantities of Roman pottery which is likely to be the result of manuring arable land with domestic debris. Over Green lies at one corner of a rectilinear field system, much of it surviving as existing boundaries, which is similar to demonstrably Roman or pre-Roman field systems elsewhere.[63] Thirteen sherds of Roman pottery found in excavations in the Bull Ring[64] hint at a farmstead, though no features of Roman date survived.

A rectilinear field system surviving as hedge lines in Sutton Coldfield.
© Michael Hodder

Relatively little pottery may have been used in these settlements. The marked difference between the quantities of Roman pottery found in the excavation at Longdales Road (over 3,000 sherds) and that at Langley Mill Farm (745 sherds) might reflect the availability of pottery. The main types found at Longdales Road were Severn Valley and Malvern wares, which were manufactured to its south-west and may have been more difficult or more expensive to obtain further north, particularly away from roads. This may have encouraged pottery manufacture at Perry Barr and Sherifoot Lane in the second century. Although it is difficult to identify the boundaries of *civitates* (administrative units of Roman Britain, based on pre-Roman tribal territories), Longdales Road is likely to have been within and possibly near the boundary of the more Romanized Dobunnic territory.[65]

Excavations at Sherifoot Lane, Sutton Coldfield, revealed the remains of a pottery kiln whose floor was supported by double arches of sun-dried clay bricks, an unusual arrangement which also occurs in south-eastern England, suggesting that the potter may have moved to Sherifoot Lane from that region. By contrast, fire-bars supported vessels in the kiln at Perry Barr. Waste pottery shows that the main products of the Sherifoot Lane kiln were jars and bowls, but tankards, flagons (handled vessels to contain and serve drinks), beakers, dishes and mortaria (mixing bowls) were also made. Jars, bowls and tankards were produced at the Perry Barr kiln. Similar vessel forms were made by the Roman pottery industry in north Warwickshire, but the tankards are a characteristic vessel form of the Severn Valley ware which may have been copied by the potters to meet local demand.[66] Fuel for the kilns would have been obtained from nearby woodland, probably managed as coppice. Sherifoot Lane is near the former Hill Wood and the Perry Barr kiln is similarly near woodland which is marked on an eighteenth-century map.[67]

These tankards and bowls were made at the Roman pottery kiln in Sherifoot Lane, Sutton Coldfield.
© University of Birmingham; Classics, Ancient History and Archaeology, photograph by Graham Norrie

The late third century and beyond

Roman rural settlements in the West Midlands enjoyed their greatest prosperity from the mid-second to mid-third centuries. From this time on, and into the early fourth century, settlements were abandoned, possibly reflecting insecurity in the country as a whole.[68] Roman pottery dating to the late third and early fourth centuries found at Longdales Road and Langley Mill Farm shows that they were both occupied into the later Roman period. In the late third century the double-ditched enclosure at Longdales Road was replaced by a ditch; circular houses and roadside plots were replaced by a small enclosure set back from Ryknield Street.[69] Mixed farming might have replaced the previous livestock specialization; charred spelt wheat found in the latest phase at Longdales Road may have been grown on the site. The upper part of the peat deposit at Aldridge Road in Perry Barr, which was radiocarbon-dated to around AD 330, also contained evidence of mixed farming. It contained pollen of cereals, cornflower (a weed of arable fields) and wetland grasses, and dung beetles indicated grazing animals.[70]

The settlements and associated features at Langley Mill Farm, Longdales Road and some other parts of the Roman landscape of Birmingham may have been abandoned before the end of the Roman period. However, the lines of some local Roman roads are still in use, including Ryknield Street near Longdales Road. The spur of land occupied by the Roman enclosures there can be identified as *Hellerelege*, mentioned in a charter of AD 669, which suggests a continuity of estate boundaries.[71] The concentrations of Roman pottery at Over Green and Wiggins Hill and the pottery found in excavations in King's Norton and the Bull Ring may indicate that some of Birmingham's medieval villages and hamlets, and the medieval town, are on the sites of Roman farmsteads.[72]

The early history of Birmingham in context

Archaeology has contributed to understanding all periods of Birmingham's past[73] but it is the sole source for the thousands of years before documented history. It enables us to observe the actions and interpret the motives of the people of prehistoric and Roman Birmingham who left no records. Unlike the documentary record, physical remains are not determined by what people write down or depict, but they are similarly subject to the vagaries of survival and the methods and extent of investigation.

Prehistoric and Roman Birmingham was markedly different to later periods. There were no villages, let alone towns, and little industry. There are, as yet, no discoveries of human remains through which we can encounter actual individuals. However, these times cannot be separated from the later, documented past. From the archaeology we can identify themes familiar in more recent history such as the movement of people, ideas, raw materials and products into Birmingham and entrepreneurialism in the establishment of a Roman pottery industry. People also influenced land use by clearing woodland, creating heathland, establishing roads and tracks and, perhaps, initiating later settlement patterns.

Notes

1   W. Hutton, *An History of Birmingham* (2nd edn, 1783), 17–25, 371–2; R.K. Dent, *The Making of Birmingham* (Birmingham, 1894), 1; C. Gill, *History of Birmingham Volume I. Manor and Borough to 1865* (London, 1952), 2–4; V. Skipp, *A History of Greater Birmingham down to 1830* (Birmingham, 1980), 11–12. For the derivation of the place name see, for example, M. Gelling, *Place-names in the Landscape* (London, 1984), 49, 263.

2   C. Chattock, *Antiquities* (Birmingham, 1884); W. Midgley, *A Short History of the Town and Chase of Sutton Coldfield* (Birmingham, 1904), 3

3   M. Hodder, *Birmingham: The Hidden History* (2nd edn, Stroud, 2011); M. Hodder, *The Archaeology of Sutton Park* (Stroud, 2013). Birmingham City Council's *Historic Environment Record* (www.birmingham.gov.uk/her) contains information on individual sites.

4   A. Jones, 'Roman Birmingham I. Metchley Roman Forts excavations 1963–4, 1967–9 and 1997', *Transactions of the Birmingham and Warwickshire Archaeological Society*, 105 for 2001 (2002), 1–133; A. Jones, 'Roman Birmingham II. Metchley Roman Forts excavations 1998–2000 and 2002, the Eastern and Southern Annexes and other investigations', *Transactions of the Birmingham and Warwickshire Archaeological Society*, 108 for 2004 (2005), 1–115; A. Jones, *Roman Birmingham 3. Excavations at Metchley Roman Fort 1999–2001 and 2004–2005. Western Settlement, the Livestock Compound and the Western Defences*, British Archaeological Reports, British Series, 354 (Oxford, 2011); A. Jones, *Roman Birmingham 4. Excavations at Metchley Roman Fort 2004–2005. The Praetentura, Central Range, Western Defences and Post-Roman Activity*, British Archaeological Reports, British Series, 552 (Oxford, 2012); A. Jones, *Roman Birmingham 5. Metchley Roman Fort, Birmingham. Excavations in the Fort Interior, 2003–2005 and 2010; Synthesis and Overview of Excavations 1963–2010; Consolidated Bibliography*, British Archaeological Reports, British Series (forthcoming).

5   A. Jones, B. Burrows, C.J. Evans, A. Hancocks and J. Williams, *A Romano-British Livestock Complex in Birmingham. Excavations 2002–2004 and 2006–2007 at Longdales Road, King's Norton, Birmingham*, British Archaeological Reports, British Series, 470 (Oxford, 2008).

6   A.B. Powell, P. Booth, A.P. Fitzpatrick and A.D. Crockett, *The Archaeology of the M6 Toll, 2000–2003*, Oxford Wessex Archaeology Monograph, 2 (Oxford, 2008).

7   T. Jones, 'Birmingham and Warwickshire Archaeological Society, the "East of Sutton" survey', *West Midlands Archaeology*, 41 (1998), 109–11; T. Jones, 'Birmingham, the "East of Sutton" survey', *West Midlands Archaeology*, 42 (1999), 146–8; M.A. Hodder and T.A. Jones, 'Birmingham's rural fringe: an archaeological survey of the Green Belt in Sutton Coldfield', *Transactions of the Birmingham and Warwickshire Archaeological Society* (forthcoming).

8   L.H. Barfield and M.A. Hodder, 'Burnt mounds in the West Midlands: surveys and excavations', in A. Gibson (ed.), *Midlands Prehistory*, British Archaeological Reports, British Series, 204 (Oxford, 1989), 5–13; L.H. Barfield and M.A. Hodder, 'Burnt mounds in south Birmingham: excavations at Cob Lane in 1980 and 1981, and other investigations', *Transactions of the Birmingham and Warwickshire Archaeological Society*, 114 for 2010 (2011), 13–46; Hodder, *Hidden History*, 28–43.

9   E. Tetlow, B. Geary, J. Halsted and A. Howard, 'Palaeoenvironmental evidence for Holocene landscape change and human activity at Tameside, Aldridge Road, Perry Barr, Birmingham', *Transactions of the Birmingham and Warwickshire Archaeological Society*, 112 (2008), 1–11.

10 Most of the dates for the prehistoric period, and some for Roman sites, are derived from radiocarbon dating, which measures the residual radioactive isotopes of carbon samples associated with archaeological remains. It provides a statistical measure which produces a likely date range rather than a single date. For clarity, this chapter uses the central date of the likely range.

11 Over the past 500,000 years there have been three main glaciations ('Ice Ages'), when ice caps covered much of Britain. The glaciations were separated by interglacials, and within each glaciation there were warm periods called interstadials. For a summary, see T. Darvill, *Prehistoric Britain* (3rd edn, London, 2010), 25–7

12 Darvill, *Prehistoric Britain*, 25–46; A. Lang and S. Buteux, 'Lost but not forgotten: the Lower and Middle Palaeolithic of the West Midlands', in P. Garwood (ed.), *The Undiscovered Country: The Earlier Prehistory of the West Midlands*, The Making of the West Midlands, 1 (Oxford, 2007), 6–38.

13 J. Evans, *Ancient Stone Implements, Weapons and Ornaments of Great Britain, 2nd edition* (London, 1897), 578–80.

14 P. Watson, 'Prehistoric finds from Birmingham reported to Birmingham City Museum', *Transactions of the Birmingham and Warwickshire Archaeological Society*, 96 for 1989–90 (1991), 95–6.

15 A.T.O. Lang and D.H. Keen, 'Hominid colonisation and the Lower and Middle Palaeolithic of the West Midlands', *Proceedings of the Prehistoric Society*, 71 (2005), 63–83.

16 M. Smith, A. Howard and M. Hodder, 'Birmingham's oldest inhabitants: a newly discovered Palaeolithic axe from Sutton Coldfield', *Past* (Newsletter of the Prehistoric Society), 66 (2010), 6–7.

17 N. Daffern and A. Clapham, *Analysis of Environmental Remains from 45 College Road, Perry Barr, Birmingham, West Midlands*, Historic Environment and Archaeology Service, Worcestershire County Council, Report 1888 (2012).

18 V. Score and T. Higgins, 'Early prehistoric clearance in Birmingham? Excavations at Banbury Street', *Transactions of the Birmingham and Warwickshire Archaeological Society*, 114 for 2010 (2011), 1–12.

19 Darvill, *Prehistoric Britain*, 57–67

20 Hodder, *Archaeology of Sutton Park*, 35–7

21 N. Daffern, *Full Analysis of Environmental Remains*

from *Land to the North of Brays Road, Sheldon Heath, Birmingham*, Worcestershire Archaeology Report 2067 (2014).

22 Hodder, *Hidden History*, 24; Hodder, *Archaeology of Sutton Park*, 38–40.

23 A. Myers, 'The Upper Palaeolithic and Mesolithic archaeology of the West Midlands', in Garwood (ed.), *The Undiscovered Country*, 22–38; Darvill, *Prehistoric Britain*, 67–75.

24 Jones, 'East of Sutton'; Hodder and Jones, 'Birmingham's rural fringe'.

25 Hodder, *Hidden History*, 24–5.

26 P. Garwood, 'Regions, cultural identity and social change, 4500–1500 BC', in Garwood (ed.), *The Undiscovered Country*, 195–215.

27 C. Rann, 'A Neolithic pit, Iron Age pit and prehistoric to early medieval palaeochannel at Bournville, Birmingham', *Transactions of the Birmingham and Warwickshire Archaeological Society*, 115 for 2011 (2012), 1–15.

28 Tetlow et al., 'Palaeoenvironmental evidence for Holocene landscape change'.

29 For example Darvill, *Prehistoric Britain*, 88–92.

30 J. Greig, 'Priorities in Mesolithic, Neolithic and Bronze Age environmental archaeology', in Garwood (ed.), *The Undiscovered Country*, 39–50.

31 Barfield and Hodder, 'Burnt mounds in the West Midlands'; Barfield and Hodder, 'Burnt mounds in south Birmingham'; Hodder, *Hidden History*, 28–44.

32 Hodder, *Archaeology of Sutton Park*, 44–9; W. Fowler, *A History of Erdington* (Birmingham, 1885), 15.

33 The statistical range of the radiocarbon dates (see note 10) is 1700–800 BC, but the sites were probably in use during a shorter period than this.

34 L.H. Barfield and M.A. Hodder, 'Burnt mounds as saunas', *Antiquity*, 61 (1987), 370–9; V. Buckley (ed.), *Burnt Offerings: International Contributions to Burnt Mound Archaeology* (Dublin, 1990); M.A. Hodder and L.H. Barfield (eds), *Burnt Mounds and Hot Stone Technology. Papers from the Second International Burnt Mound Conference, Sandwell, 12th–14th October 1990* (Sandwell, 1991); Hodder, *Hidden History*, 39–42; B. Wilkins, 'Past orders: the archaeology of beer', *Current Archaeology*, 265 (2011), 28–35.

35 Barfield and Hodder, 'Burnt mounds in south Birmingham'; Hodder, *Hidden History*, 33–8.

36 Tetlow et al., 'Palaeoenvironmental evidence for Holocene landscape change'.

37 Darvill, *Prehistoric Britain*, 211ff., 238–9; Barfield and Hodder, 'Burnt mounds in south Birmingham', 43–4.

38 Powell et al., *Archaeology of the M6 Toll*, Sites 29 and 30.

39 *Sutton Coldfield Corn Rent Map* (1824–25); W. Yates, *Map of Warwickshire* (1793).

40 D. Hurst, 'Middle Bronze Age to Iron Age: a research assessment, overview and agenda', in S. Watt (ed.), *The Archaeology of the West Midlands: A Framework for Research* (Oxford, 2011), 106–8; D. Hurst (ed.), *Westward on the High-hilled Plains: The Later Prehistory of the West Midlands*, The Making of the West Midlands, 2 (forthcoming).

41 Hodder, *Hidden History*, 45.

42 A. Jones, *Broadmeadow Close, King's Norton, Birmingham, Archaeological Excavation 2014*, AJ Archaeology, unpublished report (2015).

43 Birmingham City Council, *Birmingham Development Plan Green Belt Option Areas, Archaeology and Historic Environment Assessment, September 2013* (2013). http://www.birmingham.gov.uk/downloads/file/1749/pg6-green-belt-option-areas-archaeology-and-historic-environment-assessment-2013pdf (accessed 27 August 2016).

44 C. Coutts, *Land at Walker's Heath, King's Norton, Birmingham, Archaeological Excavation*, Archaeology Warwickshire Report, 1381 (2013).

45 Jones, 'Roman Birmingham I'; 'Roman Birmingham II'; *Roman Birmingham 3*; *Roman Birmingham 4*; *Roman Birmingham 5*.

46 Jones, *Roman Birmingham 3*, 105.

47 Jones, 'Roman Birmingham II', 88.

48 Hodder, *Hidden History*, 63.

49 G. de la Bedoyere, *Roman Britain: A New History* (London, 2006),

50 D. Smith, in Jones, 'Roman Birmingham II', 67–8.

51 de la Bedoyere, *Roman Britain*, 41–7.

52 Jones, 'Roman Birmingham I', 107–8.

53 J. Greig, in Jones, 'Roman Birmingham II', 75–80.

54 Hodder, *Hidden History*, 64.

55 A. Foard-Colby, 'Archaeological excavation at the Old Bowling Green, Parson's Hill, Kings Norton, Birmingham', *Transactions of the Birmingham and Warwickshire Archaeological Society*, 114 for 2010 (2011), 73–9.

56 D. Miller, *Archaeological Watching Brief along the Line of the Northfield Relief Road*, Worcestershire County Council Historic Environment and Archaeology Service Report, 1393 (2007); R. Taylor-Wilson and J. Proctor, 'Archaeological investigations at land off Sir Herbert Austin Way, Northfield, Birmingham', *Transactions of the Birmingham and Warwickshire Archaeological Society*, 117 for 2013 (2014), 33–48.

57 S. Ratkai, 'The pottery from the excavations', in M. Hislop, G. Demidowicz and S. Price (eds), *'Northeton... a praty uplandyshe towne...' Building Recording, Excavation and Documentary Research in King's Norton, Birmingham, 2005-2007*, British Archaeological Reports, British Series, 529 (Oxford, 2011), 114–26.

58 A.S. Esmonde Cleary, 'The Romano-British period: an assessment', in S. Watt (ed.), *The Archaeology of the West Midlands: A Framework for Research* (Oxford, 2011), 127–47.

59 B. Walker, 'The Rycknield Street in the neighbourhood of Birmingham', *Transactions Birmingham Archaeological Society*, 60 for 1936 (1940), 42–55.

60 C.J. Evans, P. Booth and M. Hodder, 'A Romano-British pottery kiln at Sherifoot Lane, Sutton Coldfield', *Transactions of the Birmingham and Warwickshire Archaeological Society*, 117 for 2013 (2014), 1–32.

61 A.B. Powell and K. Ritchie, 'North of Langley Brook (Site 29)', in Powell et al., *Archaeology of the M6 Toll*, 306–37; P. Booth, 'Romano-British period discussion', in ibid., 516–35.

62 Jones et al., *Longdales Road.*

63 Jones, 'East of Sutton'; Hodder and Jones, 'Birmingham's rural fringe'; M. Hodder, 'Continuity and discontinuity in the landscape: Roman to medieval in Sutton Chase', *Medieval Archaeology*, 36 (1992), 178–82; M.A. Hodder, 'The development of some aspects of settlement and land use in Sutton Chase' (PhD thesis, University of Birmingham, 1988).

64 S. Ratkai, 'The pottery', in C. Patrick and S. Ratkai, *The Bull Ring Uncovered: Excavations at Edgbaston Street, Moor Street, Park Street and The Row, Birmingham, 1997-2001* (Oxford, 1999), 92–171; M. Hodder, C. Patrick and S. Ratkai, 'Discussion', in ibid., 304–19.

65 M. Hodder, 'Forts, farms, fields and industries: the Roman period in West Midlands County (Birmingham, Coventry, Dudley, Sandwell, Solihull, Walsall and Wolverhampton)', in R. White and M. Hodder (eds), *A Clash of Cultures: The Archaeology of the Romano-British West Midlands*, The Making of the West Midlands, 3 (forthcoming).

66 Evans et al., 'Romano-British pottery kiln at Sherifoot Lane'; Hodder, *Hidden History*, 70–6; H.V. Hughes, 'A Romano-British kiln site at Perry Barr, Birmingham', *Transactions of the Birmingham Archaeological Society*, 77 for 1959 (1961), 33–9; P. Booth, 'Roman pottery in Warwickshire – production and demand', *Journal of Roman Pottery Studies*, 1 (1986), 22–41.

67 S. Botham, *A Plan of the Township of Handsworth in the County of Stafford* (Oxford, 1794).

68 White and Hodder, *Clash of Cultures.*

69 Powell and Ritchie, 'North of Langley Brook'; Jones et al., *Longdales Road.*

70 Tetlow et al, 'Palaeoenvironmental evidence for Holocene landscape change'.

71 Jones et al., *Longdales Road*, 91; G. Demidowicz, 'The lost Lint Brook. A solution to the *Hellerelege* Anglo-Saxon charter and other explorations of King's Norton history', *Transactions of the Birmingham and Warwickshire Archaeological Society*, 107 (2003), 111–29.

72 Hodder, *Hidden History*, 78.

73 Hodder, *Hidden History.*

Rex Angl' 7 Dux Norm[annie] Aquit[anie] 7 Com[es] An[d]...
... noster pro[?]sisse 7 dedisse ... fec' Will[elm]o ... de ...
... 7 cum om[n]ib[us] libertat[ib]; 7 liberis consuetudin[ib]; ...
... et sicu[n]d[um] ... in mea p[rese]ntia. T[este] Will[elm]o ...

... Rex Angl' ... 7 p[rese]nti carta mea ... affirmasse ...
... 7 ... 7 cum om[n]ib[us] libertat[ib]; 7 ...
... 7 honorifice p[re]d[i]co d[i]e ...
... Will[elm]o de Longo Cam[p]o ...

CHAPTER THREE

Medieval Birmingham

STEVEN BASSETT AND RICHARD HOLT

Throughout the twentieth century Birmingham's history was popularly thought to have begun in the late eleventh century and to have remained largely invisible until the late twelfth.[1] Apart from a few isolated fragments of evidence (such as its Old English name), earlier aspects of it – its Anglo-Saxon and Norman 'prehistory' – were unknown and assumed to be unknowable. The traditional account of its origins was of the eponymous *Beorma* and his fellow Anglo-Saxon immigrants having cleared away primeval woodland so as to create a village, the *hām* of the *Beormingas*.[2] Still of little importance or interest when first recorded in Domesday Book (1086),[3] it was believed to encircle a green on which stood its church, St Martin's, and which served as the village's marketplace when in 1166 Peter de Birmingham granted it the status of a borough.[4] Thereafter, it was thought, it showed little evidence of the growth of town life until the sixteenth century.[5]

Since 2000, however, the results of archaeological fieldwork, topographical analysis and a new approach to the study of the medieval ecclesiastical organization of the area of the modern conurbation have thrown light on previously hidden aspects of Birmingham's history before 1166 – in particular, on its agricultural landscape, on the origins of its secular and ecclesiastical land-units, and on the settlement's early history and topography.[6] These new insights combine to extend the history of Birmingham, at its modern extent, back into the pre-Conquest period and also to revise, redefine and fill out our understanding of its origins as a medieval borough. This new perception of Birmingham's origins and medieval history is markedly different from the traditional one characterized above.[7]

One important new form of investigation that has been applied to the Birmingham area is a study of its human landscape – that is, the evidence of roads and field boundaries as preserved in the many well-drawn maps of the manor and town existing from 1731 onwards.[8] This reveals the evolution of Birmingham's landscape from a period when the borough occupied only a relatively small area of the manor, showing that many of the latter's more important roads, and even some of its field

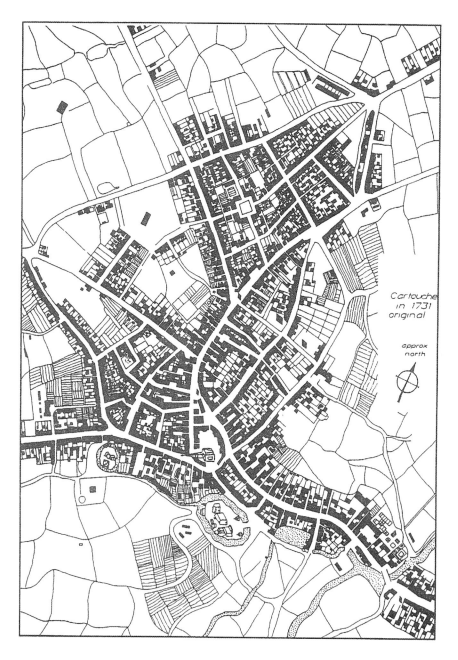

Cartouche in 1731 original

approx north

William Westley's map of Birmingham (1731), as redrawn by Lorna Watts.
By permission of Lorna Watts and the Birmingham & Warwickshire Archaeological Society

Figure 1 Important
pre-modern roads in the
manor of Birmingham
and its vicinity, shown
superimposed on the
area's relief and drainage
pattern. The probable
courses of lost lengths of
some Roman roads are
also suggested.
Map created by Duncan Probert

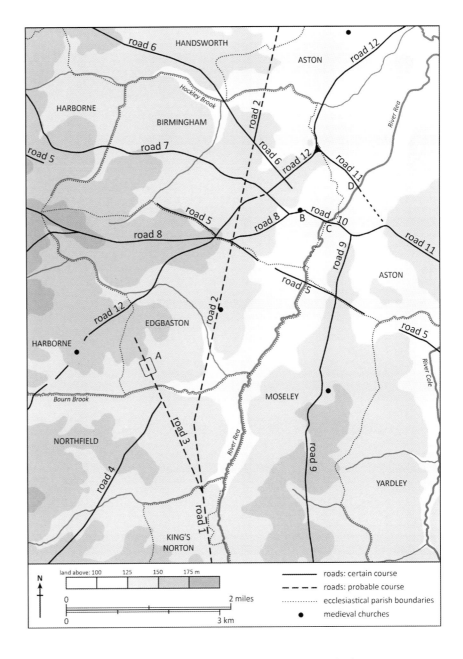

boundaries, still survive in what is today an almost completely built-up environment, while others, now lost, persisted into the nineteenth century and thus were mapped by the Ordnance Survey. Accordingly, a reliable impression has been gained of the manor's rural topography in the early eighteenth century; and this, in its broad outlines, is likely to bear a close resemblance to the topography of the Domesday manor, notwithstanding the many small-scale changes to boundaries that must have occurred in the intervening centuries. This is especially true of the manor's fertile eastern half, which appears to have been more agriculturally advanced than its western half, and therefore had a much more fully developed human landscape at an early date. The study suggests that the courses of some of the major roads that crossed the Birmingham area, and also many of the field boundaries, shared common alignments, running approximately south-west to north-east and north-west to south-east. Because these results have been set out and fully discussed in an earlier publication,[9] only a brief summary of them will be presented here.

A number of early long-distance through-routes crossed the area of the modern city, several of which are known to be of Roman construction (Fig. 1, roads 1, 4) or may confidently be supposed to be (Fig. 1, roads 2, 3); at least two others may be of pre-Roman origin (Fig. 1, roads 5, 9).[10] Yet another important early through-route ran on a north-west to south-east course through Harborne, being perpetuated today by Vivian Road, part of Harborne High Street, Harborne Road, Broad Street, Colmore Row, Steelhouse Lane, Aston Street, Aston Road and Lichfield Road (Fig. 1, road 12). This looks like one of the most important roads in the medieval manor of Birmingham, where, heading for Lichfield, it ran down the middle of the narrow outcrop of Lower Keuper sandstone that, stretching from Northfield to Sutton Coldfield, dominated the manor's natural topography.[11]

First mapped in the eighteenth century but doubtless in existence for many centuries before, the roads that ran on a generally north-west to south-east line through medieval Birmingham crossed the River Rea at Deritend (Fig. 1, C); consequently, as each approached the river its course moved progressively further off the dominant alignment. The Birmingham family's castle was situated next to the roads' joint route to the ford, and together they formed the central axis of the planned marketplace (Fig. 1, B, road 10). These roads were ones coming from, respectively, Wolverhampton, Dudley and Halesowen (Fig. 1, roads 6, 7, 8). Another ford further downstream, in Duddeston (Fig. 1, D), was probably the more important of the two for through-routes approaching the Rea from a generally eastern direction until the creation of Birmingham's marketplace. The roads from Alcester and Coventry appear initially to have crossed the Rea at this more northerly ford (Fig. 1, roads 9, 11), but subsequently they were diverted on to new courses that took them to the Deritend crossing and thus into the marketplace.[12]

The origins of the medieval manor and parish of Birmingham

It was arguably in an agriculturally productive landscape crossed by important through-routes, therefore, not in clearings hacked out of dense woodland, that the post-Roman inhabitants of the area of modern Birmingham – the *Beormingas* and their many anonymous neighbours – settled and farmed.[13] The small portion that, by 1086, constituted the manor of Birmingham had not always been a self-contained land-unit, however. In origin it appears to have been formed by the gradual, piecemeal fission of a far larger territory that, by analogy with other areas of lowland England for which there is much fuller evidence, had been created in the first post-Roman centuries. It is likely that the *Beormingas* – 'Beorma's people' – were only one among many small communities that farmed distinct parts of the territory's land, while acknowledging another nearby community's supralocal authority in political, fiscal and, at length, ecclesiastical matters. Economically self-sufficient territories of this sort were the individual building blocks out of which the earliest discernible Anglo-Saxon kingdoms were forged, by conquest or other form of amalgamation, in the course of the late sixth and early seventh centuries.[14] They often kept one or more aspects of their territorial identity in later centuries by becoming the original parish served by a minster of seventh- or early eighth-century foundation, or by retaining an important local governmental role, singly or in a group of two or more, as a hundred (the chief subdivision of a shire).[15] In this case, the territory within which the *Beormingas* lived has been tentatively identified as the huge parish that was originally served by a minster set up at an unknown date at, it seems, Harborne, which lay just west of medieval Birmingham and which by 1086 was in the hands of the bishops of Lichfield.

The origins of the English parochial system that is in use today lie mainly between the tenth and the mid-twelfth century. In the West Midlands, as in many other regions, it evolved out of an earlier one – widely known as 'the minster system' – by a long-drawn-out process that left many fragments of valuable evidence scattered about in late medieval sources.[16] This evidence can be used to form a picture of the ecclesiastical geography of the West Midlands from the seventh century onwards. It shows that, just as there was a direct geographical correlation between manors and parishes in and after the tenth century, even as far back as the seventh century the major missionary churches known as minsters had served the secular land-units of the day in the West Midlands. However, these territories, already spoken of here, were far larger than the manors referred to in late Anglo-Saxon and later sources. Accordingly, where evidence exists of how the many late medieval churches in the Birmingham area were related to each other in respect of their original status, an understanding of the area's Anglo-Saxon ecclesiastical history can be gained. This in turn can throw a little light on the extensive early Anglo-Saxon territories out of which the area's Domesday manors were formed.

Therefore, to make progress in determining the original extent of the territory within which lay the land that became the Domesday manor of Birmingham, particular attention needs to be paid to the recorded interrelationships of the medieval churches situated within the modern city.

The Anglo-Saxon minsters and other medieval churches of the Birmingham area

Not far from late medieval Birmingham were churches that meet the criteria for being recognized as former Anglo-Saxon minsters, such as Bromsgrove, Halesowen, Wolverhampton, Walsall, Lichfield St Michael's, Coleshill, Hampton-in-Arden and Wootton Wawen.[17] They had parishes that were originally very large and that, between them, encircled most of the area now occupied by the city of Birmingham. Within the latter area there were two churches, Aston's and Harborne's, that also had the distinctive characteristics of a former minster, such as dependent chapels and an extensive original parish (Fig. 2). One of these two was very probably the original mother-church of the whole Birmingham area: Harborne is undoubtedly the stronger candidate, but the evidence is not conclusive.[18]

In the early nineteenth century Harborne's parish, which always included Smethwick, was of only average size for the area, but it had initially been extensive. When first recorded in the 1270s, Edgbaston's church was a chapel subject to the church of Harborne, and it remained so until it became parochially independent around the end of the Middle Ages. In 1247 the rector of Harborne was said to be entitled to £2 13s 4d from the endowment of Handsworth parish, a claim that was upheld after a lengthy legal dispute. This shows that, although Handsworth's church had been behaving as if it were an independent parish church, not just for the manor of Handsworth but for Perry and Little Barr too, it had originated as Harborne's chapel.[19] West Bromwich also seems initially to have been part of Harborne's parish, as is suggested by the details of a long-running dispute in the twelfth century. This resulted in the rector of Handsworth's church (itself once subject to Harborne's) having his claim upheld, in 1181, that he should have control of West Bromwich's as well.[20]

The same may be true of Great Barr. Handsworth's parish included Perry and Little Barr, the latter being one of two Domesday manors called Barr. The other,

Figure 2 Medieval parishes and townships of the Birmingham area, shown at their early nineteenth-century extent.
Map created by Duncan Probert

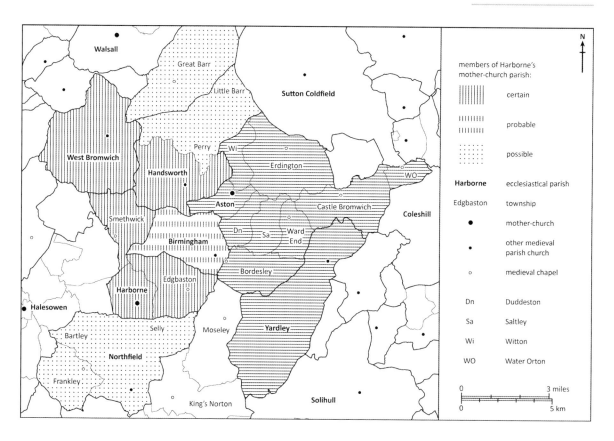

Great Barr, was a chapelry of Aldridge (which lay to the north of it), in and after the late medieval period.[21] It is very likely that, since (as their name indicates) they were created by the fission of a single land-unit called Barr, these three manors were originally served by the same mother-church. However, it is impossible to say if this role was fulfilled by Harborne (Handsworth's mother) or by Walsall (Aldridge's).[22] Similarly, it is impossible to identify the original mother-church of Northfield, which lies immediately south of Harborne. Bromsgrove (the mother-church of neighbouring King's Norton) and Harborne are equally strong candidates. At its northern end Northfield's parish contained the two manors of Selly (including the modern districts of Weoley Castle, Selly Oak and Selly Park), and also Bartley, a detached part of the larger Selly manor. Selly had almost certainly been an original part of Harborne's parish; but it is unclear if its subsequent parochial attachment to Northfield was as a result of 'manorial capture' – in 1086 the manor of Northfield and both manors of Selly were held by William fitz Ansculf – or because Northfield's church, which already existed then, had initially been a chapel of Harborne's church.[23]

The former minster at Aston had one of the largest parishes in the West Midlands, having at least six chapels subject to it at the end of the Middle Ages – those at Erdington, Little Bromwich *alias* Ward End, Castle Bromwich, Deritend (in Bordesley), Water Orton and Yardley. In the twelfth and thirteenth centuries a long, complex dispute over parochial control of Yardley was waged between the church of Aston and, separately, the Benedictine abbeys of Pershore and Alcester. Even though Pershore appears to have held Yardley since the late tenth century, and probably also before then, Aston was said to be its mother-church in three separate judgements in 1237, 1263 and 1274. In contrast to Harborne's church, Aston's had always enforced its matronal status, hence the very large size of its late medieval parish.[24] However, the likelihood of its having been the original mother-church of the entire Birmingham area is greatly diminished by the fact that it was, of course, the church of an area called Aston, 'eastern land-unit'. Directional names such as this indicate the early subordination of the area concerned to another, more important socio-economic and administrative centre. The key questions, therefore, are of the latter centre's location and, secondly, of the full extent of the much larger territory of which Anglo-Saxon Aston had initially been only the eastern part.

So far there has been no consideration of medieval Birmingham itself. Encircled as it was by land served by the churches of Harborne and Aston, it must at first have been in the parish of one or other of them; but the available sources offer few clues as to which one. On topographical grounds Harborne looks much the more likely, since in the early nineteenth century (when first mapped) its parish surrounded Birmingham's on three sides, an embrace suggesting a proprietary relationship (Fig. 2). Coupled with the evidence that Aston's name yields that the entire area of its late medieval parish had originally been socio-economically and administratively subject to somewhere to the west of it, this topographical clue points to the minster at Harborne as the original mother-church of the entire Birmingham area. So, too, does the ownership of Harborne and its church by the bishops of Lichfield in and before 1066, since it is certain that in earlier centuries important but failing minsters and their landed endowments were often taken under direct episcopal control so as to prevent them from falling under secular control.[25] Although this can no more act as proof of the matronal supremacy of Harborne's church in the area covered by most of the modern city than can the other indications rehearsed here, it adds significantly to the circumstantial evidence that it was indeed the area's mother-church.

The reason why nothing is known of the origins of St Martin's, Birmingham is probably because it became the parish church of a successful town. It is likely to be of late twelfth-century foundation and to have been set up specifically to serve the borough,[26] as is indicated by its location within a new triangular marketplace, a classic location for a borough chapel.[27] To the best of our knowledge there is no known instance in medieval Britain, Ireland, or the parts of France that were under English control at times in the late Middle Ages of a church that stood within a planned marketplace – as opposed to beside or close to it – being the parish church of the whole manor at the time of the marketplace's establishment. (Some such churches subsequently took on this role, as St Martin's did, but that is a different matter.) The borough's strong economic growth saw it rapidly transformed into 'a prosperous manufacturing and market town'[28] – a success mirrored in the rebuilding of St Martin's on a much grander scale in the mid-thirteenth century, by which time it probably had a graveyard.[29] However, it is most unusual to find a chapel of this sort serving not only the borough but also the whole manor in which it stood, as St Martin's did. It

An extract from a map of Harborne of 1790, which appears to show evidence in the local boundaries for the former existence of a substantial, squarish enclosure about St Peter's church – a feature reminiscent of the precincts within which other, better-evidenced minsters of Anglo-Saxon foundation are known to have stood.

By permission of the Library of Birmingham, Sherriff, *Map of Manor of Harborne*, 1790, MS 3202 [282533]

PLATE 7

A sample of the probably late fourteenth-century wall paintings visible in the chancel of St Martin's church until it was rebuilt in 1873–75. They show aspects of the life of St Martin of Tours.

By permission of Cambridge University Library, *Trans. Birmingham Arch. Soc.*, vol. for 1873 (1874), Plate 7

means that there was very probably a church on the manor of Birmingham before the borough's creation. If so, there can be little doubt that it stood elsewhere and that it was eventually eclipsed by its chapel, St Martin's, and then disappeared – such as occurred in almost identical circumstances at, for instance, Chelmsford and Braintree (Essex) and Lichfield.[30] Consequently, St Martin's at length served not only the borough but also the whole manor of Birmingham.

The only known candidate for recognition as Birmingham's first church is the church of the poorly documented priory or hospital of St Thomas, Birmingham, a house of Augustinian canons that stood on the north-east side of Bull (formerly Chapel) Street (Fig. 3). This hypothesis has been explored elsewhere,[31] and so only a brief summary of the argument will be given here. Sources refer to St Thomas's variously as a hospital, a house and a priory, but provide so few details of it that it cannot be reliably characterized. It was in existence by 1284–85, but its date of foundation is unknown.[32] By the time of its dissolution it had a large block of land, most of it lying adjacent to its precinct and most, perhaps all, of which it had probably acquired by the end of the thirteenth century, since thereafter the house was in decline. The land's size and compactness suggest that St Thomas's gained most of it in no more than two or three substantial blocks, and that it was almost certainly former demesne land of the Birminghams, the house's alleged founders.[33]

It is what we know of the graveyard in which it stood that points to its church having existed before the priory/hospital was founded. It was evidently a large one, not only in its extent but also in the number of burials.[34] Given that St Martin's stood in the borough's marketplace, even if it had burial rights from the outset (which is intrinsically unlikely) its graveyard must always have been small, as it still was when famously described by William Hutton in the 1780s.[35] At first most, perhaps all, of Birmingham's dead must have been buried elsewhere, in the manor's original

Figure 3 Elements of the late medieval landscape of the eastern part of the manor of Birmingham.
Map created by Duncan Probert

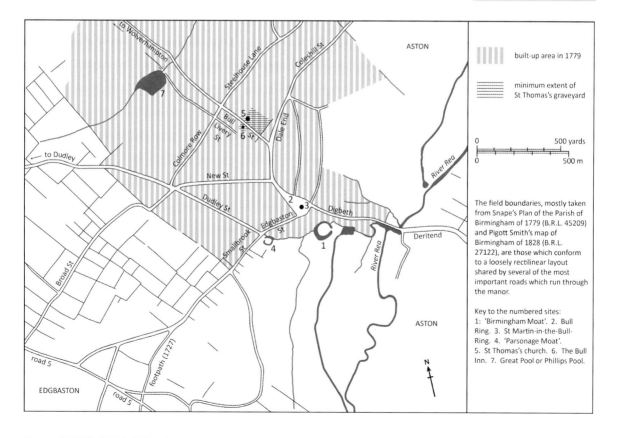

The field boundaries, mostly taken from Snape's Plan of the Parish of Birmingham of 1779 (B.R.L. 45209) and Pigott Smith's map of Birmingham of 1828 (B.R.L. 27122), are those which conform to a loosely rectilinear layout shared by several of the most important roads which run through the manor.

Key to the numbered sites:
1: 'Birmingham Moat'. 2. Bull Ring. 3. St Martin-in-the-Bull-Ring. 4. 'Parsonage Moat'.
5. St Thomas's church. 6. The Bull Inn. 7. Great Pool or Phillips Pool.

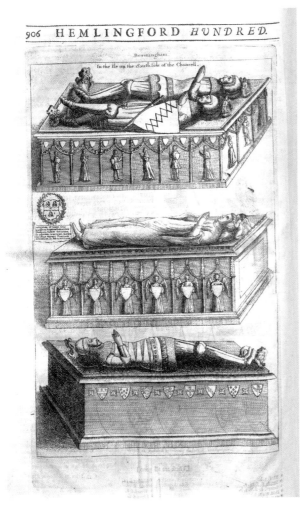

Probably Sir John de Birmingham, whose effigy of about 1390 in St Martin's church has survived largely undamaged.
© Elaine Mitchell

The four medieval tomb effigies still surviving in St Martin's church, as depicted in Sir William Dugdale's *Antiquities of Warwickshire* (1656). Much of the detail of the fourteenth-century effigies of Sir William de Birmingham and Fulk de Birmingham, seen at the top of the illustration, has since been lost.
By permission of the Cadbury Research Library: Special Collections, University of Birmingham

graveyard. That was arguably the one in which St Thomas's church stood, which therefore would have been the church in whose parish – coterminous with the manor of Birmingham – St Martin's was founded as a borough chapel.[36]

The castle and the market town

In 1086 the manor of Birmingham, as reported in Domesday Book, was an 'insignificant agricultural settlement' that had 'no sign of any distinguishing characteristics or any particular potential for growth'.[37] Valued at only 20 shillings, the lord's demesne had one plough team at work, and the nine peasant tenants – five *villani*, or villagers, and four *bordarii*, or smallholders – had just two between them.[38] Into this entirely rural landscape some important new features were inserted in the century after the Norman conquest: a castle, a created borough and probably a bridge or bridges over the Rea adjacent to the Deritend ford.

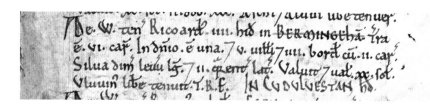

In 1166 Henry II granted Peter de Birmingham and his heirs a market that was to be held 'at his castle of Birmingham'.[39] Henry may have been doing no more than sanctioning a market that already existed, but, if so, it was probably not a long-established one. As lord of the manor, Peter was both the owner of the land and the legal master of those who lived on it. He could now hold a weekly market, charge tolls on transactions there, and exercise the necessary legal rights to ensure that the marketplace would be a safe place to visit and do business. Such grants were not unusual: we know of some 2,000 from the late twelfth and thirteenth centuries.[40] The right to hold a market had become a royal monopoly; and while many markets grew up that were never legalized by the grant of a royal charter, they could never deliver the toll revenues that their owners wanted, and, in the absence of a market court with the authority to hang transgressors on the spot, were likely to be the haunts of dealers in stolen goods and other undesirables. Unlicensed markets remained small and irregular, therefore, and did not establish themselves as permanent institutions as the Birmingham market did. Peter's purchase of a charter – and we may assume that the king demanded a suitably large fee for his valuable grant – was an investment in the future, a conscious act to increase his income from Birmingham. And his ambitions went further, well beyond fulfilling a desire to tap into the revenues that he could get from sales in the market. Peter knew, evidently, that a successful new market was essential for the fostering of a new town; and ownership of a town was an alluring prospect indeed, with the income that its lord could expect from the rents of hundreds of new tenants and the many, varied fees and fines that his town court and administration would be able to rake in on a regular basis. The twelfth century was the golden age of urban growth. Towns – which we understand to be settlements where populations with a variety of skills and occupations came together to make up communities practising a diversity of economic activities – had been growing all over western Europe since the eleventh century or earlier. The process was relatively rapid in historical terms, and Peter is likely to have been dimly aware of it. Domesday Book identifies or describes some 112 places as towns or displaying urban characteristics. Seventy years later, when Birmingham received its market charter, the number had already grown considerably – and would continue to grow until about 1300, when the area of England described in Domesday Book would now have over 500 towns of one sort or another.[41]

It was not uncommon for a twelfth-century 'created borough' to be laid out on suitable ground next to a castle, which itself may have been erected for strategic reasons at some distance from the manor house and main settlement of the manor concerned. If the castle was not a short-lived one, its presence is likely to have boosted the market's success and also to have led to its taking over the old manorial centre's role, which – as happened at Birmingham – then disappeared from both sight and local memory. In this case it appears that the castle was an earthwork-and-timber one of the sort known as a ringwork – a simple round enclosure consisting of a bank and ditch and usually having a strongly fortified entrance, within which were a hall and lesser buildings. Being on a low-lying site, its ditch may have been water-filled from the outset. The castle, which sat at the edge of the manor of Birmingham, was presumably created so as to control a crossing-point of the Rea used by several of the major long-distance roads that traversed the southern end of the Birmingham Plateau. It subsequently evolved into Birmingham's moated manor house, surviving as such into the early nineteenth century. Its precise date of origin will presumably remain unknown, but it was probably created in the late eleventh century, or perhaps in the early twelfth, in circumstances that required close control to be kept of an important river crossing on the manor of Birmingham's eastern boundary.

Establishing a new town was not a complicated procedure. Since the market would be the centre of its economic life, by Peter's time a designated marketplace generally lay at the physical centre of the new community. If it was expected to be a cattle and animal market as well as a market for corn and other foodstuffs, it was prudent to make the marketplace a large one (as was the case in Birmingham). Around it there needed to be enough house-plots for the new inhabitants, laid out along new streets or existing roadways – plots of a fairly standard size to be let at a standard rent. The purpose of such a new town was not (in the first place) to create new economic activities but to reorganize what already existed, and channel them into both old-established and new, strategically placed centres so as to create new commercial and industrial opportunities. We can envisage a twelfth-century countryside full of craftsmen, many or most of them combining their skills with farming and selling simple products to their neighbours. A new market, by drawing rural customers on a regular basis to the same place, opened the opportunity for craftsmen to sell enough to live by their trade alone.

The texts of the two market charters, with that of 1166 followed by that of 1189, in the official archive copy made by the king's chancery in the thirteenth century. The original documents given to Peter de Birmingham and his son William have not survived
By permission of The National Archives, London, C52/19 (41-42)

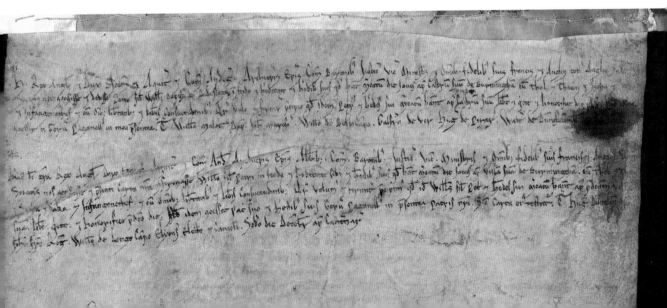

Moreover, the founders of these places knew that they had to make their towns attractive to new settlers, to offer conditions that would tempt craftsmen living in a scatter of villages across the region to move to the new centre: crucially, the newly available plots had to be much more than just places where a house could be built. They were to be 'burgages' whose tenants would be 'burgesses', full members of the new community and sharers in all its legal privileges. In a world of dependent rural tenants, where those who cultivated the land were all more or less under the control of a lord with extensive economic and legal authority over them, the burgess was a legally free man. He was subject to the lord's court, the new borough court, but it was understood that the lord's rights would be restricted to what was proper for a borough, and that the rights of the burgesses must be respected. It was these legal aspects of the town that defined it as a 'borough', a privileged place in law. In practice 'town' and 'borough' were the same, although not every place given burghal privileges developed into a town, and there were towns that were never formally boroughs. As a full member of the borough, the burgess was free of the market – that is, he paid no tolls and could trade freely without interference. He rented his burgage, but the tenancy was permanent and his heirs would inherit it without having to pay a massive fine, and he paid a cash rent that was fixed in perpetuity. And the plot was big enough for the burgess – if the town prospered, as nearly all did – to sublet or otherwise cram in new houses and to collect far more in rent than he himself paid to the lord.[42]

The new church of St Martin was built in the middle of the marketplace, which may have looked like this in the town's earliest years. Soon the rapid expansion of the decades around 1200 would turn this semi-rural scene into a bustling industrial and commercial centre with much denser housing.
© Birmingham Museums Trust

Some lords, a majority of them, had all this written down and issued as a formal charter of privileges. Others were wary of granting away privileges in perpetuity – the great Benedictine abbeys were notorious in this respect, so that major towns such as Bury St Edmunds and St Albans never received written confirmation of their liberties from their monastic owners. Other lords, it seems, just did not see the need, and perhaps especially in the earlier years of town foundation when there were fewer models to copy and when so many important transactions were still conducted orally. Birmingham fell into this latter group, and its burgesses never had a written charter. They did not need one: their privileges within the town were defined and well known, and did not change. When a piece of land in Solihull (a growing commercial settlement of the thirteenth century that also had no charter of privileges) was sold in around 1300, it was to be held of the lord of the manor 'according to the liberties and customs merchant of the market of Birmingham'.[43] The unchanging nature of these recognized liberties was acknowledged in 1529 when some details were entered into an appendix to a survey made of the manor, details that amply confirm their antiquity: in addition to enjoying freedom from tolls and other exactions, the burgess and his heirs were to pay the lord no substantial heriot or inheritance tax. Only his best weapon was to be paid, or 40d in money in default of his owning a suitable weapon (a formula often to be found in the written charters of smaller boroughs of earlier foundation).[44]

Identifying predominant trends in the medieval roads and field boundaries of the Birmingham area also allows us to measure the impact on the rural topography of the introduction of this planned borough, and of its subsequent piecemeal, partly planned, enlargement (Fig. 3). Significant road diversions were involved in order to force all traffic to pass through the new borough, which was located immediately north of an important crossing-point of the River Rea at Deritend. This site was no doubt chosen for the commercial opportunities afforded by the convergence on the Deritend ford of existing long-distance roads. It would therefore have been eminently sensible for Peter or another early member of the Birmingham family to have a bridge or bridges erected across the Rea there, thus further enhancing the new marketplace's ability to attract custom.[45]

We cannot demonstrate that Birmingham's identity as a town began immediately in 1166, or with Peter de Birmingham. Perhaps appropriate privileges were granted to tenants after his time – for example, by his son William who was careful to pay again to get his market confirmed by the new king Richard I in 1189, from which we deduce that William was taking no chances that he might lose such a valuable privilege. But it is significant that whereas Peter was granted the right to hold a market at his castle (*castrum*), William's grant stated that the market was to be held at his town (*villa*) of Birmingham.[46] An early borough foundation to coincide with Peter's purchase of the market charter is overwhelmingly probable, especially given the indications that it came into existence as a settlement all at once at some point during the twelfth century and certainly no later than 1200. Excavations in and around the area of the new Bull Ring from 1997 to 2001 found no evidence of settlement before the twelfth century. Everywhere in the area, it seems, the earliest evidence of human activities was consistent with the emergence of the new town before 1200.[47] The latter's triangular plan, the regularity of the plots fronting on to its sides, and the putative realignment of one or more of the major roads that converged on it from the east indicate that they were laid out in a single operation.

The excavations ruled out the possibility that the new town was in any way an extension of an earlier settlement. If the nine peasant households recorded in 1086 had been grouped together so that these farmers lived in a village or, more likely, a hamlet – rather than dispersed within the agricultural lands of the manor – this had certainly not been in the vicinity of the later marketplace. The older centre, as both Bassett and Demidowicz have argued, was in all likelihood in the area of the ancient ridgeway crossing the manor which has been discussed above, perpetuated in the later Colmore Row and Steelhouse Lane – indeed in the vicinity of the church of St Thomas.[48] The new market, by contrast, was located on heavier clay land better fitted for enclosure as the lord's deer-parks. Modern connotations of the word are misleading; a medieval park was wooded wasteland often unsuitable for agriculture that could nevertheless profitably be used for woodland management and grazing by captive deer. Botanical and insect evidence from the excavations around the Bull Ring confirms that before the town existed the whole area had been covered with trees and other wild vegetation characteristic of an uninhabited, wet landscape, little adapted for farming, if at all.[49]

But while this wasteland may have been unsuitable for agriculture, a considerable attraction of the new streets was the ready access of many of the house-plots to watercourses. Those along Edgbaston Street backed on to an existing stream and thus offered ideal facilities to tanners and other craftsmen requiring a ready source of water. There is biological evidence for the presence of both flax and hemp from the excavations, so that it is likely that both retting and subsequent production of linen, rope and twine were carried on in the new town. To the rear of the plots along High Street and Digbeth lay a substantial town ditch, at least seven metres wide and two metres deep and dug apparently in the mid-twelfth century to demarcate the eastern side of the town from the lord's park, later called the Little Park. This ditch, too, was a watercourse, at least in its early decades before it began both to silt up and to be filled with rubbish.[50]

The historical evidence from later years is entirely consistent with this picture of a new town founded on a new site. The rent for a burgage, once set, was fixed in perpetuity; later evidence, then, can confirm that the new town had a core of burgages rented out for 8d a year. That is what burgages are recorded as paying in the rental made in 1296, as we shall see, and still in the one from 1553, and we find this rent referred to in scattered documents from other dates.[51] That fact alone argues forcefully for the town of Birmingham having been born in a single act of planning, with standard plots laid out along either new streets or, more likely, existing routeways incorporated as streets into a town plan around the new marketplace. The lineaments on the ground of that planned development were visible throughout the succeeding centuries, until successive phases of redevelopment during the twentieth century destroyed much of it, although not all. The planning process also entailed a legal reorganization. The lords of Birmingham already had a court for their tenants, but it would hardly have done to mix the affairs of the new, free burgesses with those of the existing agricultural tenants who held by unfree, villein tenure. Now there were to be two separate areas of jurisdiction, each with its own court – the procedure that was always adopted with new town foundations. The names used in Birmingham for the two jurisdictions, the Borough and the Foreign, are also found elsewhere. Designating the town as the 'Borough' emphasized its special legal character, associated everywhere with urban growth. The earliest references that we have to these terms come from the thirteenth century, and they occur in a scatter of documentation from succeeding centuries.[52] The extent of the lordship of Birmingham, showing both the Borough and the Foreign as they were around 1300, is depicted in Figure 4.

A factor contributing to Birmingham's early growth was that local conditions must have been particularly favourable to urban development. The Arden region of north Warwickshire was wooded and under-exploited at the time of the Domesday survey, but saw considerable colonization during the twelfth and thirteenth centuries as the rising population of England generally expanded into hitherto sparsely settled areas. When woodland and previous pasture land were cleared for arable agriculture, it was usually done by individuals and small groups, so that the resulting fields took the form of private enclosed crofts rather than extensions to the open fields with

Figure 4 The manor of Birmingham in the late medieval period, based on George Demidowicz's original map.
Map created by Duncan Probert

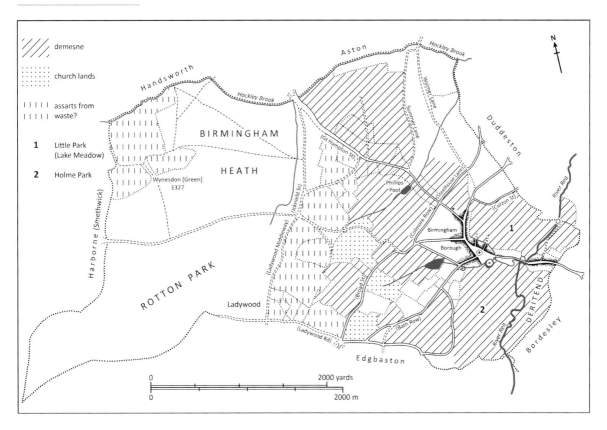

their communal agriculture. In the manors of Yardley and King's Norton we know of enclosures from the waste being made during the thirteenth century; at the same time enclosed crofts were sold in Erdington and Perry Barr.[53] The pattern was being repeated all around the new market town, and the most detailed evidence that we have comes from Bordesley, adjacent to the Deritend area. A survey of the manor made in 1291 describes its original lands as being 61 acres in demesne, with some meadow and pasture, and the peasant-held lands as eight and a half virgates (a virgate being reckoned as a family holding of some thirty acres or so). But now there were 78 tenants, free men who held lands newly asserted or cleared from the waste and who together paid £13 annually in rent. That pattern will have been repeated all around Birmingham.[54]

Birmingham in the thirteenth century

The first written reference to a Birmingham burgage comes from as late as 1232, reflecting how thin the historical record is for the town's early years. In that year the lord of Birmingham, another William, came to an agreement with a group of 16 of his tenants. All held house-plots freely for the same rent of 8d, and so in other words they held burgages. They wanted to be free of the lord's right to force them to help at his haymaking (or presumably to force them to pay in lieu of this work) and to collect ½d from them every time they brewed. It seems remarkable that they were willing to pay over £10 to secure this deal, and an annual payment of 2s in perpetuity to be taken from the burgage of William of Wyrley. That is, each of them paid 12s 6d, and would pay a further 1½d per year, and we must accept that it was worth their while to do so. Eight of the men had occupational surnames: there was a smith, a mercer, a purveyor, a tailor, and four weavers.[55] William was presumably a native of Wyrley, and others were from Bordesley, Henley and Studley – places at most 15 miles distant from Birmingham.

Specific evidence from later in the century is fragmented and thin, but highly eloquent. Not least, representatives from Birmingham were summoned to the parliament of 1275, as one of the market towns (*villate mercatorum*) which were represented that year.[56] Archaeological and historical evidence shows that Birmingham's success could be seen on the ground in several extensions to the town plan. Perhaps they had all taken place in a single act of expansion, initiated and carried out by the lords of Birmingham, or alternatively had happened as separate phases of development. Park Street was a new residential area, and Moor Street, too, was new, both encroaching on to the Little Park of the lords. There was also the expressively named New Street, laid out over what one guesses was previously the lords' demesne land.[57] While these additions to the street plan, all named in the 1296 rental, may have followed former routeways, the formal nature of their inception is demonstrated clearly in the archaeological record: the substantial, mid-twelfth-century ditch that had marked the boundary of the town was filled in where Park Street crossed it so as to allow the laying out of new burgages, and a new ditch was dug to bring water to their rear ends.[58] Perhaps the lords were reacting to informal expansion that was already taking place, as there is some evidence (mainly deposits of pottery) pointing to activity along Park Street even before 1200. In the case of New Street we see what looks like evidence of deliberate planning, however rudimentary, in the exact (and hardly accidental) 90-degree angle of the corner where it joined the existing High Street. We cannot date this process of expansion other than by assigning it to the thirteenth century, on the basis that the first boundary ditch was not filled in until well into that century while these new residential streets all existed by 1296.

It is only at the very end of the thirteenth century that we have the detailed evidence needed to fill out much more of the picture of what had happened since 1166. Our knowledge of early Birmingham has been considerably enhanced by the recent discovery of a hitherto unsuspected rental or rent-list of the tenants of the town of Birmingham, lying unrecognized in the historical records at Longleat House until identified by George Demidowicz.[59] The rental was accompanied by another, made in 1344 or 1345, which is partly illegible, and so it is the 1296 rental that gives the more complete picture. The information from the rental allows a map of the borough of Birmingham around 1300 to be reconstructed (Fig. 5). In total 248 residential properties were listed, held from the lord by 136 named people (and so there was clearly a high degree of subletting by them), and it is interesting that the precise tenurial terminology that we might expect was to an extent absent. So while 98 properties paying a rent of 8d were described as burgages, and 33 were described as half-burgages, paying 4d, there were nearly as many properties described simply as 'tenements', 'houses' or 'messuages', although many also paid a rent of 8d. Clearly all these properties were held by burgage tenure, that is freely and in heredity by fixed rents. Perhaps by the 1290s, therefore, the word 'burgage' was losing its significance, as all properties in the town were held on the same legal basis. It would be tempting to guess that the properties described as burgages were the oldest, granted to tenants in the initial planning of the town, but that was not the case, since at least one of them was located in New Street. With so many surnames being listed in this single source we can extract specific, useful information. A number of men had names taken from their occupations, reflecting the range we find in other well-documented small towns: a baker, miller, tailor, capper, chaloner (bedding-maker), carpenter, cooper, mason, mercer, tanner, glover, smith, farrier and armourer. Another group of men had locational surnames, and again we see a pattern that we meet in other towns. Immigration to Birmingham had been from its own market area, with two-thirds of the names being places within ten miles of Birmingham.

Yet we must beware of assuming that the horizons of the Birmingham craftsmen were limited to the local market, as a tantalizing reference from 1308 illustrates. With the suppression of the Knights Templar, an inventory of the Master's possessions was made, in which we find that he owned a number of 'Birmingham pieces'. The term is unexplained; the objects were doubtless small, although of high value, and seem to have been precious ornaments of one sort or another.[60]

An unusual feature of the 1296 rental is the recording of 85 people described as *chensarii* – a term usually found elsewhere as *censarii*. These 'censers' were probably a ubiquitous feature of medieval towns by this time but are seldom recorded. They were traders and craftsmen who paid an annual fee, here in Birmingham nearly all of 1d, to be free of the market – that is, to be able to buy and sell wares including their own manufactured products as the burgesses did, freely and without paying tolls.[61] The list may have included Birmingham residents who were not burgesses – men and women who did not hold from the lord by burgage tenure, or who were not otherwise recognized by the borough court as having that status. It is perhaps more likely that most were inhabitants of the Foreign or from further afield – 25 had locational surnames indicating an origin within the area of modern greater Birmingham or in the near vicinity. The list, therefore, fills out our understanding of the way in which Birmingham at the end of the thirteenth century already acted as the economic focus of its immediate region.

Despite the fortunate discovery of these rentals, medieval Birmingham remains poorly documented, and the incompleteness of the historical record is nowhere better illustrated than in the archaeological evidence for an otherwise unrecorded Birmingham speciality of the thirteenth century, a thriving pottery industry. Evidence of pottery manufacture in Deritend, in a fairly wide area including a site to the rear of the later Old Crown, emerged in the 1950s, and the more recent excavations in the city centre have pointed also to a centre of production in the region of Park Street and perhaps Moor Street.[62] The picture now is of pottery

Figure 5 Birmingham in 1350, based on George Demidowicz's original map. Map created by Duncan Probert

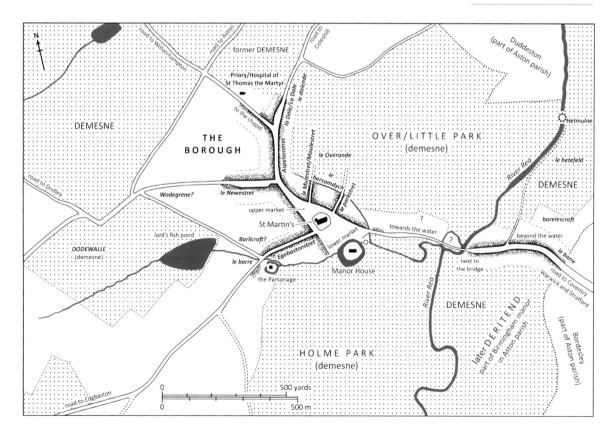

production in an extensive zone along the High Street, on both sides of the Rea, from Alcester Street in the east to the Moor Street area, a distance of some half a mile. Much of the evidence points to production in the thirteenth century and into the fourteenth, although there are signs that production in Deritend may have commenced before 1200, and indeed that pottery production in Birmingham could have begun already in the first half of the twelfth century. The archaeological evidence for later phases of pottery production in Birmingham is unclear, although the presence of post-medieval wasters in this production zone may well indicate an unbroken sequence of pottery production through the fourteenth and fifteenth centuries that has not as yet been otherwise identified.

The 1296 rental can be used to give a rough idea of the size of the town and its population. Needless to say, the calculation must be uncertain, as in the first place the purpose of the rental was to record all those paying rent to the Birmingham family from the Borough (not the Foreign), and nobody else. In an unknown number of cases, though perhaps most, these tenants of the manor will have sublet houses to people who were probably – although not necessarily – poorer, and who are not mentioned. We can be sure that the very poor are not named in such a document, and we have no idea how many such people there were. And if we cannot translate the number of properties into houses, we also do not know how extensive most of these houses were, nor how many people lived in them. Demidowicz stressed that his calculation of Birmingham's population then as being 1,250 is a cautious, minimum figure, and it is as good as any other estimate that might be based on that rental.[63] Certainly the calculation is better than any based on the previously used taxation returns of 1327 and 1332, which name respectively 75 and 69 taxpayers from Birmingham, who clearly were only the more substantial people of the town, with very many – and those the poorer – inhabitants and their households omitted.[64] On the basis of the 1296 rental we might hazard a guess that these taxations of individuals' wealth affected no more than one in twenty of the population. Actually, more fruitful than to calculate questionable population totals is to compare Birmingham with other towns. On these taxation figures, it was in, respectively, 1327 and 1332 the third largest place in Warwickshire, with the county town Warwick only marginally larger with 84 and 92 taxpayers and the regional capital Coventry with 200 and 135.[65]

Birmingham, 1300–1500

The composite picture that we have of Birmingham around 1300 is not matched until the better documentation of the sixteenth century reveals copious details of the town, its people and their activities. The damaged borough rental of 1344–45 adds little of substance to our knowledge, although there are details that enlarge the picture drawn by the rental of fifty years before. We read, for instance, of a tenement in front of *le Baterchepyng*, the Butter Market, although the existence of specialist areas within the market can hardly have been a new feature then.[66] Nor does the increased volume of surviving property deeds add very much to our understanding of the town and its people: by contrast with the handful of recorded transactions from before 1300, as many as 35 survive from the following half-century, and in all some 150 deeds from the medieval period.[67] But while this source can supply personal names and a leavening of topographical references, we lack the sources that might answer the deeper questions about Birmingham. Most importantly, we do not know how far the population decline of the fourteenth and fifteenth centuries affected the townspeople, although the evidence from other towns is of lower populations and in many cases contemporary claims of impoverishment.[68] Archaeology shows a shrinkage of settlement and activity along Park Street that began in the fourteenth century, but it is not possible to say whether other parts of the town were similarly affected.[69]

Everywhere the period saw economic and social change. All around Birmingham the rural economy continued to develop along the lines already described for the period of the town's initial growth. We see, essentially, a continuation of the conditions already remarked upon before 1300, so that when we can observe the local manors in the fifteenth and early sixteenth centuries we see that practically all tenants were freeholders, most if not all of the land was enclosed, and pastoral agriculture predominated. We can envisage a countryside, therefore, of farmers producing a large surplus of animals for meat, wool and hides, who went to the market to buy their corn, and who – more than arable farmers – had opportunities for industrial by-occupations.[70]

New economic realities in the fifteenth century will have affected Birmingham, although to an unknown extent. There are indications that the town was developing a specialism as a major cattle market, of regional rather than just local significance, where cattle often from Wales and the Marches were sold to midlands graziers and drovers who supplied major markets further to the south and east. In 1401 and 1404 there were cases in which men from Wednesbury and Tipton were accused of avoiding paying tolls on hundreds and perhaps thousands of cattle that they had sold at Birmingham. In the 1440s John Brome, the lord of Baddesley Clinton, was using his demesne land to fatten cattle that he had bought principally at Birmingham and Coventry, it seems, and then sold on. The name 'Welsh Market' that the cattle-market end of High Street had acquired by the sixteenth century seems to refer to this trade.[71] There is also reason to believe that Birmingham was becoming prominent not just as an iron-working centre, but also as a marketing centre for the iron products of an industrializing countryside, roughly speaking the area of today's Birmingham and the Black Country. The iron and coal fields of the Black Country had been exploited since at least the thirteenth century, and the cattle drovers from Wednesbury also sold iron, steel and brass, presumably to be worked up in Birmingham or further distributed. When royal purveyors were purchasing arms for the king's armouries in the early sixteenth century, they came to Birmingham to acquire weapon-bills, a standard infantry weapon. The role of marketing centre for metal goods must have been growing during the fifteenth century, and, although hard evidence is lacking, the situation that we see after 1500 with ironworkers all around Birmingham – for example, nailers in Moseley, Harborne and Handsworth, bladesmiths in Erdington and Smethwick, and scythesmiths in Erdington, Bordesley and Yardley – can hardly have come into being overnight.[72]

And what of the town's people? At the end of the fifteenth century we see a town community apparently dominated by several wealthy families through the medium of the Gild of the Holy Cross. This was a religious gild founded in the previous century to serve the parishioners of St Martin's, and most of its income was devoted to maintaining three or even four chaplains at the parish church to say masses for the souls of dead members. The remainder was used to maintain the two Deritend bridges and an almshouse for 12 aged brethren, and to pay for a common midwife. It had a large, and presumably grand, gildhall on New Street that became King Edward's School after the Reformation and whose exact site now accommodates the Odeon cinema. Ubiquitous in this period, parish gilds provided an outlet for religious sentiments as well as a social focus for local communities. There was a similar gild in Deritend, founded in 1381 to maintain St John's chapel there and its priest. It also employed a second priest to teach a grammar school – presumably at its gildhall, which seems to have been the building known to later centuries as the Old Crown House and which modern timber building analysis has now dated to about 1490.[73]

We have evidence to show that in other small towns – Stratford-upon-Avon being an excellent example – these parish gilds could transcend their religious and social functions and come to represent the borough community, especially against their lord. At Stratford the burgesses used their gild meetings to decide in advance business to be brought to the borough court. A list of 29 leading men of Birmingham from 1482 starts, significantly, with Henry Cheshire, the master of the gild; Roger Pepwall, the high bailiff of the court and town, comes second.[74]

It is not known whether the Deritend gild acted as a similar focus. Deritend perhaps had an ambiguous status within Birmingham that may have gone back to the origins of the borough; it certainly lay outside the planned area of the town around the marketplace. Its anomalous status as part of Aston parish was not only the reason for building St John's chapel, to give the inhabitants of Deritend and Bordesley a local place of worship; it was also an indication that this was originally a lordship distinct from that of Birmingham, which must have come into the possession of the Birmingham family. We do not know when that was, and it may be that in origin Deritend grew up as a rival, unlicensed market community, benefiting from

The tomb of an unknown priest of St Martin's, of the fifteenth century. This costly effigy is testimony to the wealth of the dead man and to the income that he drew from church lands and from tithes paid from the prosperous parish of Birmingham.
© Elaine Mitchell

The only non-ecclesiastical building surviving from medieval Birmingham is the impressive Old Crown, Deritend, of the late fifteenth century. Probably the hall of the Gild of St John, it was the meeting place for the Birmingham people who attended Deritend chapel, and it housed a school.
By permission of The Birmingham Civic Society

its position at the river crossing and its proximity to an established neighbouring market. Somewhat detached from the rest of the town until the building-up of both sides of Digbeth in the post-medieval centuries, medieval Deritend may always have had its own economic and social identity.[75]

Conclusion

Throughout its history the town of Birmingham has been characterized by vigorous and rapid economic and population growth. Most people will have formed that picture of its development in the eighteenth and nineteenth centuries, at any rate. Yet we see the same sort of growth during Birmingham's earlier centuries as well, and especially during its first century as a town. By 1300 it had already become an important commercial centre for quite a wide area – an area which itself was experiencing a growth of settlement, and in ways which favoured a more individual and productive agriculture, promising a more varied economic future for the whole region. Developments in the next two centuries are harder to assess, but there is good reason to believe that Birmingham's role as a market centre became ever more extensive. This happened, not least, as its rural hinterland continued to change towards a more market-based economy, favouring economic diversity and providing fertile conditions for the growth of rural industry. By 1500 Birmingham had quite clearly become a place of more than just local importance.

This contrasts strongly with Birmingham's standing in the centuries before a minor castle was placed near its eastern boundary, and a planned market settlement was laid out nearby, by no later than 1166. As we have seen, Birmingham's entry in Domesday Book indicates a manor of no apparent significance or future potential, sandwiched between the two much more important ones of Harborne and Aston. Minsters such as their churches were often had a marketplace created beside them in the eleventh or twelfth century, but neither of the latter manors displays evidence of any commercial growth in the late medieval period. Birmingham's marketplace, however, appears to have been ideally positioned to take advantage of traffic on the many well-established through-routes that converged on the Deritend crossing of the Rea, linking settlements on the Birmingham Plateau and, beyond it, in the nearer parts of the valleys of the Severn, the Avon and the Trent and their tributaries.

Peter de Birmingham deserves no credit as an exceptionally astute entrepreneur. When he planted a market settlement next to his castle and gave its inhabitants privileges, he was only doing what lay and ecclesiastical aristocrats alike customarily did so as to boost their incomes. Indeed, his decision to charge his burgesses a rent of only 8d – the normal English burgage rent was 1s (12d) – suggests no great confidence that his plantation would succeed, let alone prosper. That it did do so, and so spectacularly, may well owe something to its attractive rent, but it was chiefly on account of its geographical location, its owners' intelligent manipulation of the local landscape, and, we may well imagine, its early inhabitants' craftsmanship and skilled marketing.

Notes

1 Steven Bassett's contribution to this chapter is based, with some maturer reflections, on the following articles (where full references may be found): S. Bassett, 'Anglo-Saxon Birmingham', *Midland History*, 25 (2000), 1–27; 'Birmingham before the Bull Ring', *Midland History*, 26 (2001), 1–33. Richard Holt has similarly built upon his earlier work, principally R.A. Holt, 'The economic development of Birmingham before 1553' (MA thesis, University of Birmingham, 1975), and *The Early History of the Town of Birmingham 1166 to 1600*, Dugdale Society Occasional Papers, 30 (Oxford, 1985).

2 A better translation of Birmingham's name is 'land-unit of Beorma's people': J.E.B. Gover, A. Mawer and F.M. Stenton, *The Place-Names of Warwickshire*, English Place-Name Society, XIII (Cambridge, 1936), 34–6; M. Gelling, 'The place-name volumes for Worcestershire and Warwickshire: a new look', in T.R. Slater and P.J. Jarvis (eds), *Field and Forest. An Historical Geography of Warwickshire and Worcestershire* (Norwich, 1982), 59–78, at 68; Gelling, 'Place-names', in D. Hey (ed.), *The Oxford Companion to Local and Family History* (Oxford, 1996), 350–7, at 352. Dr Gelling told SRB (pers. comm., March 1997) that she had given up the idea that the name's final element might be *hamm* because the local topography did not allow it.

3 A. Farley (ed.), *Domesday Book seu Liber Censualis Willelmi Primi Regis Angliae*, 2 vols (London, 1783), fo. 243a; for an English translation, see J. Plaister (ed.), *Domesday Book 23: Warwickshire* (Chichester, 1976), 27, 5.

4 E.g. C. Gill, *A Short History of Birmingham from its Origin to the Present Day* (Birmingham, 1938), 10; Gill, *History of Birmingham. Volume 1: Manor and Borough to 1865* (London, 1952), 4–5; W.B. Stephens (ed.), *A History of the County of Warwick. Volume VII: The City of Birmingham*, Victoria County History (London, 1964), 4, G.E. Cherry, *Birmingham. A Study in Geography, History and Planning* (Chichester, 1994), 14; V. Skipp, *A History of Greater Birmingham down to 1830* (Studley, 1980), 14; C. Chinn, *One Thousand Years of Brum* (Birmingham, 1999), 13–14, 28.

5 Gill, *Short History of Birmingham*.

6 Bassett, 'Anglo-Saxon Birmingham'; Bassett, 'Bull Ring'. It should be noted, however, that the validity of these new methods of study is not universally accepted, being described as 'depending on later evidence, comparison and conjecture, especially for the Anglo-Saxon period': G. Demidowicz, *Medieval Birmingham: The Borough Rentals of 1296 and 1344–5*, Dugdale Society Occasional Papers, 48 (Bristol, 2008), 2.

7 Unfortunately, there is still almost no archaeological evidence of an Anglo-Saxon presence in the area covered by the modern city: M. Hodder, *Birmingham: The Hidden History* (Stroud, 2004), 77.

8 Bassett, 'Bull Ring', 6–15.

9 Ibid.

10 Hypothetical road 3 ran to the early Roman fort at Metchley (Fig. 1, A).

11 For more on roads 1–3, 4–5, 9 and 12, see Bassett, 'Bull Ring', 6–8, 11–12 (where respectively numbered 1–3, 6–7, 11 and 16).

12 For more on roads 6–8, 10 and 11, see ibid., 9–11 (where respectively numbered 8–10, 12 and 14).

13 For an authoritative account of the Birmingham area's early medieval woodland, see S.J. Wager, *Woods, Wolds and Groves. The Woodland of Medieval Warwickshire*, British Archaeological Reports, British Series, 269 (Oxford, 1998), 189–90, 193.

14 R. Faith, *The English Peasantry and the Growth of Lordship* (London, 1997), 132–4; C. Wickham, *Framing the Middle Ages. Europe and the Mediterranean 400–800* (Oxford, 2005), 305–6, 313. Exemplified in S. Bassett, 'Continuity and fission in the Anglo-Saxon landscape: the origins of the Rodings (Essex)', *Landscape History*, 19 (1997), 25–42.

15 S. Bassett, 'The administrative landscape of the diocese of Worcester in the tenth century', in N. P. Brooks and C.R.E. Cubitt (eds), *St Oswald of Worcester: Life and Influence* (London, 1996), 147–73, at 160–8.

16 J. Blair, *The Church in Anglo-Saxon Society* (Oxford, 2005), esp. chs 2–3, 7. Exemplified in S. Bassett, 'Boundaries of knowledge: mapping the land-units of late Anglo-Saxon and Norman England', in W. Davies, G. Halsall and A. Reynolds (eds), *People and Space in the Middle Ages, 300–1300* (Turnhout, 2006), 115–42, at 119–39.

17 Bassett, 'Anglo-Saxon Birmingham', 14–16; Bassett, 'Boundaries of knowledge', 119–39 (for Wootton Wawen).

18 Bassett, 'Anglo-Saxon Birmingham', 17–21.

19 Ibid., 17, and references cited there.

20 Ibid., 17, and references cited there.

21 The term chapelry indicates the area served by the priest of a public church which, lacking independent parochial status, aided a mother-church in delivering pastoral care to a portion of the latter's parish.

22 Bassett, 'Anglo-Saxon Birmingham', 18, and references cited there.

23 Ibid., 18–19, and references cited there. For the concept of 'manorial capture', see Bassett, 'Boundaries', 132–3.

24 Bassett, 'Anglo-Saxon Birmingham', 10–12, 20, and references cited there.

25 Ibid., 20–1; S. Bassett, 'The landed endowment of the Anglo-Saxon minster at Hanbury (Worcs.)', *Anglo-Saxon England*, 38 (2010), 77–100, at 84–6.

26 For a very small amount of direct evidence of twelfth-century fabric, see J.R. Holliday, 'Notes on St Martin's church and the discoveries made during its restoration', *Transactions of the Birmingham Archaeological Society*, vol. for 1873 (Oxford, 1874), 43–73, at 50.

27 How close St Martin's was, originally, to the head of the marketplace is unclear. Demidowicz believes that the latter's southern edge always adjoined the moat surrounding the Birminghams' manorial centre (*Borough Rentals*, 6, 8 and fig. 1); but this allows no room for any burgages to have been laid out along that southern frontage – hence the smaller area of the marketplace depicted in our Figure 3 (which, using Edgbaston Street

and its continuation Park Street as a key topographical determinant, represents the 'minimalist' viewpoint on this issue, whereas Demidowicz's fig. 1 represents the 'maximalist' one).

28 Holt, *Early History*, 4.

29 It certainly had one by 1296: Demidowicz, *Borough Rentals*, 8.

30 M.W. Beresford and J.K.S. St Joseph, *Medieval England: An Aerial Survey*, 2nd edn (Cambridge, 1979), 222–6; P. Drury, 'Braintree: excavations and research, 1971–76', *Essex Archaeology and History*, 3rd ser., 8 (1976), 1–143, at 134–5; S. Bassett, 'Church and diocese in the West Midlands: the transition from British to Anglo-Saxon control', in J. Blair and R. Sharpe (eds), *Pastoral Care before the Parish* (Leicester, 1992), 15–40, at 29–35.

31 Bassett, 'Bull Ring', 17–24.

32 *List of Inquisitions Ad Quod Damnum. Part I* (London, 1904), 14.

33 Bassett, 'Bull Ring', 18–19

34 Ibid., 19–21

35 Ibid., 17; W. Hutton, *An History of Birmingham to the End of the Year 1780*, 2nd edn (Birmingham, 1783), 233–4.

36 For a significantly different point of view, see Demidowicz, *Borough Rentals*, 10–12. It is argued there that the graveyard in which St Thomas's stood was no more than that of 'a new religious institution, reflecting the growing aspirations of the town', and so not the original one of the parish of Birmingham. The two roles are not mutually exclusive, however. To judge from what we know of the graveyard's probable greatest extent (Bassett, 'Bull Ring', 20), the properties close to St Thomas's chapel that are recorded in the 1296 rental (Demidowicz, *Borough Rentals*, 11) overlay earlier burials. (The encroachment of domestic properties over outlying parts of earlier graveyards is a common medieval occurrence in both urban and rural contexts.) The putative reversal of the roles of St Thomas's and St Martin's (above, at note 30), and the creation of a graveyard for the latter, would have allowed St Thomas's to be used thereafter as a hospital chapel.

37 Holt, *Early History*, 3.

38 *Domesday Book*, fo. 243a.

39 J.C. Davies (ed.), *Cartae Antiquae Rolls 11–20*, Pipe Roll Society, new series, XXXIII (Oxford, 1960), 190–1 (no. 613).

40 Holt, *Early History*, 3.

41 R. Holt, 'Society and population, 600–1300', in D. Palliser (ed.), *Cambridge Urban History of Britain* (Cambridge, 2000), I, 79–104, at 83, 96; M. Beresford and H. Finberg, *Medieval English Boroughs* (Newton Abbot, 1973), 38–40.

42 We say 'he', but there was no law that insisted that a burgess had to be a man, although it was assumed in both custom and practice. A daughter or a widow might inherit a burgage, but control of it would pass to her husband upon marriage or re-marriage. A very few widows who chose not to re-marry might function as burgesses.

43 *Calendar of Ancient Deeds in the Public Record Office*, VI (London, 1906), C5067.

44 National Archives, SC/12/4/1, 'A Survey of Birmingham made in 1529', copy in Birmingham Central Library, 94314; M. de W. Hemmeon, *Burgage Tenure in England* (Cambridge, MA, 1914), 22.

45 By the sixteenth century there were two 'great stone bridges' across the two channels of the Rea, immediately adjacent to the ford; the earliest bridges there may, however, have been of either stone or wood. Nothing is known of their date of origin: J. Toulmin Smith (ed.), *English Gilds*, Early English Text Society, Original Series, XL (London, 1870), 249; L. Toulmin Smith (ed.), *The Itinerary of John Leland in or about the years 1535–1543* (London, 1908), II, 96; Stephens (ed.), *A History of the County of Warwick: Volume VII*, 31.

46 *Cartae Antiquae*, 191, no. 614.

47 C. Patrick and S Ratkai, *The Bull Ring Uncovered: Excavations at Edgbaston Street, Moor Street, Park Street and The Row, Birmingham City Centre, 1997–2001* (Oxford, 2009), 5–6, 34, 48, 305–19.

48 Bassett, 'Bull Ring', 12; Demidowicz, *Borough Rentals*, 33.

49 Patrick and Ratkai, *Bull Ring Uncovered*, 1, 15, 55–7, 240–6, 256–8, 305.

50 Ibid., 41, 48, 55, 83–4, 109, 113, 256–8. The ditch was identified by name in the 1296 rental as *le hyrsonedych*, or later as the Hersum Ditch, a name also used in Coventry: Demidowicz, *Borough Rentals*, 8, 38; Demidowicz, 'The Hersum Ditch, Birmingham and Coventry: a local topographical term?', *Transactions of the Birmingham Archaeological Society*, 106 (2002), 143–50; and M. Gelling, 'What is a Hersumdich? Note upon the Hersum Ditch, Birmingham and Coventry', *Transactions of the Birmingham Archaeological Society*, 107 (2003), 150.

51 Demidowicz, *Borough Rentals*, 35–49; W.B. Bickley and J. Hill, *A Survey of the Borough and Manor of Birmingham made in 1553* (Oxford, 1890).

52 Stephens (ed.), *A History of the County of Warwick: Volume VII*, 73.

53 Holt, *Early History*, 6; J.B. Harley, 'Population trends and agricultural developments from the Warwickshire Hundred Rolls of 1279', *Economic History Review*, 2nd ser., 11 (1958), 8–18; Harley, 'The settlement geography of early medieval Warwickshire', *Transactions of the Institute of British Geographers*, 34 (1964), 115–30; *Rolls of the Justices in Eyre for Worcestershire, 1221*, Seldon Society, 53 (London, 1934), 448; V. Skipp, *Medieval Yardley* (Chichester, 1970), 27; Birmingham Central Library, 252445, 292201.

54 Holt, *Early History*, 6; Inquisition post mortem of Roger de Somery, *Cal. Inq. Post Mortem*, II (London, 1906), 813.

55 E. Stokes and F.C. Wellstood (eds), *Warwickshire Feet of Fines*, Dugdale Society, 11 (London, 1932), I, no. 479.

56 C.H. Jenkinson, 'The first parliament of Edward I', *English Historical Review*, 24 (1909), 234.

57 S. Buteux, *Beneath the Bull Ring: The Archaeology of Life and Death in Early Birmingham* (Studley, 2003), esp. 47–53; Hodder, *Hidden History*, 84; Demidowicz, *Borough Rentals*, 35–49.

58 Patrick and Ratkai, *Bull Ring Uncovered*, 84.

59 Demidowicz, *Borough Rentals*, from which the following information is taken.

60 E.A. Gooder, 'Birmingham pieces', *Transactions of the Birmingham Archaeological Society*, 88 (1976–77), 135.

61 Demidowicz, *Borough Rentals*, 18–19, 47–9.

62 Patrick and Ratkai, *Bull Ring Uncovered*, 92–3, 95–6.

63 Demidowicz, *Borough Rentals*, 12.

64 W.F. Carter (ed.), 'Lay subsidy for Warwickshire of 1327', *Transactions of the Midland Record Society*, 1–6 (1896–1902); Carter (ed.), *Lay Subsidy for Warwickshire of 1332*, Dugdale Society, 6 (London, 1926).

65 Holt, *Early History*, 8–9.

66 Demidowicz, *Borough Rentals*, 59.

67 Ibid., 30.

68 R.B. Dobson, 'Urban decline in late medieval England', in R. Holt and G. Rosser (eds), *The English Medieval Town* (London and New York, 1990), 265–86.

69 Patrick and Ratkai, *Bull Ring Uncovered*, 85. Recent works that present archaeological insights into this period are Buteux, *Beneath the Bull Ring*, and Hodder, *Hidden History*.

70 Holt, 'Economic development of Birmingham', 17–28.

71 Holt, *Early History*, 10–11.

72 Ibid., 18–19.

73 J. Toulmin Smith, *Men and Names of Old Birmingham* (London and Birmingham, 1864), 57; Toulmin Smith, *English Gilds*, 258–61; S. Price, *The Old Crown, Deritend, Birmingham: A Report on its History and Architectural Development Prepared for English Heritage and Birmingham City Council* (Birmingham, 1993).

74 Holt, *Early History*, 13.

75 The historical development of this part of Birmingham and its relationship to the larger settlement throughout the centuries were discussed in R. Holt, 'The historical background', in S. Litherland, *An Archaeological Assessment of the Digbeth Economic Regeneration Area and Cheapside Industrial Area*, Birmingham University Field Archaeology Unit, Report 337 (Birmingham, 1995).

CHAPTER FOUR

The Tudor and Stuart Town

RICHARD CUST AND ANN HUGHES

In his 1782 *History of Birmingham* William Hutton identified the Restoration of the monarchy in 1660 as the principal watershed in the town's development:

> the ancient and modern state of Birmingham must divide at the restoration of Charles II. For though she had before held a considerable degree of eminence, yet at this period the curious arts began to take root and were cultivated by the hand of genius … now her growths will be amazing, her expansion rapid, perhaps not to be paralleled in history. We shall see her rise in all the beauty of youth, of grace, of elegance and attract the notice of the commercial world …[1]

Hutton particularly had in mind Birmingham's spatial, demographic and economic development. Between 1650 and 1700, he explains, it expanded rapidly in terms of the area it covered and the number of its streets (from 15 to 28); its population grew around threefold (from 5,472 to 15,032); and the range of its trades and manufactures broadened and diversified, with guns, toys, shoe buckles, buttons and steel goods supplanting the swords, scythes and nails of an earlier period.[2] Of changes in politics, religion and government, however, he has much less to say until he reaches his own era of the mid-eighteenth century.

Hutton's assessment provides a useful way in to the study of Tudor and Stuart Birmingham. How well do his claims of a watershed at the Restoration stand up to analysis in the light of recent work on the development of the town? There is every indication that his knowledge of Birmingham before the eighteenth century was extremely hazy; and where he lacked concrete evidence he would tend to fall back on local legend and myth. On the other hand, his claim that the Restoration was a

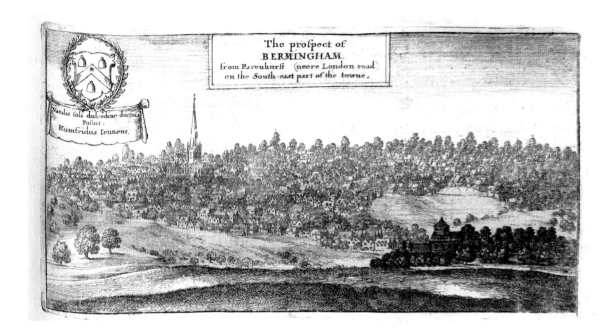

watershed for towns like Birmingham has gained considerable currency in recent scholarship;[3] and if nothing else, the remarkably rapid growth in its population suggests that transformational changes were taking place. The aim of this chapter, then, is to analyse the nature and character of these changes – starting with demographic and social developments and moving on to governance, politics and religion – to assess the extent to which 1660 was, indeed, a watershed.

Economy, society and government

For the sixteenth-century visitor, Birmingham already had a well-established identity as a centre of metalworking and manufactures. When John Leland visited the town around 1538 he approached it from the east, through Deritend, which he described as 'a pretty strete' with its half-timbered manor house (the Old Crown Inn) and St John's chapel (Fig. 1). But he also noted the presence of the 'smiths and cuttlers' who were dwelling there. As he crossed the River Rea and ascended the long main street, through Digbeth, past St Martins church and up to New Street, he ignored the tanning yards which we know from the 1553 survey clustered around the river crossing and again focused on the bustle and activity of the metalworkers:

> There be many smiths in the towne that use to make knives and all maner of cutting tools, and many lorimars that make byts, and a great many naylors. So that a great parte of the towne is mayntayned by smithes.[4]

About fifty years later William Camden journeyed to the town and formed a similar

The first known pictorial representation of Birmingham – from the mid-seventeenth century – shows a view of the town from the south-east. *The Prospect of Bermingham* by Wenceslaus Hollar was published in Dugdale's *Antiquities of Warwickshire* (1656).
By permission of the Cadbury Research Library: Special Collections, University of Birmingham

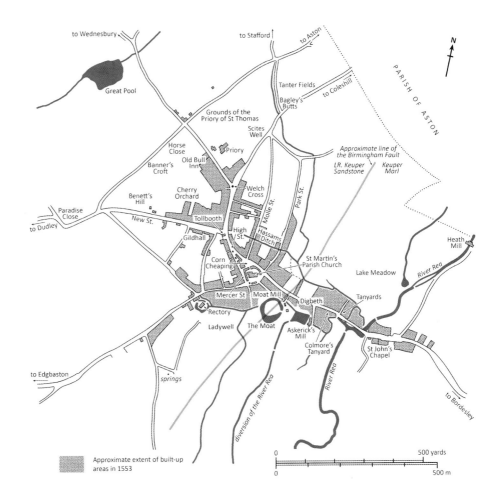

Figure 1 The Tudor town reconstructed from the survey of 1553. From *Birmingham and its Regional Setting*, published in 1950 following that year's meeting of the British Association for the Advancement of Science in the city.

Map created by Duncan Probert

impression. 'Bermincham' was a town 'full of inhabitants, and resounding with hammers and anvils for the most part of them are smiths.'[5] How far these visitors were picking up on a pre-existing image of Birmingham, and were recording what they expected to see, is uncertain. But whether or not this was the case, it is evident that Birmingham's identity in the eyes of contemporaries was firmly established. It was a bustling, industrious marketing and manufacturing centre which reverberated to the noisy production techniques of the metalworkers. This is the conventional image of early modern Birmingham; but it is worth investigating how far it should be qualified by the more prosaic evidence provided by deeds and accounts, wills and inventories, tax returns and manorial surveys.

Perhaps the hardest part of the picture to get clear is the size and rate of increase of Birmingham's population. Different sources tell different stories. Richard Holt's careful analysis of the lay subsidy of 1525 demonstrates that, in terms of the numbers of taxpaying households, Birmingham was already firmly established as the third largest town in Warwickshire, after Coventry and Warwick. But extrapolating from this to estimate population size is problematic. Holt estimates that it was probably somewhere between 1,000 and 1,400.[6] During the following twenty-five years growth appears to have been rapid. Estimates of the number of 'houseling people' (i.e. those taking Communion) in the chantry certificates of 1545 and 1547 provide figures of

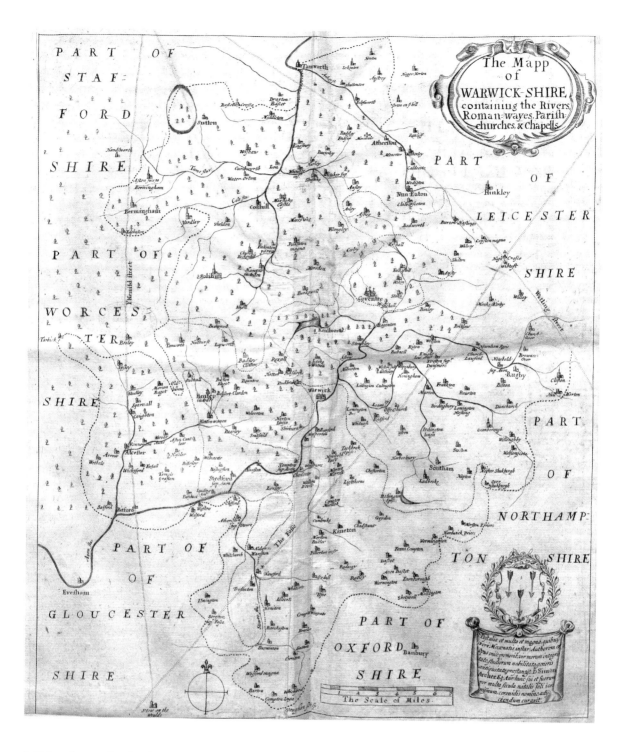

2,000 and 1,800 (evidently rounded up or down) which – using a multiplier of 1.33 to allow for non-communicating children – suggests a population of around 2,400 or 2,700.[7] A doubling of population in a twenty-five year period before the rapid growth in overall population of Elizabeth's reign would appear improbable. But even if the rate of growth suggested by these figures is exaggerated, they do confirm the impression of a dynamic, expanding local economy, attracting migrants in search of employment. The survey of households in the parish in 1563, however, offers the very different picture of a town which had recently suffered catastrophic population decline, with a total of only 200 households. John Moore has argued that this was a general phenomenon in the 1550s when the combination of 'sweating sickness' in the early part of the decade and the 'influenza' epidemic of 1556–60 produced overall population decline of 15–20 per cent, with even bigger falls in some localities. Using the conventional multiplier of 4.75 for 200 households gives a population for Birmingham in 1563 of only 950. This count of households excludes Deritend, and Moore suggests that the Birmingham figure has been rounded down from perhaps 220 or 240 (as often happened elsewhere).[8] Once these factors are taken into account we are back with a figure of between 1,100 and 1,400, similar to Holt's estimate for 1525. So it would appear that, in demographic terms, Birmingham had more or less returned to its early Tudor starting point.

Thereafter growth would appear to have been rapid, fuelled by the combination of an increasing overall birth rate and life expectancy and the attractiveness to migrant workers of Birmingham's dynamic economy. Camden's sense of a town 'full of inhabitants' towards the end of Elizabeth's reign certainly suggests as much. Hutton, in his *History*, claimed that by 1650 the population of the town had risen to 5,472, based on a rough and ready calculation that its 15 streets contained 907 houses.[9] However, the 1670 hearth tax return lists only 780 households for Birmingham and a further 92 for Deritend under Aston parish; the multiplier would suggest a lower figure of under 4,200.[10] In 1670 it was still smaller than Coventry, whose population amounted to some 6,000 people in 1,400 households, but thereafter Birmingham rapidly overtook its Warwickshire neighbour. Urban historians suggest that it was among the 15 most populous towns in England by the end of the century, with some 8,000–9,000 inhabitants and that overall, between 1650 and 1750, the town's population probably increased more than fivefold to some 24,000.[11] These indicators of rapid population growth are confirmation of the continuing capacity of the local economy to draw in workers and migrants and sustain the prosperity of its artisan classes.

Amidst all the references to metalworking and forges, it is easy to forget that in the early sixteenth century the economy of the Birmingham area was still based on agriculture. The agrarian economy of north-west Warwickshire, and the adjoining districts of south-east Staffordshire and north Worcestershire, was predominantly pastoral rather than open-field. The emphasis was on cattle rearing (and dairying by the seventeenth century) in field systems which had often been enclosed early in the Middle Ages; and by the fifteenth century Birmingham had developed a cattle market of regional importance which was still growing in the following century, when we get the first reference to the 'Bull Ring'.[12] Joan Thirsk has demonstrated that the rhythms and routines of stock rearing and dairy farming in the wood-pasture regions of England often left the peasantry with enough time to combine farming with small-scale craft and industrial production. This process

Joseph Wright (1756–93), *Farmyard near Aston Hall* (watercolour on paper). An example of a farm in Birmingham surviving from the pre-1700 period, captured in this eighteenth-century painting.
© Birmingham Museums and Art Gallery/Bridgeman Images

of what is sometimes called 'proto-industrialization' might take the form of weaving and spinning, wood turning, or, as in the Birmingham area, metalworking. The probate evidence from the sixteenth century demonstrates that a high proportion of the metalworkers combined their industrial production with farming: Thomas Haldon, a scythemaker from Erdington, whose inventory of 1569 recorded cattle, pigs, a horse and dairy-making facilities, alongside his metalworking shop and implements, is typical.[13] Clothing and tanning, both of continuing importance in sixteenth-century Birmingham, also reflected the agrarian basis of its economy.

In the late fourteenth century the town had been a centre of cloth production which was second only to Coventry within the shire. Cloth remained important to the town's economy well into the sixteenth century, with mercers prominent among the town's wealthier citizens. But its relative significance was declining, as cloth production moved out into the surrounding villages and local fulling mills (for preparing cloth) were converted to blade mills (for example at Holford Mill and Bromford Mill).[14] Birmingham also had a well-developed tanning industry which had grown out of stock rearing and cattle marketing, and throughout the period it continued to play an important role in local manufacturing. The 1553 survey showed up to a dozen tanneries along Tanners Row down by the bridge at Deritend, and tanners were among the elite of Birmingham tradesmen throughout the period. Robert Elsmore died in 1551 with an inventory worth £160, half of which was money tied up in hides and leathers which were being processed at his death. Ambrose Foxall, who died in 1670, described himself as a tanner in his will, although his inventory worth £176 contained only small amounts of leather. He had, however, acquired substantial landed property in Birmingham, Bordesley and Solihull, served as governor of King Edward's Grammar School and as bailiff of the town in the 1650s, and was described as a gentleman when serving as a tax collector in the 1640s. His son, also Ambrose, was charged for an impressive six-hearth house in Digbeth in the 1670 hearth tax return.[15] Tanning required significant investment over a long period; it might bring great rewards but it was generally an occupation for wealthier artisans. Metalworking, by contrast, required minimal capital outlay. A smith could set himself up with forge, anvil, bellows and hammer for as little as 10 shillings in the early sixteenth century, which made it an ideal occupation for a small, family workforce.[16]

The earliest evidence of metalworking in the town can be traced back to the 1379 poll tax return, which recorded the presence of several smiths. The increasing number of scattered references to Birmingham metal goods during the fifteenth century suggest that it was growing apace and, as we have seen, by the time Leland visited, the town had an established identity as a metalworking centre. This development was helped initially by its proximity to the raw materials required for the production process. Leland commented that the smiths 'have yren out of Staffordshire and Warwickshire, and see cole out of Staffordshire'.[17] Birmingham and

Charles Barber (c.1784–1854), *Bromford Forge, Erdington* (1808, pencil on paper). A small-scale forge at Bromford that was making iron in the seventeenth century. Barber's pencil sketch shows the mill wheel that powered the bellows that drove the furnace.
© Birmingham Museums and Art Gallery/Bridgeman Images

its region thus benefited from natural resources of coal, iron and water, and from the availability of a growing population of landless or near landless labourers in the surrounding region. By the second half of the seventeenth century, 61 per cent of probate inventories listing the possessions of recently deceased inhabitants in the parishes surrounding Birmingham reveal involvement in industry and commerce, and over one-third of all inventories were of people involved in metalworking, more than were engaged in agriculture.[18] Metalworking at this time was dominated by men. Women were employed in the less skilled crafts, such as nailmaking, but the metal workshops were almost entirely the preserve of 'men and boys' according to the Staffordshire historian, Robert Plot.[19]

Expansion was stimulated by two important technological advances in the mid-sixteenth and early seventeenth centuries. First, from about 1550, the blast furnace was introduced to local iron foundries, such as Cannock Wood in south Staffordshire, and this made possible the production of much larger quantities of pig iron than the old medieval bloomeries. Then, secondly, the slitting mill, introduced in the 1620s, speeded up nail and wire production by rolling sheets into the required thickness before cutting them with shears. The number of small-scale metalworkers in Birmingham and throughout the Black Country expanded rapidly in this period, so that by the time of a 1683 hearth tax survey there were 183 smiths' hearths, mostly in Digbeth and Deritend, with 15 more in Edgbaston and 78 in Aston.[20] As production expanded, so local districts developed their particular specialisms. Dudley, Stourbridge and parts of the Black Country specialized in nailmaking and wire-drawing; Walsall in bit-makers and bucklemakers; Wolverhampton in locksmiths; and Birmingham developed a particular expertise in the making of edged tools, assisted by the numerous blade mills in the vicinity of the town. The wealthier manufacturers (like the scythesmith Thomas Bache, who died in 1590 worth £250) owned their own blade mills and leased out the facilities to the small producers. Cutlery, scythes, knives and weapons became the staple of Birmingham's manufacturing. As early as 1513–14 the town was supplying large numbers of weapon bills for Henry VIII's expedition into France; and in 1643 Prince Rupert famously burned down Robert Porter's blade mill at Digbeth after he had supposedly supplied 15,000 swords to the parliamentary cause. In more settled times Birmingham's schoolmaster took pains to provide ironwork for the new library at Brasenose College. By 1689 Birmingham had also developed a specialism in gunmaking, and the Whig MP Sir Richard Newdigate promoted the interests of the local Company of Gunmakers, helping them secure contracts to supply muskets for the army in Marlborough's wars.[21]

However, what, above all, distinguished Birmingham from the surrounding towns and villages was its status as a marketing and credit centre. It was the growing scale and reach of the operations of its ironmongers which set it apart. These men were entrepreneurs who supplied the small forges with bar iron and then sold the finished product in a regional and, increasingly, a national market. Already, as we have seen, at the start of Henry VIII's reign Birmingham ironmongers were supplying the Crown with weaponry, as well as horseshoes and bridle bits. Nicholas

Coke of Aston, who died in 1558, employed a travelling salesman who was marketing his goods as far afield as Bristol and Norwich, as well as London. By the early 1600s Birmingham ironmongers were a well-established presence in the London market. The Worshipful Company of Ironmongers in London was complaining of 'foreigners' who were undercutting them and selling goods in the city outside the traditional Leadenhall market. Those they named were mainly West Midlands men, including John Jennens, the wealthiest Birmingham ironmonger of his day, who in partnership with his brother Ambrose was supplying the London market with thousands of pounds worth of iron goods each year. By 1650 a well-informed observer was claiming that most of the 'nails and petty ironwork' sold in the capital were being supplied via Birmingham.[22]

Governance

The rapidity of Birmingham's expansion, and the flexibility and enterprise of its tradesmen, owed a good deal to the system of local governance. By contemporary standards Birmingham was a relatively lightly governed town with no corporation and none of the craft guilds established in large urban centres in the Middle Ages which enabled mercantile elites to control the local economy. In the twelfth century the manor of Birmingham had been divided between the 'Borough', to the south-east, where the town developed, and the 'Foreign', mainly agricultural land to the north and west. There were separate 'courts leet' (manorial courts dealing with minor criminal matters) with an annual 'great court' for the whole manor, while a 'court baron' met fortnightly in the Borough to supervise routine administration. This latter body had a jury composed of leading townsmen, and was headed by a high bailiff, who supervised the markets and presided over town meetings, and a low bailiff, who appointed the jurors. In the late seventeenth century the low bailiff was usually a Protestant dissenter. By this time a 'parish vestry' (a committee of leading parishioners) was also operating in the town, its main responsibility the administration of the poor relief system prescribed by the Elizabethan statutes.[23] The town was relatively free from interference by other bodies or by leading landowners. The late medieval Gild of the Holy Cross, which supervised the repair of roads and bridges and provided a forum for leading townsmen to meet and, no doubt, discuss the town's affairs, was dissolved in 1545. The de Birminghams who owned the manor were probably no more than an intermittent presence in the town in the early sixteenth century, since they resided much of the time at Shutford in Oxfordshire. In 1536 their Birmingham estates were confiscated by the Crown and the manor passed through the hands of a series of absentee landlords over the following years.[24] The most important landowners in the vicinity were the Holtes of Aston, who as the local justices of the peace possessed considerable potential power to interfere in the affairs of the town. Sir Thomas Holte, 1st bart., who built Aston Hall between 1618 and 1635, was a powerful presence in the neighbourhood, but may not have been entirely welcome in Birmingham. In 1640 a group of townsmen led by Thomas Smallbrook petitioned the Crown over 'the great want of justices of peace thereabouts', which was probably an attempt to dilute Holte's influence.[25] However, the extent of the Holtes', and indeed the county bench's, capacity to interfere in the borough was limited before the civil war. The quarter sessions order books for Warwickshire reveal relatively little business relating to the town. In 1625 it was in dispute with the county justices over their liability for the repair of the bridge at Deritend; and through much of the 1630s it was in receipt of relief from the county for periodic outbreaks of plague. But beyond this, the only evidence of outside involvement related to the small change of county government: arbitrating poor relief and ratings disputes, enforcing apprenticeship regulations and providing relief for maimed soldiers.[26]

Birmingham throughout this period remained a town dominated and governed by its wealthier inhabitants. The pyramid of wealth and status in the town is indicated by analysis of two national listings of taxpayers, the subsidy return of 1525 and the hearth tax return of 1670. Holt's investigation of the former shows that about half the taxable wealth of the town was in the hands of 14 individuals (rated at £10+). Edward Birmingham, who was still lord of the manor in 1525, headed the list, with 13 wealthy burgesses who included a mercer, two graziers, a lawyer, a tanner, a scythesmith and two ironmongers. These constituted the core of the local elite. Those in the next category, 34 in all (rated at £3–£9), constituted the bulk of the town's independent craftsmen and artisans, some of whom were substantial enough to employ a workforce. The final category consisted of 109 taxpayers (rated at £1–£2) who comprised the small-scale craftsmen, including many of the smiths and nailers referred to by Leland. Birmingham emerges from this analysis as a town with a large artisan class where manufacturing was of much greater importance relative to its Warwickshire neighbours, Stratford-upon-Avon and Warwick.[27] But, like these two towns, by the late sixteenth century it was run by an oligarchy of wealthier inhabitants drawn from families such as the Colmores, the Jennens, the Kings and the Smallbrooks who filled offices such as bailiff and town steward and served as governors of King Edward's Grammar School. Relations within this group were not always harmonious. At the start of the seventeenth century there was a bitter feud between two of the town's wealthiest citizens, both mercers and ironmasters, William Colmore and Thomas Smallbrook. Colmore accused Smallbrook of embezzling the funds of King Edward's for which he had special responsibility as the governor

The imposing seat of the Holte family, Aston Hall in the mid-seventeenth century, engraved by Wenceslaus Hollar for Dugdale's *Antiquities of Warwickshire* and described by Dugdale as a 'noble fabrick ... which for beauty and state much exceedeth any in these parts'.
By permission of the Cadbury Research Library: Special Collections, University of Birmingham

entrusted with custody of its collection of deeds. Smallbrook retaliated by accusing Colmore and his son, Thomas, of assault and spreading libellous writings against him. Sir Thomas Holte intervened and the case came before the Warwick assizes and eventually before the court of Star Chamber in London. But the disputes were not finally resolved until the death of the two main protagonists by 1609.[28]

The 1670 hearth tax return provides other insights into the social and economic structure of Birmingham. In general, towns had more households exempt from paying the tax than rural communities. However, they also had more households of real if modest prosperity with three hearths, although in Birmingham there were fewer of these than in smaller towns. Of Birmingham's 780 households, almost half (365) were exempt from the hearth tax; these were not necessarily in receipt of poor relief themselves but they were mostly too poor to be ratepayers. Poor law records surviving from the 1660s show that 70 households received regular relief, with 18 more needing it occasionally, while 380 households paid the rates. The extent of poverty in late Stuart Birmingham is indicated, however, by the level of the poor rate, which was twice as costly as the hearth tax itself. In 1670 some 23 per cent of households were assessed at three or more hearths, mostly clustering around the three to five mark; only 1 per cent of houses were assessed at ten or more hearths. No inhabitant of Deritend, where 60 out of 92 households were exempt, lived in a house rated at more than three hearths. The largest houses in Birmingham according to the return were the thirteen-hearth residences of the established gentlemen: William Colemore esquire in the 'Foreign' and Mr Philip Friers and Mr Edward Crancke in the High Street. In contrast Sir Robert Holte's Aston Hall was assessed at 41 hearths. Professional men like Archdeacon Riland (eleven hearths) and Nathaniel Brooksby (eight) lived in some comfort, and, as Rowlands has pointed out, the most prosperous men associated with trade and the iron industry ranked with the minor gentry and also had substantial residences. Thirteen per cent of households were headed by women, including Widow Benson whose house had seven hearths, though

she was 'miserably poor, nothing to be found but children and raggs'. She had not paid her tax. The assessors for Birmingham's hearth tax listed households by street, so we can get some sense of the social geography of the town. They began with the 'Welch End' where there were many poor households and some new building, and then moved down the left of the High Street towards the Bull Ring, before assessing the houses on the right of the street. In the High Street prosperous and humbler households existed in close proximity. Two small houses newly built in Carr's Lane were listed before the crowded, mostly poor Digbeth, followed by Edgbaston Street, Spicer Street, New Street, Moor Street and Park Street. Finally a single forge was listed in Court Lane before a general listing of the exempt. The entries for Deritend and Edgbaston came before the fairly prosperous 'forreigne' which contained 20 chargeable houses (eight of three or more hearths) and seven exempt.[29] Despite the widespread poverty in the town, the inhabitants of later Stuart Birmingham were not short of opportunities for consumption or without cultural interests. The vast probate inventory of a prosperous mercer Samuel Kempson (d. 1667) had a total value of over £1,000. His shop sold spices, tobacco and tobacco boxes, and a whole page of the listing dealt with ribbon and lace. Many men of modest property like the cutlers Richard Dicken and Edward Mascall, the smith Richard Clarke and the shoemaker John Garner owned books.[30]

A modern photograph of Aston Hall: in the late seventeenth century it was assessed at 41 hearths for taxation purposes.
Photograph by Tony Hisgett, Wikimedia Commons

OLD BUILDINGS IN DIGBETH.

Seventeenth-century dwellings in Digbeth, Birmingham as illustrated in the Victorian period. One of a series of plates from *Buildings of Birmingham Past & Present Sketched and Described*, published by Thomas Underwood in the late nineteenth century.
Private Collection

Religious developments in the town around the time of the Reformation are poorly documented. The town's main charitable institution, the Hospital of St Thomas of Canterbury, founded in the thirteenth century, was dissolved in 1536 and the Gild of the Holy Cross, with its chantry priests, in 1545. Their property was sold off and some of the proceeds used to endow King Edward VI's Free Grammar School, founded in 1552 to provide a classical humanist education for local children.[31] With its large population of independent tradesmen and artisans, the conditions were in place for evangelical Protestantism to establish an early foothold in the town. But it is hard to get much sense of its religious character until the first references to regular weekday sermons by Puritan ministers seeking further reform of the Church during the 1630s. These were attended by the young Thomas Hall who went on to become the Presbyterian minister of King's Norton in the 1640s, committed to promoting a reformed national Church without bishops. Hall talks of having 'sat at the feet of those grave Gamaliels, your learned lecturers, Dr Burgess (minister at Sutton Coldfield), Mr Slader (minister at St Martin's in Birmingham), Mr Grent (minister at Aston) and Mr Atkins'.[32] The curate in the later 1630s and early 1640s was Francis Roberts, who became a prominent Presbyterian in London after 1643.

By the time of the civil war, the most dramatic and traumatic event in Birmingham's early modern history, the town had become renowned, or notorious, as a centre of committed parliamentarianism and zealous Puritan religion. It was, wrote the royalist politician and historian Edward Hyde, a town 'generally wicked … declaring a more peremptory malice to his majesty then any other place'. Birmingham men were credited with a decisive role in establishing parliamentarian control in Warwickshire, established when the city of Coventry refused to admit Charles I and his army in August 1642. Its inhabitants' resolve was stiffened, according to another hostile witness, William Dugdale, 'through the aid of many sectaries and schismatics which flocked unto them especially from that populous town of Birmingham'.[33] This reputation, and the town's supply of weapons to the Parliament, prompted the punitive treatment it received at the hands of the royalist commander Prince Rupert, on Easter Monday, 3 April 1643. Parliamentarian pamphlets indignantly recorded how the 'famous and well affected town of Birmingham' had attracted the particular hatred of 'Popish and prophane malignants'. The town had therefore supported a troop of horse for its defence commanded by Captain Richard Greaves of Moseley, but when the people heard of Rupert's approach, many, including the minister, urged the soldiers to withdraw, which they seem to have done. Nonetheless, the 'middle and inferior people' of the town resolved to stand on their own guard against the 'great fury' of Rupert and the cavaliers. The royalists plundered the town, destroying Porter's blade mill, and terrified local women with 'setting naked swords and pistols to their breasts'. None of the cavaliers slept that night but 'sat up revelling, robbing and tyrannising', drinking healths to Prince Rupert's dog. Much of the town was fired, and at least 14 inhabitants were slain 'in this frenzy', including a poor lunatic minister who was hacked to death on the assumption that he was Francis Roberts.

The school house at King's Norton, originally built to house the library of the leading Presbyterian minister Thomas Hall.
Photograph by Tony Hisgett, Wikimedia Commons

A royalist account pointed out that the inhabitants 'were they who first stirred up those of Coventry to resist the king' and that the town had sent 15,000 swords to the parliamentary army, but it feared, correctly, that Rupert would be denounced for the 'firing of this town, which he never commanded or countenanced'. Parliamentarians did, indeed, insist that Prince Rupert's 'burning love to England' was demonstrated in Birmingham's flames; and that the town's fate was a prime example of the 'devilish actions of the Cavaliers' and a warning to the rest of the kingdom. God's providence was, however, demonstrated for Parliament in the losses suffered by the royalists, notably the death of one of the leading Warwickshire noblemen, the earl of Denbigh.[34]

The sack and firing of the town was the most brutal aspect of Birmingham's civil war experience, but it also suffered from troop incursions and heavy taxation, including an excise on manufactures throughout the 1640s. The town was in a contested region; a local man, 'Tinker' Fox, established a parliamentarian garrison in the house of the Middlemores, a Catholic gentry family, at Edgbaston, while there were powerful royalist garrisons for much of the war at Dudley and Lichfield, and a smaller one briefly operated in Aston Hall, before being removed after a three-day siege in December 1643. The burdens of war are revealed in the town's accounts of losses to the Parliament drawn up in 1646. They had paid heavy taxation to local and national armies, donated horses to the Parliament and been heavily plundered by its Scottish allies, while 42 people had lent just over £450 to the cause at the start of the war, mostly in modest sums from £2 to £30. The inhabitants emphasized, however, that they had 'lent willingly and freely at the first out of their good affection to the parliament'.[35]

We know little of the state of opinion in Birmingham for the rest of the 1640s and 1650s apart from a fleeting glimpse of divisions among parliamentarians. In June 1650 Robert Girdler, a long-cutler and zealous parliamentarian, alleged that the schoolmaster at King Edward's, Nathaniel Brooksby, and most of the governors were 'disaffected unto the State', and had refused the 'Engagement' of loyalty to the republic. All the accused testified that they had in fact taken the oath, and the case was dismissed, but this attempt to purge the school was probably an indication of the strength of more moderate parliamentarianism in the town, and disquiet about the execution of Charles I.[36] Far from being 'sectaries and schismatics', the most influential of Birmingham's inhabitants were committed to overall 'Presbyterian' reformation of the Church, rather than to religious liberty or independent gathered congregations, and this sober Puritanism was to dominate Birmingham nonconformity after the restoration of the monarchy and the episcopal Church in 1660.

The Restoration did not bring religious and political harmony to Birmingham, many of whose inhabitants in the early 1660s seem to have been eager to continue the battles of the 1640s and 1650s. Divisions centred around the extraordinary figure of Josiah Slader, who claimed the rectory of St Martin's in 1661.[37] The respected Presbyterian minister Samuel Wills had been appointed to the living in 1646 on the presentation of Viscount Saye and Sele, probably acting as Master of the Court of Wards during the minority of the Marrow lord of the manor, but the right to present was also claimed by the widow of the long-serving but rarely resident rector Luke Smith. At the Restoration, Slader claimed he had been presented in the 1640s by Mary Smith and he was instituted to the living by the new bishop of Lichfield in October 1661. Wills, being of a 'peaceable temper', preached instead for a while at Deritend chapel, before his formal deprivation in January 1662. He left Birmingham, and then, like many Presbyterians, he refused to take the oaths required by the 1662 Act of Uniformity or to accept the revised Anglican Book of Common Prayer. Slader, on the other hand, made the required subscription on 5 August 1662, nine days before the deadline on 14 August, 'Black Bartholomew's Day'.

Slader seems to have been a charismatic and eccentric chancer; he was certainly

Prince Rupert's 'burning love' to Birmingham, exploited by parliamentarian propaganda. His dog was credited with devilish powers. The image appeared as a woodcut that accompanied a parliamentarian propaganda tract, *The Bloody Prince, Or A Declaration of the Most Cruell Practices of Prince Rupert*, published within three weeks of the sack of Birmingham.
By permission of the Cadbury Research Library: Special Collections, University of Birmingham

not the same as the godly minister mentioned by Hall, but it is not impossible that the coincidence of names inspired his impersonation. Slader's subscription prompted a petition to the bishop from prominent Birmingham men, including the schoolmaster Nathaniel Brooksby, Ambrose Foxall and Richard Smallbrook, accusing him of forging his ordination papers and masquerading as a clergyman. In extended Church court proceedings, Slader was accused of drunkenness and sexual promiscuity, of fathering a child born to his sister-in-law and, most bizarrely, of a conjuring trick in which he cut off his son's head and then replaced it before a crowd of gullible townsmen and women. While his enemies also accused Slader of radical parliamentarian sympathies, he and his supporters denounced them as 'rigid Presbyterians' who had 'fashioned' him into a 'fanatic'. Slader did have significant support in the town, with 300 names attached to a petition in his favour delivered to the bishop. Smallbrooke and his other accusers sought to discredit these supporters on largely social grounds, as non-ratepayers, young people, alehouse keepers and strangers. Evidence was given that it was the 'better sort' who had been most affronted by Slader's ministry, and it may be that the sober godliness of his opponents was not appealing to many of the town's inhabitants.

We will probably never know for certain whether Slader was a republican 'fanatic' or a wronged cavalier. What is clear from the voluminous evidence produced in the Lichfield court is that Birmingham men and women were well informed and still deeply divided over the issues that had afflicted the town so profoundly in the 1640s. It was generally accepted that Slader had operated as an apothecary, selling medicines throughout the 1650s, and his claim to the town living was eventually rejected. This prompted direct action. In the summer of 1662 12 men (including two of Slader's sons, complete with their heads) and one woman were indicted at quarter sessions for rescuing Josias Slader from custody, and on 30 January 1663 some 15 people rioted in the parish church and held it against local officials for three days. 30 January was of course the sacred day when Anglicans commemorated the regicide of Charles I, but the riot was more likely connected with the recent institution as rector of Birmingham of the impeccably royalist and Anglican archdeacon of Coventry, John Riland.[38]

We hear little of Slader after 1663, but Birmingham people remained divided over religious and political issues to the end of the Stuart period. A significant and prosperous segment of the population remained committed to Presbyterian-type religion. Such people had been committed to a reformed, staunchly Puritan national Church in the 1640s and 1650s, but such a Church became an increasingly distant possibility after 1660. Gradually Presbyterians became reconciled to becoming a distinct 'denomination' outside the established Church, achieving legal religious toleration in 1689, following the Revolution which replaced the Catholic James II with Protestant William and Mary. Throughout the period Presbyterians were subject to harassment and opposition from Anglicans who often seem to have been supported by humbler townspeople.[39]

After 1662 Birmingham became a refuge for many ejected Puritan ministers. One of these, Thomas Bladon, formerly minister of Alrewas in Staffordshire, praised it as 'an asylum, a place of refuge', and the town's lack of corporate status perhaps made it relatively free from interference by the authorities. Resident Presbyterians in 1670 included Jarvis Bryan, later pastor of the Presbyterian church in Coventry, and two of the three founding ministers of the 'Old Meeting' in Birmingham itself, William Fincher and Thomas Baldwin. The bishop of Lichfield complained of Presbyterian influence in 1669, reporting on two large 'conventicles' in both Aston and Birmingham. He insisted to the archbishop of Canterbury that it would take a troop of horse to control the 'desperate and very populous rabble'. The networks developed during the Interregnum, and inconsistent government policies, gave nonconformists resilience and breathing space. In 1672 when Charles II suspended the laws enjoining conformity through a royal 'Declaration of Indulgence', no fewer than nine houses in Birmingham were licensed for Presbyterian worship (including Baldwin's in New Street, and Fincher's in Bull Street) and one (Samuel Girdler's) for Congregationalists. The Presbyterians also asked, without success, for the Town Hall to be licensed as a meeting place.

Divisions between Anglicans and dissenters overlapped by the later 1670s with the emerging parties of Tory and Whig, and political differences were most often expressed in religious terms. Whigs campaigned for the exclusion of the Catholic James, Duke of York, from the succession, and favoured more limited monarchy and sympathized with respectable dissent. Tories defended hereditary authoritarian monarchy and the Anglican Church. Following the defeat of 'Exclusion' in the early 1680s there was a Tory reaction, enthusiastically backed in the Birmingham area by the Holtes of Aston and their clerical proteges. Divisions in Birmingham focused on King Edward's Grammar School, which was regarded as a Presbyterian stronghold. Sir Charles Holte backed an attack on the school's charter, alleging corruption on the part of the governors as well as sympathies with dissent. The charter was revoked in 1684, Brooksby was forced to resign and a new governing body was appointed in 1685, representing the 'Tory–Anglican' interest. Among the governors was John Riland, who had preached at the Restoration that 'government comes from above' and that social and political order depended on 'a religious gentry and a pious and obedient clergy'.[40] As in the controversy over Slader in the early 1660s, there is evidence in the conflicts over the school of resentment by poorer inhabitants against Presbyterians associated with a socially exclusive, self-righteously moralizing segment of the town, suggestive perhaps of early 'popular Toryism'. After the Revolution of 1688 empowered Whigs locally and nationally, a series of legal cases restored the 'old governors' and removed Brooksby's successor John Hicks, but the 'new governors' had their supporters. It was claimed they were more sympathetic to the poor; and among the witnesses on their behalf was Josiah Slader, son and namesake of the Restoration rector, who denounced Brooksby as 'an angry man' whose beatings had lamed the young Josiah, his pupil.[41]

There were other religious groups in Restoration Birmingham, including radical Protestant congregations seeking toleration outside the established Church. For example, Quaker meetings, begun in the 1650s, survived persecution more brutal than that meted out to more 'respectable' nonconformists. The frequent presentation of Quakers at quarter sessions in the early 1680s included Birmingham residents who met at the house of the prosperous Robert Rotherham, in Washwood and Saltley, assessed at nine hearths in 1670.[42] There was also a small number of Congregationalists, associated particularly with the Girdler family. And, finally, there is evidence of Roman Catholics in Birmingham, with the Middlemores of Edgbaston prominent protectors of a Franciscan mission intermittently active in the area. A Catholic chapel or 'mass house' was built in 1687, helped by donations from King James himself, only to be destroyed during the Revolution of 1688.[43]

The first meeting house, of the Presbyterians, the most significant dissenters from the established Church, was registered for worship in July 1689 under the auspices of the Toleration Act of that year, but its construction had begun almost two years earlier under the more sweeping but controversial terms of James II's 1687 Declaration of Indulgence, which, unlike the 1689 measure, also gave freedom of worship to Catholics. Eleven substantial trustees or 'proprietors' purchased the land and arranged for the construction of the substantial eight-bay building for the congregation that became known as the 'Old Meeting'. At least seven of these men had served as constables or low bailiff in the town. By 1690 the congregation had grown so large that a 'Lower' or 'New Meeting' was established in a house in Deritend, later to settle in Moor Street and to become famous under Priestley's ministry. Far from creating a modus vivendi among different religious groups, however, the 1689 Act bred Anglican resentment, and inaugurated, in David Wykes' words, a generation of 'bitter religious strife'.[44] The Holtes of Aston and their High Church vicars harassed Quakers and more respectable dissenters alike; the curate of Deritend chapel, who was the vicar's subordinate but had many nonconformist sympathizers among his congregation, often pleased neither faction. Religious and political conflict erupted in street violence at the Hanoverian succession. As Whigs and dissenters celebrated the coronation of George I, Anglican Tory crowds attacked the houses of two of the proprietors of the Presbyterian meeting, and in 1715 a rowdy 'mob' controlled the town for ten days of Church and Stuart rioting in which the Old Meeting house was badly damaged and the owner of the house in Deritend forced into ejecting the congregation.

Evidence of the presence of 'respectable' dissent in Birmingham from the later seventeenth century: 'Old' and 'New Meeting' from William Hutton, *An History of Birmingham* (1809). By permission of the Library of Birmingham, SC5/563151

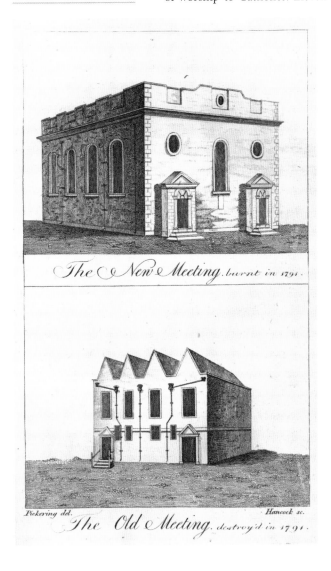

Pickering del.

Hancock sc.

The New Meeting, burnt in 1791.

The Old Meeting, destroy'd in 1791.

Conclusion

Birmingham at the end of the Stuart Age was a crowded, lively and prosperous place, although for significant numbers of the population the metalworking trades offered only a precarious living. In comparison to two hundred years earlier its population had probably increased tenfold, new streets and new housing had been built, it was at the forefront of new manufactures and fashions in the metalworking industries and it had become one of the leading commercial centres outside London.

St Martin's Church from Moat Lane from a sketch made in 1853, in John Thackray Bunce, *History of Old St. Martin's, Birmingham* (1875). This late nineteenth-century image shows surviving early modern buildings which provide evidence of the prosperity of the town at the end of the Stuart period. Bunce was editor of *Aris's Birmingham Gazette* and wrote a number of books on the history of Birmingham and its people.
By permission of the Cadbury Research Library: Special Collections, University of Birmingham

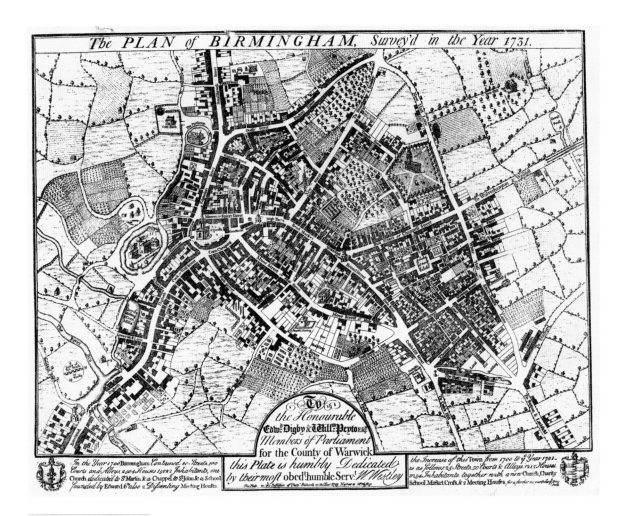

The PLAN of BIRMINGHAM, Survey'd in the Year 1731.

To the Honourable Edwd Digby & Will:^m Peyto Esq.^s Members of Parliament for the County of Warwick this Plate is humbly Dedicated by their most obed^t humble Servt W. Westley

The prospering town in the
early eighteenth century
is illustrated by William
Westley's *Plan of Birmingham
Survey'd in the Year 1731.*
By permission of the Library of
Birmingham, MAP/148760

At the same time it was also religiously and politically divided. In the aftermath of civil war its Puritan religious identity had fractured into dissenting factions, such as the Presbyterians, Congregationalists and Quakers, and these were now confronted by an aggressive and reactionary Tory Anglicanism. Religious divisions fed into political splits between Whigs and Tories as the inhabitants of Birmingham continued to re-fight the battles of the 1640s. In many respects, then, Hutton was right. The Restoration did mark a watershed in Birmingham's historical development. After this date, it was no longer just a town of local and regional significance; it had become an urban centre of national importance, encapsulating many of the dynamic forces that were to transform England in the eighteenth century.

Notes

1   William Hutton, *A History of Birmingham* (2nd edn., 1783), 41–2 (all references are to this edition).

2   Ibid., 40–52, 73–9, 82–7.

3   See, for example, P. Borsay, *The English Urban Renaissance. Culture and Society in the Provincial Town 1660–1770* (Oxford, 1989); P. Clark (ed.), *The Cambridge Urban History of Britain. Volume II, 1540–1840* (Cambridge, 2000),

4   *The Itinerary of John Leland*, ed. L. Toulmin-Smith, 6 vols (London, 1964), II, 96–7.

5   William Camden, *Britannia….*, trans. P. Holland (London, 1610), 567. William Smith, in his 1588 survey of England, described Birmingham as a town 'where great store of knyves are made; for almost all the townes men are cutlers or smiths': W.B. Stephens (ed.), *A History of the County of Warwick. Volume VII: The City of Birmingham*, Victoria County History (London, 1964), 81, http://www.british-history.ac.uk/vch/warks/vol7/ (accessed 31 December 2015). For a survey of archaeological evidence relating to Birmingham in this period, see M.A. Hodder, *Birmingham: the Hidden History* (Stroud, 2004), 136–8.

6   R. Holt, *The Early History of the Town of Birmingham 1166 to 1600*, Dugdale Society Occasional Papers, 30 (Oxford, 1985), 14–17.

7   The case for the reliability of these certificates, the rounding up or down that took place and the 1.33 multiplier is made in J.S. Moore, 'The mid-Tudor population crisis in midland England', *Midland. History*, 34 (2009), 46–50.

8   Ibid., 44–57; A.D. Dyer and D.M. Palliser (eds), *The Diocesan Population Returns for 1563 and 1603*, British Academy Records of Social and Economic History, new series 31 (London, 2005), xxxiv–l, 123.

9   Hutton, *Birmingham*, 42–4, 48.

10 The 1670 return is the fullest available for Warwickshire: T. Arkell with N. Alcock (eds), *Warwickshire Hearth Tax Returns: Michaelmas 1670*, Dugdale Society 43, British Record Society, Hearth Tax Series vol. VII (London, 2010), 453–4.

11 Clark (ed.), *Cambridge Urban History*, II, 384, 679; K. Wrightson, *Earthly Necessities. Economic Lives in Early Modern Britain* (London, 2000), 236, 243.

12 Holt, *Early History*, 10–11; Stephens (ed.), *A History of the County of Warwick. Volume VII*, 248; V. Skipp, *A History of Greater Birmingham – down to 1830* (Birmingham, 1980), 35–6; Skipp, *Crisis and Development: An Ecological Case Study of the Forest of Arden 1570–1674* (Cambridge, 1978), 38–54.

13 J. Thirsk, 'Horn and thorn in Staffordshire: the economy of a pastoral county', in Thirsk, *The Rural Economy of England* (London, 1984), 163–82; W.H.B. Court, *The Rise of the Midland Industries* (Oxford, 1938), 39.

14 Holt, *Early History*, 9–10; C. Gill, *History of Birmingham, vol. 1. Manor and Borough to 1865* (Oxford, 1952), 43–4; Stephens (ed.), *A History of the County of Warwick. Volume VII*, 255–6.

15 Lichfield Record Office, will proved, 8 October 1670;

John Izon (ed.), *The Records of King Edward's School Birmingham*, vol. VI, Dugdale Society, 30 (Oxford, 1974), 25–6, 35. The National Archives (hereafter TNA), E179/270/13.

16 Holt, *Early History*, 17–19; Court, *Midland Industries*, 39–40.

17 Holt, *Early History*, 18–19; *Leland Itinerary*, II, 97.

18 M.B. Rowlands, *Masters and Men in the West Midlands Metalware Trades before the Industrial Revolution* (Manchester, 1975), 20–1, based on over 2,000 inventories in Staffordshire and Warwickshire.

19 Ibid., 39, 160–1.

20 R.A. Pelham, 'The growth of settlement and industry 1100–1700', in British Association, *Birmingham and its Regional Setting* (Birmingham, 1950), 147–9, 154, 156; Stephens (ed.), *A History of the County of Warwick. Volume VII*, 85; Skipp, *Birmingham*, 85; Arkell with Alcock (eds), *Hearth Tax Returns*, 40.

21 Rowlands, *Masters and Men*, 26–37; Stephens (ed.), *A History of the County of Warwick. Volume VII*, 82–5; Holt, *Early History*, 20; Skipp, *Birmingham*, 44–6; Izon (ed.), *Records of King Edward's School*, VI, xi.

22 Rowlands, *Masters and Men*, 9–13, Holt, *Early History*, 20–1; Pelham, 'Settlement and industry', 152.

23 Holt, *Early History*, 11–12; Skipp, *Birmingham*, 74–5.

24 Holt, *Early History*, 11–13; Gill, *Birmingham*, 38–9; Stephens (ed.), *A History of the County of Warwick. Volume VII*, 318–19.

25 A.L. Hughes, *Politics, Society and Civil War in Warwickshire, 1620–1660* (Cambridge, 1987), 31, 42n, 55; O. Fairclough, *'The Grand Old Mansion': The Holtes and their Successors at Aston Hall 1618–1684* (Birmingham, 1984); *Calendar of State Papers Domestic 1639–40*, ed. W.D. Hamilton (London, 1877), 349–50.

26 S.C. Ratcliff and H.C. Johnson (eds), *Warwick County Records*, vols. I and II (Warwick, 1935–36), I, 15, 37, 68–9, 107, 118, 137, 171–3, 220–1; II, 12–13, 65–6, 69, 215–18, 269.

27 Holt, *Early History*, 15–17.

28 M. Fogg, *The Smallbroke Family of Birmingham* (e-publishing lulu.com, 2009), 35–44.

29 Arkell with Alcock (eds), *Hearth Tax Returns*, 55, 86, 98–100, 13, 354–61.

30 Lichfield Record Office (hereafter LRO), wills proved 4 July 1667 (Kempson); 4 March 1661 (Dicken); 20 June 1666 (Mascall); 11 March 1668 (Clarke); 24 August 1664 (Garner). About half of a sample of 50 Birmingham inventories from the 1660s reveal book ownership.

31 Stephens (ed.), *A History of the County of Warwick. Volume VII*, 6, 77–8, 549; Gill, *Birmingham*, 40–1.

32 Hughes, *Warwickshire*, 80–4; Stephens (ed.), *A History of the County of Warwick. Volume VII*, 411.

33 The account of Birmingham in the civil war is taken from Hughes, *Warwickshire*, 147, 149.

34 This account is from *Prince Ruperts Burning Love to England Discovered in Birminghams Flames* (London, 1643); *A True Relation of Prince Ruperts Barbarous Cruelty*

against the Towne of Birmingham (London, 1643); *A Letter Written from Walshall* (London, 1643); I.W. *The Bloody Prince* (London, 1643).

35 TNA SP28/186, Birmingham accounts, 11; A.J. Hopper, '"Tinker Fox" and the politics of garrison warfare in the West Midlands, 1643–50', *Midland History*, 24 (1999), 98–113.

36 Izon (ed.), *Records of King Edward's School*, VI, 24–6.

37 Stephens (ed.), *A History of the County of Warwick. Volume VII*, 364–5; A.G. Matthews, *Calamy Revised* (Oxford, 1934), 534; Maureen Harris, '"Schismatical people": conflict between clergy and laity in Warwickshire 1660–1720' (PhD thesis, Leicester University, 2015). Consistory court proceedings: LRO, B/C/5, 1662, 1663. Clergy of the Church of England Database [web resource].

38 TNA SP29/22/70, 1662, reprinted in *Quarter Sessions Order Book 1657–1665* (Warwick County Records, vol IV, 1938), xl; see also 275–6.

39 Stephens (ed.), *A History of the County of Warwick. Volume VII*, 398–9, 412–14; D.L. Wykes, 'James II's Religious Indulgence of 1687 and the early organisation of dissent. The building of the first nonconformist meeting-house in Birmingham', *Midland History*, 16 (1991), 86–102; Harris, 'Conflict between clergy and laity in Warwickshire'.

40 Riland, quoted in Hughes, *Politics, Society and Civil War*, 343.

41 Izon (ed.), *Records of King Edward's School*, VI, 53–64

42 Arkell with Alcock (eds), *Hearth Tax Returns*, 352.

43 Stephens (ed.), *A History of the County of Warwick. Volume VII*, 398–9; J. Champ, 'The Franciscan mission in Birmingham 1657–1830', *Recusant History*, 21 (1992), 40–50.

44 Wykes, 'James II's Religious Indulgence', 86, 93–6.

CHAPTER FIVE

The City of a Thousand Trades, 1700–1945

MALCOLM DICK

Whether or not Edmund Burke was accurate in describing Birmingham in the late eighteenth century as 'the city of a thousand trades', it is a catchphrase that has become associated with the town's public identity, as any internet search reveals. The label usefully draws attention to Birmingham's diverse manufacturing and commercial base and the importance of economic activity in shaping its history. It also sets Birmingham apart from other rapidly growing industrial towns such as Manchester, Leeds and Sheffield, whose economies were substantially based on one trade, respectively cotton, wool and steel. Birmingham and its surrounding district in the Black Country, with which its economy was inextricably linked, produced many different goods, mainly but not exclusively in a variety of metals. This diversity propelled the growth of the town. The economic landscape was transformed over 250 years and can be measured by the growth in population. In 1700 about 7,000–8,000 people lived in the parish of Birmingham – the figure is higher if adjacent districts such as Aston and Handsworth which later became part of the city are included – but by the early 1940s, the figure was over one million.[1] This massive expansion raises several questions: why did this growth take place, how did it happen and what changes occurred? This chapter attempts to answer these questions by considering individually and collectively how people were shaped by and shaped changing patterns of industry and trade. It explores the subject in four segments: first, how Birmingham's industrialization can be explained, and then by considering three periods: 1700–1851, 1851–1914 and 1914–1945. Ways of understanding the history of 'the city of a thousand trades' have changed over time and these perspectives are charted first.

The first historians of Birmingham's industries and trades viewed expansion through the prism of individual achievement. In an early edition of his history, William Hutton (1723–1815),[2] selected John Taylor (1710/11–75), the 'uncommon genius', who allegedly mass-produced 800,000 buttons per week; John Baskerville (1706–75), who spent 'a life of genius, in carrying to perfection the greatest of all human inventions', printing; and Matthew Boulton (1728–1809), 'genius' of 'the nursery of ingenuity' at Soho manufactory, where among other things, the steam engine was improved.[3] Hutton's heroic view was cemented in 1866 by Samuel Timmins, who saw Birmingham as the epitome of a new industrial civilization: a global example of enterprise, invention and achievement.[4] Robert K. Dent's subsequent history, which he dedicated to Timmins and which has served as a major reference source for local historians, devoted substantial space to Baskerville, Boulton and James Watt (1736–1819).[5] Subsequent writers have reacted against this approach: George Barnsby, Clive Behagg and Carl Chinn have focused on the contributions of working-class individuals to Birmingham's economic history.[6] Others, including G.C. Allen, W.H.B. Court, D.E.C. Eversley, Marie Rowlands, Victor Skipp and Barbara M.D. Smith have added significantly to our knowledge of industrial structure, individual businesses and technological change, while avoiding an overemphasis on 'genius'.[7] Eric Hopkins has provided a broad survey of the local economy within the national experiences of industrial revolution, patterns of boom and slump and changing living standards.[8] This chapter owes much to his work. Additional perspectives have located Birmingham's industries and trades in an international context. J.R. Harris looked at how eighteenth-century economic life was affected by industrial espionage, Peter M. Jones provided a major study of the region's industry as part of the industrial enlightenment and Leslie Tomory argued for gaslight as a pioneering technology-based industry not only in Birmingham, but elsewhere.[9]

There are, however, few analytical studies of the local metals industry during the Industrial Revolution, and many businesses, industrialists, traders and activities merit critical exploration, though Marie Rowlands explored the pre-1760 metalware trades within a regional context, and Guy Sjögren's research is an investigation of the cut-nail trade.[10] The ways in which migrants contributed to the economy is also important.[11] The relationship between business and landscape is crucial: Gordon Cherry produced a pioneering study and the Birmingham Historic Landscape Characterisation Project has created a digital resource for mapping the changing distribution of industry and transport.[12] Historians can also utilize the findings of other disciplines, including architectural history and

William Hutton's stone memorial shows him surrounded by his books, the tools of his trade. Hutton (1723–1815) was the first published historian of Birmingham and his concerns, prejudices and agendas have influenced the writing of the town's history ever since. This monument in St Margaret's Church, Ward End, close to where he lived in Washwood Heath, was sculpted by Peter Hollins. By permission of Keith Wadsworth

archaeology, to throw light on Birmingham's economic history.[13] Material and print culture provides ways of gaining insight into the past by exploring the historical as opposed to the aesthetic significance of paintings, prints, maps, photographs, trade cards, advertising ephemera, poetry, prose and artefacts. There are, therefore, a variety of ways to sketch the changing contours of the 'thousand trades'.

Explaining Birmingham's industrialization

Several theories have evolved to explain Birmingham's emergence as a centre of industry and commerce. William Hutton, a migrant to the town, believed that local people had special cultural characteristics: 'They possessed a vivacity I had never beheld … Their very step along the street shewed alacrity: Every man seemed to know and prosecute his own affairs … [the] inhabitants were full of industry.'[14] These traits, he believed, were due to the flourishing nature of local commerce, which, in turn, was due to the openness and freedom of the town. The reason for this was the absence of a corporation.[15] There was no urban government that could impose restrictions on economic activity, which meant that there were no guilds that could protect established elites by restricting access to trade and laying down apprenticeship regulations. It also meant that Birmingham was exempt from the provisions of the legislation of the Clarendon Code (1661–65), which excluded dissenters from public civic life and prevented nonconformist ministers from preaching within five miles of an incorporated borough. Hence, dissenters – and Hutton was one – could move to Birmingham and operate within a permissive economic environment. There are doubts about the validity of these claims. Other locations, including Wolverhampton, had similar features but did not develop as rapidly as Birmingham, and Coventry, a borough which possessed a corporation, still experienced rapid economic growth.[16]

Explaining any economic change, however, involves the interplay of changing demand from customers and the ability for this demand to be met – the supply side of this relationship. Demand from domestic and overseas consumers was important to stimulate the supply side of the economic equation. Hopkins argued that the expansion of the home market was more important than foreign demand, though this is difficult to prove given limited statistical data. Selling goods depended upon factors: agents who facilitated commerce at home and abroad, and lenders and banks who could supply credit. The extensive Archive of Soho in the Library of Birmingham has enabled historians to explore how one businessman, Matthew Boulton, pursued commercial relationships with agents and creditors.[17] Lloyd's Bank, initially Taylor and Lloyd's, founded by two local industrialists Sampson Lloyd (1699–1779) and John Taylor in 1765, invested heavily in Birmingham's growing canal network and may, therefore, have helped to create the infrastructure which was essential for customers to be reached.[18]

Overseas trade was vital as a source of raw materials and luxuries and as a market for manufactured products. Trade with Asia, Europe and the Americas was

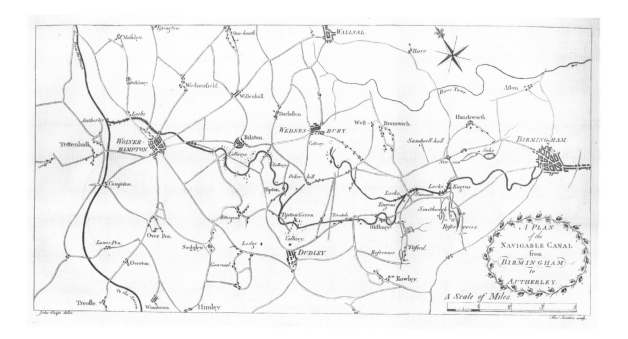

Birmingham's first major navigable canal, illustrated in Hutton's *History of Birmingham*, was opened in 1769 and connected Birmingham's manufactories with the coal mines of the Black Country. It reduced dramatically the cost of coal imported into Birmingham compared with transport by road.
By permission of the Library of Birmingham, SC5/563151

Fifteen Birmingham gun makers, including Samuel Galton, are listed in this advertisement in Bisset's *Magnificent Directory* of 1808. Published in time of war, the advert patriotically celebrates an important Birmingham industry.
By permission of the Library of Birmingham, 47154

important, as the damaging impact of the French Wars (1793–1815) revealed.[19] How far Birmingham's economy was stimulated by participation in the African slave trade and West Indian plantation slavery is a subject of debate. The Trinidadian historian Eric Williams argued that Britain's Industrial Revolution was driven by participation in the triangular trade and the plantation economies of the Americas, which supplied vast quantities of sugar to domestic consumers. Much of his evidence was based on the exports of Birmingham guns and metalware, including manillas, brass horseshoe-shaped bracelets which were widely used as a currency in West Africa.[20] The Williams thesis has been the subject of historiographical controversy, but, without necessarily accepting his argument in full, some of Birmingham's industrialists and traders clearly participated in the slave trade and slavery and made money as a result. The records of the gun-making business of Farmer and Galton show that this firm exported considerable quantities of guns to Africa as part of the slave trade. Samuel Galton junior, a Quaker, was an extremely wealthy man.[21] The involvement of the local brass industry can be asserted, but primary sources which prove an extensive connection with slavery are tantalizingly few. The firm of Boulton and Watt exported steam engines to power Caribbean sugar cane crushing machines in the early nineteenth century.[22] Slaves also reached Birmingham and were sold in the town, but the numbers were small. A Swedish visitor, Samuel Schröder, visited a slitting mill in 1749, which prepared bar iron for nail-making, owned by the Quakers Charles and Samuel Lloyd. Four men were at work, three of whom were white and received wages while one was a black slave who received only his food and clothing.[23]

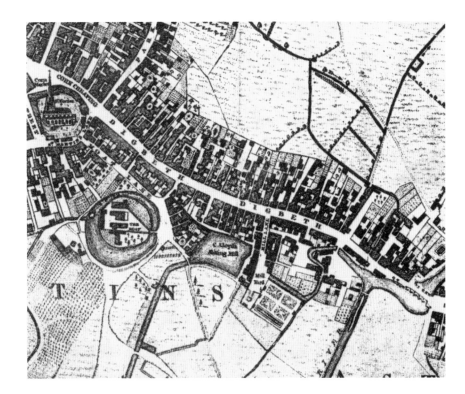

The site of Charles Lloyd's slitting mill, one of the major ironworks in Birmingham, can be identified on Bradford's 1750 *Plan of Birmingham*. Established by a Quaker dynasty of iron founders, the mill was sited in Digbeth, the traditional centre of manufacturing in Birmingham.
By permission of the Library of Birmingham, 72830

THE

FIRST REPORT

OF

THE FEMALE SOCIETY,

[1825-26]

FOR

BIRMINGHAM, WEST-BROMWICH, WEDNESBURY, WALSALL,

AND THEIR RESPECTIVE NEIGHBOURHOODS,

FOR THE RELIEF OF

British Negro Slaves.

"Remember those in bonds, as bound with them : and them that suffer adversity, as being yourselves also in the body."—HEB. XIII. 3.

That British Female Slaves are chained and manacled at the will of their Owners, is proved by the facts detailed in the official correspondence of Col. Arthur, Governor of Honduras, with Lord Bathurst, ordered to be printed by the House of Commons, on the 16th of June, 1823.

See the Letter, dated October the 7th, 1820.

See, also, the Anti-Slavery Reporter, No. 3, Mauritius, "*Women are alike subject to flogging, and the punishment of working in chains. Chains of any endurable weight may be affixed by the master to his slaves, whether men or women.*"—p. 21.

BIRMINGHAM :

Printed at the Office of Richard Peart, 38, Bull-street.

1826.

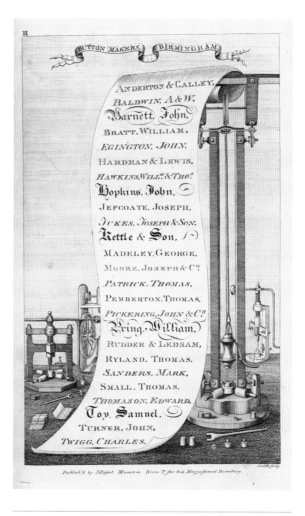

Despite the involvement of Birmingham's manufacturers in the slave trade and slavery, abolitionist activity in the town was strong. The Female Society for the Relief of British Negro Slaves (founded in 1825) was a particularly active society which was widely supported by the wives, sisters and daughters of many local businessmen.
By permission of the Library of Birmingham, MS 3173/2/1

Birmingham's button makers used sophisticated hand-operated machinery, as illustrated in this advertisement in Bisset's *Magnificent Directory*, to mass-produce their goods.
By permission of the Library of Birmingham, 47154

A 1771 advertisement for the sale of a 21-year-old male slave, in *Aris's Birmingham Gazette*, reveals that slave trading took place in the town,[24] but it is the only known example of an advert of this kind for Birmingham itself. These points do not prove that Birmingham's economy was mainly dependent upon the slave trade and slavery, but show that the connection was significant. Birmingham's involvement, of course, needs to be set alongside the leadership and participation of many local businessmen, particularly Quakers such as the Lloyds and Sturges, and their wives, sisters and daughters in the abolitionist campaigns to end the British slave trade before 1807 and slavery before 1838.[25]

As well as demand, the supply side also contributed to local economic growth. Geography and geology ensured good sources of drinking water to support a large population and provided springs and streams to power mills and for use in manufacturing processes that required cleansing.[26] The resources of the Black Country – coal, iron, limestone and clay – were also crucial in supplying industrial activity and building construction.[27] Birmingham had a long-established market which drew in arable produce and animals from the countryside. Industrial activity before 1700 based on metalworking and gun making provided a residue of skills and opportunities for later developments.[28] By the mid- and late eighteenth century, as visitors to the town pointed out, Birmingham manufacturers had developed mass-production techniques based on the division of labour and the use of sophisticated hand-operated machines, dependent on human power, dexterity and ability: the stamp and press which were used for buttons; lathes, which produced engine-turned parts; the draw bench, for drawing out wire in pin making; and sophisticated drills for gun making and other precision engineering activities.[29]

This raises the question as to whether labour was available. Birmingham's central position, a high-wage economy and opportunities for the employment of women and children drew workers not only from adjacent counties, but from Wales, Scotland, Ireland and Europe. We need to know more, however, about how skills were learned and transmitted. Opportunities for success within a booming economy also attracted potential or actual entrepreneurs. Migration occurred from abroad. Jews from Europe settled in Birmingham in the eighteenth century and created a community based on a synagogue. The first Jewish settlers were pedlars who sold toys and inexpensive metal products such as buttons and buckles which they purchased locally and sold elsewhere. Most are anonymous in the historical record, but we know about one, Samuel Harris, who converted to Christianity and was the subject of a nineteenth-century biography. Polish-born, Harris arrived in England in 1821 and secured some money from London Jews to purchase products from which he could make a living. He moved to Birmingham and travelled elsewhere buying and selling as he went, though he had to secure support from local Jews as he travelled.[30] Pedlars were at the bottom of the business hierarchy, but they provided a link between manufacturers and customers. Not all Jews were poor; some were traders and manufacturers who had sufficient status and income to be listed in a 1770 Birmingham directory.[31] One eighteenth-century Jewish businessman was Mayer Oppenheim who owned a glassworks and patented a method for manufacturing red glass.[32] Migration to the town continued and by the mid-nineteenth century traders and manufacturers in a Jewish community of several thousand contributed to Birmingham's economic life, in, for example, silverware and jewellery making.[33]

Buying, selling and the movement of labour depended upon effective transport. For much of

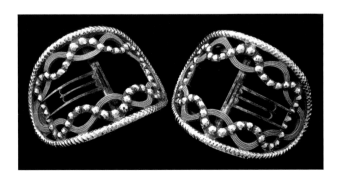

Although at the luxury end of the buckle-making trade, these silver buckles made by Willmore & Alston in 1782 represent the toys, or small metal objects, for which Birmingham became famous. By permission of Assay Office Birmingham

the eighteenth century the carrier trade used roads to move products to markets – and also to bring raw materials, foodstuffs and luxuries into Birmingham. Highways connected to rivers and ports such as Bewdley on the Severn were especially important for Birmingham. Imports were obtained and exports dispatched via coastal ports such as Bristol, Liverpool, Hull and London. The pressure upon and the poor state of the roads led to the creation of turnpike trusts to improve their quality, and canal companies in the late eighteenth century and railway companies in the nineteenth led to new forms of transport to meet industrial and trading needs. Canals moved goods more easily than road, particularly bulky products – a canal boat could carry 25 tons of coal, much more than a waggon. Canal construction in the West Midlands began locally in 1766–69, and by 1770 their value was clear: the price of coal in Birmingham from Wednesbury fell dramatically from 13s a ton to 7s 6d.[34] Other links to rivers such as the Severn, Mersey, Trent and Thames followed. By 1800 Birmingham lay at the centre of a canal network connected with all the major ports. This had massive implications for industrial development; not only was the transportation of goods cheaper, but new industries were able to locate along the canal banks. Gas Street Basin and the surviving canals are physical reminders of how important canals were by the early 1800s. Edgbaston was an exception within Birmingham; though the Birmingham and Worcester Canal crossed the parish, the development requirements in the Canal Act prohibited the construction of factories, workshops and reservoirs. Lord Calthorpe, who owned the estate, was one entrepreneur who was not keen on industrial development.[35] Edgbaston therefore developed as a prosperous suburb of middle-class housing, different from most of the town. Canals had disadvantages: movement was slow and flooding, freezing, drought and leakages could affect the operation of the network. They were suitable for moving heavy non-perishable goods

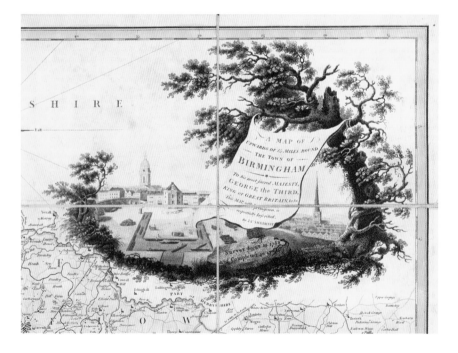

A bird's-eye view of commercial activity in central Birmingham from Sherriff's 1788 *Map of Upward of 25 Miles Round the Town of Birmingham*. Canal boats are loaded with goods as a carrier's wagon pulls into the canal basin. Interestingly, the images of the churches, St Philip's on the left and St. Martin's on the right, are in the background while commercial activity is prominently represented.
By permission of the Library of Birmingham, MAP/236/460

but not passengers or products which had to be transported quickly. The railways provided an alternative, supported by local business interests. In 1837 a route to Liverpool was opened and the completion of the London and Birmingham Railway in 1838 provided a speedy link to the capital. The terminus at Curzon Street still survives. Like the canals, railways developed rapidly and, by 1842, Birmingham was linked by rail to the ports of Bristol, Hull and Liverpool as well as London.[36]

The Black Country provided raw materials and labour, but the West Midlands region was also a focus for technological innovation: the Silicon Valley of the eighteenth century. Coke for iron smelting and new uses for the metal were developed in the Ironbridge Gorge, ceramics technology in north Staffordshire, glass manufacturing in Stourbridge and chemicals in Tipton.[37] The members of the Lunar Society, including, among others, Matthew Boulton, Samuel Galton junior, James Keir, James Watt and Josiah Wedgwood, were wealthy, well-educated and progressive. They were doers as well as thinkers, a fact which gave the West Midlands enlightenment, in which they played a part, a practical dimension that applied scientific thinking to industrial processes. The Lunar men were more than technologically minded industrialists and they were part of a wide circle that extended beyond a few well-known individuals. They have been extensively studied, but there are still opportunities to explore their interrelationships, the contribution of the Lunar women to their activities and how their ideas were translated into reality by their employees. Not all industrial activities, moreover, were dependent upon scientific knowledge and experimentation, but the existence of a West Midlands enlightenment centred upon Birmingham in the late eighteenth and early nineteenth century provided an intellectual dimension that contributed to economic expansion.[38]

As early as the 1730s, people in Birmingham were conscious that the town was industrially important. William Westley's dramatic print of Birmingham contained the following claim:

> BIRMINGHAM, a Market Town in the County of WARWICK, which by the art and industry of its inhabitants has for some years past been rendered famous all over the World, for the choice and invention of all sorts of Wares and Curiosities, in Iron, Steel, Brass &c: admired as well for their cheapness as for their peculiar beauty of Workmanship.[39]

A poem published in *Aris's Birmingham Gazette* in 1751 versified this assertion, though it also noted that, despite manufacturing success, some skills were wanting:

> Here Implements, and Toys for distant Parts,
> Of various Metals, by mechanic Arts,
> Are finely wrought, and by the Artists sold,
> Whose touch turns ever Metal into Gold;
> But 'tis in vain, alas! We boast our Skill;
> Wanting thy Arts, we are deficient still.
> O come and join us, teach us to excel
> In Casting, Carving, and in Building well;[40]

Between 1700 and 1851 the forces that enabled Birmingham to expand created a diverse economy: 'the great toyshop of Europe' according to Edmund Burke.[41] Birmingham was particularly famous for its metal buckles and buttons.[42] Hutton's 'genius', John Taylor, was particularly adept at applying the division of labour

William Westley's 1731 *East Prospect of Birmingham* prominently displays St Philip's church in an elevated position on high ground. The proportions of the building are exaggerated while the rural hinterland frames the town. Birmingham was already a busy, noisy and polluted manufacturing centre, particularly in the Digbeth area at the bottom of the hill towards the left, but this dimension of the town is barely represented.
By permission of the Library of Birmingham, MAL 14035

The EAST PROSPECT of BIRMINGHAM.

Jennens and Bettridge was the most important mid-nineteenth-century manufacturer of japanware in Birmingham. This 'gothic'-shaped tray, painted with exotic birds and embellished with decoration using coloured metal powders, was made by the firm in about 1825.
Collection of Shirley S. Baer

to mass-producing the latter: Lord Shelburne, who visited Birmingham in 1765, attributed Taylor's success to 'the breaking down of the production process enabling each employee to become highly adept through constant repetition of the same operation'.[43] Taylor also made japanware, a local trade that combined technical and artistic skills to produce items as varied as trays, tea caddies, fire screens, vases and household furniture. Yvonne Jones's study examines and describes the business histories and decorative products of this major industry. As well as Taylor, she explores other eighteenth-century japanware manufacturers, including John Baskerville, Boulton and Fothergill and Henry Clay. The most important early and mid-nineteenth-century business was Jennens and Bettridge (c.1810/13–1860/61) and their short-lived successor John Bettridge and Co. (1859–c.1869). They made high-quality products, were patronised by royalty, received visitors and trained numerous decorators.[44] The industry declined in the 1860s as a result of increased competition, declining workmanship and the rise of a new consumer product, silver electroplated decorative household items.[45]

Boulton and Watt are the two best-known Birmingham industrialists. Both had families who kept their memories alive, are commemorated in monuments, remembered in museums, including Soho House and the Science Museum, and are recorded in the Archives of Soho. Their industrial and trading activities have been widely explored, including Boulton's creation of the huge Soho Manufactory in Handsworth, which, like Taylor's button works, applied the division of labour to mass-producing toys and other metal items. He made luxury and everyday consumer goods as well as products that were suitable for companies, and he entered partnerships to manufacture ormolu, silver and coins. The latter were made at the Soho Mint next to the Manufactory. Boulton could see the potential of steam power and, with James Watt, developed a much-improved Newcomen beam engine, which could pump water, and the rotative engine, which could power machinery and was developed by other engineers to drive locomotives. These machines were built in the Soho Foundry in Smethwick.[46] Watt's chemical copying machine, which Boulton and Watt also manufactured, enabled businesses to copy documents and diagrams. His workshop, a surviving example of material culture from the time, has been recreated in London's Science Museum.[47] Boulton worked collectively with silver merchants and manufacturers to secure an Act of Parliament to establish the Assay Office in 1773 to assess (assay) quality and hallmark silver items. This institution helped to raise the reputation of local silverware and continues to operate. It also contains a major collection of locally designed and manufactured silver. Not everything Boulton did was successful; his financial management was poor and partners and managers found his neglect of practicalities frustrating, but he was an entrepreneurial visionary who was conscious of the importance of image, marketing and political lobbying. His employees paraded *en masse* to pay their respects at his funeral.[48]

Gun making was one of Birmingham's major trades in the eighteenth and early nineteenth century, expanding from its seventeenth-century origins and increasingly located in a district of Birmingham known as the Gun Quarter. Most studies of

Matthew Boulton was able to secure an Act of Parliament to establish an Assay Office in Birmingham in 1773. The Board of Guardians of the Assay Office met in the King's Head Inn on New Street whose inn sign bore an image of George III, the monarch when the Act was passed.
By permission of Assay Office Birmingham

The reputation of Birmingham's silverware was enhanced by the establishment of the Assay Office in 1773, whose collections demonstrate both silversmith skills and mass-production techniques. This sweetmeat basket was manufactured by Boulton and Fothergill in 1774.
By permission of Assay Office Birmingham

Birmingham guns have focused on their technical features, but David Williams incorporated changing technological and engineering developments within a wider industrial and economic context. By the end of the eighteenth century, the trade produced sporting and military guns and supplied both British and overseas forces with huge quantities of weaponry during the French Wars. Most businesses were small and workshop based. Concern with the quality of locally manufactured items led to the creation of the Birmingham Gun-Barrel Proof House in 1813 to test items and improve production standards. It still fulfils its original purpose and contains a museum. In 1861 Birmingham Small Arms (BSA), an amalgamation of several local gunmakers, was created to compete more effectively with the London-based Enfield

Birmingham's Gun Quarter became an important manufacturing district in the town during the eighteenth century. Tipping and Lawden was one business located in the area, decoratively celebrated in *The New Illustrated Dictionary Entitled Men and Things of Modern England* of 1858.
By permission of the Library of Birmingham, 61999

Factory.[49] How far the high-quality skills used to make and engrave locks, stocks and barrels may have been transferred to other industries such as type founding and printing deserves exploration.

The period was not one of continuous economic growth and expansion. Rising food prices could affect demand for industrial goods and war could damage as well as stimulate industry and trade. Hopkins argues that before 1793, somewhat surprisingly, wars did not have any significant effect on Birmingham exports. The French Wars between 1793 and 1815, with a brief period of peace between 1802 and 1803, were on a much larger scale and longer than previous conflicts and were accompanied by poor harvests and rising bread prices. Opportunities for exporting were severely disrupted, not only to continental Europe but, after 1812, to the United States as well. The gun and sword trades did well given their ability to supply the army and navy, but exports of iron, steel, brass and copper were affected. The coming of peace was also economically difficult as the market for munitions dramatically fell. There were additional times of distress in the 1820s, late 1830s and early 1840s.[50]

The autobiography of the radical writer George Jacob Holyoake (1817–1906) provides an insight into the economic structure of Birmingham in the 1820s and 1830s, including the importance of the small family business, female entrepreneurship and the relationships between skilled workers and independent artisans, and merchants and employers, and the beginnings of steam power in local industries. Holyoake was born in Inge Street, where his mother had a workshop attached to the house, which made horn buttons, until it failed. She had owned the business before her marriage and had several employees. His mother 'received the orders; made the purchases of materials; superintended the making of the goods; made out the accounts; and received the money; besides taking care of her growing family'.[51] Holyoake assisted her as a young boy in various hand-operated mechanical tasks, including winding copper wire, stamping and cutting. Later he worked for a tinsmith, soldering handles on to lanterns.[52] He described their neighbours. Next door, Mrs Massey 'sold cakes and tarts'; at No. 5 'there resided a neat, little, clean bright-eyed old lady, who used to charm away warts, and other small maladies'. Mr Hawksford at No. 12 was 'a baker and flour seller'; next to him lived 'a plain, busy, rosy-faced widow', who 'kept the best grocer's shop in those parts – where the butter was always fresh'. Opposite were Mr Roberts, who ground glasses for opticians, and Sally Padmore, who nursed the sick.[53] Holyoake's father was a skilled worker at the Eagle Foundry in Broad Street, a large business that contained multiple artisanal trades: whitesmiths, blacksmiths, an engine smith's casting shop and kitchen range makers. The business was a partnership and Holyoake, who joined his father, described the different approaches of the two masters – one was paternal and the other was harsh in their manner of treating the workers. Holyoake also described how 'mechanics who worked in little workshops of their own' had to sell their products to merchants: 'The men who lived in the town, and those who came miles into it, with the produce of their week's work, were kept hanging about the merchants' warehouses until nine, ten and often eleven o'clock on Saturday night, before they were paid their money.' His father was able to set himself up in business, bought machinery for turning bone buttons and hired steam power at the nearby Baskerville Mill. Holyoake was placed in charge and during that time was able to improve the process of

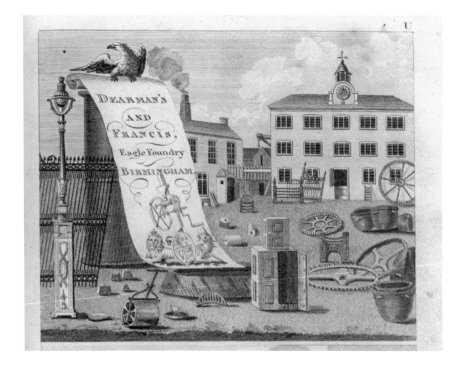

The Eagle Foundry in Broad Street produced a large variety of iron goods for industrial and domestic use, as this advertisement from Bisset's *Directory* reveals.
By permission of the Library of Birmingham, 47154

manufacturing by inventing a perpendicular drill.[54] Holyoake celebrated the local industrial structure: 'It was always a peculiarity of Birmingham that numerous small household trades existed, which gave the inmates independence, and often led – if the trade continued good – to competence or fortune.'[55] Whether Holyoake was correct or over-optimistic in his assessment of how businesses could develop at the time is open to debate.

The 1849 Birmingham Industrial Exhibition provided a showcase for the achievements of local firms, but from a national and international perspective the 1851 Great Exhibition at the Crystal Palace in Hyde Park provided a greater opportunity for advertising.[56] Initially businesses were not keen to participate as the commissioners wanted the product designer rather than the manufacturer to be credited. A compromise was reached, however, to enable both to be credited and 230 Birmingham exhibitors were represented, together with another 68 from the Black Country towns.[57] The exhibition was a showcase for the local area for two reasons. First, the building, though designed by Joseph Paxton, was constructed by local firm Fox, Henderson and Co. and sheathed in plate glass made by Chance Brothers, both of Smethwick.[58] Both firms were able to use the canal and railway networks that connected with London to supply products for construction. Secondly, the exhibition was a showcase for local products, including glass ornaments and decanters from

The Crystal Palace which housed the Great Exhibition of 1851 in Hyde Park, London, was a showcase for Britain's, and Birmingham's, industrial products. This international exhibition of manufactured goods marked the high-water mark of Britain as the 'workshop of the world'. This lithograph by Augustus Butler, c.1851, was one of many images which celebrated this monument to commerce and construction.
Courtesy of the Ironbridge Gorge Museum Trust Library & Archives, AE185.477

Bacchus and Co. and Lloyd and Somerville, and sacred and secular metalware
made by Hardman and Co. The huge glass fountain made by F. and C. Osler was
placed in the centre of the exhibition, reflecting, literally and metaphorically, the
glass carapace of the Crystal Palace. The catalogue claimed that it 'was, perhaps, the
most striking object in the Exhibition; the lightness and beauty as well as the perfect
novelty of its design, have rendered it the theme of admiration with all visitors'.[59] The
Great Exhibition displayed Birmingham and district's achievements in industrial
construction, manufacturing and design and serves as a conclusion to the first 150
years of the 'city of a thousand trades'.

Economic life, 1851–1914

Eric Hopkins provides the most up-to-date overview of the local economy in the
late nineteenth and early twentieth centuries. Detailed surveys by G.C. Allen and
the *Victoria County History* contain much additional information, though Hopkins
has revised some of the earlier judgements. Individual business achievements form
the subject of several essays in a book edited by Barbara Tilson.[60] Brass was the
premier industry at the beginning of the period and W.C. Aitken's poetic, proud

Brass &china mortise furniture   per two bolt set

2187 Ivory china ball 86
with patent keyed spindle

5362 polished brass 12
with patent keyed spindle
3in 21

2192 Ivory china
with cast brass roses 36

2191 White china
with cast brass roses 33

2188 Ivory china 49
with patent keyed spindle

2189 Ivory china 43
with patent keyed spindle

oval

oval

2190 Ivory china 49
with patent keyed spindle

and triumphalist exposition of the state of the brass industry in the 1860s reveals the range of its products, its ability to penetrate domestic and overseas markets and its shaping of energy, transport and cultural practices:

> What Manchester is in cotton, Bradford in wool and Sheffield in steel, Birmingham is in brass; its articles of cabinet and general brass foundry are to be found in every part of the world; its gas fittings in every city and town into which gas has been introduced, from Indus to the Poles – on the railways of every country and on every sea, its locomotive and marine engine solid brass tubes generate the vapour which impels the locomotive over the iron road, and propels the steam-boat over the ocean wave – its yellow metal bolts, nails, and sheathing hold together and protect from decay 'wooden walls' of our own and other countries' ships – its 'manillas', once made in tons, are the circulating medium of the natives of the Gold Coast – and its rings and ornaments of brass, sent out in immense quantities, are the chief decorations of the *belles* on the banks of the distant Zambesi.[61]

Timmins's book, in which Aitken's essay appeared, was a celebration of the local economy at a time when it was the workshop of the world and a manifestation of the so-called Victorian Boom. This lengthy volume, which remains the most valuable printed primary source for Birmingham's Victorian industry, describes more than

The manufacture of many different kinds of brass products was a staple of Birmingham's metal industries in the nineteenth century. The catalogue of William Tonks, Sons & Co. (1880) advertises brass door furniture to the prospective purchaser.
By permission of the Library of Birmingham, L62.65

a thousand trades. Elihu Burritt's *Walks in the Black Country* is a similarly valuable source for the 1860s.[62] Birmingham experienced considerable prosperity in the 1850s and 1860s, but recession arrived during 'The Great Depression' (1873–96), when changing tastes, declining incomes and foreign competition affected demand for jewellery, brass items, buttons and guns. A recovery set in towards the end of the century.[63] By the 1850s Birmingham's railway network provided a means of stimulating access to raw materials and the selling of products at home and abroad. The building of Snow Hill and New Street stations, in 1852 and 1854, destroyed homes and disrupted lives in the areas where they were built. At the same time they stimulated local construction firms, including Fox and Henderson, and led to the enhancement of retail businesses in the town centre. Heavy engineering expanded and Tangyes in Smethwick was one firm that was particularly important.[64] Birmingham also became a centre of railway carriage manufacturing in Saltley.[65] Local businesses were diversifying and adapting to new demands.

Birmingham's Jewellery Quarter developed in the nineteenth century as a metalworking district, not exclusively devoted to jewellery trades. It also illustrates the responsive nature of the economy.[66] The Museum of the Jewellery Quarter, the Pen Museum, Newman Brothers Coffin Furniture Factory and J.W. Evans Silver Factory are heritage centres which illustrate the material culture, industrial organization and outputs of large and small manufacturing industries in the area at the time.[67] Steel pen production, a descendant of the eighteenth-century toy trades, developed through the activities of numerous inventors and entrepreneurs, including John Mitchell (1794–1854), William Mitchell (1806–45), Josiah Mason (1795–1881), Joseph Gillott (1799–1872) and John Sheldon (1802–63). Though emerging in the early nineteenth century, its post-1851 experience witnessed the concentration of production in a few large companies which were able to benefit from economies of scale. By the end of the century, Birmingham businesses were the most important makers of steel pens in the world and supplied children, clerks and correspondents with a cheap means for communicating and record keeping.[68] Another firm which had its manufactory in the Jewellery Quarter was Elkington's, which introduced the electroplating of nickel with a thin layer of silver after 1840. The business also produced other decorative items in silver, gilt and bronze. It was extremely successful: its workforce expanded from 500 in 1850 to 1,000 by 1870, doubling in size again by 1914.[69] Hardman and Co. was a major local manufacturer of secular and ecclesiastical gilt and brass metal products and stained glass.[70]

Birmingham was home to other trades that catered for a growing demand for luxury household items and foodstuffs. Patricia Coccoris has drawn attention to a local glass designer who achieved an international reputation. George Piercy Tye (1810–79) was a die-sinker and seal engraver in Great Charles Street. In the 1850s he took out various patents for a hyacinth bulb vase with a metal support, which ingeniously kept a flowering hyacinth upright. The product was marketed in Britain, exported to the empire and its manufacture was copied in Europe and the USA. *The Garden* in 1880 commented: 'The originator lived long enough to see his design reproduced in many and most artistic patterns, till they have become handsome drawing room ornaments.'[71] Cadbury's catered for consumers of cocoa and chocolate, another type of taste. The company was founded in 1831 by the Quaker, John Cadbury (1801–89), but its expansion was limited until the business moved to a green-field site to the south of Birmingham in 1879, a transition which was orchestrated by his sons, Richard (1835–99) and George (1839–1922). The site, which was renamed Bournville, also became the location for an adjacent garden village which provided well-built homes and gardens.[72] Cadbury's was an example of the advent of innovative food processing firms within the local economy before 1914.[73]

Many of the workers in Birmingham's industries were women, especially in the pen trade and food processing, but traditionally the role of women in businesses has been ignored. Even feminist historiography, according to Jennifer Aston, has 'argued that by 1850, middle-class women had been removed from public life and restricted to the domestic, private sphere where they were separated from family businesses and therefore economically dependent on male relatives'.[74] Aston and Katherine Jenns, however, have shown that there were many women in business in the late nineteenth and early twentieth centuries.[75] Women traded in a variety of manufactures, including rope making, the gun trade, button making, nail making and steel rolling; as blacksmiths, coopers, japanners, tin-workers, founders and umbrella makers; in jewellery and silver-smithing; as gilt toy makers, stonemasons, ironmongers, saddlers, platers, boat builders, upholsterers, cabinetmakers and brushmakers. Through an analysis of directories, Aston has shown that between 1849 and 1900, between 4.4 and 8.2 per cent of businesses in the centre of Birmingham were owned by women.[76] Birmingham's small business structure, the limited application of expensive technology and its growing importance as a market in its own right made it relatively easy for women without access to considerable wealth to set up in business.

By 1914 small businesses that employed less than one hundred workers dominated the economy, but there were nine businesses that employed more than 1,000 within Birmingham's then political boundaries. Cadbury's was the largest with 6,000. Two businesses benefited directly from the emerging demand for motor vehicles: Dunlop's with 4,000 and Austin with 2,000

In the 1820s Cadbury's catered for a growing taste for cocoa and chocolate. A 'chocolate box' view of the shop in Bull Street, Birmingham, from *A Century of Progress* (1931), celebrated the success of the business. Private Collection

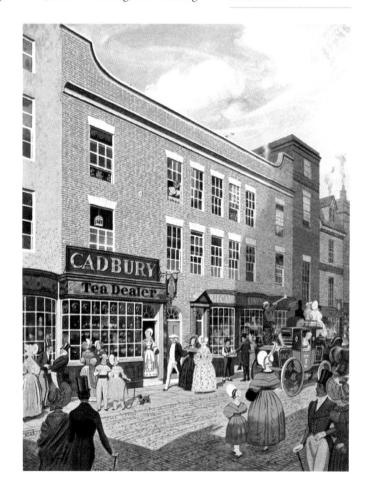

workers. The screw producers, Nettlefold's, had 4,000 employees; Buttons Ltd, an amalgamation of four button-making firms, had 2,000; and the electroplaters, Elkington's had 2,000. Perry and Co., the largest producer of steel pen nibs, employed 1,500, followed by two manufacturers of railway carriages: the Metropolitan Railway Carriage Co. and Brown, Marshall and Co., with 1,100 each.

Economic life, 1914–1945

The First World War illustrates how Birmingham's industry and workforce were affected by global influences outside the direct control of local people. Initially the war depressed the economy as demand for peacetime products fell: unemployment increased, wages were cut and the cost of living rose. The requisition of horses for the armed forces badly affected deliveries of goods. Unemployment fell as men were recruited into the armed forces and government contracts stimulated the economy.[77] Shell shortages and the failure of industry to meet military demand led to increasing state intervention to manage the supply side of the economy. In 1915 the newly established Ministry of Munitions created the government-controlled National Shell Factory in Washwood Heath, which manufactured the standard 18-pounder and 4.5-inch shells for British artillery. Private firms, subject to government influence, also contributed to the war effort. BSA, which had been facing recession before the war, expanded rapidly. It produced 1.6 million Lee-Enfield rifles, as well as revolver cartridges, shell cases and Lewis automatic machine guns. The Lewis gun was originally an American invention and, under licence, 145,397 were made by BSA during the war. BSA also produced thousands of motorcycles which were crucial for military communications work. In 1913 the firm employed 4,000 workers, but in 1918 the number had risen to nearly 14,000 and 25 per cent were women. Kynoch's, at Witton, produced both high explosives and rifle ammunition. By the end of the war it employed 18,000 workers, many of whom were women. A hand grenade, the Mills bomb, was also manufactured in Birmingham by the Mills Munitions Factory in Grove Street and Bridge Street West.[78] The nearby Black Country manufactured tanks and TNT and firms in the Jewellery Quarter produced military buttons and medals. Wolseley Motors manufactured 4,000 cars for war purposes and Austin at Longbridge, which had a workforce of 20,000 at the end of the war, produced aeroplanes, aero engines and trucks. Cadbury's received large orders to produce chocolate for the troops.[79] Though much of the University of Birmingham was requisitioned for use as a military hospital and students and staff were called up to serve in the armed forces, science and engineering academics and students were enrolled to support local industry. Research was conducted into poison gas and its detection, dyes for uniforms, explosives and anaesthetics, partly to overcome the previous dependence on imported German chemical products before the war. Members of staff were also engaged to inspect and test the quality of locally manufactured ammunition and explosives.[80] Local industries and employment patterns were transformed during the war, but not without difficulties: government

THE 1907, LONG PATTERN BAYONET

THE FORE SIGHT

ACTION OPEN READY FOR LOADING

COMPLETE SECTION SHOWING ACTION NOT COCKED

THE BOLT

THE BACK SIGHT

PART SECTION SHOWING ACTION COCKED

TOP VIEW OF THE RIFLE

THE BRITISH SERVICE RIFLE
(The Lee-Enfield Short Pattern Mark III .303 Barrel)
MADE BY THE B.S.A. CO. LTD. AND USED BY
BRITISH & COLONIAL TROOPS IN THE GREAT WAR.

policy initiatives collided with local practicalities and there was tension between management and labour.[81]

There were also tragedies. Two of the directors of pen-makers Brandauer and Co., Frederick and Hermann Brandauer, were defined by the state as 'enemy aliens', given their German origins; they were removed from the board and their shares were confiscated. Frederick had been resident in Britain for thirty years and, in 1894, had become a naturalized British subject. He had, however, not renewed his status and he was arrested in 1917. Old and infirm, he was interned in a detention camp on the Isle of Man. Frederick was faced with deportation to Germany and killed himself with a drug overdose in 1918. Shortly after, Frederick Shramm, a friend and agent for the business and a naturalized British subject, also committed suicide. The firm continued in business, trading under the same name, and contributed to the war effort by manufacturing cartridges for Lee-Enfield rifles.[82]

In March 1918 newspaper journalists were provided with a tour of the city's industries. A subsequent report in *The Times* described how work was geared to the demands of conflict. Total war had shaped the local production of tanks, shells, grenades, fuses, rifles, machine guns, artillery and aircraft:

> throbbing with energy directed to a single and unalterable purpose – the winning of the war … Birmingham and its environs form a vast mass of smithies and workshops, in which tens of thousands of men and women, boys and girls, are toiling night and day to manufacture military implements. What we have seen – and it is only a part of the direct war work which is being carried out in this area has been a revelation.[83]

Close to victory, this end-of-war summary reflected the forecast in 1915 of the British Commander-in-Chief, Sir John French, who described the conflict as 'a struggle between Krupps and Birmingham', a reference to the importance of the huge armaments firm in the Ruhr to the German war effort. Local manufacturing played its part in contributing to the Allied victory in 1918, as revealed in individual business histories, which outlined how local firms contributed to the conflict.[84] Despite these observations, as John Bourne pointed out, no definitive, analytical history of how Birmingham's economy adapted to and contributed to the war has been written.[85]

The inter-war period is frequently portrayed as a time of industrial failure, depression and high unemployment. The slump after the war affected Birmingham badly as demand for armaments fell; women were forced to leave employment and returning soldiers found it difficult to find work. However, as Birmingham was not economically dependent upon coal, textiles, iron manufacturing and ship building, it weathered the 1920s and 1930s more effectively than the industrial north, Wales and Scotland. Unemployment, despite some fluctuations, remained consistently below national averages. By the mid-1930s, Birmingham was experiencing a labour shortage. Birmingham benefited from the varied nature of its industrial base, so while the gun trade and jewellery making declined, the production of motor vehicles, electrical goods, aluminium, plastics, metal tableware and food processing increased. The motor industry acted as a leading sector, demanding products used in manufac-turing, including glass, chrome, rubber and copper wire, providing high wages to workers, an increase in road construction and the development of tram and bus routes. It also stimulated building as suburban living became increasingly possible for middle- and working-class employees.[86] The rise in living standards also led to an increase in the retail and leisure industries, including the building of dance halls, cinemas and public houses. There are many remaining examples of co-op stores in Birmingham which were originally opened in the inter-war period.[87] Large firms became larger, not least by combining with or taking over other businesses, as Morris did with Wolseley. The standard unit of business in Birmingham, however, remained the small firm, as Eric Hopkins has convincingly shown. By the outbreak of the Second World War, the vast majority of businesses employed less than one hundred workers.[88] Unlike their larger rivals, their histories need to be better known.

One of the largest local firms was Cadbury's, employing 10,000 by 1927. During the inter-war years it benefited financially from high consumer demand for cocoa and chocolate, good worker–management relations and its ability to provide a range of social, educational and welfare benefits for its employees,[89] which included free toothbrushes and dental powder for employees under the age of 16.[90] J.B. Priestley, the novelist and socialist, visited Cadbury's and the Bournville suburb as part of his observational tour of England in 1933. The location, the business and its workforce were in contrast to other parts of industrial Birmingham he visited. He was impressed by the colossal size of the works – 'really a small town engaged in the manufacture of cocoa and chocolate' – its methods of production, the wellbeing of the workers and the facilities provided for employees. 'Here,' he wrote, 'in a factory run for private profit are nearly all the facilities for leading a full and happy life.' Priestley, though, was concerned how such a paternalistic system damaged the independence of workers:

> Pensions, bonuses, works councils, factory publications, entertainments and dinners and garden parties organized by the firm … easily create an atmosphere that is injurious to the growth of man as intellectual and spiritual beings, for they can easily give what is, when all is said and done, a trading concern for private profit a falsely mystical aura.[91]

A bird's-eye view of the Bournville works in 1931 shows the vast extent of the Cadbury factory, its semi-rural surroundings and the emerging Bournville housing estate: a visual celebration of the factory in the countryside from Cadbury's own promotional literature.
Private Collection

Perhaps the most striking dimension of the business in the inter-war period was its attention to marketing, not only to consumers but also to the wider public. A former employee, John Bradley, has analysed and illustrated the evolution of the Cadbury brand since the beginning of the business, and Jo-Ann Curtis has explored the iconography of Cadbury advertising between the wars, especially how women were represented in publicity material.[92] The quality, breadth and depth of Cadbury's marketing in the inter-war period was extraordinary. The firm produced adverts, histories, a works magazine and publications on its varied activities. *A Century of Progress* was written in 1931 by T.B. Rodgers, the editor of the *Bournville Works Magazine*, 'mainly for circulation to the Firm's customers and others associated with them in business'. The 89-page booklet was a history and a contemporary description of the firm's business and social accomplishments. More importantly, it was expensively produced: an embossed art-deco cover in gold lettering included a dramatic modernist image of the factory on the front. Its visual impact was enhanced by the many well-reproduced colour images as well as black-and white photographs and other illustrations on virtually every page.[93] A second, 64-page pamphlet, full of

A dramatic celebration of 100 years of Cadbury's manufacturing activities reveals the nineteenth-century Bull Street premises overshadowed by the modernist factory at Bournville. The two images enclose an African hut, a reference to the West African origins of the basic raw material, cocoa, and a reminder of how the Empire serviced Birmingham's economy at the time.
Private Collection

Smiling women workers pack Neapolitans in a pristine packing room: another example of how Cadbury's wanted to be positively portrayed in its literature.
Private Collection

sepia photographs, probably dating from the late 1930s, was presented as a personal invitation to visit the factory and Bournville village. It claimed: 'If the place where we work is fresh and bright and airy, the people healthy and cheerful, the work as interesting as it can be made, it is bound to show in the goods we produce.' Employees were named and their working day was followed, the contribution of West African cocoa workers was stressed and chocolate's healthy ingredients – fruit, nuts, eggs and milk – were described. The firm's provision of leisure, sport, education, work councils and pensions were illustrated, the latter accompanied by a photograph of male workers receiving free sun-ray treatment.[94] The pamphlet was an exercise in marketing to the public, but at a time when there was a high demand for labour in Birmingham, before war broke in 1939, it was also an advert for potential employees.

Compared to the economic experience of Birmingham between 1914 and 1918, industry during the Second World War has received more attention.[95] As Bourne has written, the city 'reprised its role in the First World War as a major supplier of munitions'.[96] State planning for the war was more advanced in 1939 than in 1914. Prior to the conflict, the government created and paid for so-called 'shadow factories', to build aero engines and aircraft. They were linked geographically and managerially to motor-manufacturing plants which meant that technology, expertise and manpower could be transferred relatively easily once war commenced. Shadow factories were created at Acocks Green and Solihull (Rover), Cofton Hackett (Austin) and Castle Bromwich (Morris). The latter became particularly famous for manufacturing the Spitfire fighter plane and Lancaster bomber. Other businesses also contributed to supporting the war effort, including BSA, which made guns, ammunition and motorcycles as it had in the First World War, as well as a collapsible military bicycle that was used by paratroopers. Another existing firm, Cadbury's, established Bournville Utilities Limited, which employed 2,000 workers, many of whom were existing Cadbury employees, to make aeroplane parts, rockets and respirators. Businesses in the jewellery trades made components for radar equipment, rifles and aircraft, and radio parts were produced by Birmingham's electrical industries. The demands of total war meant that the local economy was directed centrally or by locally established committees, made up of civil servants, managers and trade union representatives. Several firms were concentrated into larger units and major labour shortages had to be overcome. The latter problem was difficult to resolve and was tackled by the dilution of existing skills, recruitment of new workers from the existing population, including women, juveniles and the disabled, the direction of labour from elsewhere in the UK and immigration from Ireland.[97]

The University of Birmingham played a more extensive role in the local economy and the international Allied war effort than it had between 1914 and 1918. The demand for scientific research and manpower was significantly greater. Metallurgists and engineers were engaged even before the war had started to test bullet and shell cases and propeller blades manufactured locally, and subsequently they developed new hydraulic control mechanisms for gun turrets. The best-known contributions were in physics. In 1940 John Randall (1905–84) and Harry Boot (1917–83) developed the cavity magnetron, which was crucial in the development

The *Sentinel* sculpture by Tim Tolkein commemorates the history of Spitfire manufacture at Castle Bromwich during the Second World War. The artist is a great-nephew of the author J.R.R. Tolkein, who spent part of his boyhood in Birmingham, and the sculpture was made in the Black Country.
Birmingham Museums Trust
Wikipedia residency, Wikimedia Commons

of radar. Two academic refugees from Nazism, Rudolf Peierls (1907–95) and Otto Frisch (1904–79) contributed to the science which led to the creation of the atomic bomb.[98]

One important difference from Birmingham's experience in the First World War was that the city was now easily reached by German heavy bombers, which were directed to destroy Birmingham's industrial capacity. A major air raid on 19 November 1940 inflicted severe damage and killed many workers at BSA, but despite the destruction and loss of life, production recovered by early 1941. The same raid damaged local roads, the canal system and disrupted the pipes that moved fresh water to Birmingham from the Elan Valley in Wales. Again, recovery was rapid. Several businesses were not bombed at all: a remarkable survival was Serck Radiators Limited in Tysley, only a few hundred yards from the BSA works in Small Heath. It made all the radiators and oil coolers which were fitted to Spitfires and Hurricanes during the Battle of Britain.[99] Despite the physical damage to Birmingham, bombing only temporarily disrupted production, transport and the water supply, though this is not to minimize the impact the war had on residential property and people's lives.

This photograph from the diary of Sir Raymond Priestley, Vice-Chancellor of the University of Birmingham from 1938 until 1952, records the impact of the bombing of Birmingham during the Second World War. Priestley kept a regular weekly diary that gives details of bomb damage to university buildings at Mason College in Edmund Street in 1941 and the effects of the conflict on both staff and students.
By permission of the Cadbury Research Library: Special Collections, University of Birmingham

Conclusion

There are other ways in which the history of Birmingham's industries and trades could have been written: one might have focused on the great entrepreneurs and inventors of the past or told the stories of famous firms.[100] An interesting approach would be to investigate the objects that were designed, made and distributed by local businesses, and what their history reveals about changing patterns of design, production, skills and taste. There is also more to find out about the role of science, skills and technology transfer in shaping industrial change. Within a chronological framework, this chapter has looked at how thinking about the past and using different evidence can offer new ways of seeing. The contributions of women and migrants are stories that are only beginning to be uncovered. Small businesses as well as large ones deserve further exploration and the less well known need to be rescued from the condescension of posterity.

The writing of history is shaped by our beliefs and prejudices and the types of evidence we consider to be important. Source material is inevitably partial and some parts of the past are better supplied with data than others. The descendants of Matthew Boulton, James Watt and John Cadbury took care to preserve archival material that presented the achievements of these captains of industry. We know little about most businesses, and even less about their workers before the recent past, but tantalizing indicators are provided by a directory entry or trade card detail. Newspapers, archaeological evidence, buildings, images, material culture, ephemera, diaries, family archives and oral history recordings provide opportunities for new narratives and meanings. It is an exciting task not only to reinvestigate the known, but also to dig beneath the existing landscape of the city of a thousand trades.[101]

Notes

1 P.M. Jones, *Industrial Enlightenment: Science, Technology and Culture in Birmingham and the West Midlands, 1760–1820* (Manchester, 2008), 34; GB Historical GIS / University of Portsmouth, Birmingham District through time | Population Statistics | Total Population, A Vision of Britain through Time, http://www.visionofbritain.org.uk/unit/10104180/cube/TOT_POP (accessed 18 May 2016).

2 C.R. Elrington, 'Hutton, William (1723–1815)', *Oxford Dictionary of National Biography* (hereafter *ODNB*) (Oxford, 2004), online edn, http://www.oxforddnb.com/view/article/14317 (accessed 1 January 2016).

3 W. Hutton, *An History of Birmingham* (2nd edn, Birmingham, 1783), 74, 90–3, 271–2; P. Hamilton, 'Taylor, John (1710/11–1775)', *ODNB*, online edn, http://www.oxforddnb.com/view/article/50560 (accessed 29 December 2015); J. Mosley, 'Baskerville, John (1706–1775)', *ODNB*, online edn, http://www.oxforddnb.com/view/article/1624 (accessed 1 January 2016); J. Tann, 'Boulton, Matthew (1728–1809)', *ODNB*, online edn, http://www.oxforddnb.com/view/article/2983 (accessed 1 Jan 2016). Hutton did not name Boulton, presumably because, unlike the other two, he was still alive.

4 S. Timmins (ed.), *The Resources, Products and Industrial History of Birmingham and the Midland Hardware District* (London, 1866).

5 R.K. Dent, *Old and New Birmingham* (Birmingham, 1880), Dedicatory Page, 111–19, 138–41, 265–72; J. Tann, 'Watt, James (1736–1819)', *ODNB*, online edn, http://www.oxforddnb.com/view/article/28880 (accessed 1 January 2016).

6 G.J. Barnsby, *Birmingham Working People* (Wolverhampton, 1989); C. Behagg, *Politics and Production in the Early Nineteenth Century* (London, 1990); C. Chinn, *They Worked all their Lives: Women of the Urban Poor in England, 1880–1939* (Manchester, 1988); C. Chinn, *Poverty amidst Prosperity, The Women of the Urban Poor in England, 1834–1914* (2nd edn, Lancaster, 2006).

7 G.C. Allen, *The Industrial Development of Birmingham and the Black Country 1860–1927* (London, 1929); W.H.B. Court, *The Rise of the Midlands Industries 1600–1838* (London, 1938), 149–259; D.E.C. Eversley, 'Economic and social history: industry and trade, 1500–1880' and B.M.D. Smith, 'Economic and social history: industry and trade, 1880–1960', in W.B. Stephens (ed.), *A History of the County of Warwick. Volume VII: The City of Birmingham*, Victoria County History (London, 1964), 81–208, http://www.british-history.ac.uk/vch/warks/vol7/ (accessed 31 December 2015); V. Skipp, *History of Greater Birmingham down to 1830* (Birmingham, 1980); V. Skipp, *The Making of Victorian Birmingham* (Birmingham, 1983); M.B. Rowlands, *Masters and Men in the West Midlands Metalware Trades before the Industrial Revolution* (Manchester, 1975), 125–46. See also J.B. Smith, 'The economic history of Birmingham', in C. Chinn (ed), *Birmingham: Bibliography of a City* (Birmingham, 2003), 157–80. C. Chinn, *Birmingham: The Great Working City*

(Birmingham, 2002) is a good general introduction to the diverse economy of 'the city of a thousand trades'.

8 E. Hopkins, *The Rise of the Manufacturing Town: Birmingham and the Industrial Revolution* (2nd edn, Stroud, 1998); E. Hopkins, *The Making of the Second City 1850–1939* (Stroud, 2001).

9 M. Berg, *The Age of Manufactures 1700–1820: Industry, Innovation and Work in Britain* (2nd edn, London, 1994); J.R. Harris, *Industrial Espionage and Technology Transfer: Britain and France in the Eighteenth Century* (Aldershot, 1998); Jones, *Industrial Enlightenment*; L. Tomory, *Progressive Enlightenment: The Origins of the Gaslight Industry, 1780–1820* (Cambridge, MA, 2012).

10 Rowlands, *Masters and Men*; G. Sjögren, 'The rise and decline of the Birmingham cut-nail trade, c.1811–1914', *Midland History*, 38.1 (2013), 36–57. The website 'Grace's Guide to British Industrial History' is an extremely valuable resource for the history of industries, firms and transport developments, http://www.gracesguide.co.uk/Main_Page (accessed 18 May 2016); Revolutionary Players is a digital resource of images and text devoted to West Midlands history during the Industrial Revolution, www.revolutionaryplayers.org.uk (accessed 18 May 2016). For an example of an archaeological investigation, see C. Hewitson (ed.), *The homes of our metal manufacturers. Messrs R.W. Winfield and Co.'s Cambridge Street Works and Rolling Mills, Birmingham, Archaeological Excavations at the Library of Birmingham, Cambridge Street*. British Archaeological Reports British Series 579 (Oxford, 2013).

11 See Carl Chinn, 'The Peoples of Birmingham', in this volume.

12 G.E. Cherry, *Birmingham: A Study in Geography, History and Planning* (Chichester, 1994); A. Axinte, *Mapping Birmingham's Historic Landscape* (Birmingham, 2015); www.birmingham.gov.uk/hlc (accessed 18 May 2016).

13 P. Leather, *A Guide to the Buildings of Birmingham: An Illustrated Architectural History* (Studley, 2002); P. Ballard (ed.), *Birmingham's Victorian and Edwardian Architects* (Wetherby, 2009); A. Foster, *Pevsner Architectural Guides: Birmingham* (New Haven, CT, and London, 2005); M. Hodder, *Birmingham: The Hidden History* (Stroud, 2004), 133–68.

14 Hutton, *History*, 63; discussed in Harry Smith, 'William Hutton and the myths of Birmingham', *Midland History*, 40.1 (2015), 53–73.

15 Hutton, *History*, 328.

16 Allen, *Industrial Development*, 26–8; Hopkins, *Manufacturing Town*, 5; Jones, *Industrial Enlightenment*, 61–200.

17 Hopkins, *Manufacturing Town*, 13–15.

18 K. Sampson, '"A bank of unquestionable substance": Lloyds first one-hundred years' *History West Midlands*, 3 (2015), 40–2; J.M. Price, 'Lloyd, Sampson (1699–1779)', rev., *ODNB*, online edn, http://www.oxforddnb.com/view/article/37682 (accessed 3 January 2016).

19 Hopkins, *Manufacturing Town*, 15–16, 36–7, 70–5.

20 E. Williams, *Capitalism and Slavery* (London, 1964),

esp. 81–2; C. Harris, 'Birmingham manufacturing industries and the European slave trade', in Harris (ed), *Three Continents, One History: Birmingham and the Transatlantic Slave Trade and the Caribbean* (Birmingham, 2008), 74–80; M. Sherwood, *After Abolition: Britain and the Slave Trade since 1807* (London, 2007), 59–64.

21 B.M.D. Smith, 'The Galtons of Birmingham: Quaker gun merchants and bankers, 1702–1831, *Business History*, 9.2 (1967), 132–50; W.A. Richards, 'The import of firearms into West Africa in the eighteenth century', *The Journal of African History*, 21.1 (1980), 43–59; H. Smith, 'Galton, Samuel (1753–1832)', *ODNB*, online edn, http://www.oxforddnb.com/view/article/105102 (accessed 1 January 2016). The Galton Archives are in the Library of Birmingham.

22 J. Tann, 'Steam and sugar: the diffusion of the stationary steam engine to the Caribbean sugar industry 1770–1840', *History of Technology*, 19 (1997), 63–84.

23 C. Evans and G. Ryden, *Baltic Iron in the Atlantic World in the Eighteenth Century* (Leiden, 2007), 189; D.I. Callaghan, 'The black presence in the West Midlands, 1650–1918', *Midland History*, 36.2 (2011), 186.

24 'Advertisement for the sale of a Creole slave', *Aris's Birmingham Gazette*, 11 November 1771.

25 M. Dick, 'Joseph Priestley, the Lunar Society and anti-slavery', in Dick (ed.), *Joseph Priestley and Birmingham* (Studley, 2005), 65–80; A. Tyrrell, 'Sturge, Joseph (1793–1859)', *ODNB*, online edn, http://www.oxforddnb.com/view/article/26746 (accessed 4 January 2016).

26 Allen, *Industrial Development*, 28–9; 'Economic and social history: mills', in Stephens (ed.), *A History of the County of Warwick. Volume VII*, 253–69.

27 Cherry, *Birmingham*, 11–32.

28 See chapters by Stephen Bassett and Richard Holt and Richard Cust and Ann Hughes in this volume.

29 Hopkins, *Manufacturing Town*, 6–10.

30 C. Roth, *A History of the Jews in England* (3rd edn, Oxford, 1964), 228–30; B. Naggar, *Jewish Pedlars and Hawkers 1740–1940* (Camberley, 1992); T.M. Endelman, *The Jews of Georgian England 1714–1830* (Ann Arbor, MI, 1999), 166–91.

31 *Sketchley and Adam's Tradesman's True Guide and Universal Directory of Birmingham* (Birmingham, 1770).

32 A. Engle, 'Mayer Oppenheim of Birmingham', in Engle (ed.), *Readings in Glass History* (Jerusalem, 1974).

33 M. Dick, 'Birmingham Anglo-Jewry c.1780 to c.1880: origins, experiences and representations', *Midland History*, 36.2 (2011), 195–214.

34 Cherry, *Birmingham*, 35.

35 Cherry, *Birmingham*, 34–5, 48; Hopkins, *Manufacturing Town*, 27–30; S.R. Bracebridge, *The Birmingham Canal Navigations, vol. 1, 1768–1846* (Newton Abbott, 1974).

36 Hopkins, *Manufacturing Town*, 30, 54, 78.

37 P.K. Wilson, E.A. Dolan and M. Dick (eds), 'Introduction', in *Anna Seward's Life of Erasmus Darwin* (Studley, 2010), 3–5.

38 R.E. Schofield, *The Lunar Society of Birmingham* (Oxford, 1963); J. Uglow, *The Lunar Men* (London, 2002); Jones, *Industrial Enlightenment*, 22–160; J. Mokyr, *The Enlightened Economy: An Economic History of Britain, 1700–1850* (New Haven, CT, and London, 2009), 79–144; D. Wootton, *The Invention of Science: A New History of the Scientific Revolution* (London, 2015), 476–508.

39 William Westley, *Prospect of Birmingham* (1732).

40 'A Letter from a Mechanick in the busy Town of Birmingham', *Aris's Birmingham Gazette* (1751). T. and P. Berg, *R.R. Angerstein's Illustrated Travel Diary, 1753–1755* (London, 2001), provides descriptions of many British, including Birmingham and Black Country, industries from the perspective of a Swedish observer.

41 C. Gill, *History of Birmingham, vol, 1, Manor and Borough to 1865* (Oxford, 1952), 137.

42 S. Mason, *Jewellery Making in Birmingham 1750–1995* (Chichester, 1998); buttons could also be made from other products such as horn, tortoiseshell and pearls: George Hook and Company, *The Birmingham Pearlies: An Account of the Pearl Shell Industry in Birmingham* (Smethwick, 2001).

43 Y. Jones, *Japanned Papier Maché and Tinware 1740–1940* (Woodbridge, 2012), 113–15.

44 Ibid., 113–38, 144–64.

45 Ibid., 7–11.

46 George Demidowicz has researched the sites of the three Soho works and his book, *The Soho Industrial Buildings: Manufactory, Mint and Foundry*, is forthcoming from History West Midlands.

47 http://www.sciencemuseum.org.uk/watt

48 E. Delieb, *The Great Silver Manufactory: Matthew Boulton and the Birmingham Silversmiths, 1760–1790* (London, 1971); J. Tann, *Birmingham Assay Office 1773–1993* (Birmingham, 1993); R. Doty, *The Soho Mint and the Industrialization of Money* (London, 1998); N. Goodison, *Matthew Boulton: Ormolu* (London, 2002); S. Mason (ed.), *Matthew Boulton: Selling What All the World Desires* (New Haven, CT, and London, 2009); M. Dick (ed), *Matthew Boulton: A Revolutionary Player* (Studley, 2009); K. Quickenden, S. Baggott and M. Dick (eds), *Matthew Boulton: Enterprising Industrialist of the Enlightenment* (Farnham, 2013); J. Tann and A. Burton, *Matthew Boulton: Industry's Great Innovator* (Stroud, 2013); R.L. Hills, *James Watt, vol 2: The Years of Toil, 1775–1785* (Ashbourne, 2005); R.L. Hills, *James Watt, vol 3: Triumph Through Adversity, 1785–1819* (Ashbourne, 2006); B. Marsden, *Watt's Perfect Engine: Steam and the Age of Invention* (Duxford, 2002); B. Russell, *James Watt: Making the World Anew* (London, 2014).

49 D. Williams, *The Birmingham Gun Trade* (Stroud, 2009); D. Williams, 'Birmingham and Wellington's muskets', in A. Watts and E. Tyler (eds), *Fortunes of War: The West Midlands at the Time of Waterloo* (Alcester, 2015), 22–5.

50 Hopkins, *Manufacturing Town*, 62–80; M. Dick, 'The West Midlands in war and peace', in A. Watts and E. Tyler (eds), *Fortunes of War: The West Midlands at the Time of Waterloo* (Alcester, 2015), 6–10.

51 G.J. Holyoake, *Sixty Years of an Agitator's life, Vol 1* (London, 1900), 10, 15–16; E. Royle, 'Holyoake, George

Jacob (1817–1906)', *ODNB*, online edn, http://www. oxforddnb.com/view/article/33964 (accessed 29 December 2015).

52 Holyoake, *Sixty Years*, 19.

53 Ibid., 13–14

54 Ibid., 19–24.

55 Ibid., 10–11.

56 J. Prinsen, 'Birmingham Exhibition of Manufacturers and Arts 1849', *History West Midlands*, 4.1 (2016), 4–8; 'Art and Industry'. This spring edition of *History West Midlands* is devoted to the Great Exhibition.

57 J. Davis, *The Great Exhibition* (Stroud, 1999), 71, 79.

58 http://www.gracesguide.co.uk/Fox,_Henderson_and_Co (accessed 1 January 2016); http://www.gracesguide.co.uk/ Chance_Brothers_and_Co (accessed 1 January 2016). Many of the iron castings were made by the Woodside Iron Works and Foundry in Dudley: http://www. gracesguide.co.uk/Woodside_Ironworks_and_Foundry (accessed 1 January 2016).

59 *The Industry of all Nations: The Art Journal Illustrated Catalogue* (London, 1851), 32, 92–3, 255.

60 Hopkins, *Second City*, 33–48; Allen, *Industrial Development*, 3–369; Eversley, 'Industry and trade, 1500–1880'; Smith, 'Industry and trade, 1880–1960'; B. Tilson (ed), *Made in Birmingham: Design and Industry, 1889–1989* (Studley, 1989).

61 W.C. Aitkin, 'Brass and brass manufacturers', in S. Timmins (ed.), *The Resources, Products and Industrial History of Birmingham and the Midland Hardware District* (London, 1866), 229.

62 E. Burritt, *Walks in the Black Country and its Green Borderland* (London, 1869).

63 R.A. Church, *The Great Victorian Boom 1850–1973* (London, 1975), and S.B. Saul, *The Myth of the Great Depression* (2nd edn, London, 1975), examine critically two labels commonly applied to characterize the late nineteenth-century British economy.

64 W.B. Owen, 'Tangye, Sir Richard (1833–1906)', rev. H.C.G. Matthew, *ODNB*, online edn, http://www. oxforddnb.com/view/article/36413 (accessed 1 January 2016); R.E. Waterhouse, *A Hundred Years of Engineering Craftsmanship: A Short History … of Tangyes Ltd, Smethwick, 1857–1957* (London, 1957).

65 Cherry, *Birmingham*, 49–52, 62.

66 Mason, *Jewellery Making*; J. Cattell and B. Hawkins, *The Birmingham Jewellery Quarter: An Introduction and Guide* (London, 2000); J. Cattell, S. Ely and B. Jones, *The Birmingham Jewellery Quarter: An Architectural Survey of the Manufactories* (London, 2002); F. Carnevali, 'Golden opportunities: jewelry making in Birmingham between mass production and speciality', *Enterprise and Society*, 4 (2003), 272–98; R.A. Church and B.M.D. Smith, 'Competition and monopoly in the coffin furniture industry, 1870–1915', *The Economic History Review*, NS, 19.3 (1966), 621–41.

67 http://www.birminghammuseums.org.uk/jewellery; http:// www.penroom.co.uk/; http://www.coffinworks.org/; http:// www.english-heritage.org.uk/visit/places/j-w-evans-silver-factory/ (all accessed 18 May 2016).

68 J.T. Bunce, *Josiah Mason: A Biography* (Birmingham, 1882), 30–42; B. George, *A Birmingham Master of Manufacturing and Innovation: John Sheldon, Toymaker, Pencil Maker and Silversmith* (Penrith, n.d.); J. Berkeley, *From Pens to Particle Physics: The Story of a Birmingham Family Business* (Birmingham, 2011); B. Jones (ed.), *People, Pens and Production* (Birmingham, 2013); B. Jones, 'Words, birds and Birmingham pens', *History West Midlands*, 1.3 (2013), 18–19; F. Terry Chandler, 'Women, work and the family: Birmingham 1800–1870' (PhD thesis, University of Birmingham, 1995).

69 Skipp, *Victorian Birmingham*, 54–5; http://www. gracesguide.co.uk/Elkington,_Mason_and_Co (accessed 18 May 2016).

70 M. Fisher, *Hardman of Birmingham: Goldsmith and Glasspainter* (Ashbourne, 2008).

71 P. Coccoris, *The Curious History of the Bulb Vase* (Birmingham, 2012), 85–117.

72 I.A. Williams, *The Firm of Cadbury 1831–1931* (London, 1931); C. Chinn, *The Cadbury Story: A Short History of Cadbury* (Studley, 1998); D. Cadbury, *Chocolate Wars: From Cadbury to Craft – 200 Years of Sweet Success and Bitter Rivalry* (London, 2010); H.M. Davies, 'Cadbury, John (1801–1889)', rev. Christine Clark, *ODNB*, online edn, http://www.oxforddnb.com/view/article/37254 (accessed 31 December 2015); I.A. Williams, 'Cadbury, George (1839–1922)', rev. Robert Fitzgerald, *ODNB*, online edn, http://www.oxforddnb.com/view/article/32232 (accessed 31 December 2015).

73 Others established before 1914 included Alfred Bird and Sons, Typhoo Tea and HP Sauce.

74 J. Aston, 'Female business ownership in Birmingham 1849–1901', *Midland History*, 37.2 (2012), 189, criticizing the separate spheres theory in L. Davidoff and C. Hall, *Family Fortunes: Men and Women of the English Middle Class, 1780–1850* (2nd edn, London, 2002).

75 K. Jenns, 'Female business enterprise in and around Birmingham in the nineteenth and twentieth centuries' (PhD thesis, University of Birmingham, 1997); Aston, 'Female business ownership', 187–206; J. Aston, 'Female business owners in England 1849–1901' (PhD thesis, University of Birmingham, 2012).

76 Aston, 'Female business ownership', 191–2.

77 Hopkins, *Second City*, 129–42; J. Bourne, 'War', in C. Chinn (ed), *Birmingham: Bibliography of a City* (Birmingham, 2003), 224–6, 234–6; J. Bourne, 'Introduction: the midlands and the Great War', *Midland History*, 39.2 (2014), 159–61; Sian Roberts, *Great War Britain: Birmingham Remembering 1914–18* (Stroud, 2014), 10–14, 56–66.

78 http://www.voicesofwarandpeace.org/portfolio/mills-munitions-workers/ (accessed 29 December 2015).

79 http://www.voicesofwarandpeace.org/portfolio/cadbury/ (accessed 29 December 2015).

80 D. Drummond, 'The university and the war effort', in E. Ives, D. Drummond and L. Schwarz, *The First Civic University: Birmingham, 1880–1980. An Introductory History* (Birmingham, 2000), 174–87.

81 Hopkins, *Second City*, 129–42.

82 Berkeley, *From Pens to Particle Physics*, 15.

83 Quoted in Roberts, *Birmingham Remembering*, 56–7.

84 G. Frost, *Munitions of War: A Record of the Work of B.S.A. and Daimler Companies during the World War 1914–1918* (Birmingham and Coventry, 1919); Kynoch, *Notes on Kynoch War Work* (Birmingham, 1918, 1919); Birmingham City Council, 'Austin – the war years', in *A Brief History of Austin and Longbridge*, http://www.birmingham.gov. uk/cs/Satellite?c=Page&childpagename=Lib-Central-Information-Services%2FPageLayout&cid=1223092632871 &pagename=BCC%2FCommon%2FWrapper%2FWrapper (accessed 20 December 2015).

85 Bourne, 'War', 224; Bourne, 'Introduction', *Midland History*, 162.

86 R.A. Church, *Herbert Austin: The British Motor Car Industry to 1941* (London, 1979); R.A. Church, *The Rise and Decline of the British Motor Industry* (Cambridge, 1995).

87 *History of the Birmingham Co-operative Society Limited 1881–1931* (Birmingham, 1931); C.J. Shelley, 'The politics of co-operation: consumer co-operative societies in Birmingham and Bristol 1880–1921' (PhD thesis, University of Birmingham, 2007).

88 Hopkins, *Second City*, 143–9.

89 Williams, *Cadbury*; Chinn, *Cadbury Story*; Cadbury, *Chocolate Wars*. The social welfare measures took place under Lawrence Cadbury: R. Fitzgerald, 'Cadbury, Laurence John (1889–1982)', *ODNB*, online edn, http://www.oxforddnb.com/view/article/46801 (accessed 31 December 2015).

90 Hopkins, *Second City*, 147.

91 J.B. Priestley, *English Journey* (Harmondsworth, 1977), 88–98.

92 J. Bradbury, *Cadbury's Purple Reign: The Story behind Cadbury's Best-loved Brand* (Chichester, 2008); J. Curtis, 'Cadbury's angels: the depiction of women and the Bournville Works', http://www.connectinghistories.org.uk/wp-content/uploads/2015/07/sb-cadburys-angels-print.pdf (accessed 30 December 2015).

93 T.B. Rodgers, *A Century of Progress 1831–1931: Cadbury Bournville* (Birmingham, 1931).

94 *Bournville: An Invitation* (Birmingham, n.d.).

95 A. Sutcliffe and R. Smith, *History of Birmingham, III, Birmingham 1939–1970* (London, 1974), 14–56; D. Thoms, *War, Industry and Society: The Midlands 1939–45* (London, 1989); C. Chinn, *Brum Undaunted: Birmingham during the Second World War* (Birmingham, 1996).

96 Bourne, 'War', 227.

97 Sutcliffe and Smith, *Birmingham*, 14–56.

98 M.H.F. Wilkins, 'Randall, Sir John Turton (1905–1984)', rev., *ODNB*, online edn, http://www.oxforddnb.com/view/article/31584 (accessed 31 December 2015); C.S. Nicholls, 'Boot, Henry Albert Howard (1917–1983)', rev., *ODNB*, online edn, http://www.oxforddnb.com/view/article/30833 (accessed 31 December 2015]); D. Drummond and E. Ives, 'The return to war', in E. Ives, D. Drummond and L. Schwarz, *The First Civic University: Birmingham, 1880–1980. An Introductory History* (Birmingham, 2000), 281–92; R.H. Dalitz, 'Peierls, Sir Rudolf Ernst (1907–1995)', *ODNB*, online edn, http://www.oxforddnb.com/view/article/60076 (accessed 29 December 2015); Rudolf Peierls, 'Frisch, Otto Robert (1904–1979)', rev. Xavier Roqué, *ODNB*, online edn, http://www.oxforddnb.com/view/article/31127 (accessed 29 December 2015).

99 Sutcliffe and Smith, *Birmingham*, 25–35.

100 For a recent well-illustrated example of a history of 15 different trades, see R. Shills, *Birmingham's Industrial Heritage 1900–2000* (Stroud, 2002).

101 A number of current and former students have discussed aspects of Birmingham's industrial and trading history with me or shared the results of their research. Tom Gidlow received an undergraduate research scholarship from the College of Arts and Law at the University of Birmingham for the summer of 2015 and provided some of the evidence which has been used in this study. Roger Bruton, Jenni Dixon, Duncan Frankis, Kate Iles, Dawn MacQueen, Mary Nejedly, Guy Sjögren, Janet Sullivan and Sue Tungate have conducted research into aspects on 'the city of a thousand trades' before 1945, and I have benefited greatly from their work.

CHAPTER SIX

Birmingham: A Political Profile, 1700–1940

ROGER WARD

Unrepresented in Parliament, unincorporated until 1838, Birmingham was politically unimportant within a region judged by John Money to have been unable 'to advance any … claim to significance in the affairs of the nation'.[1] Dissatisfaction with dependence on the county and with the town's own internal governance, based as it was on the ancient institutions of manor and parish supplemented by local Improvement Acts, did not surface with any degree of consensus until after the French Wars (1793–1815). In the period of reform beginning in 1828, however, Birmingham became a major focus of radicalism, its Political Union a model for others and its leader, Thomas Attwood ('King Tom'), a figure of national stature.

Achieving both parliamentary status in 1832 and incorporation in 1838, Birmingham became, for the ensuing half-century, a leading centre of radicalism, especially in the agitation for further parliamentary reform under the leadership of John Bright in 1867 and Joseph Chamberlain in 1884.[2] Not especially prominent in the two leading pressure groups of the 1840s and 1850s, Chartism and the Anti-Corn Law League, Birmingham blossomed in the 'Liberal Golden Age' of the 1860s and 1870s, pioneering new forms of political organization (the 'caucus') and earning a reputation for dynamic local government ('municipal socialism'). The reputation earned at this time for efficient, well-managed local government lasted well into the next century.

The transformation in Birmingham's hitherto sluggish local government was indelibly associated with the name of Joseph Chamberlain, who built a local power base which he was able to project into national politics and bequeath as a legacy to his sons, especially Neville. The Liberal split over Irish Home Rule of 1886 was a seminal moment in British politics and had powerful repercussions locally. After a short internal struggle Chamberlain succeeded in wrenching Birmingham politics out of its accustomed track and forging a Unionist alliance with Conservatives which would dominate both parliamentary and municipal politics for two generations. Opposition from an enfeebled Liberal Party was succeeded between the wars by the challenge of the nascent Labour Party. An electoral breakthrough in 1929, sparked by the leadership of Oswald Mosley, proved ephemeral, however, and Unionist dominance was resumed in the 1930s.

The hegemony of Unionism in a city overwhelmingly industrial and working class defied the perception that social class was increasingly becoming the principal determinant of political allegiance and has been described as Birmingham 'exceptionalism', until the Second World War once again altered the trajectory of Birmingham politics.

The town in 'the long eighteenth century'

In 1716 a group of citizens petitioned Parliament in vain for an Act of Incorporation. According to William Hutton, the town's first historian, the petition carried only 27 signatures – an indication that the move lacked support from among the town's elite. In a celebrated and oft-replicated judgement, Hutton argued that the absence of a mayor, corporation and trade guilds was a principal reason for the dynamic rise of Birmingham: 'a town without a charter,' he argued, 'is a town without a shackle'.[3] The unincorporated status of the town was also regarded as its attraction to dissenting immigrants who contributed so much to its economy, since the restrictive legislation imposed on dissenters during the previous century did not apply to unincorporated towns.[4]

How long could the town be governed in this way? In 1760 'the town of 30,000 still had the institutions of a rural parish'.[5] There were clear deficiencies, particularly in maintaining law and order. Birmingham experienced periodic riots, usually sparked by dissatisfaction with food prices at times of depression and by sectarian hatreds. The most serious were the 'Church and King' riots of July 1791, when the houses of leading dissenters were sacked and their chapels burned in retaliation for their suspected sympathy for the French Revolution, the chief victim being the scientist and Unitarian minister Joseph Priestley. These events necessitated the intervention of the county justices and militia.[6]

By the time these riots occurred the government had responded to the need to fill gaps in the government of towns such as Birmingham. 1769 saw the passage of an Improvement Act, known locally as the 'Lamp Act' since a priority was the lighting of the streets. It was supplemented by a further four Acts, the last in 1828, each one supplementing the powers of the nominated Streets Commission as the principal authority in the town. The evidence suggests that this arrangement worked to the satisfaction of most citizens until the post-Napoleonic years. Although there were times when the Commission was criticized for inertia, it was generally regarded as efficient. It guided the town through both the canal and the railway age, with the

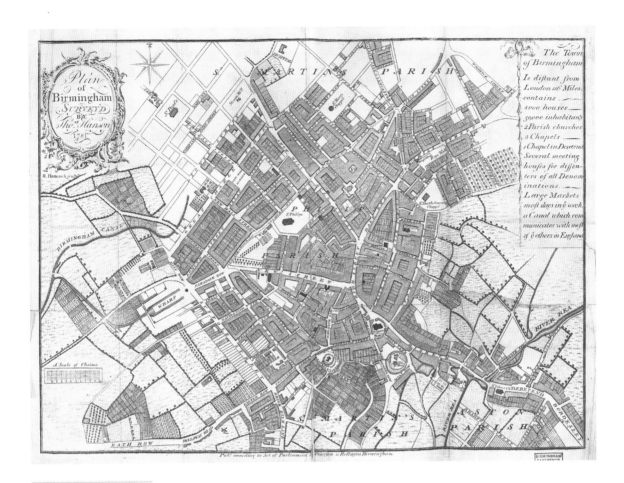

Birmingham in 1781 surveyed
by Thomas Hanson and
published in William Hutton's
History of Birmingham of the
same year. Hutton described
Birmingham as 'a town
without a shackle'.
By permission of the Library of
Birmingham, MAP/174790

An artist's depiction of the
sacking of Joseph Priestley's
house and laboratory at
Fairhill, Sparkbrook, during
the Church and King riots
of 1791.
By permission of the Library of
Birmingham, D/5 70480

attendant reconstruction, and it had left a legacy of impressive public buildings, notably the Town Hall and the Market Hall, by the time of its abolition in 1851.[7]

By the late eighteenth century the parliamentary system, 'Old Corruption', was widely denounced as a scandal. Various efforts at reform, however, were frustrated until, with the outbreak of the French Wars in 1793, advocacy of reform became stigmatized as seditious by an authoritarian government. One of the defects was the lack of representation for industrial towns such as Birmingham and Manchester. Some 400 Birmingham freeholders qualified for the vote in Warwick county elections, but elections almost invariably resulted in the return of country gentlemen with little knowledge of Birmingham, although, according to R.B. Rose, several MPs and local peers, such as Lord Dartmouth, did their best to uphold Birmingham's interests.[8] In 1812 a town meeting censured Sir Charles Mordaunt for his 'great inattention to applications of great importance in this town and neighbourhood'. Another county MP, D.S. Dugdale, confessed that he had no more than a rudimentary knowledge of Birmingham industries.[9]

Increasingly conscious of the growing need for corporate action, in 1783 Birmingham entrepreneurs, led by the manufacturing chemist Samuel Garbett (1717–1803), formed the Birmingham Commercial Committee, the forerunner of the Chamber of Commerce which had a continuous existence from 1813.[10] But there was no great pressure for direct representation, probably because elections were often the occasion of riot. Instead, Birmingham entrepreneurs focused upon the traditional methods of petitioning, lobbying and soliciting the help of sympathetic MPs and peers. The third Lord Calthorpe, busy developing his lucrative estate in

Birmingham's newly built Town Hall was proudly celebrated in a variety of media. This silver and mother-of-pearl snuff box commemorates an important expression of Birmingham's civic pride.
By permission of Assay Office Birmingham, photographer Alexandre Parré

Edgbaston, acted on behalf of the town, presenting no fewer than fourteen petitions between 1820 and 1831. These methods were successful. An Act of Parliament in 1783 established the Assay Office and another in 1813 the Gun-Barrel Proof House.[11]

Wars with France between 1793 and 1815 provided opportunities for Birmingham business but also brought hazards that made corporate organization necessary. The government's response to Napoleon's Continental System, designed to lock British trade out of mainland Europe, was to issue Orders-in-Council in 1812 in an attempt to ban trade with France and its satellites.[12] A storm of protest persuaded the government to modify the Orders, though too late to prevent war with the United States, with which the town did considerable trade.

During the campaign against the Orders, Thomas Attwood (1783–1856), high bailiff, came to prominence as the leader of the movement outside Parliament.[13] He and his partner in Attwood and Spooner's bank, Richard Spooner, were also prominent in the successful agitation against the renewal of the East India Company's monopoly of Asian trade.[14] Attwood, a fanatical currency reformer, agitated against Peel's Bank Act of 1819 and bombarded Parliament with pamphlets and letters arguing for the issue of paper currency which, he believed, would revive trade and reduce unemployment. A 'High Tory' in his early days, Attwood's frustration with Lord Liverpool's Tory government drove him closer to the camp of parliamentary reformers.[15] However, it was not Attwood but George Edmonds (1788–1868), the son of a Baptist preacher, schoolmaster and journalist, who became the main spokesman for the reformers.

Thomas Attwood, leader of the Birmingham Political Union, holds the Declaration of the Union in his hands. The BPU, which campaigned for parliamentary reform and the extension of the vote, put Birmingham on the national political map for the first time and the historian Edward Pearce has described Attwood as 'a blazing credit to Birmingham'.
By permission of the Cadbury Research Library: Special Collections, University of Birmingham

Two leading advocates of reform, Major John Cartwright and Francis Burdett MP, created a national network of Hampden Clubs. Curiously, Birmingham was not represented at the initial delegates' meeting in London but, on the initiative of Edmonds, a meeting was held on Newhall Hill on 22 January 1817 to launch a Birmingham Hampden Club. This meeting, attended by a reputed 25,000, was the first of many on this spot over the succeeding fifteen years. Various initiatives followed. Days before the Peterloo Massacre in July 1819, a meeting was held to elect a 'Legislative Attorney', Sir Charles Wolseley, and to send him to Westminster as Birmingham's representative. Stunts of this kind were treated by the Home Office as seditious and arrests and prosecutions followed, Edmonds being sentenced to nine months' imprisonment. When released he was given a hero's welcome in Birmingham. He later studied law and became Clerk of the Peace. Until his death in 1868 Edmonds was ever-present on reform platforms. A popular figure, he was an important link between working men and the elite figures who led the reform movement and its 'union of classes'.[16] In 1827, on the initiative of Sir Charles Tennyson, a motion was proposed in the House of Commons to transfer the representation of the notoriously corrupt borough of East Retford to Birmingham. In support, a meeting was convened in Beardsworth's Repository, the largest local indoor venue, which resulted in the sending of a petition bearing 4,000 signatures to Parliament. Tennyson's motion was rejected, as was a similar effort by Lord John Russell. Meanwhile, Attwood won converts to his ideas for currency reform as a means of alleviating distress. The passage of the 1829 Catholic Emancipation Act by Wellington's government inspired the hope that a Tory government might turn to parliamentary reform. When Wellington set his face firmly against it, Attwood shifted tack and declared himself a Radical. A successful banker and a man of 'fizzing energy', he cast himself in the role of leader of a renewed reform movement.[17]

On 14 December 1829 Attwood and Joshua Scholefield (1775–1844),[18] a merchant, took the initiative in convening a meeting in the Royal Hotel to form a Political Union for the Protection of Public Rights, and in the following week a set of rules was drawn up, signed by 28 persons. On 30 January 1830 a reputed 15,000 people gathered in Beardsworth's Repository, with George Muntz (1794–1857)[19] in the chair, to found the Birmingham Political Union (BPU). Attwood was named president. Some 5,000 persons subsequently became paid-up members. Attwood was explicit that the BPU must act legally and constitutionally to 'meet, consult, resolve and petition'. He characterized the campaign for parliamentary reform not as innovative but as a demand for the restoration of the traditional rights of the people under the Crown, frequently ending his addresses with the mantra 'God Bless the King'. The Union hymn, composed by the Revd Hugh Hutton, reinforced these principles:

> See, see we come. No swords we draw
> We kindle not war's battle fires
> By union, justice, reason, law
> We'll gain the birth right of our sires

In June William IV, thought to be more favourable to reform, succeeded George IV, and in July France erupted in revolution. The BPU held a dinner for 4,000 at Beardsworth's Repository to celebrate 'the July Days', but Attwood once again insisted on peaceful agitation: 'the constitution and nothing but the constitution'. Hopes mounted in November with the replacement of Wellington's government by a Whig government headed by Lord Grey and committed to reform. This marked the beginning of a tortuous parliamentary struggle, culminating in the passage of the Great Reform Act in June 1832.

In the course of that struggle Attwood made his name as an impresario of popular protest. Union rallies held on Newhall Hill were carefully orchestrated events with marching bands, professional singers, flag waving and the presentation of medals, and presided over by the Birmingham banker in his trademark sealskin coat. Attendance at one, on 31 October 1831, was claimed to be over 100,000. At the largest, in May 1832, *The Times* reported an attendance of 250,000. The BPU's

"THE GATHERING OF THE UNIONS."
ON NEW HALL HILL, BIRMINGHAM.
Drawn on Stone from Sketches taken during the Three successive Meetings in May 1832.
by HENRY HARRIS, Birmingham.
Printed by G. Hullmandel

Henry Harris's representation of the Birmingham Political Union's rallies held on Newhall Hill in May 1832. Thousands attended to support these calls for reform in a festive atmosphere.
© Mary Evans Picture Library

example was followed elsewhere, with many other Unions adopting its rules.[20] Its peaceful example, however, was not universally imitated and there were outbreaks of violence in Derby, Nottingham and Bristol in October 1831. With the Lords rejecting the Bill and Grey briefly resigning, a crisis was reached and even Attwood contemplated forming a National Guard. Fortunately for the town the moment passed. When the Great Reform Act was passed, the BPU claimed to have united the town in a union of the middle and working classes. The BPU passed into legend – Birmingham leading the struggle for reform under its gallant leader, 'King Tom'.[21]

How justified was this myth, so influential in Birmingham's subsequent history? Early historians ignored the popular dimension and represented the struggle for reform as essentially a parliamentary battle between Whig and Tory. Carlos Flick, followed by Eric Hopkins, dismissed the myth as largely a fiction. In Flick's words, 'the BPU was a local creation and it never transcended its provincial origins and character'.[22] These judgements seem not to account for both elite and popular opinion. On 19 May 1832 Grey thanked Attwood for the part he had played ('we owe our situation entirely to you') and four days later, at a great banquet in the Mansion House, Attwood was granted the Freedom of the City of London. On his return to Birmingham he was feted as a hero. Attwood's chief biographer, David Moss, strikes a better balance between myth and reality, while more recent historians have no

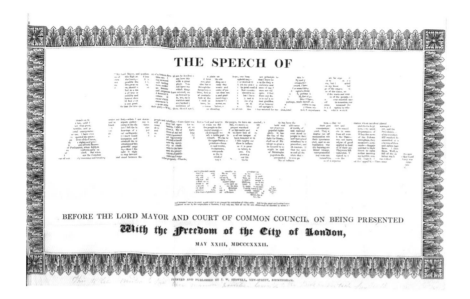

THE SPEECH OF

[decorative text forming the name "ATTWOOD"]

BEFORE THE LORD MAYOR AND COURT OF COMMON COUNCIL, ON BEING PRESENTED

With the Freedom of the City of London,

MAY XXIII, MDCCCXXXII.

PRINTED AND PUBLISHED BY J. W. SHOWELL, NEW-STREET, BIRMINGHAM.

Birmingham's celebration of the granting of the Freedom of the City of London to Thomas Attwood on 23 May 1832. The honour was recognition by the City of Attwood's national importance.
By permission of the Cadbury Research Library: Special Collections, University of Birmingham

doubt of the significance of the BPU, with Attwood described by Edward Pearce as 'a blazing credit to Birmingham'.[23] The gratitude of leading Whig politicians is readily explained. As Antonia Fraser commented, Attwood 'managed popular anger'.[24] For better or worse, his influence served to combat those forces in society making for violent revolution. The rough-sharpened swords of the Scots Greys remained in their scabbards, at least in the midland region, and especially in a town noted for arms production and therefore feared.

Historians have also argued over the validity of the BPU's boasted 'union of classes' with its implications for Birmingham's evolving political culture. In Clive Behagg's view, this concept obscures conflicts of interest between the middle and lower classes and overlooks the discrete organizations of the latter.[25] George Barnsby reinforced the argument in his study of local working-class organizations.[26] Behagg feared that this might remain a minority view and he has proved correct. What has been called 'the Briggs model', elaborated in the corpus of work on Birmingham by Asa Briggs, while not denying conflicting class interests, traces the propensity for cross-class cooperation to the structure of industry in the town; the proliferation of small firms, face-to-face relations between masters and men and the opportunities for social mobility.[27] Observations by informed contemporaries such as Richard Cobden and John Stuart Mill tend to bear out these interpretations.

Chartist sequel

In Birmingham's first parliamentary election, Attwood and Scholefield were returned unopposed. Disillusion, however, followed swiftly: not the promised 'dawn of liberty' but legislation, and in particular the new Poor Law, which provoked bitter resentment. Attwood, alienated by the rejection in Parliament of his currency ideas, joined those advocating further parliamentary reform. He can therefore be regarded as an early leader of Chartism, so named after the People's Charter drawn up by William Lovett. He was deputed to present to Parliament a monster petition bearing over a million signatures, only for it to be rejected in the Commons by 235 votes to 46.[28]

The BPU, dissolved in 1834, was reconstituted in 1837 and the rallies on Newhall Hill resumed. Attwood persisted in advocating peaceful and constitutional means but the tide of opinion turned towards the robust advocacy of Feargus O'Connor, ex-Irish MP and editor of the *Northern Star*. A People's Convention was held in London in July 1839 but when it met hostility from the authorities the delegates reconvened in Birmingham. Scenes of disorder provoked the intervention of the Home Office which, at the request of the Birmingham magistrates, sent a contingent of Metropolitan police to the town. On arrival the police were attacked by a mob and days of riot and destruction followed, necessitating military intervention.[29] The 'Bull Ring' or Chartist riots left the town sullen and subdued.[30] The locus of Chartism moved north.[31]

These events marked the end of Attwood's political career and the beginning of his descent into obscurity. In December 1839 he resigned from Parliament to be replaced by G.F. Muntz. He died in March 1856 and lies buried in the churchyard of Hanley Castle. Only with difficulty was £800 raised to pay for a memorial statue (in contrast to the £50,000 raised on the death of Richard Cobden). A few years later, in 1865, the bank with which his name was associated collapsed. For a brief time deemed 'the most popular man in England', Attwood was the first Birmingham man to have built a national reputation. His 'Birmingham School of Political Economy' was then eclipsed until Joseph Chamberlain sought to give it new life.[32]

Richard Doyle's satirical representation of the police response to Chartist protest in Birmingham's Bull Ring in 1839. Doyle later worked as an illustrator for *Punch* and Charles Dickens. This sketch lay undiscovered for over 100 years in the Library of Congress until uncovered in 2015 by Professor Ian Haywood of the University of Roehampton.
Courtesy of Library of Congress, Caroline & Erwin Swann Collection No. 774

The man who requested Home Office assistance to quell the Chartists was Mayor William Scholefield, son of Joshua, while one of the newly appointed magistrates involved in the prosecution of rioters was Philip Muntz, brother of George. These men were, classically, poachers turned gamekeepers. Stalwarts of the BPU, they had led the demand for the incorporation of the town under the terms of the Municipal Corporations Act of 1835, in the formulation of which Joseph Parkes, a Birmingham lawyer and Whig 'wire-puller', played a major part.[33] The Privy Council responded positively and the Charter of Incorporation was delivered to the town in October 1838. The high bailiff, William Scholefield, was charged with carrying out elections to a town council. Birmingham, divided into 13 wards, elected 48 councillors, who then chose 16 aldermen, all from among the elected body, thus necessitating by-elections to make up the council of 64. Scholefield was elected 'Charter' mayor, in what proved to be a very hot seat.

In these first municipal elections all seats were contested, although the electorate remained small.[34] All were won by Liberals of either the Radical or Whig variety. The Tories expressed their frustration by challenging the legal validity of the Charter. The government had its own concerns, reluctant to appoint as magistrates men who had so recently been depicted as agitators. It insisted on changes to the proposed bench of magistrates and withheld police powers. It was an unhappy baptism but, to general surprise, when Sir Robert Peel became prime minister in 1841 he granted full police powers to the council and followed it up in 1842 with a confirmation of the legality of the Charter. A man so often seen in the town as an enemy was mourned as a hero on his death in 1850 and commemorated with a handsome statue.[35]

The town council enjoyed the legal and police powers envisaged by the 1835 Act but the Streets Commission retained its functions. Having no premises of its own, the council was obliged to go cap-in-hand to the Commission, which graciously loaned a room in the Town Hall 'when such room is not otherwise engaged'.[36] Not until after the passage of the Public Health Act of 1848 and Rawlinson's Report recommending the amalgamation of all local powers did the town council finally come into its own. The Improvement Act of 1851 gave the council full powers in the parliamentary borough of Birmingham and the various Streets Commissions in the area were abolished.

Thirteen years of uncertainty had taken their toll. In the official history of the corporation, J.T. Bunce declared that the council had sunk into 'practical anarchy', in which 'many of the ablest and most influential citizens shrank from taking their just share in local government'.[37] Into this vacuum stepped small businessmen, a 'shopocracy', whose leading figure was a scandal-mongering journalist and failed manufacturer, Joseph Allday. For Bunce, Allday epitomized all that was wrong with Birmingham's local government. His 'pot-house' followers determined policies in the Woodman Tavern in Easy Row or in Allday's wife's tripe-shop in Union Street. Their major concern was to keep down the rates, hence the label 'Economists'.[38] Allday's instinct for scandal, however, was not always misplaced and he did good service in exposing brutality in the borough jail at Winson Green, which resulted in the death of an inmate in 1853.[39] The resignation of Allday in 1859 weakened the hold of the Economists and was followed by a decade of cautious advance in public provision, associated chiefly with Alderman Thomas Avery, the scale-maker, who acted as a bridge between the 1850s and the municipal dynamism of the 1870s.[40]

Mid-Victorian years

During the 1840s the two most prominent pressure groups were the Chartists and the Anti-Corn Law League. The events of 1839 had been a shock and it is hardly surprising that many in the town backed away from Chartism. Those who continued to campaign tended to be drawn from the working class, their principal mentor being Arthur O'Neill, pastor of the Chartist church in Newhall Street who, like many others, had been imprisoned in Stafford jail for his speeches.[41] O'Neill was a teetotaller and a pacifist and this made him *persona grata* to middle-class Radicals who recoiled from physical force. In particular, O'Neill had good relations with Joseph Sturge (1793–1859), labelled by his biographer 'a moral Radical'.[42] Sturge and his brother Charles were corn merchants and Quakers. Joseph Sturge had been a prominent campaigner against slavery, was a passionate member of the Peace Society and a philanthropist on a grand scale. He had served the town as a Streets Commissioner and a councillor. Rejecting violent means did not imply rejection of all the aims of Chartism, and early in 1842 Sturge founded the National Complete Suffrage Union (NCSU) to bridge the gap and restore the union of classes. Eighty-seven delegates attended the founding conference in the Town Hall in April. Sturge confirmed his support for the People's Charter but, believing Chartism to have become tainted by association with 'violent and improper conduct', he called for the Charter to be replaced by a Bill of Rights. Sturge, however, was asking Chartists to repudiate their past activities for which over 400 had suffered imprisonment. O'Connor mobilized his supporters to reject what he regarded as a middle-class hijack and, at the second NCSU conference, Sturge's proposition was rejected. By 1845 the NCSU had withered away. In 1844 Joshua Scholefield died and Sturge insisted on standing in the by-election in defiance of the Liberal committee's support for Joshua's son, William. The Liberal vote was split and Richard Spooner sneaked in – the only Tory to represent Birmingham in Parliament between 1832 and 1886.[43]

Joseph Sturge, publisher of the *Corn Trade Circular*, was a valuable source of intelligence to the Anti-Corn Law League (ACLL) and a friend of fellow Quaker John Bright (1811–89), co-leader with Richard Cobden of the League. As in the case of Chartism, there was widespread local support for the League. In 1839 the town council petitioned Parliament for the abolition of the Corn Laws, widely believed to be keeping the price of bread artificially high. The Chartists, too, supported abolition but mutual suspicion stood in the way of cooperation with the ACLL. In Birmingham, however, the ACLL never acquired deep roots. Charles Geach, mayor in 1847, successful banker and later MP for Coventry, explained this in terms of industrial structures.⁴⁴ The ACLL strongholds were to be found in Manchester and the Lancashire textile manufacturing districts, the bulk of its funds raised from 'the lords of a thousand spindles'. The abolition of the laws in 1846, beginning the progression to free trade, was nevertheless welcomed in Birmingham.

With rare exceptions, nineteenth-century Birmingham's MPs were chosen from local men with a record of success in business and public service. The earliest exception was John Bright, a cotton spinner from Rochdale, a former leader of the ACLL with a reputation for stirring oratory. From 1847 to 1857 Bright represented Manchester, which he regarded as his natural home. But Bright was summarily rejected in 1857 because of his opposition to the Crimean War. His moral stature was enhanced, especially among nonconformists, but at the cost of a nervous breakdown from which he never completely recovered. In July 1857 George Muntz died, creating a parliamentary vacancy. Not only was Bright damaged goods, but many Birmingham Liberals were Palmerstonian in their outlook on foreign affairs, sympathizing with the oppressed nationalities of Europe, with Russia perceived as the worst of the oppressors. Bright's supporters, however, prevailed and the Liberal committee agreed that Bright, who was convalescing in Scotland, should be approached. Sturge consulted with Bright and returned with a letter of acceptance. Three days later Bright was elected unopposed and in his absence. It would be over a year before he was fit enough to address his constituents.

Cobden approved of Bright's move to Birmingham, which he famously described as a town where 'there was more social equality and a greater faith in democratic principles' than in Whiggish Manchester. The Birmingham Liberals hoped that Bright would reinvigorate the campaign for further parliamentary reform. In his first address in October 1858 he aroused enormous enthusiasm by appealing to the tradition of the BPU and lauding its veterans such as Edmonds. The campaign was slow to catch fire, but by the mid-1860s it had done so. Once again Birmingham

John Bright, MP for Birmingham from 1857 until his death in 1889, was a Quaker with a radical reputation who made a major contribution to extending the franchise in the nineteenth century.
By permission of the Cadbury Research Library: Special Collections, University of Birmingham

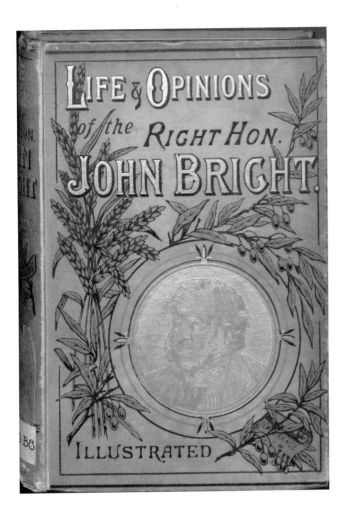

Published in 1887, this decorated and illustrated book celebrated the life and opinions of John Bright MP.
By permission of the Cadbury Research Library: Special Collections, University of Birmingham

became the scene of huge rallies, this time at Brookfields, a mile outside the town centre. One such, on 27 August 1866, attracted an estimated crowd of between 150,000 and 200,000 people, an event replicated on 22 April 1867. Bright's organizational skills, his parliamentary experience and his eloquence proved invaluable. In popular perception it was John Bright, 'the People's Tribune', who was the chief author of the Second Reform Act in August 1867, which added over one million, mostly urban householders, to the electoral registers. This achievement ensured for Bright an unassailable ascendancy, amounting to reverence, in Birmingham politics until his death in 1889.[45]

The Liberal Golden Age

The 1867 Act was followed five years later by the abolition of the hustings, to be replaced by the secret ballot. The Third Reform Act of 1884 enfranchised rural labourers, increasing the size of the electorate from 3 to 5 million. These changes created a mass electorate and transformed the nature and organization of politics. Arguably, modern politics was made in Birmingham.

In 1865, in anticipation of coming changes, a group of leading Liberals met to form the Birmingham Liberal Association (BLA). Its first president was Philip Muntz (1839–1908), its secretary George Dixon (1820–98) and its treasurer John Jaffray (1818–1901),[46] co-owner of the *Birmingham Daily Post*. Reputedly the instigator of this new organization, dubbed by Disraeli the 'caucus', was William Harris, an architect and surveyor. It had a pyramidical structure. Committees were established at the base, in each of the town's 16 wards. The ward committees sent representatives up an ascending and reducing system of committees topped by a management committee and finally by an executive committee at the apex. The transmission of ideas and opinions from base to apex and apex to base was thereby facilitated, all managed by a secretary, a role in which Francis Schnadhorst (1840–1900), a tailor, excelled.[47] The annual meeting of the caucus – at first the '400', then the '600' and finally the '2,000' – was a mobilizing political rally addressed by leaders, including Bright and Joseph Chamberlain. The caucus became the subject of bitter controversy. To its defenders it was a means of giving full expression to democratic opinion; to its critics it was a means by which a small oligarchy of leaders could exercise domination and deny minorities a voice and a share of representation. Both views have validity. Its critics, however, paid the caucus the compliment of imitation and the structure of the BLA became a standard model of political organization.[48]

Its effectiveness was proved in 1868, in the first general election following the passage of the Reform Act. A modest redistribution had awarded two-member boroughs an extra seat, and in an effort to enhance Tory urban representation, Disraeli had introduced a 'minority clause' which allowed each voter to 'plump' his two votes on a single candidate. The Birmingham Conservative Association (BCA) fielded two candidates, S.S. Lloyd, a banker, and Sebastian Evans, a journalist and litterateur. To defeat Disraeli's 'fancy franchises', the caucus arranged the distribution of the Liberal vote evenly over their three candidates, Muntz, Bright and Dixon, who were duly elected. So demoralized was the BCA by the power of the caucus that it was unable to muster a single candidate six years later. To be a Tory in Radical Birmingham was, as one commentator put it, to belong to a 'forlorn hope'.[49]

The caucus was already focused on the unsatisfactory nature of municipal affairs. The most eloquent critic of the town council was George Dawson, the outstanding member of a remarkable group of nonconformist ministers active in Liberal politics. Dawson, described by Charles Kingsley as 'the best talker in England', was an inspirational and charismatic preacher, his sermons avidly absorbed by some of the town's elite. Decorating his sermons with analogies from business and the life of the street, he urged his communicants to take up civic responsibilities – to become town councillors and Guardians of the Poor.[50] In 1861 Dawson was the central figure of a group which launched the satiric magazine, the *Town Crier*, to expose and ridicule Economists and others standing in the way of progress.[51] Dawson's supporters sought out the big businessmen whose expertise might transform the municipal scene. One such was Joseph Chamberlain (1836–1914), screw manufacturer, canvassed by William Harris and persuaded to stand for the town council. He was elected unopposed for St Paul's ward in 1869. For a time Chamberlain was fully engaged in business, from which he was able to retire with a substantial fortune in 1874, but he had been singled out by fellow Radicals as a born leader. In November 1873 he was elected mayor of Birmingham, a seminal moment in the history of the town.[52]

The key issue which brought Chamberlain and other leading members of the BLA into politics was the inadequacy of educational provision. In March 1867 George Dixon convened a meeting at his house, 'The Dales' in Augustus Road, Edgbaston, to found the Birmingham Education Society (BES) with the central object of raising funds to pay the school fees of poor children. Generous subscribers included Chamberlain and his father, also Joe, who had moved his family to Birmingham from London. The researches of Jesse Collings exposed the gravity of the problem: approximately half of the town's children between 3 and 15 received little or no schooling.

Members of the BES concluded that philanthropy was an inadequate response. Again Dixon took the initiative.[53] In January 1869, with education at the top of the government's agenda, a pressure group, the National Education League (NEL), was formed to campaign for a national system which would be universal, compulsory, free and unsectarian. Dixon became president and the League's parliamentary spokesman, Chamberlain chairman of the executive committee. To replace the existing voluntary system managed by the Churches, the majority by the Anglican Church, with only tiny state support, would prove immensely expensive. The Gladstone government shrank from such a radical solution. Whenever education was under discussion, sectarian dispute became intense. Dixon, an Anglican, tried manfully to keep sectarianism at bay but was unable to prevent the NEL being increasingly perceived as a nonconformist pressure group. The militant line pursued by Chamberlain and by Robert Dale (1829–95),[54] founder and chairman of the Central Nonconformist Committee, did little to allay these suspicions.

W.E. Forster's Education Act of 1870 was a compromise. The voluntary schools were given time to improve and a degree of financial help while a new body, the School Board, was to be established in areas where provision was inadequate. The School Board, elected every three years, was to consist of 15 members and would be dependent for its financing on a precept from the rates. Electors would each have 15 votes which could be 'plumped'. In the first election to the Birmingham School Board in December 1870 the caucus over-reached itself, putting up 15 candidates while the Anglicans, led by S.S. Lloyd, put up only eight and the

The Chamberlains at Highbury, the family home at King's Heath on the outskirts of Birmingham. The photograph, which probably dates from the 1890s, shows from left to right, Joseph Chamberlain's sons Neville and Austen, Joe himself, his daughter Hilda and his third wife Mary.
By permission of the Cadbury Research Library: Special Collections, University of Birmingham

Catholics a single candidate, who came triumphantly at the head of the poll. 'The Bible Eight' therefore prevailed, the outraged nonconformists finding themselves in a minority. Partisanship was intense and the Radicals used their control of the town council to block, illegally, the transfer of finance. No progress could be made until the election of 1873.

With George Dixon fully occupied in Parliament, the executive role in the NEL was filled by Chamberlain, who led an uncompromising attack on the government. He thus made his debut in national politics as a militant nonconformist, the apprentice of Dale and the other conspicuously politicized nonconformist pastors of Birmingham. As he informed Radical allies such as John Morley, editor of the *Fortnightly Review*, and Sir Charles Dilke, he was fully prepared to smash up 'that whited sepulchre called the Liberal party' – an 'instrumentalist' approach to party which presaged the future course of his career.

While the NEL met with frustration on the national scene, in Birmingham the caucus learned from its previous mistake and took control of the School Board in December 1873. With Chamberlain elected chairman progress in school building became rapid. During Chamberlain's three years at the helm, 13 new schools were built to the impressive Gothic designs of John Henry Chamberlain, 'the caucus architect', the beginning of a programme which rolled out over 30 new schools in the thirty-two year existence of the School Board.[55]

Laying the foundations of the cult of Chamberlain

Combining the mayoralty with the chairmanship of the School Board, Chamberlain presided over a transformation which fulfilled the hopes of those Radicals who had long preached 'the civic gospel'. His two and a half years of office are one of the most chronicled episodes in Birmingham history, not only 'the most outstanding mayoralty in English history',[56] but one that set standards of municipal administration beyond the boundaries of the town. In 1874 Mayor Chamberlain withdrew from business to concentrate entirely on politics, with an intensity that lasted his lifetime.[57]

The achievement was real enough though the legend tended to grow with the telling. From one perspective it was a catching-up exercise, the municipalization first of gas and then of water having already been secured by over 50 municipal authorities. But in Birmingham it was achieved with impressive speed and efficiency. Chamberlain used 'the despotic authority' conferred on him by the caucus to acquire and reform these utilities. Birmingham had few corporate assets but Chamberlain was able to channel the profits of gas into improvements in physical and cultural facilities.[58]

His most innovative project was the Improvement Scheme made possible by the Artisans' Dwelling Act of 1875. Characteristically Chamberlain went beyond the central purpose of the Act, which was to promote slum clearance, and used it to launch a grand scheme of urban development to establish Birmingham's status as 'the Midlands Metropolis'. With Corporation Street as its focus, the Improvement

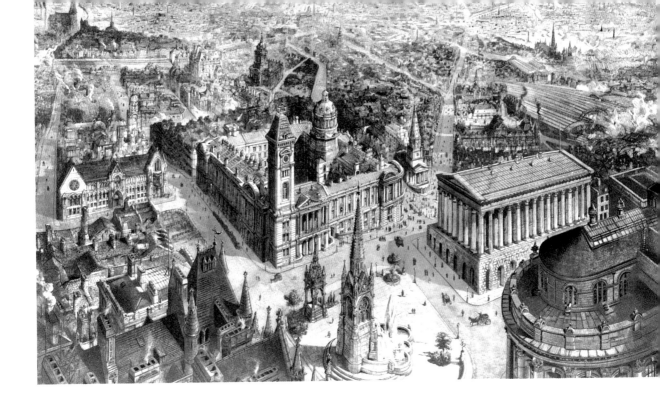

Birmingham's new civic buildings depicted in the *Bird's Eye View*, published in 1886. The School of Art, the Council House and the museum cluster around Chamberlain Square and its fountains. In the background can be seen the smoke of Birmingham's manufactories and to the right, the huge glass canopy of New Street station.
Private Collection

Scheme would ultimately furnish the town with the shops, restaurants, inns, theatres, offices and law courts in which it was deficient. Parallels were made with the work of Haussmann in Paris, and Corporation Street was dubbed 'Rue Chamberlain'. Central Birmingham was vastly improved but not without controversy. While the Improvement Scheme led to the demolition of noxious slums, it also entailed the loss of premises which could not be described in this way, and the council shrank from providing municipal housing to replace the demolished dwellings.[59] The Scheme also entailed a considerable addition to the borough debt, and by the time, in 1879, that construction began to replace demolition, the buoyant economy of the early 1870s, so favourable to Chamberlain's expansionist schemes, had given way to depression. 'Rue Chamberlain' would not be completed at the Aston end until the turn of the century. However, the abundant evidence of civic improvement impressed Birmingham citizens: 'high Victorian Birmingham really did bear some resemblance to a promised land, a holy city'.[60] Chamberlain reaped a great personal and political dividend from his efforts. The cult of Chamberlain as 'father of modern Birmingham' persisted beyond his lifetime and it was an image he carefully cultivated. Throughout the national political career on which he embarked he nursed the interests of Birmingham. In 1890 a visiting journalist, Julian Ralph, writing for a New York journal, conferred on Birmingham the much-valued accolade of 'the best governed city in the world', praising many aspects of an administration operated on lines of business efficiency and run by businessmen.[61]

Even while deeply engaged in the enterprise of Birmingham, Chamberlain cast around for a parliamentary seat. After suffering defeat in Sheffield in 1874, pressure was brought to bear on Dixon to stand down and Chamberlain took his place at

Westminster in 1876, Dixon replacing him as chairman of the School Board, a post he filled with much distinction. Chamberlain's unopposed election marked the beginning of an unbroken career of thirty-eight years representing Birmingham. At Westminster Chamberlain led a small band of Radicals. Recognizing the need to shake off the taint of militant sectarianism, he wound up the NEL and in May 1877 convened a meeting of delegates in Birmingham to found the National Liberal Federation (NLF). A notable *coup* was to secure the presence of Gladstone, and Chamberlain ensured that he received a rapturous welcome. The NLF was the national extension of the caucus and was Birmingham-dominated. As president, Chamberlain claimed the Liberal general election of 1880 as a victory won by the NLF.[62]

The Birmingham Conservative Association meanwhile was struggling to establish itself. In 1877, on the model of the caucus, the '300' was born and in the election of 1880 the BCA managed to field two candidates, the larger-than-life soldier and travel writer Captain Burnaby and the heir to the Calthorpe estate, the tongue-tied A.C.G Calthorpe.[63] Burnaby's combative efforts invigorated the Tories, but the three Liberals – Bright, Muntz and Chamberlain – were safely returned.

Bright's patronage secured Chamberlain's appointment as president of the Board of Trade in Gladstone's second administration. His tenure of office was relatively undistinguished in legislative terms but furnished him with valuable experience. In the run-up to the election of 1885 he launched a series of inflammatory reform proposals, dubbed 'the Unauthorised Programme'.

The main achievement of this administration was the passage of the Third Reform Act (1884), followed by a Re-distribution of Seats Act, largely abolishing the list system of election. Birmingham received four extra seats and was divided into seven constituencies. The Liberals won all seven contests in 1885, in spite of a vigorous Tory challenge headed by Lord Randolph Churchill.

For the first time Free Trade vs. Fair Trade was a serious issue, but this was dwarfed by the problem of Anglo-Irish relations. Chamberlain joined Gladstone's third administration as president of the Local Government Board in January 1886, but resigned in March when Gladstone declared his intention of legislating for Irish Home Rule. The resulting crisis was seminal for British politics and profound in its effect on Birmingham. Chamberlain, up to that time an advocate of land and local government

Birmingham Borough Council presented this elaborately bound illuminated address to Joseph Chamberlain to memorialize his period as mayor of the town between 1873 and 1876.
By permission of the Cadbury Research Library: Special Collections, University of Birmingham

The illuminated address presented to Joseph Chamberlain also records the council's thanks for his services to Birmingham.
By permission of the Cadbury Research Library: Special Collections, University of Birmingham

reform, was adamantly opposed to Irish independence. His resignation and his attempts to rally Radical opposition to the Irish Home Rule Bill placed him at the centre of the storm. Birmingham politics was thrown into turmoil and remained so for years.

Chamberlain's position was precarious but he persisted with his opposition to the Bill, which was defeated in June, with 93 Liberals voting against, at least two-thirds of whom were Whig followers of Lord Hartington. Parnell, famously but hardly objectively, labelled Chamberlain as 'the man who killed Home Rule'. It was now a question of mere survival. Chamberlain formed the National Radical Union, little more than 'a family and friends party', and relied heavily on the support of the Tory leaders, Salisbury and Balfour, who protected the Liberal Unionists against Tory vengeance. Chamberlain's main asset was that five of the seven Birmingham MPs shared his support of the Union and in the election of July 1886 were unopposed. Of the two Gladstonians, one (Broadhurst) fled the city while the other (Cook) was defeated by Chamberlain's close ally and friend, Jesse Collings. One seat was sacrificed to the Tories and was occupied by Henry Matthews, a protégé of Lord Randolph. Matthews became the first Tory to represent Birmingham since Spooner in 1844 and, appointed Home Secretary by Lord Salisbury, the first Catholic to sit in a British Cabinet.

Birmingham, therefore, was represented by seven Unionist MPs, but the situation remained unstable. In 1888 the Gladstonians captured the ward associations and Chamberlain responded by throwing in his lot with Hartington and concentrating his organizational skills on building up the Liberal Unionist Party. The first test came in March 1889 when John Bright's death necessitated a by-election in the Central Division. Rejecting Tory claims to the seat, Chamberlain brought forward Bright's eldest son, John Albert Bright, whose victory showed that Birmingham Unionism was no mirage. Between this key by-election and Chamberlain's death in 1914 Birmingham's parliamentary representation was monopolized by Unionists. It was an astonishing achievement and one fully acknowledged by Unionist Party leaders, who were content to leave west midland politics ('the Duchy') in Chamberlain's capable hands.[64] In 1895 Chamberlain entered Salisbury's Cabinet as Secretary of State for the Colonies. His advocacy of social reform was muted by political reality, and the Empire absorbed his energies. While espousing the platitudes of the age (the Anglo-Saxons as a great governing race) and not oblivious to the value of patriotic sentiment, Chamberlain's view of Empire was primarily materialist: the colonies were 'underdeveloped estates' and cried out for improvement on the Birmingham model.

His studies of imperial trade made him aware of the declining competitiveness of British industry and by the end of the 1890s Chamberlain had ceased to be a Free Trader. He had begun to explore the possibilities of imperial preference in discussions with colonial leaders at successive Colonial Conferences. This experience made him aware that this could not be done on a free trade basis. In the search for imperial profit, attention focused on South Africa, with its recently discovered diamond and gold deposits in the Boer Republic of the Transvaal. Chamberlain, having narrowly escaped disgrace over his alleged involvement in the Jameson Raid (December 1895), put pressure on the Boers, aided and abetted by his High Commissioner in South Africa, Sir Alfred Milner. In 1899 this precipitated a war labelled 'Joe's War' by Lord Salisbury.[65] After a series of ignominious British defeats,

A souvenir of Joseph Chamberlain's seventieth birthday celebrations in 1906. Shortly after the lavish civic festivities, Chamberlain suffered the stroke that ended his political career. He died in 1914.
By permission of the Cadbury Research Library: Special Collections, University of Birmingham

the Boer states were annexed in 1900. Chamberlain seized the opportunity, in an atmosphere of public and press jingoism, to urge the PM to dissolve Parliament. 'Joe's election' had the desired result – a slightly increased Unionist majority.[66] Confounding expectations, the Boers did not surrender and launched a destructive guerrilla war. By the time peace was made in May 1902 imperialism was past its peak and the Unionist government discredited, though Chamberlain, in contrast to his fellow ministers, largely escaped censure.

By the time that Salisbury retired in July 1902, giving way to his nephew Arthur Balfour, Chamberlain was in a negative frame of mind, depressed by the government's Education Act, which alienated many nonconformists, the prospect of coming electoral defeat and the decline of his own influence in Cabinet. He was ready for a new departure, a new 'Unauthorised Programme', and it came in a speech in Birmingham on 15 May 1903, which marked the start of the tariff reform campaign. In September he resigned to concentrate his formidable energies on this cause. Tariff reform was well received by midlands industrialists but opposed by other powerful interest groups. Fatally, Chamberlain failed to win over

organized labour, split his party and sparked a Liberal revival. In the 1906 election the Unionist Party suffered a humiliating defeat, only Birmingham and, to a lesser extent, the West Midlands responding positively to tariff reform. In July 1906, after remarkable birthday celebrations in Birmingham, Chamberlain suffered a stroke and was incapacitated until his death in 1914. Tariff reform was the legacy he handed to his political heir, Austen Chamberlain (1863–1937).[67] It proved a heavy burden.[68]

The BLA met humiliating electoral defeat in 1892 and 1895 and went into steep decline. While it retained the loyalty of elite families such as the Cadburys, Tangyes and Oslers, it failed to recruit a new generation of members.[69] In its weakness it reached out to organized labour, a number of whose leaders sought representative status. The most powerful trade union leader in Birmingham was W.J. Davis, president of the Brassworkers' Society. Chamberlain's patronage secured him membership of the School Board in 1873 and the town council in 1876 but, following the Liberal split in 1886, he remained a Gladstonian. In 1892 he stood for Parliament, unsuccessfully, as a 'Lib-Lab'. Other prominent 'Lib-Labs' were Eli Bloor (Glassworkers) and J.V. Stevens (Tinplate Workers). Both were elected to the city council, Stevens spectacularly defeating Austen Chamberlain in 1889. Bloor also stood for Parliament in 1892 but lost his council seat in the same year.

The Lib-Labs sought the endorsement of the Birmingham Trades Council (BTC) but opinion within the Council was divided once socialist societies emerged to seek independent labour representation.[70] The most influential of these societies in the 1880s was the Social Democratic Federation (SDF), eclipsed in the following decade by the Independent Labour Party (ILP). Securing representation proved to be an uphill struggle. John Haddon (SDF) sought election to the council five times between 1887 and 1889, only to be defeated on each occasion. In 1897 Robert Toller (Gasworkers) was elected for Saltley, becoming the city's first Labour councillor to be elected without Liberal support.[71] In the general election of 1892 both Davis and Bloor stood unsuccessfully as 'Lib-Labs'. Some consolation came in the following year in the form of appointments to the magistracy of Bloor and William Gulliver, the first president and later secretary of the BTC. In the general election of 1906 John Stevens ('Lib-Lab') put up an impressive but losing performance in East Birmingham against Sir Benjamin Stone and was defeated again in December 1910. Bruce Glasier (ILP) and James Holmes (Railway Servants' Union) were also defeated in 1906 and two Labour candidates, J.J. Stephenson and Fred Hughes of the Birmingham Socialist Centre, were defeated in January 1910. In 1914, in a city council of 120 members, a mere six identified themselves as Socialists and nine were 'Lib-Labs'. The council also included three women, the first two elected in 1911. The Unionist stronghold proved unassailable in spite of the fact that the BTC had a large membership and was one of the first to affiliate to the Labour Representation Committee (1900), which became the Labour Party (1906). The weakness of trade unionism in Birmingham can be traced to the absence of a single dominating union and the proliferation of smaller unions, which made combined action difficult even if consensus could be arrived at.

The struggle of labour for recognition in the electoral system was matched by that of women, who were expressly denied the vote in the Great Reform Act. By the latter half of the century their right to vote and to be members of School Boards and Boards of Guardians was acknowledged, but their claim to vote in parliamentary elections, let alone sit in Parliament, was repeatedly rejected in spite of the efforts of MPs such as John Stuart Mill and Sir Charles Dilke, who persuaded both Chamberlain and Bright to vote in favour in 1878 – votes they both later regretted. Women's agitation for the right to vote took organized form in the wake of the Second Reform Act, but the great majority of suffragists were middle class and their approach non-violent.

Edward Steel Harper II (1878–1951), *Portrait of Mrs Alfred C. Osler* (1917–18, oil on canvas). Osler was an energetic campaigner for votes for women and a member of one of Birmingham's leading manufacturing families.
© Birmingham Museums & Art Gallery/Bridgeman Images

Everything changed in 1903 with the formation of the Women's Social and Political Union (WSPU) by the formidable Pankhursts. In the face of repeated rejections, the women's movement turned violent.

In 1909 the wave of violence reached Birmingham. On 17 September Prime Minister Asquith came to the city to make two speeches in defence of Lloyd George's People's Budget. When he arrived at Bingley Hall for a meeting, with Arthur Chamberlain in the chair, he was met with a barrage of roof-tiles thrown from a neighbouring building by two suffragettes. A series of violent actions culminated with a final attack on the PM as he left New Street station. Ten suffragettes were arrested and were subjected to force-feeding in Winson Green prison. In the two years before war broke out there was a tide of violence, including arson which destroyed the Carnegie Library at Northfield, window smashing, attacks on the cathedral and the slashing of a painting by Romney in the art gallery by Bertha Ryland, a relation of the Lord Mayor. Among Birmingham MPs, Austen Chamberlain was a leading opponent of women's suffrage, though Leo Amery offered support.[72]

The best-governed city

In the years following Ralph's enthusiastic description there was a loss of momentum in civic policy making, which reflected tougher economic conditions. As Asa Briggs wrote: 'what had occurred was a loss of faith in an adventurous policy of civic development. Politics became more cautious and horizons narrowed.'[73] The council, ignoring criticisms of the destruction wrought in realizing the Improvement Scheme, remained opposed to municipal house building and only with reluctance embarked on minor developments. It also lagged behind other local authorities in the municipalization of electricity supply and transport, critics suggesting that the city's motto 'Forward' could more appropriately be replaced by 'Backward'. In 1892, however, the city embarked on a long-term plan to bring Welsh water the seventy miles from the Elan Valley to Birmingham. Not completed until 1904, the scheme was a magnificent achievement, the reservoirs and dams of great architectural quality. Ironically Chamberlain, reflecting the prevailing sense of pessimism about the economic prospects of the region, counselled against it because of its impact on the borough debt.[74] Fortunately he was ignored, but he made an important contribution to the city by his initiative in converting Mason College into the University of Birmingham. Although it continued to show reluctance to build houses, the council, under the leadership of J.S. Nettlefold (1866–1930), the son-in-law of Arthur Chamberlain, placed itself in the forefront of the movement for town planning.[75] When Nettlefold lost his Edgbaston seat in 1911, having opposed his uncle's tariff reform scheme, the baton was picked up by his cousin Neville Chamberlain (1869–1940),[76] who succeeded him as chairman of the Housing and Town Planning committee and continued with his plans for zoning the city. The Greater Birmingham Act of 1911 was a notable *coup*. The physical size of the city was more than doubled and its population increased from 520,000 to 840,000. On the eve of the First World War, the city council was in robust health.

The construction in the late nineteenth century of the Elan Valley dams, reservoir and pipeline to Birmingham was a major civic and engineering achievement for Birmingham Corporation.

Harrington Mann's portrait of Joseph Chamberlain, the first Chancellor of the University of Birmingham, painted in about 1900. Chamberlain played a major role in fundraising for the newly established university.

Required to steer the city through the myriad changes wrought by the war, Birmingham City Council proved admirably efficient: among its many tasks were the compiling of a National Register, the introduction of food and fuel rationing in advance of a central government scheme and coping with refugees in conjunction with the Birmingham Citizens' Committee. Meanwhile, the loss of 150,000 adult males to the armed services did not preclude a massive contribution by Birmingham industries to war production.[77]

While the war brought Austen Chamberlain into the War Cabinet in 1915, in Birmingham it was Neville who was proving to be Joe's true heir. Rooted in Birmingham business (Elliott's Metal, Hoskins, BSA), he progressed from councillor in 1911 to alderman in 1914 and Lord Mayor in 1915. His unhappy spell as director of National Service in Lloyd George's coalition government from December 1916 to August 1917 confirmed his deep distrust of the PM and of the ways of Westminster. Resignation saw him return to Birmingham as Deputy Lord Mayor. Ample evidence that he had inherited his father's Radical instincts included the establishment of the city's unique Municipal Bank and the consolidation of the city's musical tradition through the establishment of the CBSO. Austen, who moved from Highbury to 11 Downing Street in 1903 and was never again resident in Birmingham, remained the Unionist figurehead but it was Neville who took control. His appetite for politics whetted by what he felt to be his dismal failure in government, he assumed leadership of the combined Unionist Party (BCUA) and cast around for a parliamentary seat. Meanwhile, he concentrated his energies on restoring the Unionist machine to its pre-war efficiency. The Liberal Party, split between Lloyd George and Asquith, remained in the doldrums while the Labour Party bore the scars of wartime division between pacifists and 'patriots'. It was no surprise that, with the end of the war in November 1918, the coalition government led by Lloyd George won an overwhelming endorsement from the electorate, now expanded to include women over 30.[78]

BRITAIN'S FIRST MUNICIPAL SAVINGS BANK

The Romance of a Great Achievement

J. P. HILTON

In 1916 Birmingham's Municipal Savings Bank was created to raise money for the war effort by attracting savers to invest. It was a major civic achievement of Neville Chamberlain as Lord Mayor of Birmingham. His scheme was supported by the local socialist politician Eldred Hallas, who later became the town's first Labour MP.
Private Collection

Between the wars

The re-casting of the electoral system added five additional constituencies to Birmingham's seven and all 12 returned Unionists with unassailable majorities; Neville in Ladywood, Austen in West Birmingham. The most intriguing result came in Duddeston which elected Eldred Hallas, an official of the Municipal Workers' Union. With a background in the ILP and Labour Party, Hallas had a claim to be the city's first Labour MP. However, the circumstances were peculiar. Hallas and W.J. Davis were leading members of a patriotic labour organization, the British Workers'

A triptych of Oswald Mosley campaigning as Labour candidate in the Smethwick by-election of 1926. Mosley had a varied political career. Initially a Unionist MP, in 1918 he defected to Labour and pursued a radical agenda for economic and social reform. In that year he unsuccessfully contested Birmingham Ladywood, but was elected for Smethwick in 1926. He left Labour and set up the New Party in 1931, which became the British Union of Fascists in 1932. By permission of the Cadbury Research Library: Special Collections, University of Birmingham

League. Hallas had given Neville Chamberlain stalwart support in his campaign to establish the Municipal Bank. Duddeston was his reward. The pull of Labour, however, proved too strong and within a year Hallas crossed the floor of the House. In 1922 he stood down, to be replaced by E.V. Hiley, former town clerk and ally of Neville Chamberlain.[79]

In the Lloyd George coalition Austen Chamberlain was a reluctant Chancellor of the Exchequer. With economy and society in disarray and the National Debt ten times its pre-war level, this was a poisoned chalice, which he gratefully surrendered in March 1921 when his party leader, Bonar Law, was forced to retire through ill health, Austen taking his place. Mutual distrust between Lloyd George and Austen had dissipated, Austen becoming convinced that the 'Welsh wizard' was the indispensable national leader and a bulwark against socialism. Austen's loyalty to Lloyd George led him to spurn opportunities to become PM and provoked the famous party revolt against him at the Carlton Club on 19 October 1922, which brought an end to the coalition. Both Lloyd George and Austen resigned. Bonar Law returned to assume the leadership of the party and the premiership and to call a general election, the first of three in three years. Neville's fortunes were to take a dramatic turn. While Austen stood aloof, Neville found himself valued by both Bonar Law and his successor in 1923, Stanley Baldwin, and in quick succession Neville filled the offices of Postmaster General, Minister of Health and, briefly, Chancellor of the Exchequer. The glittering prize which Austen had spurned now lay within Neville's reach.

In the stutter of the three elections, the Unionist machine in Birmingham once again proved itself the most efficient in the country. With full-time agents in each constituency, a female agent to concentrate on female recruitment and the backing of Sir Charles Hyde's formidable newspapers, the *Post* and *Mail*, it dwarfed the fading Liberal Party and the impoverished Labour Party which, in contrast, had only one full-time agent which it shared with the Trades Council, and the support of the weekly *Town Crier*, the circulation of which never exceeded 2,000.[80] The result was the maintenance of the Unionist monopoly. Nevertheless the BLP was making progress. Its share of the vote rose from 22 per cent in 1918 to 38 per cent in 1924. In the election of that year it won its first parliamentary seat, a trade union official, Bob Dennison, defeating Sir Herbert Austin in the King's Norton division, while Neville Chamberlain survived the challenge of Oswald Mosley (1896–1980) in Ladywood by a mere 77 votes. In Mosley the BLP had found a new and charismatic leader, who, like Churchill in the 1880s, sought a quick route to fame by attacking the Birmingham stronghold.

Mosley, the son of a Staffordshire baronet, had served in the army and the Royal Flying Corps. In 1918 he had been elected Unionist MP for Harrow but had revolted against the coalition government over its policy of 'meeting terror with terror' in Ireland. In 1924 he defected to the Labour Party. After losing Ladywood, in 1926 Mosley won a by-election in Smethwick and continued the work of galvanizing the Labour Party in the area.[81]

Meanwhile, Joe's successors were installed in key positions in Baldwin's second government – Austen as Foreign Secretary and Neville as Minister of Health, arguably the outstanding members of the government of 1924–29. While Austen negotiated what was considered at the time to be the diplomatic triumph at Locarno, Neville piloted a remarkable programme of social and local government reforms.[82] Two other Birmingham MPs, Sir Arthur Steel-Maitland and Leo Amery, were also members of Baldwin's Cabinet, marking a peak of Birmingham influence in government.

During the General Strike (3–12 May 1926), Birmingham workers surprised trade union officials by the 'completeness of the response'.[83] The changing structure

Extracts from the front page of Birmingham Labour Party's *Town Crier* newspaper, published on 30 April 1926, immediately before the start of the General Strike.
By permission of the Cadbury Research Library: Special Collections, University of Birmingham

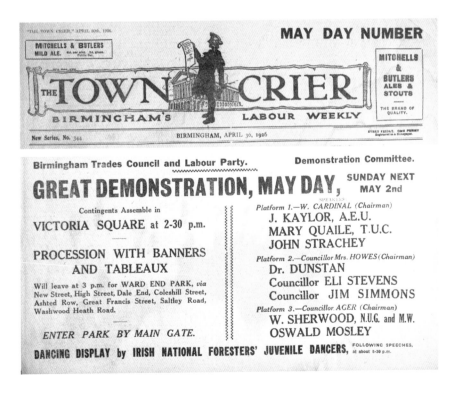

of Birmingham industry was proving favourable to union recruitment and 'for the first time in the history of the city large numbers of Birmingham workmen acted as a class'.[84] Anger generated by the prosecution of trade union leaders and incidents of victimization encouraged the BLP to look to a brighter future. Mosley had subsidized the *Town Crier* and channelled funds to each of Labour's candidates. Above all, he excited crowds with his platform bravura. Oliver Locker-Lampson, MP for Handsworth, had the temerity to debate with Mosley in the Rag Market on 13 May 1929. He suffered humiliation, the *Town Crier* reporting that he had been 'rolled in the dust'. 1929 proved to be the BLP's *annus mirabilis* and seemed to mark the demise of Birmingham 'exceptionalism'. Ironically, the Unionists regained King's Norton, but the BLP seized six of Birmingham's 12 seats, mainly in the inner city. The result that most shocked the Unionists was Austen Chamberlain's narrow squeak, by 43 votes, in West Birmingham. Mosley's efforts earned him a place in Ramsay Macdonald's second Labour government as Chancellor of the Duchy of Lancaster with special responsibility for unemployment, which was rising alarmingly. Within weeks he was at odds with his colleagues. His plans, embodied in the Mosley Memorandum, were rejected in Cabinet and then by the Parliamentary Labour Party. He appealed to the party conference at Llandudno where once again his proposals were rejected, though by a narrow majority. Mosley's association with Labour was over. He resigned in February 1931, going on to form the New Party and later the British Union of Fascists.[85]

These events and the economic crisis, for which Macdonald's government had no answers, dealt a devastating blow to the BLP. In the general election of October 1931 Labour suffered humiliation. All 12 Birmingham seats reverted to the Unionists with huge majorities. Amid violent scenes, the New Party candidates polled less than 1,000 votes and lost their deposits. This result was replicated in 1935, in the last general election for a decade. Birmingham 'exceptionalism' had been restored. Both Chamberlains returned to office, Austen briefly as First Lord of the Admiralty, while Neville was quickly promoted to Chancellor of the Exchequer and in May 1937 succeeded Baldwin as PM. Austen's hopes of returning to the Foreign Office had been thwarted by Baldwin but from the backbenches he became the chief spokesman of those warning against the deteriorating international situation and the threat posed by Hitler's Germany. 'His last years,' wrote his biographer, 'were among the most fruitful and distinguished in his career.'[86] Austen's death in March 1937 was a loss to his country at a critical time.

The BLP, having suffered in October 1931 'the most crushing defeat ever inflicted on a political party in this country', endured further humiliation in the municipal elections in November, its representation on the city council reduced to barely a quarter of its composition.[87] This proportion did not improve significantly during the remainder of the decade, by which time the membership of the council had increased to 136.

Domination of the council by the BCUA throughout the inter-war years did not imply stagnation. The Radicalism injected into Unionism by 'the Chamberlain tradition' was never entirely absent. In education, medical services, transport and housing Birmingham's record was progressive. In these years Birmingham built more than 100,000 houses; even Walter Greenwood, Labour Minister of Health,

Sir James Gunn's 1938 painting of Neville Chamberlain as prime minister, a replica of the original which hangs in the Carlton Club in London. Chamberlain was an authoritative PM until his career ended with the outbreak of the Second World War.
© The University of Birmingham Research and Cultural Collections

acknowledged that the city was in the forefront of planning and construction. Although the council always retained a bias towards private ownership, to facilitate which had been a major objective of the Municipal Bank, it built 50,000 municipal houses, more than any other local authority, in well-planned estates away from the city centre.[88] Long before Margaret Thatcher, Birmingham pioneered the right to buy. A serious problem of rundown back-to-backs and terraces in central districts persisted. The complimentary analysis of Birmingham's local government made by Julian Ralph in 1890 remained valid.

It was to the chagrin of Neville Chamberlain, an archetypal Victorian paternalist employer and the most successful social reformer of the inter-war years, that his energies as PM were diverted into foreign policy.[89] Whatever criticisms can be made of Chamberlain, he, more than any other leading politician, was responsible for the rearmament on which Britain embarked in earnest in 1936, at a time when much public opinion was beguiled by fantasies of security based on the League of Nations. While he pursued peace with the dictators, a leading historian of the period commented that he 'never failed in vigilance for the defence of Britain'.[90] Winston Churchill praised his role in promoting rearmament, though demanding a higher tempo. Chamberlain insisted on priority being given to the RAF, which arguably saved Britain in 1940. His critics then and since criticized his reluctance to rearm at a faster rate, and his concession of Czechoslovakia to Hitler in the Munich Treaty of September 1938 has, in spite of efforts at revisionism, been consistently condemned.[91]

At the time, the Munich Treaty raised Chamberlain to the pinnacle of international popularity. Leo Amery, MP for Sparkbrook and a critic of Chamberlain, found his constituents 'delirious with enthusiasm'. But Munich, contemptuously violated by Hitler in March 1939, ultimately savaged his reputation. Amery was not the only Birmingham MP critical of the policies pursued. The most outspoken was the recently elected MP for King's Norton, Ronald Cartland.[92] Cartland died at Dunkirk in 1940, by which time Churchill had replaced Chamberlain as PM. Neville Chamberlain died of cancer in November 1940 and with him into the grave went Birmingham 'exceptionalism'. 'With his passing the name of Chamberlain virtually disappeared from Birmingham's affairs.'[93]

Conclusion

Much evidence supports the dominant interpretation of Birmingham's political history: the interlocking economic and social power of an elite which, reinforced by relatively benign labour relations, produced firm leadership, epitomized above all by the Chamberlain dynasty, and long periods of near-monopolistic party domination in the nineteenth and twentieth centuries: first, Liberal/Radical followed by Unionist. This interpretation has been challenged as underplaying or obscuring the conflicts of interests, of class, of ideology which one would expect to find in a city as large and as diverse as Birmingham. The result has been a rich and varied body of historical interpretation.

Council House, Birmingham.

An early twentieth-century postcard of the Council House, home of Birmingham's civic government.
By permission of Mary Harding

Notes

1 J. Money, *Experience and Identity. Birmingham in the West Midlands 1760–1800* (Manchester, 1977), 275.

2 For a challenge to the association of Birmingham with radicalism, see D. Leighton, 'Municipal progress, democracy and radical identity in Birmingham, 1838–1886', *Midland History*, 25 (2000), 115–42.

3 W. Hutton, *A History of Birmingham* (Birmingham, 1783), 328.

4 Hutton's view, though persuasive and much reproduced, has met with scepticism among more recent historians, for example E. Hopkins, *Birmingham. The First Manufacturing Town in the World* (London, 1989), 100–1.

5 C. Gill, *History of Birmingham Vol.1. Manor and Borough* (Oxford, 1952), 73.

6 Gill, *History of Birmingham*, 144–7; and J. Stevenson, *Popular Disturbances in England 1700–1832* (London, 1992), 174–7. J. Atherton, 'Rioting, dissent and the Church in late eighteenth century Britain: the Priestley Riots of 1791' (PhD Thesis, University of Leicester, 2014), is the most thorough exploration of the causes, nature and aftermath of the riots.

7 Gill, *History of Birmingham*, 154–99. See also D. Fraser, *Power and Authority in the Victorian City* (Oxford, 1979); A. Peers, *Birmingham Town Hall: An Architectural History* (Farnham, 2012), 11–37.

8 R.B. Rose, 'Political history to 1832', in W.B. Stephens (ed.), *The Victoria History of the Counties of England. Vol. VII: The City of Birmingham* (London, 1964), 270–98, http://www.british-history.ac.uk/vch/warks/vol7/ (accessed 31 December 2015). For a discussion of 'grassroots' politics in this period, see J. Money, 'Taverns, coffee houses and clubs: local politics and popular articulacy in the Birmingham area, in the age of the American Revolution', *The Historical Journal*, 4.1 (1971), 15–47.

9 D. Cannadine, *Lords and Landlords: The Aristocracy and the Towns 1774–1967* (Leicester, 1980), 149–51.

10 G.H. Wright, *Chronicles of the Birmingham Chamber of Commerce 1813–1913 & of the Birmingham Commercial Society 1783–1812* (Birmingham, 1913).

11 Hopkins, *Birmingham*, 43–50; C. Behagg, 'Attwood, Thomas (1783–1856)', *Oxford Dictionary of National Biography* (hereafter *ODNB*) (Oxford University Press, 2004), online edn, http://www.oxforddnb.com/view/article/878 (accessed 7 December 2015).

12 J. Uglow, *In These Times. Living in Britain through Napoleon's Wars 1793–1815* (New York, 2014), 444–54.

13 D. Read, *The English Provinces c.1760–1960: A Study in Influence* (London, 1964), 57.

14 A. Webster, *The Twilight of the East India Company. Anglo-Asian Commerce & Politics 1790–1830* (Woodbridge, 2009).

15 D.J. Moss, *Thomas Attwood. The Biography of a Radical* (Montreal and Kingston, 1990); and Moss, 'A study in failure: Thomas Attwood, M.P. for Birmingham, 1832–1839', *Historical Journal*, 21.3 (1978), 545–70.

16 S. Thomas, 'Edmonds, George (1788–1868)', *ODNB*, online edn, http://www.oxforddnb.com/view/article/74226 (accessed 6 December 2015).

17 E. Pearce, *Reform! The Fight for the 1832 Reform Act* (London, 2003), 4–7.

18 R.W. Davis, 'Scholefield, Joshua (1774/5–1844)', *ODNB*, online edn, http://www.oxforddnb.com/view/article/24814 (accessed 7 December 2015).

19 S. Timmins, 'Muntz, George Frederick (1794–1857)', rev. Matthew Lee, *ODNB*, online edn, http://www.oxforddnb.com/view/article/19551 (accessed 7 December 2015).

20 See N. LoPatin, 'Ritual, symbolism and radical rhetoric: political unions and political identity in the age of parliamentary reform', *Journal of Victorian Culture*, 3.1 (1998), 1–29.

21 R. Ward, *City-State and Nation. Birmingham's Political History 1830–1940* (Chichester, 2005), 20–32.

22 C. Flick, *The Birmingham Political Union and the Movements for Reform in Britain 1830–1839* (Hamden, CT, and Folkestone, 1978), 12–16; and Hopkins, *Birmingham*. See also N. LoPatin, *Political Unions, Popular Politics, and the Great Reform Act of 1832* (London and New York, 1999).

23 Moss, *Thomas Attwood*; and Pearce, *Reform!*, 4–7.

24 A. Fraser, *Perilous Question. The Drama of the Great Reform Bill 1832* (London, 2013), 277.

25 C. Behagg, *Politics and Production in the Early Nineteenth Century* (London and New York, 1990); and Behagg, 'Custom, class and change: the trade societies of Birmingham', *Social History*, 4.3 (1979), 455–80. See also D. Smith, *Conflict and Compromise. Class Formation in English Society 1830–1914. A Comparative Study of Birmingham and Sheffield* (London, 1982).

26 G. Barnsby, *Birmingham Working People. A History of the Labour Movement in Birmingham 1650–1914* (Wolverhampton, 1990); and Barnsby, *Socialism in Birmingham and the Black Country 1850–1939* (Wolverhampton, 1998).

27 A. Briggs, *Victorian Cities* (London, 1963), 184–8; Briggs, *History of Birmingham Vol. 2. Borough & City 1865–1938* (Oxford, 1952); E. Hopkins, 'Birmingham during the Industrial Revolution: class conflict or class co-operation?', in L. Kriesberg, M.Dobkowksi and I. Wallimann (eds), *Research in Social Movements, Conflict & Change. Volume 16* (Greenwich, CT, and London, 1993), 16, 117–37; and T. Tholfsen, 'The artisan and the culture of early Victorian Birmingham', *University of Birmingham Historical Journal*, 4 (1954), 146–66.

28 For the relationship between the BPU and Chartism, see C. Behagg 'An alliance with the middle class: the Birmingham Political Union and early Chartism', in J. Epstein and D. Thompson (eds.), *The Chartist Experience* (London, 1982), 59–86.

29 For the events of 1839, see T. Tholfsen, 'The Chartist crisis in Birmingham', *Chartism International Review of Social History*, 3.3 (1958), 461–80.

30 Behagg sees the events of July 1839 as proof of class divisions in the town: 'the middle class radicals after a

brief flirtation with the principle of universal suffrage turned on the Chartists with appalling ferocity'. Behagg, *Politics and Production*, 17.

31 M. Weaver, 'The Birmingham Bull Ring riots of 1839: variations on a theme of class conflict', *Social Science Quarterly*, 78.1 (1997), 137–48; see also D.M. Taylor, 'To the Bull Ring! Politics, protest and policing in Birmingham during the early Chartist period' (MA thesis, University of Birmingham, 2013).

32 Ward, *City-State*, 39–40. For Attwood and incorporation, see N.C. Edsall, 'Varieties of radicalism: Attwood, Cobden and the local politics of municipal incorporation', *The Historical Journal*, 16.1 (1973), 93–107.

33 See N. Lo Patin, '"With all my oldest and native friends". Joseph Parkes: Warwickshire solicitor and electoral agent in the age of reform', *The Parliamentary History Yearbook* (2008), 96–108; P.J. Salmon, 'Parkes, Joseph (1796–1865)', *ODNB*, online edn, http://www.oxforddnb.com/view/article/21356 (accessed 7 December 2015).

34 E.P. Hennock, *Fit and Proper Persons: Ideal and Reality in Nineteenth Century Urban Government* (London, 1973), 10–14.

35 Gill, *History of Birmingham*, 214–71. For the early years of the council, see also A. Briggs, 'Social structure and politics in Birmingham and Lyons (1825–1848)', *The British Journal of Sociology*, 1.1 (1950), 67–80.

36 J.T. Bunce, *History of the Corporation of Birmingham Vol. 1* (Birmingham, 1878), 174.

37 Ibid., 297.

38 For the Economists, see S.G. Checkland, 'The Birmingham Economists, 1815–1850', *The Economic History Review*, NS, 1.1 (1948), 1–19.

39 R. Ward, 'Joseph Allday. Scapegoat for municipal backwardness', *Birmingham Historian*, 32 (2008), 18–22.

40 Hennock, *Fit and Proper Persons*, 106–11. For the mid-Victorian period, see also Leighton, 'Municipal progress'.

41 S. Roberts, *The Chartist Prisoners. The Radical Lives of Thomas Cooper (1805–1892) and Arthur O'Neil (1819–1896)* (Bern, 2008).

42 A. Tyrell, *Joseph Sturge and the Moral Radical Party in Early Victorian Britain* (Bromley, 1987); Tyrrell, 'Sturge, Joseph (1793–1859)', *ODNB*, online edn, http://www.oxforddnb.com/view/article/26746 (accessed 7 December 2015).

43 Ward, *City-State*, 34–7.

44 Ibid., 5.

45 B. Cash, *John Bright. Statesman, Orator, Agitator* (London and New York, 2012), 259–62. P.T. Marsh, *Joseph Chamberlain. Entrepreneur in Politics* (New Haven, CT, and London, 1994), 153; and M. Taylor, 'Bright, John (1811–1889)', *ODNB*, online edn, http://www.oxforddnb.com/view/article/3421 (accessed 7 December 2015).

46 V.E. Chancellor, 'Dixon, George (1820–1898)', *ODNB*, online edn, http://www.oxforddnb.com/view/article/7697 (accessed 7 December 2015); P. Ballard, 'Jaffray, Sir John, first baronet (1818–1901)', *ODNB*, online edn, http://www.oxforddnb.com/view/article/104637 (accessed 7 December 2015).

47 B. McGill, 'Francis Schnadhorst and Liberal Party Organization', *The Journal of Modern History*, 34.1 (1962), 19–39; E. Taylor, 'Schnadhorst, Francis (1840–1900)', rev., *ODNB*, online edn, http://www.oxforddnb.com/view/article/37938 (accessed 7 December 2015).

48 H.W. Crosskey, 'The Liberal Association, the "600" of Birmingham', *Macmillan's Magazine* (February 1877), in Ward, *City-State*, 62–5. For the caucus, see also T. Tholfsen, 'The origins of the Birmingham caucus', *The Historical Journal*, 2.2 (1959), 161–84.

49 R. Ward, '"Leader of a forlorn hope": Sampson Samuel Lloyd and Birmingham Conservatism', *West Midlands Studies*, 13 (1980), 34–9.

50 Hennock, *Fit and Proper Persons*, 61–79; and I. Sellers, 'Dawson, George (1821–1876)', *ODNB*, online edn, http://www.oxforddnb.com/view/article/7347 (accessed 7 December 2015).

51 S. Roberts and R. Ward, *Mocking Men of Power. Comic Art in Birmingham 1861–1911* (Birmingham, 2014)

52 P.T. Marsh, '"No one has the right to be happy in this brutal world": Joseph Chamberlain's first forty years', *History West Midlands: Joseph Chamberlain, Man, Politician and Icon*, 2.2 (2014), 9–13; R. Ward, '"Made in Birmingham": Joseph Chamberlain's early political career', *History West Midlands: Joseph Chamberlain, Man, Politician and Icon*, 2.2 (2014), 18–22.

53 J. Dixon, *Out of Birmingham. George Dixon (1820–98) Father of Free Education* (Studley, 2013). See also P. Auspos, 'Radicalism, pressure groups, and party politics: from the National Education League to the National Liberal Federation', *The Journal of British Studies*, 20.1 (1980), 184–204.

54 R. Tudur Jones, 'Dale, Robert William (1829–1895)', *ODNB*, online edn, http://www.oxforddnb.com/view/article/7015 (accessed 7 December 2015).

55 The best account of these events is to be found in Dixon, *Out of Birmingham*, 136–73. See also Auspos, 'Radicalism, pressure groups, and party politics'.

56 Marsh, *Joseph Chamberlain*, 58.

57 For a challenge to the belief in Liberal dominance in Birmingham's local politics, see C. Green, 'Birmingham's politics, 1873–1891: the local basis of change', *Midland History*, 2.2 (1973), 84–98.

58 Marsh, *Joseph Chamberlain*, 48–61; and T. Hunt, *Building Jerusalem. The Rise and Fall of the Victorian City* (London, 2004), 232–84.

59 C. Chinn, *Homes for People: 100 Years of Council Housing in Birmingham* (Birmingham, 1991), 4–5, and for inter-war developments, 37–74.

60 V. Skipp, *The Making of Victorian Birmingham* (Studley, 1983), 187.

61 J. Ralph, 'The best-governed city in the world, (Birmingham)', *Harper's New Monthly Magazine*, 81 (June/November 1890), 99–111.

62 Marsh, *Joseph Chamberlain*, 116–20.

63 R. Ward, 'Monumental soldier', in B. Hall (ed.), *Aspects of Birmingham* (Bradford, 2001), 120–30.

64 M.C. Hurst, *Joseph Chamberlain and West Midlands Politics 1886–1895*, Dugdale Society Occasional Papers,

15 (Oxford, 1962). For the development of local politics in this period, see I. Cawood, 'The Unionist "compact" in west midland politics 1891–1895', *Midland History*, 30.1 (2005), 92–111.

65 A. Roberts, *Salisbury. Victorian Titan* (London, 2000), 736–9.

66 R. Jay, *Joseph Chamberlain. A Critical Study* (Oxford, 1981), 248–9.

67 D.J. Dutton, 'Chamberlain, Sir (Joseph) Austen (1863–1937)', *ODNB*, online edn, http://www.oxforddnb.com/view/article/32351 (accessed 7 December 2015).

68 Marsh, *Joseph Chamberlain*, 581–631; and Ward, *City-State*, 155–77.

69 R. Ward, 'The strange death of Liberal Birmingham', *Journal of Liberal History*, 82 (2014), 16–25.

70 J. Corbett, *The Birmingham Trades Council 1866–1966* (Birmingham, 1966).

71 Barnsby, *Birmingham Working People*, 303.

72 Barnsby, *Birmingham Working People*, 373–80; P. Bartley, *Votes for Women 1860–1928* (London, 1998); Bartley, 'Moral regeneration: women and the civic gospel in Birmingham 1870–1914', *Midland History*, 25.1 (2000), 143–58; and N. Gauld, 'The fight for the vote', *History West Midlands: Breaking the Chains? Women in the West Midlands 1870–1945*, 2.4 (2014), 13–16.

73 Briggs, *History of Birmingham*, 89–91

74 Ward, *City-State*, 147.

75 G. Cherry, *Birmingham. A Study in Geography, History and Planning* (Chichester, 1994), 102–7; and M.F. James, 'Nettlefold, John Sutton (1866–1930)', *ODNB*, online edn, http://www.oxforddnb.com/view/article/101218 (accessed 7 December 2015).

76 A.J. Crozier, 'Chamberlain, (Arthur) Neville (1869–1940)', *ODNB*, online edn, http://www.oxforddnb.com/view/article/32347 (accessed 7 December 2015).

77 Briggs, *History of Birmingham*, 200–25

78 D. Dilks, *Neville Chamberlain, Vol.1 1869–1929* (Cambridge, 1984), 142–80.

79 R. Ward, 'Eldred Hallas, Birmingham's first Labour MP?', *The Birmingham Historian*, 33 (2009), 23–9; see also R. Ward, 'Hallas, Eldred (1870–1926)', *ODNB*, online edn, http://www.oxforddnb.com/view/article/105127 (accessed 6 December 2015).

80 P. Drake, 'The *Town Crier*, Birmingham's labour weekly', in A. Wright and R. Shackleton (eds), *Worlds of Labour. Essays in Birmingham's Labour History* (Birmingham, 1993), 103–26.

81 R. Skidelsky, *Oswald Mosley* (London, 1975); Skidelsky, 'Mosley, Sir Oswald Ernald, sixth baronet (1896–1980)', *ODNB*, online edn, http://www.oxforddnb.com/view/article/31477 (accessed 7 December 2015).

82 Dilks, *Neville Chamberlain*, 419–42.

83 R.P. Hastings, 'Aspects of the General Strike in Birmingham 1926', *Midland History*, 2.4 (1974), 250–73; see also *The Nine Days In Birmingham, The General Strike 4–12 May, 1926* (Birmingham, 1976).

84 R.P. Hastings, 'The Birmingham Labour movement 1918–1945', *Midland History*, 5.1 (1979), 78–92.

85 M. Pugh, *Hurrah for the Blackshirts. Fascists and Fascism in Britain between the Wars* (London, 2006).

86 D.J. Dutton, *Austen Chamberlain. Gentleman in Politics* (Bolton, 1985), 300.

87 *The Town Crier*, 30 October 1931.

88 Cherry, *Birmingham*, 112–24.

89 D.J. Dutton, *Neville Chamberlain* (London, 2001), 32–5

90 R.A.C. Parker, *Chamberlain and Appeasement. British Policy and the Coming of the Second World War* (London, 1993), 287.

91 R. Ward, *The Chamberlains. Joseph, Austen and Neville 1876–1940* (Oxford, 2015).

92 K. Olson, *Troublesome Young Men. The Rebels who Brought Churchill to Power in 1940 and Helped Save Britain* (New York, 1996), 15–20.

93 A. Sutcliffe and R. Smith, *History of Birmingham Vol. 3. Birmingham 1939–1970* (London, 1974), 14.

CHAPTER SEVEN

The Policy and Practice of Enlightened Education

RUTH WATTS

Birmingham's educational history from the later eighteenth century to the present day has been punctuated by periods of distinctive 'enlightened' education.[1] Both policy and practice have been shaped by gender, class, ethnicity and location. The expansion, urbanization and changing geography of the city, moreover, has provided the context that framed any initiatives, but was education in the town and city ever truly enlightened?

Enlightenment for a few? 'Lunaticks', radical educationalists and Birmingham's educational history, 1780–1868

Formal education and learning in England were permeated by class and gender considerations. The most reputable schooling was the classical education given in the few 'public' schools, which, despite their name, were by this period elitist institutions, largely restricted to the wealthy and privileged. Many of their students would go on to the only two English universities, the equally elitist Oxford and Cambridge. Endowed grammar schools, varying in efficacy and size (although most were small by later standards), offered a similar education to the middle ranks of society, usually as day schools. They too could lead to a university education. All of these were for boys only. Rich girls could scramble into some education, mostly at home, possibly at a fashionable boarding school. Education for the emergent middle classes was generally private, variable and often either of dubious quality or unavailable; that for the large majority of the population was sparse, usually very limited in both scope and duration and actually perceived as dangerous in the eyes of many of the powerful in society.

There was little formal education available for the young in the rapidly growing town of Birmingham in this period. For both boys and girls of the middle classes there were a range of private schools, often small and ephemeral. The nonconformist Birmingham and Edgbaston Proprietary School, situated at Five Ways on the Hagley Road from 1841, was one example that became a successful modern school for boys, though it offered classics also. For Anglican boys of the middling ranks[2] there was the King Edward VI Grammar School, but this had suffered a prolonged bleak period. The foundation authorized some elementary teaching for poor boys and girls but, despite some temporary reforms in the 1780s, the reputation of King Edward's had fallen very low – 'the worst school in England' according to Dr Jeune who became its head in 1831. His appointment and two successive Acts of Parliament enabled better administration and use of the foundation's lucrative funds to build a

Alfred H. Green (fl. 1844–62), *Ann Street School, Birmingham, 1855* (oil on canvas). Early elementary schooling is illustrated in Alfred Green's painting of Ann Street school. A Quaker-run school for children aged from 3 to 12 years, it opened in 1826. The site is now occupied by Birmingham's Council House.
© Birmingham Museums and Art Gallery/Bridgeman Images

The Proprietary School at Edgbaston was a successful modern school for boys. J. Handley's *Views and scenery of Birmingham*, published in 1874, illustrates its elegant buildings located at Five Ways on the Hagley Road, west of Birmingham.
By permission of the Cadbury Research Library: Special Collections, University of Birmingham

An old foundation reformed: the new Charles Barry-designed building for King Edward VI Grammar School for boys is captured by Charles Radclyffe in about 1840 as part of a busy street scene in *Views in Birmingham and its Vicinity*.
Courtesy of Newman University Library

new Grammar School (the Tudor Gothic building designed by Sir Charles Barry in New Street). The curriculum was extended and, with four elementary schools added, the school quickly was 'lifted … into the front rank … of English schools'.[3]

There were also some charity schools for the poor, in particular the Blue Coat Anglican charity school for both sexes (although girls were always a minority), and a Protestant dissenting charity school founded by Unitarians in 1760 for all denominations and, after 1813, exclusively for girls. It is difficult, however, to assess how much provision there was for the vast majority. As the town's population swiftly expanded, trebling in size between 1780 and 1833 to c.150,000, the education provided was generally inadequate both in extent and quality.[4] The chief growth was in Sunday schooling which steadily increased from 1784 until 1831, when 40 per cent of working-class children attended, largely those schools run by dissenters. This was lower than either Liverpool or London but somewhat ahead of other big towns and cities, although these large urban centres all lagged behind the national average.[5]

Between 1809 and 1813 four monitorial schools were founded by the Lancasterian (nonconformist) and National (Anglican) Societies which provided elementary schools for the working classes on religious lines. The Lancasterian School in Severn Street was as successful as such a school could be. Such developments gave opportunities to some working-class children, but even those who did attend often stayed no longer than a year, although they might supplement this by Sunday school and/or evening classes.[6] Further elementary schools were established, especially after 1833 when government grants became available to assist the religious societies build and provide for elementary schooling. Even so, in 1838, out of 55,000 children aged 5 to 15 in Birmingham, less than half attended any kind of school, and many of those who did went to private dame schools which might offer little scholastic education. The growth of government inspection and grants to elementary education and the expansion in numbers of schools, including those established by the growing number of Roman Catholics in Birmingham, meant that more children – 39 per

Birmingham & Midland Institution & Free Library.

Extended education for men and women: the Birmingham and Midland Institute and Free Library, illustrated here in Handley's *Views and scenery of Birmingham*, was one of a number of initiatives to improve the education of adults.
By permission of the Cadbury Research Library: Special Collections, University of Birmingham

JOSEPH PRIESTLEY. L.L.D: F.R.S.

Publish'd by J.Sewell Cornhill 1 Jan.ʸ 1791.

Joseph Priestley, scientist, nonconformist clergyman, political radical and member of the Lunar Society, was a particularly important educational reformer in the late eighteenth century. He lived in Birmingham from 1780 to 1791. This *Portrait of Joseph Priestley, LLD, FRS*, published in 1791, is from the Priestley Collection by Samuel Timmins.
By permission of the Library of Birmingham, MS 3004/11

cent in 1868–69 – experienced formal schooling, but for many it was of short duration. A large number were really illiterate. Evening schools, Sunday schools, ragged and reformatory schools supplied varying needs to some extent, while the Quakers and other dissenters set up adult Sunday schools. Other initiatives led eventually to the excellent Birmingham and Midland Institute in 1854, while colleges for men training for teaching, medicine and the ministry were opened. However, Birmingham, as elsewhere, was in need of educational reform and expansion.[7]

Within this picture, echoed to a greater or lesser extent throughout the country, there were significant pockets of enlightened thought and practice. Most Sunday schools in the late eighteenth century only taught simple Bible reading but the Old and New Meetings in Birmingham (ostensibly Presbyterian but in reality Rational Dissenting or Unitarian, then a proscribed form of Christianity), attracted many pupils because they were open to all and stressed a broad secular education and democratic organization. This radical thrust was not surprising considering the provenance of these developments. From 1780 the minister at the New Meeting was Joseph Priestley, already famed not only for his polemical theology but also as a leading scientist and a radical educational reformer. Influenced, like many dissenters, by John Locke, but even more so by David Hartley, whose work he propagated, Priestley stressed an associationist psychology which concluded that people were formed through individual associations and circumstances, not innate causes or divine intervention. All human beings, therefore, needed extensive intellectual education, suitable experience and rational reflection to attain moral, religious and intellectual progress.[8] The education should be scientific both in method and content, with empirical and experimental subjects such as modern history and natural philosophy (science), encouraged along with English literature – all new subjects in schools and higher education. Priestley's scientific and educational enthusiasm was shared by others in the small but vital Lunar Society of which he became a leading member. 'Lunaticks' such as James Watt, Matthew Boulton and Josiah Wedgwood were leading the Industrial Revolution, which excited Priestley; their explosive mixture of technological, scientific and artistic developments seemed to prove that they were mastering sources of knowledge in a way that would change and power the world. Members such as Erasmus Darwin, Thomas Day and Richard Edgeworth (together

Hazelwood School,
Birmingham, where Matthew
and Rowland Hill, the sons
of educational reformer
Thomas Wright Hill, offered
a radical, democratic and
modern education for
middle-class boys.
By permission of the Library of
Birmingham, WK-E1-414

with his daughter Maria), like Priestley, wrote educational books professing the 'enlightened' ideas that suffused their work, whether literary or industrial, and their living.[9]

Priestley and other Unitarians made further contributions to 'enlightened' education in Birmingham. From a society established in Priestley's time, the largely working-class teachers from the boys' schools of the Old and New Meetings formed a democratic Brotherly Society in 1796 which gave further education to ex-members of the boys' schools, all largely working class, and lectures on science and mechanics to factory workers. They also ran debates and their own scientific investigations. From this Society and those associated with it came the 'cast-iron philosophers' – artisans lectured to by Thomas Clark; Thomas Carpenter's Artisans Library; and the 'Philosophical Institution' of 1880–81. From these ventures emerged men who became well known in Birmingham, including the educational reformer Thomas Wright Hill who with his wife Sarah founded Hill-Top, a secondary school for boys. This led to Hazelwood School from 1819 to 1833, run by Hill's sons, principally Matthew who later became Recorder of Birmingham, and Rowland, later the founder of the penny post. The educational mix of practical, vocational and intellectual education that the Hill brothers had themselves received, underpinned by the educational teachings of Priestley and Maria Edgeworth, were the basis of the educational practice of the school, where a modern curriculum was taught through the association of ideas through drama, models, maps, illustrations, diagrams and practical methods, including oral teaching of languages. The school's organization, like its teaching, was designed to stimulate self-disciplined but energetic and entrepreneurial qualities and much pupil participation. Hazelwood, while outraging some, became a showpiece for those who wanted to reform middle-class education such as Jeremy Bentham, and educated many who were to be leading Birmingham inventors, scientists, local leaders and Liberal politicians.[10]

These developments and initiatives largely favoured men, with women included in theory but, in reality, only on the periphery, although Priestley's granddaughter, Catherine Finch, for example, later ran a school for girls where science was taught, including astronomy and conchology. Such progressive ideas were confined to a small proportion of the population, led by a group who became unpopular to the point of persecution in the conservative reaction to the French Revolution. Nevertheless, the late eighteenth century especially was a period which may be considered 'enlightened' in many respects. As elsewhere, informal education was supplied through local lectures, booksellers' shops, circulating libraries, book clubs, musical events and theatres. From 1821 Birmingham had its own Society of Arts which began to hold exhibitions and, very importantly, it was the home of the Baskerville press and a great manufactory for steel pens – a significant techno-logical improvement in communication. Yet it was not until the 1860s that the great developments in establishing a free library took place.[11]

Civic education? Birmingham's educational history, 1868–1902

This period was one of immense transformation in education in England. From the 1850s, movements for reform led to successive Royal Commissions and Acts of Parliament which reformed, expanded or stimulated change at all levels of education. Improvement and developments in kind, quality and number were urged, and often resisted, throughout the whole system – if that is not too kind a term for the somewhat chaotic proliferation of educational provision that emerged. Overall the result was greater educational opportunities for many disadvantaged groups, not least the poor, women and girls, although by the turn of the century the majority of the population still lacked anything like equal opportunities in education.

During this period, Birmingham won renown as a leader in educational and civic progress. Dominated by a liberal elite in which Quakers, Unitarians and other dissenters, women as well as men, played a prominent role, it was characterized by its 'civic gospel' which transformed Birmingham physically and intellectually. It was actually in the struggle for a national system of education that Birmingham first emerged as an enlightened leader.[12] Its Education Society of 1867 soon flourished at the centre of the National Education League, fighting for free, unsectarian and, eventually, compulsory elementary education for all, run locally and paid for by local rates. Such demands were partially met by the 1870 Education Act which empowered the ratepayers, both men and women, in each district to elect a School Board which, after what was already provided by the religious bodies and private schools was taken into account, should provide school places for all children in the area. Birmingham eagerly exploited what gains were granted, pre-empting later laws on compulsory schooling until the age of ten. Such initiatives accelerated when the largely noncon-formist Liberals won control of the new School Board from 1873. Under the successive chairmanship of the Unitarian Joseph Chamberlain and the Liberal Anglican George Dixon, Birmingham created a model School Board.[13] In 1876 Chamberlain proudly catalogued the Board's early achievements in providing extra places for the 22,263 children for whom there was no room in the private and provided provision of 1871. Chamberlain delightedly extolled the building of new schools and the Board's 'wise economy' of using well-chosen architects (the firm of Martin and Chamberlain – no relation) to construct solid, durable, 'inviting' buildings which were 'light, cheerful and airy'. They had spacious and well-ventilated separate classrooms and were outstanding for the size and character of their playgrounds.[14] These schools, indeed, were revolutionizing the urban landscape.

Chamberlain also praised the Board for having an ample number of liberally paid teachers and an efficient local inspectorate, and blamed the problems over collecting school fees on the 'excessive interference and centralisation' of the government's Education Department, which prevented 'universal free schools' as in other

Oozells Street school, one of the creations of the Birmingham School Board, exemplifies the state-of-the-art elementary schools that offered educational opportunities to children. The Ikon Gallery now occupies this Grade II listed building designed by the architectural partnership of Martin and Chamberlain. Courtesy of Marketing Birmingham

countries.[15] With compulsory schooling, school fees certainly became a huge burden on working-class parents, yet even after free elementary education was introduced from 1891, the parents' level of poverty still determined the quality of the school that the child was likely to attend.[16]

Nevertheless, the Board constantly expanded existing provision. It also gained schools from the Aston, King's Norton and Harborne School Boards when the city boundaries were extended in 1891. By 1900 a total of 56,868 children were being educated by the Birmingham School Board. In line with national developments, the elementary curriculum was extended, especially for those who stayed on at school, and special subjects were added to the basic curriculum. However, this was governed by gendered attitudes, boys being steered towards technical and scientific subjects while girls had compulsory needlework and could take various housewifery subjects. At the same time, Birmingham used existing and new legislation to establish special schools and evening schools and to make inroads into a public provision of quasi-secondary education. It established a male-orientated Municipal Technical College day school from 1897 and it made special provision for the extra education of pupil teachers – predominantly girls. From 1890 it set up a day training college for women elementary teachers. It was one of the few Boards to take advantage of grants from the Science and Art Department to develop higher-grade schools where maths, science and commerce, together with English, geography and French, could be studied by boys and girls who had achieved standard VI or VII and were able to take this ground-breaking opportunity. Significantly (and to the educational establishment's surprise), girls responded very positively to these developments, including maths. Nationally, however, stridently expressed fears over both rate funding and the 'pressure' of intellectual work, especially on girls, led to the 1902 Education Act which ended both the democratic School Boards and higher-grade schools.[17]

Birmingham shone in several other educational advances of this period, stimulated by national improvements stemming from Royal Commissions and Education Acts which reformed 'public' and endowed schooling, and by significant, although often much opposed or ignored, changes in girls' education, especially the opening up of the new public exams to them and the establishment of what was to become known as 'secondary' education.[18] In 1876 the liberal civic reformers established a non-sectarian, proprietary school for girls – Edgbaston High School. This was the first secondary school for girls in Birmingham and, despite the jeering of some, soon proved both its academic excellence and the way it could transform girls' lives. Offering a broad modern academic curriculum, many school activities (including a magazine), acting in plays, various musical and artistic activities, a garden and other clubs and even games (including cricket, to the derision of the local press), and, just as revolutionary, sensible school clothing, the school demonstrated that it was among the most progressive of this new type of school for girls.[19]

And it soon had a rival. The 1869 Endowed Schools Act enabled reforms of the King Edward's foundation for which nonconformists especially had been agitating, especially an opening up of the governing bodies on which a number of them now vigorously participated, and an extension of institutions and the numbers

On the blackboard:
a'b'c'd' is the elevation of a cube. Draw the plan, and a new elevation on a vertical plane making an angle of 45 with the

of youngsters educated by the foundation. From 1883 there were three grammar schools for boys, while the old Grammar School became the High School. Even more revolutionary was a high school and two grammar schools for girls.[20] King Edward VI High School for Girls (KEHSG) built up a strong academic tradition, stressed individual responsibility and social concern and tried to develop the potential of all pupils. It offered a range of activities including practical work such as a jewellery section. Both the girls' high schools soon engaged in the new university opportunities on offer to women. (The University of London opened degrees to women in 1878, while colleges offering degree courses, but not degrees, at Cambridge and Oxford had been emerging since 1868.) By 1893, for example, KEHSG was responsible for 6 per cent of all girls successful in the Cambridge tripos and 4 per cent of successful London BAs.[21]

The two girls' high schools owed much to their first headmistresses, Alice Cooper and Edith Creak, both of whom had taken advantage of the best of the new qualifications opening up for those who dared to become professional secondary school teachers. So had Margaret Nimmo, head of the new King Edward's Grammar School for Girls, whose school, although it had fewer resources, opened up even more opportunities to girls than the two high schools, since its fees were lower and, like the boys' grammar schools, 50 per cent of its pupils were either on remitted fees or on the foundation, thus making it possible for successful pupils from elementary

Birmingham was a pioneer in providing higher-grade schools for older elementary pupils. This girls' class at Waverley Road higher-grade school in 1896 shows that girls could study maths and science, when opportunities for girls to study these subjects were very limited.
By permission of the Library of Birmingham, WK-B11-5154

schools to attend. It is hard to convey the sheer novelty of all these developments and the refreshing openings they offered to Victorian girls, whether they were going into employment or likely to have a largely domestic life. From travelling on the school buses to the excitement of having the opportunity to attend a school headed by a woman with a degree, ex-scholars recalled the happy enthusiasm of daughters from the wealthier professional and business classes as well as the less well-off lower middle and upper working classes.[22]

The high schools, especially, were outstanding and unusual for the pioneering opportunities they offered to girls in the new scientific subjects, albeit chiefly biology and physiology rather than the physical sciences. KEHSG, for example, had some of the first highly qualified female science teachers, and many successful girls went on to university, usually Cambridge, to read science, some of whom became distinguished scientists themselves. Both high schools used the new Mason Science College to enable their girls to advance further. Founded by a local businessman and philanthropist, Josiah Mason, in 1880, Mason College was open to all. This gave women a chance of higher education, especially after the college's science and engineering curriculum expanded to meet the degrees of the Victoria and London universities.[23] Mary Sturge went from Edgbaston High to become one of the first four female scholars at Mason College, before going to London University to study medicine, eventually becoming one of Birmingham's early women doctors. Such women exemplified an impressive aspect of Birmingham's developments in secondary education. King Edward's Boys High School also had outstanding achievements in science, as perhaps could be expected from a town which prided itself on its industrial and technological standing.[24] Indeed, it was even more involved with Mason College, took more pupils, had better facilities and even greater success in science, a gendered aspect of life true of education at every level in Birmingham.[25] However, notwithstanding gendered and class differences, the authorities in Birmingham were proud of the fact that educational prospects were enlarging for all.

Mary Sturge was one of the first four female scholars at Mason Science College. She is pictured here in the November 1900 issue of *Edgbastonia*, the monthly magazine delivered to the homes of the wealthy residents of Edgbaston.
By permission of the Cadbury Research Library: Special Collections, University of Birmingham

Mason College allowed women, as well as men, a chance of higher education. The college magazine regularly reproduced photographs of students during the 1890s and these are almost the only surviving photographic records of individual students.
By permission of the Cadbury Research Library: Special Collections, University of Birmingham

MISS MARY D. STURGE, M.D. LOND.
(From a Photograph by H. J. Whitlock, Birmingham.)

In the 1890s Mason Science College absorbed the science departments of the Queen's Faculty of Medicine – another prestigious development in Birmingham intellectual life – and the women's training college for teachers, first established by the School Board. In 1898 the expanded college qualified as a university college and then, in 1900, it was transformed into the University of Birmingham, linked to the local industrial and business community. This university, generously endowed and supported by members of the liberal nonconformist elite, stressed its commitment to science, engineering and commerce – supposedly masculine subjects – yet from the first it proudly asserted that men and women were admitted on equal terms. Its inclusion of education and arts certainly attracted many women, although they were also to be found in other subjects including medicine and commerce. At the beginning, however, the university was very small, and it was based in New Street until the site at Edgbaston could be developed.[26] Nevertheless, this first civic university in England soon became a model for the new universities of Britain.[27]

Mason College, founded by businessman Josiah Mason in 1880, was located in Edmund Street. In 1900 it became the University of Birmingham and continued its strong links with local industry and business.
By permission of the Cadbury Research Library: Special Collections, University of Birmingham

An expanding system, 1902–44

The new university was certainly a symbol of the professed enlightened attitude to education of those who munificently fostered it. By 1913 student numbers had grown from 678 to 1,013, the site at Edgbaston with its magnificent new buildings had been opened and, alongside its inherited curriculum, innovative courses in practical applied science such as malting and brewing and practical mining had

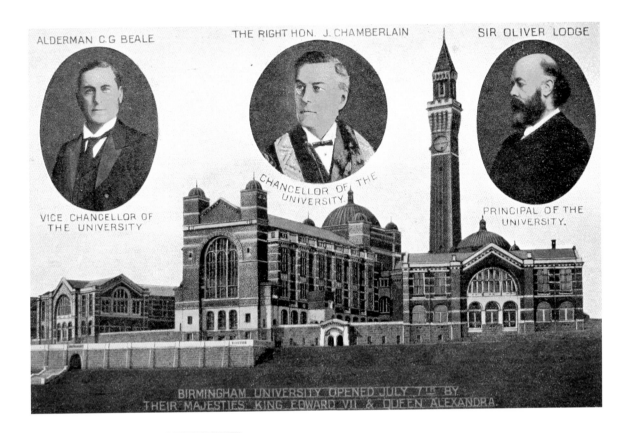

The University of Birmingham at its new site in Edgbaston. This souvenir postcard for the royal visit at the 1909 opening includes portraits of individuals closely associated with the new buildings: Joseph Chamberlain, the first Chancellor, Oliver Lodge, the first Principal, and Charles Beale, the first Vice-Chancellor.
By permission of the Cadbury Research Library: Special Collections, University of Birmingham

Margery Fry was the first warden of University House in Birmingham, the first purpose-built hall of residence for women in Britain. She was one of the first women governors of the King Edward's School Foundation and was noted for her work in penal reform. This pastel by Charles Haslewood Shannon captures Fry in 1915.
© The University of Birmingham Research and Cultural Collections

been established. A less prestigious development, although very important in terms of strengthening student numbers, particularly of women and those in arts, was the metamorphosis of the old Department of Education into one led by an 'Organising Professor of Education'.[28]

Over the next forty years the university was to grow in both quality and quantity of provision. The upheavals of two world wars and the prolonged recession of the inter-war years affected it adversely, however, exacerbating the financial and thus development problems which tested it from the start. Among other difficulties, although successive scientific and engineering subjects, followed by medicine, gradually moved to Edgbaston, it proved impossible to move the Arts Faculty and newer faculties and departments there. The resulting split site and lack of room was a constant source of frustration and irritation. The university also reached out into the local community, especially through its joint committee with the Workers' Educational Association (WEA). The building of Queen's Hospital and the opening of the glorious Barber Institute of Fine Arts and of the Students' Union added substantially not only to the quality of the university's provision for its students and staff, but also to local life. The university, in turn, relied on its local area for its students, many of whom had few financial resources and often needed grants of some kind to continue. Many students went into teaching, particularly

The art deco Barber Institute of Fine Arts. The building was opened in 1939 as a cultural centre at the University of Birmingham.
© The Barber Institute of Fine Arts, University of Birmingham

women. Despite the West Midlands coming out of recession quicker than elsewhere, however, the university's numbers did not grow in the 1930s as much as those in other provincial universities. Nevertheless, backed by grants from national and local government and others, and industrial support particularly for science and engineering, the university built up its academic strength and reputation. Indeed, in the Second World War the university's scientific research, especially in physics and related disciplines, contributed significantly both to the Allied success and to its international reputation.[29]

Other higher education institutions were also established in Birmingham: Saltley, a Church of England residential training college for men, founded in 1850; Anstey College of Further Education in 1897; and the Selly Oak colleges of Woodbrooke, Kingsmead, Fircroft, Carey Hall and Westhill, comparatively small colleges founded by various Christian sects mostly to educate for missionary, social or teaching services and for personal development. From 1919 they cooperated loosely under a Central Council.[30]

Birmingham also developed some strong centres of further and technical education to meet the demands of local manufacturers. Thousands of students, mostly part-timers and the vast majority male, attended the Municipal Technical School to study technical and scientific subjects, with some taking advanced classes and various national exams. 'Women's classes' in cookery, dressmaking, laundry and millinery were separate and popular, but financial difficulties from 1914 onwards prevented much expansion of them. From 1927 the Birmingham Central, Handsworth and Aston Technical Colleges were recognized as Colleges of Further Education and by 1939 about 10,000 students attended them. Exciting new subjects such as micro-chemistry, opthalmics, aeronautics, microbiology and radio service work were offered in a wide range of science and engineering courses. From 1927 the Central Technical College (BCTC) became an approved institution for teaching external degrees and other qualifying exams in pharmacy for the University of London. Pharmacy and biology, indeed, were scientific areas where women began to flourish, even taking degrees by 1943–44. A new course for the London University diploma in nursing and physiology up to and at degree level became increasingly popular with women, as did commercial courses.[31] Such education, however, was class-based as well as gendered. Subjects associated with crafts and manual occupations were less esteemed by the wealthier in society.

Similarly, the school system, while expanding in the early twentieth century, remained divided by gender, class and religion. The 1902 Act abolished School Boards in favour of Local Education Authorities (LEAs) – in Birmingham run by the city council – which had control over all elementary education and could establish fee-paying secondary schools, modelled on existing endowed secondary schools, not the previous higher-grade schools. This was a bitter disappointment to the Liberals, now divided between Liberals and Liberal-Unionists. Nevertheless, within the Conservative and Unionist domination which lasted fifty years, there was sufficient, if by no means complete, consensus over education for the Liberal George Kenrick and his cousin Byng Kenrick to be elected as successive chairs of

education throughout this period. To the hierarchy of secondary provision already in Birmingham were added three new municipal secondary schools – Central, Waverley and George Dixon – formed from the former two higher-grade schools and the Municipal Day Technical School. With the changing of Birmingham's boundaries in 1911, more secondary schools were added. Yet, despite the efficient administration of the Education Committee, Birmingham slipped from its place in the vanguard of progressive secondary education to near the bottom. Even before the Hadow Report of 1926, it began to reorganize and expand provision for pupils over 11, but this was within the elementary system, a cheaper option. The system remained dominated by the King Edward schools, themselves troubled by issues of finance and access in these financially stringent years. An elaborate system of free places and maintenance grants was constructed to provide a narrow scholarship ladder both to these and to the council secondary schools, but many parents could not afford the costs, especially to the King Edward schools. This situation was compounded by the preference of employers – with whom council leaders were closely linked – and perhaps parents, for apprenticeship and industrial training. LEA scholarships were also awarded to pupils from LEA schools, although more boys gained these than girls, probably because there were more secondary places for boys.[32]

Severe cuts by national government in the 1930s reduced capital spending generally

Students at Westhill College, Selly Oak, in 1927. Originally a teacher-training institution, it was incorporated into the University of Birmingham in 2001.
By permission of the Cadbury Research Library: Special Collections, University of Birmingham

in education. Teachers' salaries were cut and a bar on married women teachers was stringently applied. Nevertheless, in Birmingham there were experiments in the senior elementary schools such as the promotion of education in world citizenship and experimentation in council schools in environmental, drama, media and outdoors education – Birmingham being acknowledged as leading the development of playing fields as part of schooling. It also won repute for its provision of evening play centres for children; developing community centres as places of education; and its nursery schooling, a provision pioneered in Birmingham by Caroline Bishop and Julia Lloyd. Primary education was improved and expanded.[33]

At the same time from the 1900s, Birmingham became a leader in the great expansion of the school medical services – providing in itself a social revolution.[34] Its Hygiene subcommittee, on which unusually a number of women sat, administered much of this. Birmingham was divided into districts overseen by school medical officers (SMOs) – many of them women – who ran school aural, ophthalmic and dental clinics, and visited both hospitals and specialist provision for children in a variety of special, residential, day and open-air schools – the latter being another field in which Birmingham led. School nurses followed up inspections with visits to both schools and homes. Some SMOs researched into the malnourishment of children while, from 1932, medical, psychological and social care were combined in the pioneering Child Guidance Clinic. The Special Schools subcommittee, run by a succession of women chairs in an area in which Birmingham was a recognized leader, did much for children suffering crippling diseases and sight and hearing problems, leading to national recognition especially for its chair from 1903–13, Ellen Pinsent, despite councillors disagreeing over the treatment of an increasing selection of the 'feebleminded'.[35] All in all there was a much more scientific approach to the management of public health, although Ian Grosvenor and Kevin Myers have pointed out the social and moral imperatives of what became largely a system of middle-class control and surveillance of working-class lives.[36]

Education for all? 1944 onwards

There is no space here to detail the vast educational developments from the mid-twentieth century to the present. Public education in Birmingham from 1939 until 1970 has been termed 'a story of steady progress under major handicaps', with further, secondary and primary education becoming successive foci of attention.[37] The 1944 Education Act which established a new statutory system of free primary, secondary and further education, compulsory to the age of 15, was welcomed by all political parties. Proposals to implement it fully were eagerly made but the damage and major dislocation caused by the Second World War and the ensuing cost of reconstruction delayed such plans, particularly those to give girls more equal provision of secondary education. Until the 1960s Birmingham lagged behind most other cities in class sizes and teacher numbers, leading the way only in its home teaching service for sick children. It was slow to establish comprehensive schools

The Curzon building at
the City Centre campus of
Birmingham City University.
A university from 1992, it
was formerly the City of
Birmingham Polytechnic,
which developed from
the nineteenth-century
Birmingham College of Art.
Courtesy of Birmingham City
University

and the reaction to 10/65, the Labour government's request for plans for comprehensive reorganization, unearthed bitter disagreements over single-sex schooling,
parity of esteem, social engineering and availability of choice. Developments in
schooling certainly took place, but it was not until educational expenditure increased
in the 1990s and Tim Brighouse became Chief Education Officer for ten years that
Birmingham's educational reputation in schooling was restored, and, indeed, the
city became a 'beacon' for others. Throughout all this, the King Edward's schools
maintained their place at the top of the schooling hierarchy, although they, like all
schools, were affected by the changing school structures and terminology resulting
from the politics and ideologies of the late twentieth and early twenty-first centuries.[38]

In further and higher education there was much expansion. In 1956 the Central
Technical College became the first College of Advanced Technology in the country,
transforming into the University of Aston in 1964. Various other colleges opened
in the 1960s offering courses in commerce, art, crafts, food and domestic arts. By
the 2010s, indeed, Birmingham's further and higher education had altered out of
recognition, with the old training colleges disappearing or transforming and the
emergence of large colleges of further education and four universities – Aston, City
and Newman, plus the original University of Birmingham. The latter, finally united
on the Edgbaston site from 1961, has expanded to around 28,000 students, developed
its site (including a number of off-campus centres) and its remit academically,
incorporated Westhill College and has become a high-ranking university both
nationally and internationally.

Importantly in this, as in all educational provision in Birmingham, especially in the second half of the twentieth century, there is a history of how the increasingly ethnically and racially diverse nature of the population contributed to and yet became often a contested issue in education. Ian Grosvenor, particularly, has analysed both LEA initiatives and the active responses of black communities from the 1960s.[39] The rich cultural and social history of late twentieth-century Birmingham is explored elsewhere in this book, but, as the Black Pasts, Birmingham Futures Group has shown, educational stories, both within formal institutions and without, need to be told and listened to.[40]

There are many educational stories, both of individuals and of groups differentiated by class, gender, religion, ethnic origin and location, which could enrich this brief overview of Birmingham education. Hopefully this chapter has shown how Birmingham's response to changing educational demands, although sometimes no more than required, has at times and in different ways been truly enlightened.

The library buildings at Newman University. Founded as Newman College of Higher Education in 1968, it gained full university status in 2013.
Courtesy of Newman University

Chancellor's Court, University of Birmingham.
Courtesy of The University of Birmingham

Notes

1 'Enlightened' here means progressive, even radical: in the vanguard of educational thinking of the time.

2 'Class' was not referred to until the turn of the century.

3 V. Skipp, *The Making of Victorian Birmingham* (Studley, 1983), 121–3; R.G. Wilson, 'The schools of King Edward', in J.H. Muirhead (ed.), *Birmingham Institutions* (Birmingham, 1911), 540–3; C. Gill, *History of Birmingham Vol. 1 Manor and Borough To 1865* (London, 1952), 389–91

4 W. Barrow, 'The town and its industries', in J.H. Muirhead (ed.), *Birmingham Institutions* (Birmingham, 1911), 42–3; M.B. Frost, 'The development of provided schooling for working-class children in Birmingham 1781–1851' (MLitt thesis, University of Birmingham, 1978), 29–37; E. Bushrod, 'The history of Unitarianism in Birmingham from the middle of the eighteenth century to 1893' (MA thesis, University of Birmingham, 1954), 155–6.

5 Frost, 'Development of provided schooling', 34–7, 41–4, 48, 54; Gill, *Birmingham*, 79–82, 133.

6 Ibid., 131–3.

7 Ibid., 383–5, 392–8; Skipp, *Victorian Birmingham*, 120–8.

8 Joseph Priestley, 'Introductory essays to Hartley's theory of the human mind' (1790; 1st edn 1775), in *The Theological and Miscellaneous Works of Joseph Priestley*, ed. J.T. Rutt, 25 vols (1817–31), III, 167–96.

9 R. Watts, 'Joseph Priestley and his influence on education in Birmingham', in Malcolm Dick (ed.), *Joseph Priestley and Birmingham* (Studley, 2005), 48–52.

10 William Matthews, *A Sketch of the Principal Means which have been Employed to Ameliorate the Intellectual and Moral Conditions of the Working Classes in Birmingham* (1830), 6–18, 22–5; Watts, 'Joseph Priestley', 56–9 – for greater detail see the whole chapter 48–64.

11 R. Watts, *Gender, Power and the Unitarians in England, 1760–1860* (London, 1998), 128, 132; Gill, *Birmingham*, 135–41, 300–2, 433–6.

12 This broadly characterized the idealism promulgated by nonconformist ministers such as the Unitarians George Dawson and Henry Crosskey and the Congregationalist Robert Dale. Quaker social and religious idealism led to similar results. An important caveat has been argued cogently by Andy Green in '"The anarchy of empire": reimagining Birmingham's civic gospel', *Midland History*, 36.2 (2011), 163–79, in which he critiques George Dawson's ideology as actually being embedded in an imperialist, racist view. Christine Heward similarly points out that despite the Education League courting the support of working men, it did not put them forward for office or as candidates for the Board – C. Heward, 'Compulsion, work and family: a case study from nineteenth-century Birmingham', in R.K. Goodenow and W.E. Marsden (eds), *The City and Education in Four Nations* (Cambridge, 1992), 148.

13 A. Briggs, *History of Birmingham Vol. II Borough and City 1865–1938* (London, 1952), 100–5; A.H. Coley, 'The council schools', in J.H. Muirhead (ed.), *Birmingham Institutions* (Birmingham, 1911), 367–73

14 J. Chamberlain, *Six Years of Educational Work in Birmingham* (delivered to the Birmingham School Board, 1876; this edn 1896), 5–15.

15 Ibid., 14–24.

16 Heward, 'Compulsion, work and family', 129–57; C. Chinn, 'Was separate schooling a means of class segregation in late Victorian and Edwardian England?', *Midland History*, 13.1 (1988), 95–112.

17 Coley, 'Council schools', 369–77; D. Bishop et al., *The City a Light and a Beacon: A Guide to Birmingham Education Archives* (Birmingham City Council and the History of Education Society GB, 2001), 2–12; M. Vlaeminke, *The English Higher Grade Schools. A Lost Opportunity* (London, 2000).

18 'Public' used here in the peculiar English sense of the elite endowed boarding schools which arrogated the term to themselves from the seventeenth century. In the nineteenth century new 'public' schools were built to educate 'gentlemen' when there was an expansion of both the better-off middle classes and railways. See J. Lawson and H. Silver, *A Social History of Education in England* (London, 1973), 179, 202, 206, 300–6.

19 J. Whitcut, *Edgbaston High School 1876–1976* (Birmingham, 1976), 37–51, 55–60.

20 The high schools took pupils until 18; the grammar schools had a leaving age of 16 for boys and 17 for girls.

21 R. Watts, 'From lady-teacher to professional: a case study of some of the first headteachers of girls; secondary schools in England', *Educational Management and Administration*, 10.4 (1998), 339–45.

22 Ibid., 340–4; Whitcut, *Edgbaston High*, 60–3.

23 B. Jones, *Josiah Mason 1795–1881: Birmingham's Benevolent Benefactor* (Studley, 1995), 88–97.

24 Ibid., 342–3. Another proprietary school for girls – the 1890 Edgbaston Church of England College for Girls – although also good on science, was relatively small at first; Birmingham City Library (BCL) No. 4216, *Edgbaston Church of England College for Girls Limited Minute Book 18 November 1890–30 November 1904*.

25 KESB Archives, *King Edward VI Governors' Order Book, 29th July 1887–29th June 1892*, 20, 77, 160–1; *30th September 189 –30th May 1900*, 156–7, 176, 349, 442, 522; University of Birmingham Special Collections (UBSC), Pbx7795.s7, *Mary Darby Sturge M.D. Obit. March 14, 1925*.

26 Based on Mason College Calendars and Reports in the Cadbury Research Library (CRL) at the University of Birmingham: see UB/MC/E/2–4; UB/MC/H/1/12–17 *The Mason Science College (from 1892 with Queen's Faculty of Medicine), Birmingham. Calendar(s) for the Session(s) 1891–7*; UB/MC/H/2/1 *Mason College's Reports 1891–7*; UC 5/1 *Mason University College, Birmingham (with Queen's Faculty of Medicine), Calendar(s) for the Session(s) 1898 and 1899*.

27 E. Ives, 'The struggle for the charter', in E. Ives, D. Drummond and L. Schwarz, *The First Civic University: Birmingham 1880–1980. An Introductory History* (Birmingham, 2000), 104.

28 CRL UC 5/I *University of Birmingham Calendar(s) for the Sessions(s) 1900–1913* (including Council, VC and Principal's Reports).

29 D. Drummond, 'The inter-war years', 191–215; E. Ives, 'Charles Grant Robertson', 216–36; L. Schwarz, 'In an unyielding hinterland, the student body 1900–45', 237–70; D. Drummond and E. Ives, 'The return to war', 271–93; E. Ives, 'Stress, hope and frustration', 294–315, all in Ives et al., *First Civic University*; CRL UC 5/I *University of Birmingham Calendar(s) for the Sessions(s) 1923–1940* (including Council, VC and Principal's Reports).

30 M.V.C. Jeffreys, 'University of Birmingham Institute of Education', *Educational Review*, 1.2 (1949), 67–76; University of Birmingham pamphlet, *Institute of Education 1947–1950* (Edinburgh [?1950]).

31 CBEC *Reports* 1903–44; *BCTC Reports* 1939–45.

32 D. Adams, 'From consensus to conflict? Continuity and change in the structure for secondary education in Birmingham (1902–2000)' (MPhil thesis, University of Birmingham, 2004), 20–70; Briggs, *Birmingham*, 236–44; CBEC *Reports and Minutes*.

33 I. Grosvenor and K. Myers, 'Progressivism, control and correction: local education authorities and educational policy in twentieth-century England', *Paedagogica*

Historica, 42.1/2 (2006), 232–3; Birmingham City Archives, Selly Oak Nursery, Acc. 2011/036, Box 1: *Annals of the Birmingham Nursery Schools Association 1903–1919*.

34 Briggs, *Birmingham*, 244, 246–7.

35 CBEC *Minutes* and *Reports* 1913–45, including *Hygiene Sub-Committee Minutes, Medical Reports* 1937–40; *Report on the Child Guidance Clinic* 1938, 1–6; A. Brown, 'Ellen Pinsent: including the "feebleminded" in Birmingham, 1900–1913', *History of Education*, 34.5 (2005), 535–46; F. Wilmot, 'Birmingham and the Open Air School movement', *History of Education Society Bulletin*, 64 (1999), 102–12.

36 Grosvenor and Myers, 'Progressivism, control and correction', 225–47.

37 A. Sutcliffe and R. Smith, *History of Birmingham, Vol. III: Birmingham 1939–1970* (London, 1974), 332.

38 Ibid., 333–51, 357–62; Adams, 'From consensus to conflict?', 71–170.

39 I. Grosvenor, *Assimilating Identities. Racism and Educational Policy in Post 1945 Britain* (London, 1997), esp. 149–84.

40 See, for example, I. Grosvenor, R. McLean and S. Roberts (eds), *Making Connections* (Birmingham, 2002).

CHAPTER EIGHT

Art, Design and Architecture

SALLY HOBAN

Birmingham's artistic, design and architectural history has been fashioned by industry, patronage, civic power, creativity and individual talents and enterprise. In 1949 M.J. Wise claimed that 'since 1700 a ... secret of Birmingham's industrial success has lain in the adaptability of its trades to meet the changing demands of both local and world markets'. This adaptability reflected the widespread provision of vocational instruction in the arts, which culminated in 1885 with the establishment of the nationally important Birmingham Municipal School of Art (BMSA) and other institutions which were linked to specific trades. As well as education, Birmingham made important contributions to the Arts and Crafts Movement, art deco, modernism, surrealism and brutalism. The interrelationship of trades, education and cultural movements has shaped the evolution of local art, design and architecture.

The late eighteenth and early nineteenth centuries

Birmingham provided a fertile environment for independent artisans to set up in business in the town's expanding commercial centre or the emerging Jewellery Quarter, where painters, engravers, printmakers, jewellers, toy makers, enamellers, japanners, goldsmiths and silversmiths thrived and adapted their output to new styles and fashions. In 1785 24 artists were advertising their services to prospective patrons in the town, including James Millar.[1] Millar exhibited at the Royal Academy in the 1780s and his sitters included John Baskerville in 1774, the poet John Freeth in 1790, Francis Eginton, a stained-glass artist and associate of Matthew Boulton in

1796, and the family of Robert Mynors, a leading Birmingham surgeon in 1797.[2] His self-portrait (1766) is one of the first images created by a Birmingham artist and the earliest known self-portrait.[3] Formal art instruction was rare in the town until 1801, when Joseph Barber (1757–1811) taught drawing at an academy in Great Charles Street, and Samuel Lines (1778–1863) held drawing classes in Newhall Street from 1807. Young designers and commercial artists in Birmingham most likely trained as apprentices or in family firms with occasional professional supplementary tuition.

Artisans and manufacturers capitalized on commercial opportunities; they were aware of the need for good design in order to compete in international markets, but before the Municipal Art Gallery opened in 1885 there was limited opportunity for trainee artists and designers to see high-quality examples to emulate. One opportunity came through miniature painter James Bisset, who was the proprietor of 'Bisset's Modern Museum' in New Street, a concoction of late eighteenth-century enterprise, entertainment and spectacle. With free admission, the 'museum' offered the curious and those seeking an education in fashion, design and contemporary taste the chance to see jewellery, toys, fancy miniatures, ornaments, fashionable hair devices and paintings. A watercolour portrait miniature by Bisset is attributed as a self-portrait of the artist and entrepreneur within his museum, surrounded by his carefully curated exhibits.[4] Bisset's *A Poetic Survey round Birmingham* (1800) was accompanied by his ambitious *Magnificent Directory* and demonstrates his awareness of the power of marketing. This guidebook, poetic ode to the town and commercial trade directory captures the intersection between the growing commerce

Joseph Barber, *Trade card for Birmingham Union Fire Office*, c.1790. Barber came to Birmingham to work as a decorator in the japanning trade. David Cox and the engraver William Radclyffe were among his pupils. Courtesy of the Royal Birmingham Society of Artists, photograph by James White

An example of the engraver's art: title page from Bisset's *Magnificent Directory* (1808). By permission of the Library of Birmingham, 47154

of the city and its decorative arts through the inclusion of beautifully engraved trade illustrations to accompany the advertisements. Growing commerce provided a ready market for the engravers' skills through the proliferation of advertisements, trade and calling cards.

Samuel Lines came out of this busy background of engravers, metalworkers, japanners and decorative artists. He was also father to a Birmingham dynasty of artists – his five sons all pursued careers in art.[5] Lines was born near Coventry and was apprenticed to a Birmingham clock-dial enameller and decorator in 1794.[6] In 1809 he joined with fellow Birmingham artists including Charles Barber, John Vincent Barber and Moses Haughton the Elder to form a life-drawing academy in Peck Lane, New Street. Its success led to a move to larger premises in Union Passage in 1814. Lines is best known for his landscape scenes and topographical images of the centre of Birmingham as it transformed into an industrial city. One example, *View from No. 3 Temple Row West, Birmingham* (1821), depicts two male figures discussing the view from on top of the building, the fields in the background contrasting with the growing commercial centre of the town.[7] *Birmingham from the Dome of St Philip's in 1821* has become one of the most famous views of Birmingham in the early nineteenth century, and captures the town's industrial transformation by merging a south-westerly view towards Christ Church with a more traditional pastoral scene in the foreground, depicting land that was developed soon after the painting was completed.[8] Lines was also instrumental in the founding of the Birmingham Society of Artists.

David Cox (1783–1859), an artist with a national reputation, worked predominantly in watercolour and oils. Cox was born in 1783 in Deritend and studied drawing with Joseph Barber before apprenticeship to a Birmingham miniature painter.[9] Cox's career began with scene painting at the Theatre Royal in Birmingham. This occupation took him to London in 1804, but he retained links with his native town, exhibiting regularly at the Birmingham Society of Arts and becoming a member in 1842. He exhibited at the Royal Academy and combined professional painting with art instruction, including *A Treatise on Landscape Painting* (1813–14) and *The Young Artist's Companion* (1819–20). Cox lived in Hereford and London

but he moved back to Birmingham in 1841, living in Harborne.[10] *Birmingham Horse Fair*, of around 1845, depicts the fair which was held at Holloway Head. The scene provides a record of the business of trading within Birmingham with its focus on horse traders and the animals, the buildings of Birmingham merely hinted at in the background.[11] *The Skylark* (1849) is reputed to depict a pastoral scene near Harborne, with a farmer and his young family observing a skylark which flies above them.[12] It provides a contrast to the bustling town scene that is captured in *Birmingham Horse Fair*.

Samuel Lines (1778–1863), *Birmingham from the Dome of St Philip's Church, 1821* (oil on canvas). Lines's painting shows the expansion of the town in the early nineteenth century.
© Birmingham Museums and Art Gallery/Bridgeman Images

David Cox (1783–1859), *The Skylark* (1849, oil on canvas). Cox was born in Deritend in Birmingham, the son of a blacksmith. The location of the landscape is meant to be near Harborne.
© Birmingham Museums and Art Gallery/Bridgeman Images

A new School of Design was formed in 1842 to improve the quality of practical design for local trades. Government grants supported the school and teaching was based on the nationally approved art instruction scheme. A decade later the School of Design moved from the Society of Arts rooms – the Society had been founded in 1829 to encourage art education – to the Midland Institute Building and the Birmingham Society of Arts moved into the New Street Gallery. In 1868 the Society received royal patronage from Queen Victoria and became known as the Royal Birmingham Society of Artists, which remains the city's pre-eminent organization for working artists.[13]

The impressive neo-classical portico of the Royal Birmingham Society of Artists' premises in New Street is captured in Joseph Southall's *The Old Portico* (1912).
Courtesy of the Royal Birmingham Society of Artists, photograph by James White

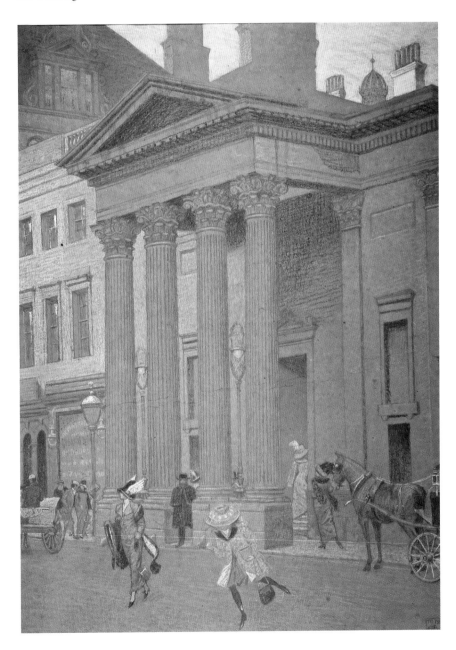

Nationally important buildings were constructed in Birmingham during the eighteenth and early nineteenth centuries. St Philip's church (1709–25), in Colmore Row, is a highly decorative example of the English Italian Baroque and was designed by the Warwickshire architect Thomas Archer (1668–1743).[14] The parish church was extended between 1883 and 1884 by J.A. Chatwin and in 1905 the chancel was refitted by Philip Chatwin.[15] In that year it became Birmingham's Anglican Cathedral. Birmingham Town Hall, which opened in 1834, was a purpose-built concert hall to house Birmingham's famous triennial music festivals and also a space for public use. The successful design in the classical style was submitted by Joseph Hansom and Edward Welch. Building began in 1832 and the opening event was held in October 1834.[16] St Chad's Roman Catholic Cathedral (1839–41) is an important example of the Gothic Revival style and a major work by Augustus Pugin. St Chad's was the first Catholic cathedral to be built in England since the Reformation.[17]

St Philip's Church.

St Philip's church from William Hutton's *History of Birmingham* (1809).
By permission of the Library of Birmingham, SC5/563151

The late Victorian period and the beginning of the twentieth century: the Arts and Crafts Movement

Birmingham's civic gospel in the late nineteenth century provided a municipally sponsored backdrop against which art and design flourished. The opening of the Municipal Art Gallery in 1885 provided a free educational resource for creative practitioners in the city, and its management committee was keen to stress that the institution did not 'fall into the mistake, so often made, of thinking that painting and sculpture are the only branches of art worthy of consideration'.[18] Examples of both traditional 'high' art and industrial design were included in its displays. The management committee was drawn from the municipal and industrial elite and some members were also responsible for the Birmingham Municipal School of Art. These included the industrialist William Kenrick and John Thackray Bunce. As editor of the *Birmingham Daily Post*, Bunce was a leading figure in the promotion and encouragement of local arts.[19] The School of Art's building in Margaret Street was designed by the Birmingham architect John Henry Chamberlain (1831–83) in the neo-Venetian style, and was a physical manifestation of the ideals of the civic gospel made possible through the links between art, industry, private and public finance and aspiration in the city.[20]

Edward Richard Taylor (1838–1912) was headmaster between 1877 and 1904.[21] He introduced unique 'Art Laboratories' to provide practical training for male and female students in enamelling, metalwork, stained-glass design manufacture, embroidery, stone carving, fresco and jewellery that could be applied in a trade. His new system of art instruction, which he named 'Executed Design', broadened traditional art instruction, which relied primarily on repetitive drawing and copying from antique casts and existing designs on paper. Executed design gave students the opportunity to construct the designs that they had created, so giving them tangible objects to show potential employers or commercial clients in the employment market. In *Drawing and Design for Beginners*, Taylor argued that students must have 'knowledge of the properties of the material, of the process of execution and of the purpose or use to which the object should be put',[22] an idea embedded in the teachings and practice of the Arts and Crafts Movement. Taylor's system received praise. The work of students and staff from the BMSA was lauded in *The Studio Magazine*, *The Artist* and other decorative arts magazines for its technical achievements and the impact of Taylor's teaching. In 1894 the Museum and School of Art Committee's report for the quarterly meeting of Birmingham City Council stated that 'the school is the best and most complete School of Art in the UK'.[23] Representatives from art schools in Manchester, Nottingham and Glasgow visited the school and there was also a visit from the Belgian government.[24] By 1900 the examiner's report of the Arts and Crafts designer William Lethaby stated:

> the school stands so high as compared with other Art Schools known to me that, if my report were to be mostly comparative, I could say nothing more than that Birmingham stood first, or amongst the very first, in the kingdom.[25]

Original watercolour sketch of the design for Birmingham Town Hall attributed to W. Harris (1831). This painting was submitted as part of the architect's winning competition entry.
By permission of Assay Office Birmingham and supplied courtesy of TownHall/Symphony Hall

A contemporary image of the domed Round Room at Birmingham Museum & Art Gallery.
Courtesy of Marketing Birmingham

Birmingham Municipal School of Art, Margaret Street. The building was designed by Birmingham architect John Henry Chamberlain and opened in 1885.
Courtesy of Birmingham City University

Many women students were drawn to enamelling and metalwork at the school, as well as the more traditional subjects of painting, leatherwork or embroidery. The demand was so great that, in 1901, Art Laboratory Two was increased in size due to the number of male and female students who wanted to take practical enamelling classes.[26] As a result, a number of women who had trained in executed design were able to take up highly paid jobs in industry or set up their own businesses.[27] Several middle-class women studied in the advanced level classes, thus acquiring highly developed practical skills to set up in business. They included Georgina Gaskin (1866–1934) who designed critically acclaimed Arts and Crafts enamelled jewellery with her husband Arthur.[28] Florence Stern (b. 1869) was a professional metalworker producing predominantly jewellery and silver flatware decorated with enamel and semi-precious stones.[29] Mary Jane Newill (1860–1947), who also taught at the School of Art, worked in textiles and stained glass.[30] Kate Eadie (b. 1879) produced jewellery and enamels.[31] Florence Camm (1874–1960) designed and produced a silver and enamel casket with fellow student Violet Holden which was to be presented to John Thackray Bunce to commemorate his being awarded the Freedom of the City of Birmingham. This commission illustrates the links between the executed design skills of the women students and civic patronage.[32] Florence Camm worked professionally from the family firm of T.W. Camm Ltd in Smethwick and became a stained-glass designer of international repute.[33]

The paucity of surviving registers makes it difficult to ascertain the number of women who came from working-class backgrounds, but one student, Caroline 'Carrie' Copson (b. 1883), produced exquisite jewellery in the Arts and Crafts

Edward Richard Taylor (1838–1912) was the first headmaster of Birmingham Municipal School of Art and a major innovator in the teaching of art and design. *Edgbastonia,* July 1894.
By permission of the Cadbury Research Library: Special Collections, University of Birmingham

A needlework class at Birmingham Municipal School of Art in about 1900.
By permission of Birmingham City University Art & Design Archives, SA/AT/28/2/4

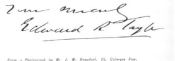

style. Her father was a watch-case maker and her mother a laundress.[34] Copson studied at the Vittoria Street School for Jewellers, a branch school of the Municipal School of Art, under the tutelage of Arthur Gaskin[35] and became a self-employed jeweller.[36] A silver fruit bowl and silver and enamel lamp and shade by Copson in the permanent collection at the Victoria and Albert Museum were exhibited at the Paris International Exhibition in 1914, demonstrating the international reach of Birmingham's professional women designers at this time.[37]

As well as the opportunity to take part in executed design classes, women students had access to both male and female life models.[38] This was rare in art teaching and gave women graduates seeking employment as fine artists, illustrators and stained-glass designers an advantage when seeking professional commissions that involved the accurate representation of the human figure. A fine example of a female nude drawing from life produced by Florence Camm is in the School of Art archive at Birmingham City University. Camm studied at the BMSA on a part-time basis between 1898 and 1909,[39] and the life drawing experience that she gained is also reflected in the exquisite facial expressions and features in arguably her greatest work in stained glass, a series of windows illustrating scenes from the story of Dante and Beatrice. These were designed and produced for the Turin International Exhibition and were awarded the Grand Prix in three classes against competition from designers

Arts and Crafts Movement brooch designed and made from silver, gold, glass and mother-of-pearl in Birmingham by Carrie Copson, c.1905.
© Victoria & Albert Museum, London

The Last Judgement, 1897, by Edward Burne-Jones. This window is one from a series by the artist in St Philip's Cathedral.
© Alastair Carew-Cox

across Europe, and the Diploma of Honour for the entire exhibition.[40]

Taylor appointed some acclaimed Arts and Crafts practitioners as teachers, and networks of professional influence came with them, including access to patrons and opportunities for students to capitalize on these professional links. William Morris's daughter, May, lectured at the BMSA for around ten years. She also acted as an external examiner of embroidery and needlework for the school's local prizes.[41] Sir Edward Burne-Jones, William Morris and Ford Madox Brown were also associated with the school as examiners of students' work, donated examples of their commissions for use in student classes and visited the school to meet with students.[42]

One major commission in the Arts and Crafts style were the stained-glass windows produced by the Birmingham-born artist Sir Edward Burne-Jones (1833–98) for St Philip's, where the artist himself was baptized.[43] Produced by Morris and Company, the glass was financed through the patronage of Emma Villiers-Wilkes.[44] The windows depict *The Ascension* (centre, east, completed in 1885), *Nativity* and *Annunciation to the Shepherds* (north-east) and *Crucifixion* (south-east, both completed 1887–88). Their colours, dominated by reds and blues, and the monumental, attenuated figures are typical of Burne-Jones's and Morris's late work. *The Last Judgement*, completed in 1897, was a separate commission, and is a memorial to Bishop Bowlby of Coventry who died in 1894.[45]

Probably inspired by Ford Madox Brown's history of Manchester murals in the Great Room of Manchester Town Hall (1879–93), John Thackray Bunce, chairman of the subcommittee of the Museum and the School of Art, persuaded the city council's Estates Committee that students from the School of Art should produce a series of oil paintings representing scenes from Birmingham's history for Birmingham Town Hall, placing their work at the heart of Birmingham's civic and public life. The panels were executed and exhibited from 1892 to 1902.[46] They were medieval-inspired, romantic, heroic works in the Pre-Raphaelite style. Only an image of Joseph Priestley escaping the Priestley riots suggests anything of Birmingham's Radical past, and there is nothing to show the political reform movements of the 1830s, or indeed, apart from Priestley again, the Midlands Enlightenment encapsulated by the industrial achievements of Boulton and Watt. The panels were removed ahead of renovation work in 1927 and ten canvases were rehung at the Historical Museum in Cannon Hill Park. They were last seen photographed in an exhibition catalogue in 1939 to mark the opening of Elmdon Airport.[47]

The emphasis on hand production at the BMSA had to be balanced with the requirements of local trades, which used machinery to mass-produce inexpensive jewellery. This tension was probably never fully resolved. A new market for Arts and Crafts goods, however, thrived in Birmingham and artists, small-scale manufacturers and designers capitalized on the fashion. The number of art metalworking companies in the city increased from 16 in 1886 to 54 in 1915, reflecting the middle-class demand for art metalwork, including Liberty & Co. (Cymric) from 1903, the Birmingham Guild of Handicraft from 1898 onwards, and the Art Jewellery Company.[48]

Aside from the production of works in the Arts and Crafts style, through Joseph Southall (1861–1944) and Kate Bunce (1856–1927) Birmingham was also home to a revival in tempera painting.[49] Bunce's *The Keepsake* and Southall's *Beauty Receiving the White Rose From Her Father* (1898–99) reveal this development. Southall also worked in fresco, including *Corporation Street in 1914* for the Municipal Art Gallery.

In the late nineteenth century two local artists, Walter Langley (1852–1922) and Edwin Harris (1855–1906), were drawn to the peace, light and mild climate of the Cornish fishing village of Newlyn where they set up a colony of working artists to capture the everyday lives of local fishing people. Walter Langley was born into a Birmingham working-class family, attended Hurst Street Unitarian Mission School and was apprenticed to a lithographic printer.[50] He studied drawing and industrial design at the Birmingham School of Design and won a scholarship to study decorative design at the South Kensington Schools, but was increasingly drawn to painting. One of Langley's watercolours is *Old Market Hall and Fountain* (1880), which depicts a fashionably dressed young lady standing alone in front of the decorative splendour of the fountain in the Old Market Hall in Birmingham, and provides a record of the market hall at the time. Langley's work in Newlyn was much more dramatic, and included *Never Morning Wore to Evening but Some Heart Did Break* (1894).[51] Edwin Harris was born in Ladywood and trained at Birmingham School of Art where he also taught, and he had moved to Newlyn by 1883.[52] He returned to Birmingham in 1895 where he set up his own studio. *The Fisherman's Daughter* (c.1890)[53] is lighter in tone than Langley's later work and Harris's subjects are more rooted in the tradition of conventional Victorian genre painting.

Walter Langley (1852–1922),
*Old Market Hall and
Fountain, Birmingham* (1880,
watercolour on paper).
© Birmingham Museums and Art
Gallery/Bridgeman Images

Early twentieth century: art deco and early modernism

The clean lines of modernism and art deco in the inter-war years made an impact on Birmingham artists, designers and architects, including William Bloye. There are several surviving buildings from this period, including Odeon cinemas, Elmdon Airport and the Barber Institute (1936–39). This building at the University of Birmingham combines elements of art deco with modernism and Scandinavian classicism. Described as the finest surviving work by the architect Robert Atkinson, the building houses a music auditorium with decorative interior, libraries, a lecture hall and art galleries.

The sculptor William Bloye (1890–1975) was born in Birmingham and studied at the BMSA and the Royal Academy of Art.[54] He joined the Royal Army Medical Corps between 1915 and 1917 and in 1919 was appointed full-time teacher of modelling at the BMSA. In 1921 and 1922 the school funded him to spend two four-week periods with Eric Gill at his workshop in Ditchling in Sussex. Here Bloye learned stone carving and letter cutting, and the influence and inspiration of Gill can be seen throughout Bloye's work, most notably in the clean, geometric lines of a series of low-relief Portland stone carvings at Birmingham's Hall of Memory (1925). Entitled *Call, Front Line* and *Return*, they are closely packed, linear figural compositions with a dynamic sense of movement. Bloye established his own studio in Small Heath and in 1929 he became Head of Sculpture at the BMSA.

The concert hall in the Barber Institute of Fine Arts at the University of Birmingham. The building was designed by Robert Atkinson and opened in 1939.
© The Barber Institute of Fine Arts, University of Birmingham

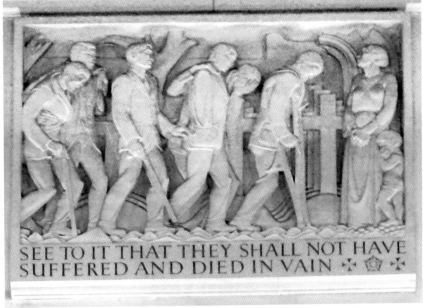

Some 51 examples of Bloye's work have been recorded in Birmingham,[55] but the works of the 1920s and 1930s in particular reflect British modernism in sculpture. The most representative include four relief figures executed in Portland stone representing *Wisdom*, *Fortitude*, *Charity* and *Faith* (1932), situated on the top-storey corners of the façade of the Legal and General Assurance building at 7–8 Waterloo Street. These figures are carved in profile with no extraneous details within the compositions and are presented against art deco styled backgrounds. Two heads in

Portland stone that form the capitals and pediment sculptures on the entrance façade of New Oxford House, also in Waterloo Street, are also typical of Bloye's work from this period and also owe a debt to Eric Gill. These attenuated and graceful figures reflect the Egyptian Revival style that swept the decorative arts alongside art deco in the late 1920s. Sporting venues and public houses in Birmingham also featured sculpture by Bloye, with *The Running Stag* low-relief stone carving on the exterior of Perry Barr greyhound track (1929) absolutely typical of the art deco style, with its streamlined, graceful depiction of the animal. Despite Bloye's contribution to British modernism and art deco in the 1920s and 1930s, he is perhaps best remembered today for his monumental, three-dimensional bronze group statue of Boulton, Murdock and Watt on Broad Street, which was completed in 1956.

Birmingham artists and designers made an important contribution to surrealism in art and brutalism in architecture. Emmy Bridgwater (1909–99) worked within a network of national and local surrealist artists. The Birmingham Surrealists were a dynamic and passionate group of artist friends who met at cafés in Birmingham and at their leader Conroy Maddox's home.[56] Their subversive work challenged the art establishment in the city, which in the main favoured artworks in the realist tradition. Members of the group included the painters John Melville, William Gear and Oscar Mellor, and Desmond Morris, the painter and anthropologist.[57] Bridgwater was born in Edgbaston and initially trained at the Birmingham School of Art in the 1920s before continuing her training in Oxford and at the Grosvenor School of Art in London.[58] By the mid-1930s she was becoming interested in surrealism and had returned to Birmingham. Surrealist artists were interested in the liberation of the imagination through art; how the unconscious and dream-like states could be accessed and expressed through painting and drawing using free association and Freudian psychoanalysis. Surrealist artworks combined elements and motifs drawn from the everyday conscious world with mysterious and often unsettling images from dreams. An important method in the composition of surrealist art was the process known as automatism, in which the composition was created by the artist through automatic drawing, where the hand is allowed to move automatically across the paper or canvas, thus liberating the artist's subconscious and imagination. Bridgwater became a critically acclaimed automatist in British surrealist art.[59] An untitled ink drawing by Bridgwater presents the viewer with a dreamlike landscape containing recognizably human body parts in the foreground.[60] Her oil painting *Night Work is About to Commence* (1940–43) seemingly depicts a ship at sail diagonally across the canvas in an unspecified setting.[61] Bridgwater's dreamlike paintings and automatic drawings force her viewers to interrogate the subject matter before them, but also provoke us to question our own thoughts, imagination and emotions as we encounter them. Bridgwater also wrote surrealist poetry, and in 1942 she contributed to the surrealist magazine *Arson*, and held a solo exhibition at Jack Bilbo's Modern Art Gallery in London.[62] She lived in London and Birmingham at this time, providing a link between the national artists and her own group in Birmingham. In 1947 one of her paintings was chosen to be shown at the International Surrealist Exhibition in Paris.[63] She signed the declaration of the Surrealist Group in England, which reaffirmed the group's commitment to the original principles of surrealism and cemented her reputation as a surrealist artist of international stature.

In post-war modernist and brutalist architecture, the work of the Birmingham architect John Madin (1924–2012) has been often unappreciated in the city but is now receiving increasing critical acclaim.[64] The economic hardships of the post-Second World War period began to ease in the later 1950s at the same time as a new generation of designers and architects, very much inspired by the European modernism of the 1930s disseminated through the Bauhaus designers in Germany, European émigrés in London and Scandinavian design, were beginning their careers. This new generation of designers brought post-war modernism into all areas of the decorative arts and architecture. Madin's ambition was to bring the modernist aesthetic to Birmingham. As early as 1940 he wrote: 'I hope to see in the near future a greater and more beautiful Birmingham, and I also wish that I should be one of those men who with care and sympathy, be able to graft our City into the finest in the World.'[65]

As finances improved in the 1950s, Birmingham City Council considered plans for a new civic centre in the city. Attempts had been made to create a grand civic complex in the pre-war period[66] and the need to rebuild and develop the city in the post-war period was recognized and publicly promoted by the Bournville Village Trust, for example, in its research project and report *When We Build Again*.[67] This contains a rallying call for the creation of a new Birmingham: 'When, therefore, we talk of rebuilding Birmingham we are not primarily concerned with the problems of war damage, but we do advocate seizing the opportunity the war has created to look at our city anew and to plan its rebuilding with a new vision.'[68] Madin's vision of a new Birmingham became an important part of the rebuilding.

John Madin was born in Moseley and aspired to be an architect from an early age.[69] He trained at the Birmingham School of Architecture in Margaret Street and in his final year spent time in Scandinavia, where he saw European modernist architecture, and later visited the USA where he met Frank Lloyd Wright and Bauhaus pioneer Walter Gropius.[70] Madin became an associate member of RIBA in 1950 and opened his own architectural practice in Birmingham. The Engineering Employers Federation headquarters (1954) was Madin's first major building; he also designed the interior furnishings scheme and fittings for this commission and throughout his career the interior decoration of his buildings was heightened through the inclusion of contemporary works of art, perhaps most notably the John Piper mosaic mural in the entrance foyer of Chamber of Commerce House in Edgbaston (1961). At the time of writing, the future of this building and the Piper mural remains uncertain.

A number of Madin's post-war buildings have been demolished, including the BBC's Pebble Mill studios in Edgbaston (1971), the NatWest Tower (1974), the Birmingham Post and Mail building (1966) and the Amalgamated Engineering building (1961). However, much of his residential work, including low- and high-rise flats on the Calthorpe Estate in Edgbaston, has survived. Madin's landmark brutalist building, Birmingham Central Library in Paradise Circus, was demolished in 2016. Described as 'the finest example of the Brutalist aesthetic in Birmingham, and a civic project of European importance',[71] the library, a linked wing to the Council House and the Conservatoire were the only buildings to be completed from Madin's original civic scheme that would have covered all the Paradise Circus site. Madin's model showing his vision for the area was displayed in 1965, and featured new additions among the existing Town Hall and Council House buildings, including a library, concert hall, student residences, a restaurant tower with a viewing platform and a monorail terminal. Water gardens and landscaped areas were an integral part of the scheme, which linked the Council House with Baskerville House on Broad Street, and reflected the key modernist belief in open spaces, the natural environment and light and open air as an integral part of planning. Cars and pedestrians were segregated.[72] Madin's plans were approved by the city council in 1968 but only a part of his architectural grand vision of the future was completed.

Construction of Madin's new library took place between 1969 and 1973. When Birmingham Central Library opened in 1974, it was the first in western Europe to be designed as a cultural centre for the city, including a lending and reference library, a lecture hall and children's and music departments in one space.[73] It was also the largest public library in Europe. However, with the backlash against brutalist architecture in the 1990s, the library fell from favour and was considered an eyesore by many in the city and beyond. Madin's original concept envisaged casing the building in either travertine marble or Portland stone. However, for financial reasons, the exterior was finished in a cheaper option of pre-cast concrete with a stone aggregate. As Alan Clawley states, had the building been finished in Portland stone or limestone it could not have been condemned as a 'concrete monstrosity';

John Madin's Chamber of Commerce House, Harborne Road, Edgbaston. The building is constructed of marble, Portland stone, aluminium and glass.
© University of Birmingham, photograph by Phyllis Nicklin, 1960

problems with the concrete panels were cited by the council in 1999 as a reason to demolish the building.[74] The central reference library is the most striking element of Madin's composition, an eight-storey inverted ziggurat supported by external piers, contrasting with the smaller, curved adjacent lending library wing. Madin's vision was to provide library users with a sense of awareness of each floor and the building as a whole. Madin designed the reference and lending library complex around an open atrium containing a public square, with four entrances. This space was later glazed and enclosed in the 1990s to create Paradise Forum, which was leased to a property company and quickly filled with fast-food outlets and restaurants.[75] This removed Madin's original modernist vision of a space around and through the library complex in which the public could interact with the buildings.

As critics have noted, the demolition of John Henry Chamberlain's nineteenth-century library in the 1970s and, in 2016, of Madin's replacement library are both examples of Birmingham's propensity 'for sweeping away its recent past to make way for the latest fashion'.[76] From the late eighteenth century onwards, Birmingham as

John Madin's Birmingham Central Library, photographed in 2008. This striking example of brutalism was demolished in 2016. Photograph by tedandjen, Wikimedia Commons

Frank Taylor Lockwood's watercolour *Surviving Bombed Houses in Gooch Street, Birmingham*, c.1950, demonstrates how Birmingham artists have depicted the changing face of the city.
Courtesy of the Birmingham Royal Society of Artists. © the artist's estate

a transforming and developing city was reflected in its art, design and architectural output. The changing fashions and new styles in art and design, both followed and created by Birmingham's creative communities and practitioners, have helped to create our image of the city itself. Birmingham artists and designers have also documented the changing face of the city, both in the past and in the present, providing us with an invaluable record through art and design of how the city has grown, been transformed and continues to change.

Notes

1   S. Wildman, *The Birmingham School* (Birmingham, 1990), 5.

2   Ibid., 33.

3   Ibid., 32.

4   Birmingham Museum and Art Gallery (BMAG), acc. P40'68.

5   C. Wan, 'Samuel Lines and Sons: rediscovering Birmingham's artistic dynasty 1794–1898 through works on paper at the Royal Birmingham Society of Artists' (PhD thesis, University of Birmingham, 2012); L.H. Cust, 'Lines, Samuel (1778–1863)', rev. A. Peach, *Oxford Dictionary of National Biography* (hereafter *ODNB*) (Oxford University Press, 2004), online edn, http://www.oxforddnb.com/view/article/16724 (accessed 5 December 2015).

6   Cust, 'Lines, Samuel (1778–1863)'.

7   BMAG, acc. 31'93.

8   BMAG, acc. 1893P72.

9   S. Wildman, 'Cox, David (1783–1859)', *ODNB*, online edn, http://www.oxforddnb.com/view/article/6520 (accessed 2 December 2015).

10 Ibid.

11 BMAG, acc. 55'09

12 BMAG, acc. 1947P76; David Cox, *The Skylark*, cat. entry 12, in *RBSA: A Place for Art* (Birmingham, 2014), 72.

13 B. Flynn, 'A place for art', in *RBSA: A Place for Art*, 12–14.

14 A. Gomme, 'Archer, Thomas (1668/9–1743)', *ODNB*, online edn, http://www.oxforddnb.com/view/article/628 (accessed 5 December 2015).

15 A. Foster, *Birmingham*, *Pevsner Architectural Guide* (London and New Haven, CT, 2005); T. Slater, 'The Pride of the Place': *The Cathedral Church of St Philip, Birmingham, 1715–2015* (Birmingham, 2015).

16 A. Peers, *Birmingham Town Hall: An Architectural History* (Farnham, 2012).

17 Foster, *Birmingham*, 47–52.

18 'Birmingham Corporation Museum and Art Gallery', *The Magazine of Art*, 10 (1887), 361.

19 S. Hoban, 'Bunce, John Thackray (1828–1899)', *ODNB*, online edn, http://www.oxforddnb.com/view/article/104428 (accessed 5 December 2015).

20 G.C. Boase, 'Chamberlain, John Henry (1831–1883)', rev. M.W. Brooks, *ODNB*, online edn, http://www.oxforddnb.com/view/article/5047 (accessed 2 December 2015); Foster, *Birmingham*, 69–73; J. Holyoak, 'John Henry Chamberlain', in P. Ballard (ed.), *Birmingham's Victorian and Edwardian Architects* (Birmingham, 2009), 168–70.

21 Birmingham Archives and Heritage, L78.1 TAY, 502220, 'A Notable Art Master, an Appreciation of Edward R. Taylor' (Birmingham Municipal School of Art, n.d.).

22 E.R. Taylor, *Drawing and Design for Beginners* (London, 1893), 101.

23 Birmingham City University, Birmingham Municipal School of Art (hereafter BMSA) Management Subcommittee Minutes (hereafter Minutes), 26 June 1894, BMSA Archive.

24 BMSA Minutes, 14 January, 1896.

25 BMSA Minutes, 13 February, 1900, private proof of Examiner's Report 1900, prepared for members of the management subcommittee.

26 BMSA Minutes, 12 February 1901.

27 S. Hoban, 'The Birmingham Municipal School of Art and opportunities for women's paid work in the Arts and Crafts movement' (PhD thesis, University of Birmingham, 2014).

28 A. Crawford, 'Gaskin , Georgie Evelyn Cave (1866–1934)', *ODNB*, online edn, http://www.oxforddnb.com/view/article/66046 (accessed 5 December 2015).

29 Birmingham Assay Office, acc. A.0 144 and A.0. 143, silver spoons; *Birmingham Gold and Silver*, exhibition catalogue (Birmingham, 1973).

30 *Kelly's Directory of Birmingham* (1909, 1910, 1911).

31 *Kelly's Directory of Birmingham* (1912).

32 The casket is held in the permanent collection at BMAG, and is illustrated in *The Studio Magazine*, XXIII (1901), 122.

33 Hoban, 'The Birmingham Municipal School of Art', ch. 5; S. Hoban, 'Camm, Florence (1874–1960)', *ODNB*, online edn, http://www.oxforddnb.com/view/article/100972 (accessed 5 December 2015).

34 1881 Census, RG11/3036; 1901 Census, RG13/2839.

35 W.T. Whitley, *The Studio*, L, issue 210 (n.d.), 298.

36 1911 Census, no page number given.

37 Fruit bowl, V&A collection, CIRC,617,1954; pendant, V&A collection, CIRC.618-1954.

38 BMSA Minutes, 23 April 1901, memorial from 24 women students to Edward Taylor, April 1901, requesting a life class. Taylor authorized a class for women to meet on Monday, Wednesday and Thursday evenings.

39 BMSA, extant School of Art registers.

40 BMAG, acc. 1988M58.1, 1988M58.2 and 1988M58.3; Minutes of the Uniting Conference, 21 October 1932, Turin, BMAG Camm Scrapbook, no acc. number, 106.

41 BMSA Minutes 9 July 1895, 11 August 1899, 10 October 1899, 14 June 1900, 19 February 1904.

42 BMSA Minutes, 27 October 1885, 25 September 1894.

43 C. Newall, 'Jones, Sir Edward Coley Burne-, first baronet (1833–1898)', *ODNB*, online edn, http://www.oxforddnb.com/view/article/4051 (accessed 5 December 2015).

44 Foster, *Birmingham*, 45.

45 For a detailed examination of the commission, see B. Mireur, 'The stained glass windows of the Cathedral Church of St Philip the Apostle' (MA thesis, University of Nice, 2003).

46 'The wall paintings by art students in the Town Hall, Birmingham', *The Studio*, 1 (1893), 237–40. The works included *The Guild of the Holy Cross*, Kate Bunce; *Birmingham Riots – The Escape of Priestley 1791*, Charles March Gere (a study of this work has survived in the BMSA Archive); *Laying the Foundation Stone of the Guildhall*, Sidney Meteyard; *Edward VI Restoring to Birmingham the Lands of the Guild of the Holy Cross for the maintenance of a Grammar School*, Janette Bayliss; *Leland's Visit to Birmingham*, Henry Payne (the study for

this work is documented in a private collection in 1984); *William de Bermingham bringing vassals to join Simon de Montford*, T.S. Lones; *Instrumental Music*, Sidney Meteyard; *Vocal Music*, Henry Payne; *Dr Johnson's Visit to his friend Hector at Warren's Bookstall*, Walter Staimer; *Dr Sacherverrel's entry into Birmingham*, Bernard Sleigh; *Alm's Houses, Lench's Trust*, Kate Bunce; *Richard de Bermingham doing homage to William Fitz Ansculf, Lord of Dudley, 1070*, G.T. Tarling; and *Birmingham Pikemen Attacked by Rupert's Cavalry, Camp Hill, Birmingham, 1843*, G. Bernard Benton. It is possible that the entire commission was not completed.

47 A. Crawford, *By Hammer and Hand* (Birmingham, 1984), 63.

48 Analysis of data in *Kelly's Directory of Birmingham* (1886, 1915).

49 Tempera is a method of painting that utilizes egg yolk, water and powdered pigments. The technique was common until the late fifteenth century for the production of easel pictures. G. Breeze, 'Southall, Joseph Edward (1861–1944)', *ODNB*, online edn, http://www.oxforddnb.com/view/article/64535 (accessed 5 December 2015); J. Marsh, 'Bunce, Kate Elizabeth (1856–1927)', *ODNB*, online edn, http://www.oxforddnb.com/view/article/64730 (accessed 5 December 2015).

50 T. Cross, 'Newlyn School (act. 1882–c.1900)', *ODNB*, online edn, http://www.oxforddnb.com/view/article/64487 (accessed 2 December 2015).

51 Both works are in the permanent collection at BMAG.

52 Cross, 'Newlyn School'.

53 Private collection; see *RBSA: A Place for Art*, cat. no. 26.

54 S. Hoban, 'Bloye, William James (1890–1975)', *ODNB*, online edn, http://www.oxforddnb.com/view/article/104427 (accessed 2 December 2015).

55 G.T. Noszlopy, in J. Beach (ed.), *Public Sculpture of Birmingham* (Liverpool, 1998).

56 T. Hilton, 'Conroy Maddox obituary', *The Guardian*, 19 January 2005.

57 J. Jenkinson, 'Emmy Bridgwater obituary', *The Independent*, 23 October 2011.

58 L. Rüll, 'Emmy Bridgwater: a family and artistic chronology', in T. Sidey (ed), *Surrealism in Birmingham 1935–1954* (Birmingham, 2000), 52–56; and *Emmy Bridgwater (1906–99) Modern British Surrealist* (The Leicester Galleries, London, undated).

59 Jenkinson, 'Emmy Bridgewater'.

60 Emmy Bridgwater, *Untitled ink drawing*, BMAG, acc. 2000P7.

61 Emmy Bridgwater, *Night Work is About to Commence*, BMAG, acc. 2001P8.

62 T. del Renzio and D. Scott, *Surrealism in England 1936 and After* (Canterbury, 1986), 65.

63 Jenkinson, 'Emmy Bridgwater'.

64 For example, A. Clawley, *John Madin* (London, 2011).

65 J. Madin, extract from 'The future of Birmingham', 17 December 1940, quoted in Clawley, *John Madin*, Foreword.

66 A series of proposals for a civic centre and exhibition hall on the current site of Centenary Square and the Convention Centre were made between 1918 and 1958. For details, see Foster, *Birmingham*, 144.

67 *When We Build Again, A study based on research into conditions of living and working in Birmingham* (Birmingham, 1941).

68 *When We Build Again*, 2.

69 Clawley, *John Madin*, 5.

70 Ibid., 8.

71 Foster, *Birmingham*, 77.

72 For details of the plans and illustrations, see Clawley, *John Madin*, 104–7. The original Central Library in Birmingham was designed by Martin and Chamberlain in 1864–65, at the height of the civic gospel in the town, after Birmingham adopted the Free Libraries Act in 1860. Following a serious fire in 1879, the library was rebuilt by John Henry Chamberlain in his typical Italianate Renaissance style, but his building was demolished in 1974 to be replaced by Madin's complex.

73 Foster, *Birmingham*, 77.

74 Clawley, *John Madin*, 110.

75 Ibid., 116.

76 Ibid., 107.

CHAPTER NINE

Industry and Illness: Investing in Health and Medical Provision

JONATHAN REINARZ

During the eighteenth century the delivery of healthcare in Birmingham changed significantly as residents funded, built and gradually turned to medical institutions when caring for the ill, starting with a workhouse, a general hospital and dispensary. Not surprisingly, the attention of scholars has in the past concentrated on these early institutions, as well as prominent members of Birmingham's medical community who outshone their medical brethren, largely because they gained appointments in these buildings, and occasionally undertook some original research. While the challenges faced by the town's residents were to some extent common to other regions, they were also unique to a religiously diverse and rapidly expanding industrial town. Unlike some rural or economically vulnerable, single-industry districts, Birmingham was able to invest in healthcare, given the accumulation of wealth in the community and a considerable number of middle-class inhabitants.[1] With the establishment of a medical school in the town in 1828, Birmingham became the centre for medical knowledge production and communication in the midlands region. The town's commercial success further permitted its inhabitants from the middle of the nineteenth century to supplement its medical infrastructure with a comprehensive collection of specialist hospitals. By the end of the nineteenth century Birmingham supported a plethora of medical institutions, some of which achieved national reputations.

Despite the proliferation of hospitals during these years, improvements in the health of Birmingham's population were very much dependent on developments and reforms in other sectors. The importance of nutrition and public health to the growth of the British population since 1700 has been emphasized in these debates.[2] Significantly, this view was most forcibly advanced by a professor of social medicine

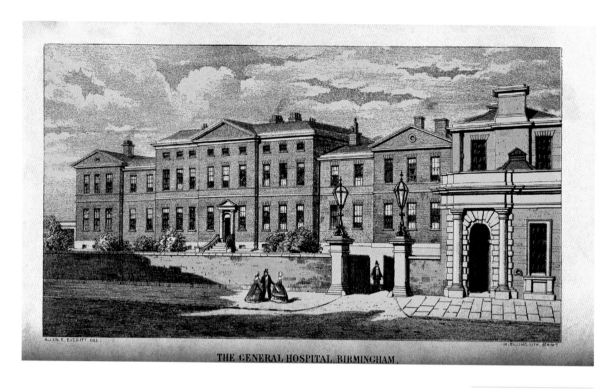
THE GENERAL HOSPITAL, BIRMINGHAM.

at the University of Birmingham, Thomas McKeown, his arguments concerning population growth having since been referred to as the McKeown thesis. He became one of the most influential figures in the development of the social history of medicine, mainly by downplaying the impact of therapeutic factors on mortality decline.[3] This shift in approach was characteristic of the work of medical historians in the 1980s and 1990s, and is equally noticeable in recent historical research on Birmingham's healthcare. That said, the history of medicine's unfolding in the city remains incomplete, and retains its earlier institutional focus; much work continues to employ a traditional biographical approach and emphasizes progress in medicine despite the existence of serious health inequalities that continue to the present day; there is also neglect of the medical careers of women and ethnic minorities who settled in the region, especially after 1950. While the literature perpetuates some myths and contains many gaps, it certainly conveys the powerful role of the hospital in the collective imagination. This chapter attempts to summarize the most influential and recent historical work on Birmingham's healthcare through the Georgian and Victorian periods. In the process, it charts the emergence of the city's comprehensive hospital services, which continue to sit at the heart of medical services in the midlands.

In 1767 Birmingham's 24,000 inhabitants were served by only a handful of qualified practitioners: 20 surgeons and only three university-trained physicians. The wealth of the local community, however, supported at least 11 druggists[4] and an ever-growing number of itinerant and unlicensed practitioners, who flogged their wares in local markets and newspapers as aggressively as any toymaker. To many

One of more than a dozen hospitals in Birmingham by the end of nineteenth century, the General was also the largest local hospital supported by voluntary donations. Its domestic appearance is emphasized in this nineteenth-century coloured lithograph by Allen Everitt.
Wellcome Library, London

orthodox practitioners it must have seemed a very crowded, if rapidly growing and potentially lucrative marketplace. To residents familiar with other industrial centres, it appeared a relatively healthy town, due partly to its distinctive natural landscape. A town on a hill, Birmingham's soils drained well and it possessed few cellar dwellings, which were common in places like Liverpool. As a result, Birmingham's inhabitants were less regularly visited by outbreaks of waterborne diseases.[5] According to local surgeon Thomas Tomlinson as early as 1769, epidemics in the town were both rare and in decline.[6] His work, along with that of other contemporary writers, popularized the view that a manufacturing town was a healthy town, an association that would go unchallenged for at least the next half century. Luxury appeared to pose greater threats to the health of the local population, which reached 52,250 in 1792, for most of the town's labourers, according to their workhouse surgeon, ate and drank too well. Perhaps it also seemed that too few spent their earnings on Birmingham's 37 surgeons and eight physicians. Although able to access the services of orthodox practitioners through membership of friendly societies,[7] most labourers avoided reliance on private doctors. Nor were medical institutions the first place to which many sick residents turned, for they were only just beginning to emerge: a workhouse infirmary was constructed in 1766 and a general hospital opened thirteen years later. By 1792 the town also possessed a general dispensary where the poor could obtain medicines, though not beds, without payment of a fee.

For most of Birmingham's inhabitants, the medical safety net, such as it existed, was the Poor Law. This form of medical provision for the lower orders had existed throughout the country since at least the seventeenth century. Medical relief was managed locally, largely by parish officers who engaged practitioners to dispense their services and wares, often on a contract basis.[8] If such expenses appeared unsustainable, as they did in Birmingham, alternative methods of organizing services were introduced. Institutional provision for Birmingham's poor had existed since

Bisset's *Magnificent Directory* (1808) carried advertisements for physicians, surgeons, apothecaries and chemists practising in the growing town.
By permission of the Library of Birmingham, 47154

The Old Workhouse on Steelhouse Lane, showing the Infirmary Wing 1766. The workhouse was central to the provision of healthcare, to the town's destitute sick. College of Medical and Dental Sciences, University of Birmingham

1733 when a workhouse was erected in Lichfield Street. A separate infirmary, costing £400, was added in 1766.[9] The medical wing accommodated 400, or less than 2 per cent of the town's population. Not surprisingly, it soon became overcrowded. Many workhouses across the country not only admitted the sick and aged, but also the infectious and mentally ill.[10] Some pressure was relieved by, for example, sending pauper lunatics to private madhouses. As a result, a new workhouse was not built until 1852 in Winson Green. Although the workhouse continued to admit infectious cases,[11] the institution never entirely shed its Poor Law associations, despite early efforts to medicalize its services.[12]

Strain on the workhouse was greatly relieved following the construction of a general hospital. Founded in 1765 by Dr John Ash, a Coventry-born and Oxford-educated physician, this voluntary hospital was intended for those who were without legal settlement in the parish, and who were therefore unable to access the existing Poor Law medical services. The project was not undertaken on purely altruistic grounds, for it allowed Ash to root himself in his adopted community and substantially enhance his profile.[13] Unlike the rate-funded workhouse, the general hospital, like other local charities, raised money through voluntary subscriptions. Following initial collections, Ash purchased a site on Summer Lane, though money ran out, possibly because of surplus wealth being invested in canals; building work ceased and the hospital lay abandoned for a decade.[14] Donations resumed in 1768, following the completion of an expensive canal network and the inauguration of a musical fundraiser held in St Paul's chapel. The hospital opened its doors to patients in 1779. Among those who joined Ash on the staff of the hospital was Shropshire physician William Withering. Best known for his book on the foxglove, Withering tested this folk remedy on his private patients as well as his hospital patients, and, in the process, transformed it into medical orthodoxy.[15]

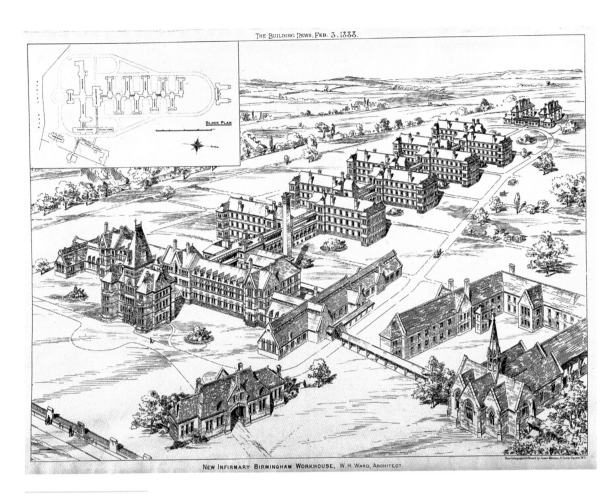

THE BUILDING NEWS. FEB. 3. 1888.

BLOCK PLAN

NEW INFIRMARY BIRMINGHAM WORKHOUSE, W. H. WARD, ARCHITECT.

New Infirmary Birmingham Workhouse, built at Winson Green in 1852, from *The Building News*, February 1888. Wellcome Library, London.

The music festival that had helped reinvigorate Ash's project became a triennial event from 1784.[16] Nationally, music and medicine enjoyed a symbiotic relationship,[17] and there were numerous artistic highlights at Birmingham's festival; as well as regular performances of Handel's oratorios, it saw the first performance of Mendelssohn's *Elijah* in 1846. By this time the festival, which was held in the Town Hall, was outperforming all other sources of funding, raising more than £10,000 in 1826, £4,500 of which was profit. At the time the hospital relied on just over 1,000 ordinary subscribers and a yearly income of less than £2,000, which barely covered the costs of treating 1,500 inpatients and more than twice that number of outpatients annually.[18]

Given the cultural role of the general hospital in the community, it is perhaps unsurprising that Birmingham's general dispensary was regarded as the less prestigious medical institution. While the general hospital has been the subject of a disproportionate number of historical studies, not least John Bunce's 1873 account,[19] dispensaries have been comparatively neglected by historians. Dispensaries offered an alternative and influential model for the delivery of healthcare and found many local champions, including the manufacturer Matthew Boulton, the dispensary's first treasurer. Initially located in Temple Row, the dispensary treated 280

William Withering moved to Birmingham in 1775. He is best remembered for his book on the medical use of the foxglove, the plant he holds in this copy by Gunnar Ekblom of von Breda's *Portrait of William Withering* (1792).
University of Birmingham Research & Cultural Collections

Charitable musical entertainments directed funds towards the general hospital. This copper medal, engraved by T. Halliday, was struck to celebrate the first Musical Festival held in the Town Hall in 1834.
By permission of Assay Office Birmingham, photographer Alexandre Parré

patients in 1794 and 2,723 in 1807, the year before it moved to Union Street. In addition to honorary physicians and surgeons, paid staff included an apothecary, who prepared medicines for 2,523 outpatients in 1818, while nearly 400 women were delivered of their children at home by the charity's midwives.[20] Perhaps its greatest, and most frequently overlooked, contribution to local healthcare was the 95,413 vaccinations carried out by its staff between 1793 and 1866.[21] So well regarded was this cost-effective form of healthcare that a series of regional branches were opened from 1872. Besides introducing additional local residents to institutional healthcare, many young medical practitioners began their careers at such institutions, albeit still largely intending to work their way up the medical hierarchy and into the service of the region's prestigious general hospitals.

One such enterprising young practitioner was John Darwall, appointed physician to the dispensary in 1822. Son of a clergyman at the general hospital, Darwall began his medical career as a surgeon's apprentice before walking the wards of the large London teaching hospitals and attending lectures at Edinburgh's medical school. Completing an innovative MD thesis on the diseases of artisans (1821), Darwall appears to have been the first Birmingham practitioner to have made the connection between industry and illness, and to have undertaken post-mortems in order to confirm causes of death.[22] While it would take some time for doctors to accept the links between poor health and specific industrial materials and processes,[23] hospital staff used such information productively and began to target local businesses more carefully when seeking donors. In this way, industry continued to prove beneficial to health in Birmingham. Identifying dangerous occupations gained added importance, due partly to the declining profits of the triennial music festivals in the 1870s. A solution to the crises repeatedly proclaimed in hospitals' annual reports was proposed by Sampson Gamgee, an outsider to Birmingham, like Ash, and a surgeon since recognized for his role in the development of aseptic surgery.[24] Gamgee suggested that the precarious state of the hospitals' finances could be rectified by canvassing local workers for their support. A 'Working Men's Fund' was first organized in 1869 to raise funds to enlarge Gamgee's own institution, Queen's Hospital. A subsequent attempt to solicit one Saturday's earnings from this constituency for 'the various medical charities' of the town in 1873 raised £4,700, and led to the establishment of an annual Hospital Saturday, which rapidly surpassed all other regular sources of funding.[25] The first initiative nationally to generate income for multiple hospitals, the fund augmented donations by encouraging competition between local workshops and provincial cities. Accounting for £10,867 raised in 1891, the Hospital Saturday Fund developed into a successful Hospital Contributory Scheme in the twentieth century. Birmingham retained its reputation as a centre of excellence in emergency medicine when it opened the Accident Hospital, under its Australian clinical director William Gissane, in 1941.[26]

Civic competition fostered other innovative initiatives, including the establishment of provincial schools of medicine. The first appeared in Manchester in 1824, the second in Birmingham a year later.[27] Unlike the town's general hospital, this medical institution was established by a locally born and educated surgeon, William Sands

From a series taken by architectural photographers Bedford, Lemere & Co., this photograph of a ward in 1897 at Queen's Hospital, Birmingham, opened in 1841, shows nurses and their patients.
By permission of the Cadbury Research Library: Special Collections, University of Birmingham

Cox. Like Darwall, Cox looked to lesions, not humours when considering disease. He came from a medical family, which worked to his advantage when establishing his school. Initially apprenticed to his surgeon father, Edward Townsend Cox, William travelled to London, where he walked the wards of Guy's and Thomas's, the capital's premier teaching hospitals. While there, he lodged with Edward Grainger, the Birmingham-born anatomist and founder of the Webb Street Anatomy School, who advised Cox to organize a course of medical instruction in the midlands. Before doing so, the young surgeon ventured to Paris where he undertook further training in botany and dissection. On his return to Birmingham, Cox was appointed surgeon to the general dispensary and climbed the first rung of the career ladder. Soon after, his ascent gained pace after he advertised and delivered his own course of anatomical lectures in the family residence in Temple Row in 1825, presumably after acquiring the unclaimed body of a pauper from the workhouse, where his father was a surgeon. From this series of demonstrations emerged an actual medical school, initially at Snow Hill, before it was relocated to a disused place of worship opposite the Town Hall in 1834.[28]

When the school successfully obtained a royal title in 1836, fundraising improved. Local inhabitants desiring a connection to the school donated books to its library, while doctors deposited specimens in the museum, which was central to instruction.[29] Never short of bodies for dissection, Cox acquired far greater sums of money when he drew the venture to the attention of a wealthy patient, the Revd Samuel Warneford. A recognized benefactor of midland medical charities, Warneford offered his support at a price. Although first and foremost a medical school, the institution, at Warneford's behest, included a theological seminary so that the school, in addition to medical practitioners, produced a stream of Anglican clergymen in a region that was attracting nonconformists. In 1841 a purpose-built teaching hospital, Queen's Hospital, opened in Bath Row. A parliamentary charter merged the two institutions in 1843, creating Queen's College. Modelled on an

J. Pardon, *Portrait of William Sands Cox* (1835?). Cox's portrait resembles that of his mentor, Astley Cooper, which hangs in the Royal Colleges of Surgeons, London.
University of Birmingham Research & Cultural Collections

THE QUEEN'S COLLEGE AT BIRMINGHAM.

Oxford college, the school offered local families a 'safe' alternative to sending their boys to London for medical training. Housed in residential wings, students attended chapel daily and were superintended by a warden.

Given Birmingham's thriving local economy and transport links, the school was potentially the nucleus for a university of the midlands. Instead, its difficulties accumulated. In 1851 student numbers declined, leaving theology the only successful department. In retrospect little else could be expected, as this period was one of nonconformist revival, with the town supporting twice as many nonconformist as Anglican places of worship. Excluded from full admission to the college, Birmingham's nonconformist community, together with Cox's other critics, established a rival school of medicine, affiliated with the town's general hospital, to which many influential citizens shifted their allegiance. With Warneford's death in 1855, Cox's funding finally dried up. Unwilling to quit his medical 'business', Cox ignored the school's problems and, eventually, the Charity Commissioners were called in to investigate the institution. Given Queen's College's chartered status, an Act of Parliament was required (and passed in 1864) to dissolve the institution. Four years later, the schools finally merged, and a universally popular medical college began to operate on transparent lines. By this time, the school's reputation had recovered, though Sands Cox's had not. His death in 1875 elicited an unusually brief report in the minutes of the teaching hospital he founded. The school, on the other

The Queen's College at Birmingham, engraving by T. Underwood. Created in 1843, Queen's College was modelled on an Oxford college.
College of Medical and Dental Sciences, University of Birmingham

hand, eventually amalgamated with Mason's College in 1892, forming what became the University of Birmingham in 1900.[30]

Long before this, medical training in Birmingham had expanded beyond the intensive study of anatomy to include new subjects and specialties, including physiology, botany, surgery and the diseases of women and children. As already recognized in many nineteenth-century trades, a division of labour proved equally beneficial to the production of medical knowledge. Representatives of orthodox medicine were initially hostile to any narrowing of practice, but the public appeared to demand the sort of specialization more often associated with quacks, who frequently declared themselves experts on particular organs or diseases. In some respects, orthodox medical practice was to blame for any splintering of expertise. Many of the first general hospitals excluded specific diseases and groups of patients, usually pregnant women, children, the mentally ill, as well as those afflicted with venereal disease, leaving rich pickings for anyone prepared to treat such cases. Localized pathology, as taught to Cox in the Parisian medical schools, provided a further rationale for those prepared to focus their attention on specific bodily systems.[31] Others saw specialization as a route to fame and fortune,[32] leading them, like Ash, to found local specialist hospitals, starting with orthopaedic (1817),[33] eye (1823) and ear hospitals (1843), when unable to attain coveted posts at the existing general hospitals. In the late nineteenth century resistance to specialization weakened, spurring the growth of other institutions: a dental hospital (1858), children's hospital (1861), women's hospital (1871) and a charity for skin diseases (1881).[34] When an Act of Parliament was passed in 1845 to encourage the establishment of mental asylums, Birmingham became the first borough council in England to open an asylum under the Act.[35] Land to build a second asylum at Rubery was purchased in 1876.

While the borough asylum, with its 200 beds, was very different from these small specialist hospitals, the dental hospital's early history is generally illustrative

Women medical students at the University of Birmingham Medical School, c.1915–16. Hilda Shufflebotham, later Dame Hilda Lloyd, is sitting in the front row, second from the right.
Private Collection

Students studying botany in 1923. The study of botany was long-established in medical training in Birmingham.
By permission of the Cadbury Research Library: Special Collections, University of Birmingham

Winson Green Mental Hosp.

Birmingham was the first borough council in England to open an asylum under the 1845 Act. Posted in 1921, the card shows All Saints Mental Hospital at Winson Green.
By permission of Mary Harding

of this specialization process, and an example of the way in which Birmingham's more modest medical charities operated, expanded and became professionalized in these years. Like Sands Cox, the founder of the town's dental charity, Samuel Adams Parker, was the son of a local surgeon, the venereologist Langston Parker. Trained in London with eminent dental practitioners, the younger Parker set up his medical institution to advance his career and expand his dental knowledge. Parker's Dental Dispensary was founded in 1858, a year after the establishment of the British Odontological Society, clearly an auspicious moment to undertake this special venture. Technological and institutional developments were also favourable to the initiative: reclining dental chairs had first been introduced to practice in 1858, and a dental charter was passed by the Royal College of Surgeons in 1859. Almost immediately, hospitals seemed reluctant to appoint anyone without the Licentiate of Dental Surgery (LDS) qualification. The first appointment of an LDS-qualified surgeon in Birmingham occurred in 1861, when the general hospital elected Parker to be its dental surgeon.[36]

Although claiming to be the town's sole dental institution, Parker's charity faced competition. The annual reports of the general hospital, for example, advertised in 1837 that staff had pulled 1,600 teeth, and numbers more than doubled by 1864. The general dispensary also offered dental treatment, though it ceased reporting cases after 1860. While this suggests that this work had begun to consolidate at a single specialist dental hospital, the children's hospital also acquired dental tools

Instruments for personal dental care were manufactured in Birmingham. A tooth-cleaning set for a wealthy customer made by Joseph Taylor in 1797 consisted of a sterling silver and bristle toothbrush, tooth-powder box and tongue scraper all contained in a red morocco case.
By permission of Assay Office Birmingham

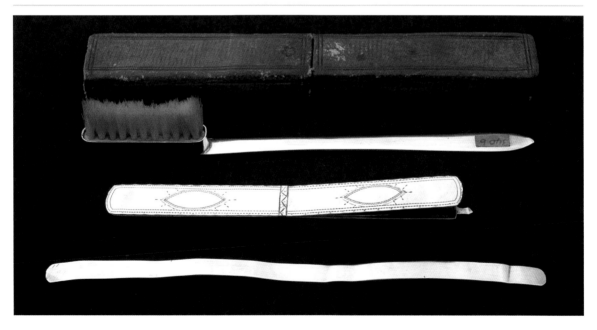

and reported four patients whose teeth required extraction in 1861, the year the hospital opened. An equivalent number were removed in the first month of 1862 alone, and hospital purchases in 1873 included a dental chair. Unorthodox practitioners also offered dental services, perhaps explaining why they were attacked in Parker's publications.[37] Of 264 medical advertisements appearing in Birmingham's newspaper, *Aris's Gazette*, between 1840 and 1870, 10 per cent were dental related, making these the fourth most common quack treatments peddled in the periodical's pages; these were surpassed only by general cure-alls (51), cosmetics (35) and medicines for respiratory diseases. In general, advertised dental goods and services included dentifrices, enamels, dentures, as well as painless extractions. One must also consider the numerous folk practices that continued to be employed in this and other areas of healthcare into the next century.[38]

When the dental charity commenced operations, like most specialist medical institutions, it started on a small scale. Opening its doors between nine and ten on one morning a week, its staff treated 645 patients and performed 725 operations during the charity's first year. By the 1860s cases had reached approximately 2,500 annually and, in 1863, the dental dispensary moved to 2 Upper Priory, where it shared premises with the homeopathic institution. Not only was this a reminder of dentistry's quack heritage, but its staff also frequently advertised, as was common among most medical pretenders. Although against the accepted rules of respectable medical practice, the strategy was effective and the charity was soon able to operate out of larger premises on Broad Street (1871). In 1878 the Dental Act placed Britain's 1,800 dentists on a sounder professional footing with the formation of the British Dental Association. Its members, like physicians, surgeons and apothecaries two decades earlier, could subsequently add their names to a register of recognized dental practitioners kept by the General Medical Council.[39] When the hospital moved to Newhall Street in 1882, it appeared little different from the town's other medical charities. If anything, it even added some prestige to the city's profile, its inhabitants being able to claim one of the world's first dental hospitals, preceded by only Baltimore (1839) and London (1840). The city eventually surpassed its rivals when it became the first to offer recognized degrees in dentistry. When the first representatives of the dental profession received knighthoods in 1884 and 1886, the transformation of dentists' professional status appeared complete. Although Parker died in obscurity in 1896, the hospital's reputation increased. Not only had it gained the support of the city's leading families, but it moved into purpose-built facilities in 1904. A few years later, programmes designed to examine systematically the mouths of school children revealed the full extent of the challenges that faced dental professionals.

Most specialist hospitals did not occupy buildings that were specifically built to house a medical charity. Birmingham's children's hospital, for example, opened its doors in 1861 in what had been a disused college of higher education, and the former site of an eye hospital.[40] Founded by the Edinburgh-trained physician Thomas Heslop, it had 16 beds, but more than doubled in size when its services moved into a former lying-in hospital on Broad Street. Serving a younger and needier cohort

of patients, the hospital appointed a greater proportion of nurses to inpatients than the town's other hospitals. Both the average age of hospital patients and nurses declined in these years.[41] By 1900, when nursing had become an occupation for young, systematically trained women, the children's hospital had expanded to 62 beds and treated 15,000 patients annually. Only from this date were women admitted to Birmingham's medical school to train as doctors, not just as nurses and midwives. The children's hospital had become the city's third biggest hospital by throughput, but staff regretted that it still had the highest death rate. While this might have indicated the need for such an institution locally, its organizers faced considerable opposition when proposing the children's medical charity nearly a decade after the country's first children's hospital opened in Great Ormond Street. The poor health of its earliest patients is best explained by the deleterious living conditions of those families residing nearest the hospital. Medicine had its limits, as McKeown and others have suggested, and further progress in health required more than the establishment of hospital services.[42] Improvement in the health of infants and of the town's poor inhabitants required better food, sanitation, as well as improved housing stock, priorities which the town's council appeared unwilling to address.[43] These improvements took many years to reach some members of the community.

Information on the history of public health in Birmingham before Alfred Hill's appointment to the post of Medical Officer of Health in 1872 is scattered. In previous years, measures were often improvised, as when an epidemic of cholera threatened the region in the 1830s, and were occasionally more effective than previous histories of the unreformed Poor Law might lead one to think.[44] By the 1870s, however, regular sanitary surveys of the town and its 383,000 residents were conducted by a permanent Board of Health. The population, with an average life expectancy of 35 years, inhabited 73,000 dwellings,[45] approximately 50 per cent of which comprised back-to-back houses located in some of the town's poorest wards. The worst slums, regarded at the time to be as 'lethal as any disease-ridden tropical marsh',[46] were removed following the commercialization of the town's centre under the Artisans' and Labourers Dwellings Act (1875). Moreover, when slums were cleared, the motive was often profit rather than concern for the 'plight of the poor'.[47] The quality of the town's private slaughterhouses and the food sold in its markets improved considerably after the appointment in 1858 of a borough public analyst, a post Hill assumed in 1866. As Medical Officer of Health, Hill regularly turned his attention to outbreaks of infectious disease. At this time, nearly 43 per cent of Birmingham's deaths resulted from six diseases: measles, scarlet fever, whooping cough, typhoid fever, diarrhoea and phthisis, leaving the borough with an average death rate of 25 per 1,000 inhabitants. While universal education was said to have encouraged the spread of infectious diseases among children gathered in schools,[48] a fever hospital, opened in Winson Green in 1875, allowed for the isolation of the town's infectious cases. The construction of sewers and the closure of open wells further reduced the impact of waterborne diseases such as typhoid. In his first two years in office, Hill closed 3,000 contaminated wells,[49] and, in the 1880s, he was still closing nearly 400 annually. Moreover, in 1878, nearly 6,000 pan privies were introduced to the borough's dwellings, raising the total to 28,660, and another 3.5 miles of sewers were constructed that same year. By this time, water was more often piped directly into, or near, homes by a local authority that controlled and filtered its own water supply.

An ambitious plan to transport water from the Elan and Claerwen rivers in Wales was planned under the Birmingham Corporation Water Act (1892) and completed in 1904, by which time John Robertson had become Birmingham's second Medical Officer of Health. At Hill's retirement in 1903, his department employed 200 staff, including female health inspectors (appointed in 1899), who made 11,000 visits in their first year.[50]

While some maternal support had been offered by existing medical charities, a hospital specifically for women was a relatively late development in Birmingham. Opened in 1871, with eight beds, the women's hospital was originally restricted to those suffering from pelvic disease, primarily ovarian tumours. As such care was not offered by existing institutions or private practitioners, the hospital from its outset potentially served a wider class of patients than was common at voluntary hospitals. It was also the first hospital in Birmingham to appoint women practitioners to its staff, beginning with a Miss Harding as

The transport of fresh water from the Elan Valley in Wales provided a vital public health improvement for the people of Birmingham. This plan shows the position of the works on the watershed and is taken from *The Future Water Supply of Birmingham* by Thomas Barclay (1898). By permission of the Cadbury Research Library: Special Collections, University of Birmingham

Alfred Hill, Birmingham's Medical Officer of Health, 1872–1903. This photograph of Hill commemorates his term as president of the Society of Medical Officers of Health from 1886 to 1888. Wellcome Library, London

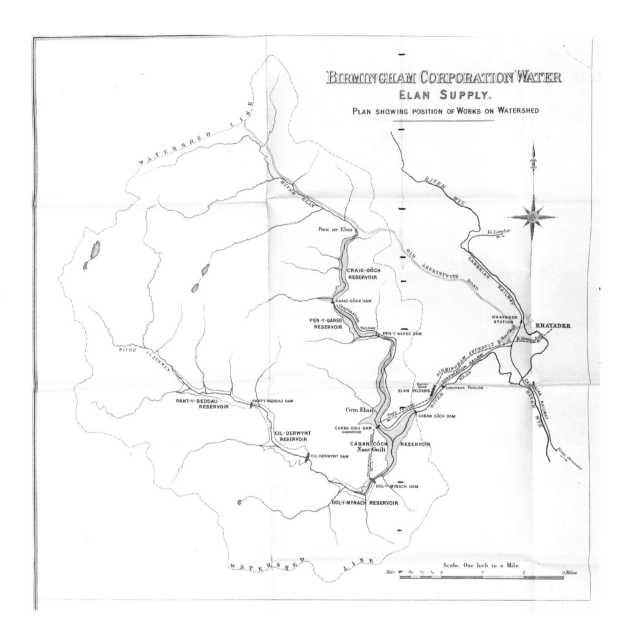

Lady Dispenser; in later years, patients were attended by Hilda Lloyd, who became the first women president of a Royal College.[51] Enlarged in 1878, the women's hospital moved out of city-centre premises at the Crescent and into the suburbs in Sparkbrook. There its staff continued a reputation for innovation, if not daring in the operating theatre. Its best-known member of staff, another outsider to Birmingham, was the surgeon Lawson Tait, who operated alongside physician Thomas Savage. Son of a butler, Tait trained in Edinburgh and served as assistant to James Simpson, the most renowned obstetrician in the kingdom due to his role in discovering the anaesthetic properties of chloroform.[52] Following Simpson, Tait operated painlessly, performing ovariotomies (the removal of diseased ovaries) under aseptic conditions

in four cottage wards designed 'specifically for the treatment of Ovarian and Kindred Tumours'.[53] According to one study, so controversial was this operation that it could only be undertaken in an outlying and free-thinking provincial town, far removed from the wider scrutiny (and control) of the capital.[54] The majority of patients treated at the hospital were admitted with post-obstetric trauma and chronic conditions, such as prolapsed uteri, which accounted for 35 per cent of attendances in the institution's first five months.[55] Despite the staff's best precautions, the hospital recorded high levels of mortality in its first years. Within a short period, however, its mortality rate had declined dramatically to 9 per cent in 1881, before plummeting to 1 per cent in 1892. As a result of his results in the operating theatre, Tait achieved an international reputation, and many students and trans-Atlantic admirers visited Birmingham.[56] Closer to home, many city inhabitants began to recognize that a level of treatment and innovation existed in hospitals which was not replicated in patients' homes, or offered by their private practitioners. This included X-rays, which were incorporated into clinical practice due to the efforts of local radiological pioneer Major Hall-Edwards.[57] As a result, in the twentieth century hospitals cemented their central place in local medical services and began to serve a much wider social class than would ordinarily have accessed institutional care before.

The Crescent was the site of the Women's Hospital from 1871 until it moved to Sparkbrook in 1878. The hospital is the building on the far left of the photograph.
College of Medical and Dental Sciences, University of Birmingham

Jacob Epstein, *Portrait bust of Dame Hilda Lloyd* (1951). Lloyd was the first woman medical professor at the University of Birmingham and the only woman in the twentieth century to be a president of a Royal Medical College, in her case that of the Obstetricians and Gynaecologists.
University of Birmingham Research & Cultural Collections

Conclusion

While the story of medicine and healthcare in Birmingham is representative of developments in many nineteenth-century English provincial towns, Birmingham's experience was also unique, not least given the nature of the local economy. As 'a town of a thousand trades', Birmingham's industrial base was diverse and dependable, for it was not reliant on a single, vulnerable industry. The strength of the local economy throughout the nineteenth century permitted a degree of hospital construction and reconstruction not seen in other towns and cities. Financial crises occurred, even in Birmingham, given ever-increasing levels of investment in institutional medicine. Nevertheless, despite having established an unrivalled range of voluntary hospitals, Birmingham was advantageously placed to weather financial storms. Besides pioneering an impressive number of medical innovations, Birmingham developed new sources of funding, not least through the municipalization of gas and water services. In times of plenty, schemes such as workplace collections promoted the growth of medical services and permitted hospital boards of management to invest in technologies that would attract individuals who had not previously sought admission to hospital. Unlike under-resourced regions, Birmingham's services did not need enhancement when the National Health Service was introduced in 1948. When buildings for all classes of patients were relocated to a new hospital centre in Edgbaston a decade earlier, this concentration of medical services was unprecedented in all but a few cities.[58]

Whether these innovations directly improved the health of the town's inhabitants is more contentious. More research is required. Birmingham's hospital services may have been well developed and financed before the introduction of a National Health Service, but historical studies of medicine in the region have focused on what might be described as the town's prestige projects, thereby neglecting the wider field of healthcare. Despite more focus on the twentieth century, there is scope for more work on the history of medicine in Birmingham in the last century, and not only on new specialties, such as oncology and genetics, but also maternity services and accident and emergency medicine. In contrast with the city's medical school and general hospital, primary care, community and public healthcare services have received far less scholarly attention. Also overlooked have been the deprived communities that made up Birmingham, which became more diverse throughout the twentieth century.

The new hospital centre in Edgbaston, which provided a concentration of medical services and medical education. The Medical School and Hospital were opened by George VI and Queen Elizabeth in 1939.
University of Birmingham Research & Cultural Collections

Notes

1   C. Chinn, *Poverty and Prosperity: The Urban Poor in England, 1834–1914* (Manchester, 1995), 77.

2   T. McKeown, *The Modern Rise of Population* (London, 1976).

3   B. Harris, 'Public health, nutrition, and the decline of mortality: the McKeown thesis revisited', *Social History of Medicine*, 17.3 (2004), 379–407.

4   J. Lane, *A Social History of Medicine: Health, Healing and Disease in England, 1750–1950* (Abingdon, 2001), 162.

5   I. Cawood and C. Upton, '"Divine providence": Birmingham and the cholera pandemic of 1832', *Journal of Urban History*, 20.10 (2013), 1–19.

6   T. Tomlinson, *Medical Miscellany* (London, 1769), 203–4; J. Reinarz, 'The transformation of medical education in eighteenth-century England: international developments and the West Midlands', *History of Education*, 37.4 (2008), 559–60.

7   E. Hopkins, *Industrialisation and Society: A Social History, 1830–1951* (London, 2000), 52.

8   J. Lane, *The Administration of an Eighteenth-century Warwickshire Parish: Butlers Marston* (Oxford, 1973), 17–21.

9   J. Reinarz and A.E. Ritch, 'Exploring medical care in the nineteenth-century provincial workhouse: a view from Birmingham', in J. Reinarz and L. Schwarz (eds), *Medicine and the Workhouse* (Rochester, NY, 2013), 142.

10 L. Smith, 'The pauper lunatic problem in the West Midlands, 1815–1850', *Midland History*, 21 (1996), 101; L. Smith, 'Duddeston Hall and the "trade in lunacy" 1835–65', *Birmingham Historian*, 8 (1992), 16–22.

11 A.E. Ritch, 'Medical care in the workhouses in Birmingham and Wolverhampton, 1834–1914' (PhD thesis, University of Birmingham, 2015).

12 G. Hearn, *Dudley Road Hospital, 1887–1987* (Birmingham, 1987).

13 R. Waterhouse, 'Portrait of a marginal man: Dr John Ash and his career', in J. Reinarz (ed.), *Medicine and Society in the Midlands, 1750–1950* (Birmingham, 2007), 12–26.

14 J. Reinarz, *The Birth of a Provincial Hospital: The Early Years of the General Hospital, Birmingham, 1765–1790* (Stratford-upon-Avon, 2003).

15 W. Withering, *An Account of the Foxglove and Some of its Medical Uses* (Birmingham, 1785); T.W. Peck and K.D. Wilkinson, *William Withering of Birmingham* (Bristol, 1950).

16 A. Elliott, *The Music Makers: A Brief History of the Birmingham Triennial Music Festivals, 1784–1912* (Birmingham, 2000).

17 J. Brewer, *The Pleasures of the Imagination: English Culture in the Eighteenth Century* (London, 1997), 375.

18 J. Reinarz, *Health Care in Birmingham: The Birmingham Teaching Hospitals 1779–1939* (Woodbridge, 2009), 27.

19 J.T. Bunce, *A History of the Birmingham General Hospital and the Musical Festivals 1768–1873* (Birmingham, 1873).

20 F. Badger, 'Delivering maternity care: midwives and midwifery in Birmingham and its environs, 1794–1880' (PhD thesis, University of Birmingham, 2014).

21 J.A. Langford (ed.), *A Century of Birmingham Life, Vol. II* (Birmingham, 1868), 143–5.

22 J. Reinarz and A. Williams, 'John Darwall (1796–1833): the short yet productive life of a Birmingham practitioner', *Journal of Medical Biography*, 3.3 (2005), 150–4.

23 T. Carter, '"Brass poisoning" in Birmingham: the rise and fall of a syndrome, 1860–1910', in J. Reinarz (ed.), *Medicine and Society in the Midlands, 1750–1950* (Birmingham, 2007), 152–66.

24 H.M. Kapadia, 'Sampson Gamgee: a great Birmingham surgeon', *Journal of the Royal Society of Medicine*, 95.2 (2002), 96–100.

25 M. Gorsky and J. Mohan with T. Willis, *Mutualism and Health Care: British Hospital Contributory Schemes in the Twentieth Century* (Manchester, 2006), 23–4.

26 S.H. Harrison, 'Accident surgery – the life and times of William Gissane', *Injury*, 16 (1984), 145–54.

27 J.T.J. Morrison, *William Sands Cox and the Birmingham Medical School* (Birmingham, 1926), 22.

28 Reinarz, *Health Care in Birmingham*, 48–51.

29 J. Reinarz, 'The age of museum medicine: the rise and fall of the medical museum at Birmingham Medical School', *Social History of Medicine*, 18.3 (2005), 419–37.

30 E. Ives, D. Drummond and L. Schwarz, *The First Civic University: Birmingham 1880–1980. An Introductory History* (Birmingham, 2000), 42–5.

31 G. Weisz, *Divide and Conquer: A Comparative History of Medical Specialization* (Oxford, 2005).

32 L. Granshaw, 'Fame and fortune through bricks and mortar', in L. Granshaw and R. Porter (eds), *The Hospital in History* (London, 1989).

33 M.W. White, *Years of Caring: The Royal Orthopaedic Hospital* (Studley, 1997).

34 Reinarz, *Health Care in Birmingham*.

35 S. Lamb et al., *All Saints Hospital* (Birmingham, 1997).

36 R. Cohen, *The History of the Birmingham Dental Hospital and Dental School 1858–1958* (Birmingham, 1958).

37 S.A. Parker, *Remarks on Artificial Teeth* (Birmingham, 1862), 56.

38 Reinarz, *Health Care in Birmingham*, 94–6.

39 D. Richards, 'Final chapters in the campaign to effect dental registration', *Bulletin of the Society for the Social History of Medicine*, 23 (1978), 23–6.

40 R. Waterhouse, *Children in Hospital: A Hundred Years of Childcare in Birmingham* (Birmingham, 1962), 24–5.

41 S. Wildman, 'Changes in hospital nursing in the West Midlands, 1841–1901', in J. Reinarz (ed.), *Medicine and Society in the Midlands 1750–1950* (Birmingham, 2007), 98.

42 R. Woods, 'Mortality and sanitary conditions in the "best governed city in the world" – Birmingham, 1870–1910', *Journal of Historical Geography*, 4.1 (1978), 35.

43 C. Chinn, *Homes for People. 100 Years of Council Housing in Birmingham* (Birmingham 1991), 2.

44 Cawood and Upton, '"Divine providence"', 3.

45 MOH annual report, 1878.

46 A. Wohl, *Endangered Lives: Public Health in Victorian Britain* (London, 1984), 286.

47 C. Chinn, *Homes for People: Council Housing and Urban Renewal in Birmingham 1849–1999* (Studley, 1999), 5.

48 MOH annual report, 1878, 9.

49 E. Hopkins, *Birmingham. The First Manufacturing Town in the World* (London, 1989), 53.

50 R.J. Proctor, 'Infant mortality: a study of the impact of social intervention in Birmingham 1873–1938' (MPhil dissertation, University of Birmingham, 2011), 45–71.

51 R. Watts, *Women in Science: A Social and Cultural History* (London, 2007), 189.

52 J. Shepherd, *Lawson Tait: The Rebellious Surgeon (1845–1899)* (Kansas, 1980), 6.

53 J. Lockhart, '"Truly, a hospital for women": The Birmingham and Midland Hospital for Women 1871–1901' (PhD thesis, University of Warwick, 2002), 58.

54 J.E. Sewell, 'Bountiful bodies: Spencer Wells, Lawson Tait and the birth of British gynaecology' (PhD thesis, Johns Hopkins University, 1990), 159.

55 Ibid., 56.

56 Ibid., 209.

57 A.M.K. Thomas and A.K. Banergee, *The History of Radiology* (Oxford, 2013), 7.

58 C. Clifford, *QE Nurse 1938–1957* (Studley, 1997), 16.

Printing and the Printed Word

CAROLINE ARCHER-PARRÉ

Birmingham is Britain's most historically important centre of printing outside London. Through its connections with William Caslon the elder, England's first native type founder, and John Baskerville, the famous printer, Birmingham became *the* centre of European printing during the mid-eighteenth century. Its contribution to printing history, however, extends beyond Caslon and Baskerville, and for three centuries the city's printers, type founders,[1] engravers,[2] book makers, newspaper makers and typographic educators have combined to make the region not only a local but also national and international typographic force, which in 2014 boasted 718 printing firms employing 7,860 people and turning over £731,598,000 annually.[3] But it is not simply economics that makes Birmingham's printing trade significant. Its products are a reflection of its changing intellectual, social, spiritual and commercial life, which has been preserved through the production of books, broadsides, ballads, newspapers and a range of general printing.

This chapter considers the history of Birmingham's printing industry and its products from the arrival of its first printer in the early eighteenth century to the advent of computer technology in the mid-twentieth century.

Books, ballads and broadsides

From the thirteenth century Birmingham's chapels and chantries, guilds and schools ensured there was a significant community of clergy and scholars with a requirement for books and manuscripts. By the mid-seventeenth century the town's learned men had their literary demands satisfied by books brought from London and sold through local booksellers,[4] whose presence was an indication of the town's educational position and literary capacity. Birmingham's educated communities comprised writers as well as readers, and John Rogers (c.1500–55),[5] clergyman and Bible translator from Deritend, is the first known published author connected with the town, who in 1548 rendered into English Philip Melancthon's *Weighing of the intern*.[6] This was the start of a literary culture in the town which generated numerous publications, political tracts and sermons written by local authors such as John Barton (c.1605–75), headmaster of King Edward's School;[7] Francis Roberts (1609–75), vicar of St Martin in the Bull Ring;[8] and Thomas Hall (1610–65), master of King's Norton Grammar School.[9] However, as a result of restrictions on the press, their texts had to be printed in London.[10] In 1712 the town's earliest known printer, Matthew Unwin, established a printing shop near the church of St Martin, rendering it unnecessary for Birmingham authors to turn to the capital for the publication of their books. In 1717 Unwin issued the first book printed in the town: *The Martyrdom of King Charles the First: A Sermon Preached on the 30th of January*.[11] Two years later, in 1719, the town's second printer, Henry Butler, issued his first book, *A help against sin*;[12] and Thomas Warren, better known as a newspaper printer, became something

Title page of *The Martyrdom of King Charles the First: A Sermon Preached on the 30th of January*, 1717, the first known book printed in Birmingham. The battered condition of the type and the unevenness of the impression are typical of the period.
By permission of the Library of Birmingham, LS SC/103

A Letter press printer from *The Book of trades or Library of the Useful Arts*, (1806). This artist's impression shows the inside of a printing house, with a wooden press in the foreground, a compositor standing at the type case and holding a composing stick in his left hand and printed sheets drying overhead.

By permission of the Library of Birmingham, 087.11806

of a celebrity when in 1733 he produced Samuel Johnson's first book, a translation of Lubo's *Account of Abyssinia*.

Unwin and Butler established their presses in Birmingham in response to a lively literate market and their services relieved the town's authors from the inconvenience and expense of engaging with the London press. At the start of the eighteenth century the quality of printing in England was at a particularly low level and Birmingham's early printed books were no exception:[13] they were roughly produced, composed using inferior type and printed on substandard paper by poorly skilled men using rudimentary wooden presses typical of the era. They were typographically unexceptional publications and yet they were significant as they marked the start of Birmingham's book printing trade.

How Unwin and Butler acquired their typographic knowledge is not known: possibly they visited London to obtain both the skills and the necessary equipment. It would have been costly for the aspiring printers to furnish themselves with all the material needed to set up shop, for they not only required wooden hand presses but also expensive metal type, which either had to be brought from London or imported from Europe because the town had, as yet, no resident type founder. In addition, paper in the early eighteenth century was costly and had to be obtained from outside the town. They would also have needed to employ additional hands in order to perform the many and varied tasks required of printing. Equipment and workmen necessitated workshop space with specially reinforced flooring to bear the weight of the metal type. Unwin and Butler were both located in premises around High Street, New Street and the Bull Ring – a district that became the nucleus of Birmingham's eighteenth-century printing trade – where conditions were often squalid and cramped, with the ever-present danger from a lethal combination of paper, oil, turpentine and candle-light.[14] However, from these unpropitious surroundings the printers issued books to satisfy affluent readers and their private libraries. Although reading and writing were no longer confined to the clergy, the town's authors were insufficient in number to sustain two book printers, and both Unwin and Butler found it necessary to offer general printing services in addition to book printing. It is likely that they produced a range of ephemeral items such as invitation and trade cards, tickets and letterheads for the same educated and prosperous buyers who purchased their books.[15]

Between 1700 and 1750 the population of Birmingham increased from 16,000 to 42,350, and there was a commensurate increase in the number of printers from two at the start of the century to 42 by the mid-eighteenth century, supplying the town's growing demand for reading matter.[16] While Birmingham's eighteenth-century book printers supplied a country-wide market, Birmingham's general printers, before the development of efficient transport and postal systems, were wholly dependent upon the immediate community for work.[17] To sustain the trade, the town needed to generate a significant amount of work in order to keep the presses occupied and enable the printers to make a return on their investment. Evidently, there was insufficient work to go round, as all Birmingham's printers supplemented their income by offering allied services such as book dealing and print selling, publishing, bookbinding, paper and ink making, or by operating circulating libraries. Over 50 per cent of the town's printers also ran additional, non-allied businesses such as auctioneering, button making and brewing, or offered their services as chemists, victuallers, hosiers, tavern keepers, estate agents or singing masters.[18] The trade was male-dominated: eighteenth-century women were prohibited from establishing printing businesses, but were allowed to inherit from family members. Between 1712 and 1799 four of the town's printing shops had female proprietors: the first, Esther Butler, was the widow of the town's second printer, Henry Butler, who continued her husband's business for fourteen years between 1758 and 1772; Sarah Baskerville, widow of John, maintained his type foundry and print shop for just two years (1775–77), as did Elizabeth Ralph, widow of a copperplate printer; Susannah Martin, widow of Robert, continued the business for thirteen years from 1797 until her own death in 1810. Of the ten known female proprietors in the nineteenth century, Sarah Turner, widow of Thomas, who traded as a bookseller, printer, stationer and music seller, was by far the longest serving, operating her business for twenty-one years between 1819 and 1840.[19]

While Unwin and Butler produced clerical and learned publications for affluent buyers with private libraries around the country, there were a growing number of printers producing cheap print for an expanding, if less erudite, local public. Eighteenth-century Birmingham developed a vibrant culture of street literature as the town's printers issued increasing numbers of the broadsides and chapbooks that formed the primary reading matter of the poor. These were cheaply printed using metal type and printed on wooden hand presses; small in format (11 x 6 cm), the publications comprised just a few pages, which were printed in a single colour using battered type on substandard paper: T. Brandard and S. Bloomer of Edgbaston Street were the foremost printers of this ephemeral, low-quality work. Priced at just one penny, the subjects included juvenile literature or moral tales, such as *The good child's amusing riddle-book*, or *Miss Maria Wilkins the only child of Mr and Mrs Wilkins who thought themselves superior to their neighbours*, and *Diamonds and toads: or, Humility rewarded, and pride punished*. Chapbooks and broadsides also carried news of

An Introduction to the Knowledge of Medals, 1775, was printed by John Baskerville's widow Sarah, one of only a handful of female printers in the town. Sarah is known to have printed two books only (the other being an edition of Horace); both were re-issues of works previously published by her husband. By permission of the Cadbury Research Library: Special Collections, University of Birmingham

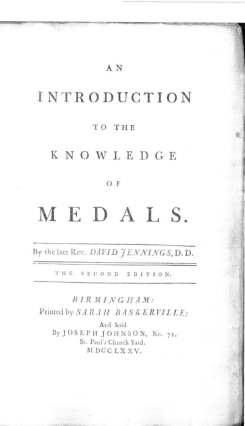

sensational and shocking crimes, executions, riots and wars and many were advertised as 'adorned with cuts' – woodblock illustrations that generally had little to do with the contents. In the absence of any local wood engravers the cuts were purchased out of town, and their battered condition indicates that they had already been used and reused for many publications. These ephemera were sold by itinerant chapmen who touted their goods in the street either from small tables or pinned to the wall.

Eighteenth-century Birmingham was also an important centre for ballad printing, cheap, flimsy and ephemeral items of literature for the poor, usually printed and sold as a single sheet. John Freeth (1731–1808) was Birmingham's leading exponent of the genre and his political ballads were published in twelve volumes and distributed nationally between 1766 and 1805.[20] The best-known of his books was *The Political Songster*, printed by John Baskerville in 1771 – not, however, as cheap literature for the poor, but as an expensive volume for the typographically discerning. Birmingham's ballad printing had its heyday in the mid-nineteenth century but the trade had almost ceased by 1890. During this period more than fifty ballad printers established themselves in the town: some were transient and vanished after issuing just a few titles, others were more permanent and prolific. Some of the leading nineteenth-century ballad printers, such as Theophilus Bloomer, Joseph Russell, William Pratt, William Wright, Thomas Watts and William Jackson,[21] remained in the town for up to thirty years and produced in excess of 500 titles.[22] For the principal exponents of the trade, ballad printing was a lucrative business: when Joseph Russell died in 1840 he left £12,000 – the proceeds of nineteen years in the trade – to George J. Holyoake (1817–1906), secularist and newspaper editor, for the purpose of setting up a secular school in the town.[23] Most ballad printers, however, struggled to make a living and worked from meagre premises in back alleys, frequently changing address and supplementing their income through allied or non-allied trades. It was a perilous business and more than one such printer ended up in Warwick jail for printing seditious literature: Joseph Russell was tried and imprisoned for six months in 1819 for printing and selling an edition of William Hone's *Political Litany* parodying the Prince Regent, which had been bought from Russell's shop by an informant.[24]

Birmingham's musical appetite was not confined to cheap ballads. In 1741 Michael Broome (1700–75), singing master, musician and psalmodist, established himself as a printer, engraver, publisher and seller of music, trading from the sign of 'Purcell's Head' in Lichfield Street, usefully located near Sawyer's Assembly Room where subscription concerts were held. So successful was Broome's business that in 1751 he moved to Colmore Row, became the father of the Birmingham Musical Society,[25] and engraved and printed many musical publications such as *Divine Harmony* (1750) and *The Catch Club or pleasant musical companion* (1757) which were sold by Thomas Aris.[26] Broome appears to have been well thought of in the local trade, and collaborated with John Baskerville on an edition of John Pixell's *A collection of songs with their recitations and symphonies*: the title page and preliminary matter were printed by Baskerville and the 'plates engrav'd and printed by M Broome in Birmingham, 1759'. The town's appetite for music ensured that

The Bloody Gardener's Cruelty, a broadside ballad printed by T. Bloomer of Edgbaston Street between 1821 and 1827. The themes of murder, courtship, a cruel mother and love which transcends social boundaries were as popular as the multitudinous and monstrous typefaces used to convey the story.
By permission of the Cadbury Research Library: Special Collections, University of Birmingham

Broome had no shortage of outlets from which to sell his printed music, for between 1741 and 1850 no less than 82 music sellers traded in the town.[27]

While Birmingham printers issued a plethora of cheap print, the town also had its share in the casting of type and the crafts of punch cutting and the production of matrices.[28] In the eighteenth century England's native type founding was restricted in production and poor in manufacture, and type of quality had to be imported from

Holland. William Caslon (1692–1766) was born in Cradley, Worcestershire, and served an apprenticeship as an engraver of ornamental gun locks and gun barrels, at which Birmingham excelled.[29] In 1716 Caslon moved to Clerkenwell, London's traditional centre of gun making, jewellery and printing,[30] from where he expanded his business to cutting tools for bookbinders and letters for bookbindings, and later embarked on cutting punches for printing types. Whether by genius, trial and error, or through the exchange of knowledge between craftsmen in the nearby trades, Caslon was able to transfer the engraving skills he had acquired in Birmingham to punch cutting, and in doing so he claims the distinction of being England's first type founder. The revolution in letters effected by Caslon was important, for it was no longer necessary to go to Holland for superior types:[31] the gun-lock engraver from Cradley rescued English type founding and gave the country a range of letters which, with only one exception, the types of John Baskerville, remained unsurpassed.

John Baskerville (1707–75) from Wolverley, Worcestershire, was the pre-eminent punch cutter, type founder and printer of the eighteenth century who, with no training in the typographic craft, created the typeface that bears his name, improved the printing press, experimented with wove paper, reconsidered the production of printing inks and took a wholly new approach to the design of books.[32] Baskerville dominates not just Birmingham's but Europe's eighteenth-century printing industry. However, he was not the first punch cutter to trade in the town; that honour goes to George Anderton (?–1763), an engraver who was also one of the earliest English provincial letter founders.[33] From his workshop in Temple Street he attempted letter founding and in 1753 printed a specimen of Great Primer roman and italic (of which no example survives), thus pre-empting Baskerville's efforts by four years.

Baskerville arrived in Birmingham in about 1726, 'having trained in no occupation': he established a school in the Bull Ring from which he taught handwriting and, by 1736, he was also carving headstones.[34] In 1740 he began manufacturing japanware,[35] a trade from which he amassed a fortune and which enabled him to return to his first passion, lettering, a skill he adapted to printing in order to accommodate his love of letters. Like Caslon before him, Baskerville transferred his skills and knowledge across trades and applied his understanding of letters to type design, creating a typeface more beautiful than had hitherto been seen. To print his new letters Baskerville needed a printing press that was more

Odes, Cantatas, Songs, etc. divine, moral, entertaining (1773), published on behalf of the poet, priest and composer John Pixell by William Fletcher, a printer and seller of music who traded in the town from 1769 to c.1806.
By permission of the Cadbury Research Library: Special Collections, University of Birmingham.

Joyce Francis drew this image of John Baskerville in the 1930s for the Birmingham School of Printing. It is a version of the only known portrait of Baskerville, painted by James Millar c.1774, which is now in the collection of Birmingham Museums Trust.

By permission of Caroline Archer-Parré

Following Baskerville's death, his printing equipment, type and punches were sold in 1785 to the French dramatist Beaumarchais who used the material to print the entirety of the banned works of Voltaire. After nearly two hundred years, the punches were repatriated when the Parisian typefounder Charles Peignot presented the surviving punches to Cambridge University Press on 12 March 1953.

Photograph by Alexandre Parré, reproduced by permission

steady and refined than the wooden hand presses common in the eighteenth century. Baskerville made adjustments to the press, which enabled him to print more evenly and regularly than had previously been possible. His presses were no different to those used by other printers, but they were built with greater precision. He also adapted his experience of flat-grinding metal plates in japanning to the production of accurately made brass platens to present a perfectly flat printing surface.[36] His ink, which probably owed much to his experience in mixing varnishes for his japanned ware, was deeper and smoother than that used by other printers; and his experiments with wove paper may also owe something to his familiarity with papier mâché from his japanning works.

Unlike most other local printers, Baskerville aimed at the high end of the market and sought not just a local but national and international clientele. Baskerville spent nearly five years and a fortune in perfecting his typeface, which was first revealed in 1757 when he issued a quarto edition of Virgil's *Bucolica, Georgica et Aeneis*, widely recognized as a masterpiece of printing, which 'went forth to astonish all the librarians of Europe'.[37] The first of over fifty titles emerging from the Baskerville Press, 'Virgil' was composed in Baskerville's own distinguished and legible type, which he displayed on pages devoid of the decoration hitherto so common in European books. His typography was revolutionary in its minimalism and demonstrated his belief in the 'beauty of letters',[38] which were enhanced by being printed on hot-pressed glossy paper using a new ink and new methods of printing of his own invention. Baskerville selected his books with care; as he wrote: 'It is not my desire to print many books, but such only as are books of Consequence, of intrinsic merit of established Reputation, and which the public may be pleased to see in an elegant dress.'[39] 'Virgil' was quickly followed in 1758 by Milton's *Paradise Lost* and *Paradise Regain'd* and over the course of eighteen years Baskerville printed more than fifty editions,[40] aimed at an international market of discerning, affluent buyers, who purchased his books either by subscription or through the London bookseller Robert Dodsley (1704–23).[41] There were plenty of local buyers including John Ryland and Matthew Boulton, an impressive list of aristocrats, Oxbridge fellows, librarians and clergy, and international purchasers including Benjamin Franklin. Baskerville's books not only marked the zenith of Birmingham book making, they were a defining moment in English printing: his books influenced the subsequent course of European typography and placed Birmingham at the centre of eighteenth-century printing.[42]

Baskerville did not work alone but employed all the hands he needed to progress his venture, including the brothers Robert, William and Thomas Martin and the punch cutter John Handy. William Martin learned punch cutting with Baskerville and after his master's death continued in the trade. Martin cut 'Baskerville-inspired' type for the printer William Bulmer (1757–1830) and also for the Shakespeare Press in around 1790.[43] In 1785 the newspaper proprietor Myles Swinney announced that he had added type founding to his other occupations. They were the first punch cutters in Birmingham to follow in Baskerville's footsteps. Both Swinney and Martin entered into the business for profit and cast type for sale as well as for their own use. With Swinney and Martin, type founding in Birmingham effectively came to

PUBLII VIRGILII

MARONIS

BUCOLICA,

GEORGICA,

ET

AENEIS.

BIRMINGHAMIAE:
Typis JOHANNIS BASKERVILLE.
MDCCLVII.

THE

Holy Bible,

CONTAINING THE

OLD TESTAMENT

AND

THE NEW:

Translated out of the

Original Tongues,

AND

With the former TRANSLATIONS
Diligently Compared and Revised,

By His MAJESTY's Special Command.

APPOINTED TO BE READ IN CHURCHES.

CAMBRIDGE.
Printed by JOHN BASKERVILLE, Printer to the UNIVERSITY
M DCC LXIII.
CUM PRIVILEGIO.

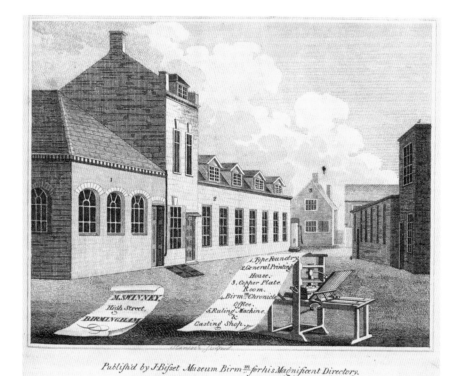

Publifh'd by J.Bisset Museum Birmm. for his Magnificent Directory.

An engraved advertisement for Swinney's printing house, as it appeared in Bisset's *Magnificent Directory* of 1808, shows a wooden printing press outside his modern manufactory. Swinney traded in Birmingham as a printer, newspaper publisher, bookseller, bookbinder, stationer and type founder – as well as stamp agent and pharmacist – between 1770 and 1812.
By permission of the Library of Birmingham, 47154

an end, although as late as 1800 Samuel Hobday of Digby Street described himself as a 'typographical letter cutter',[44] and in 1823 the ingenious Dr William Church (c.1778–1863), an American inventor living in Bordesley Green, developed and patented the first typesetting machine from premises near Walmer Lane in 1822, although it never went into production.[45]

Specialists and generalists

As printing spread in the provinces it had a great effect on the trade, for compositors and printers were no longer tied to London and regional printers could obtain the services of London men of varied experience.[46] Alongside the printing of books, ballads and broadsides, Birmingham also developed a range of specialist printers and products including newspapers, which owed their existence to incomers. In 1732 Thomas Warren printed and published the *Birmingham Journal*, the town's first newspaper, the success of which can perhaps be measured by the arrival of Thomas Aris, a stationer from London who moved to Birmingham and started a printing business in High Street in 1740 having seen an opportunity in the town for newsprint.[47] In 1741 he launched the *Birmingham Gazette* which had an unbroken life until November 1956, when it merged with the *Birmingham Post*, a paper founded by John Frederick Feeney, also an immigrant from Ireland via Liverpool. Newspaper printing was an early specialism in the town as the need to provide readers with up-to-date information necessitated that printers concentrated on newspaper production alone, rather than diversifying into other fields.[48]

The majority of general printers working in eighteenth- and nineteenth-century Birmingham were prepared to take on any type of work including the ephemera required of town and trade; even Baskerville was not above printing ladies' calling cards and pocket accomptants for gentlemen.[49] In 1740 copperplate printing emerged as a separate specialist process or as a sideline for the town's general letterpress printers, when George Anderton established himself as Birmingham's first copperplate engraver.[50] Engraving – the process of incising a design on to a hard flat surface – was a skill familiar to Birmingham's eighteenth-century craftsmen working in the gun, glass, jewellery and metalworking industries. In the printing trade, engraving was used as a method by which to reproduce prints or illustrations on paper by incising lines into an intaglio plate of copper; some of Birmingham's established engravers transferred their skills to copperplate engraving for printing. It was a process appropriate for more refined work where cost and quantity were not crucial and Birmingham's eighteenth-century engravers initially applied their skills to the production of musical scores and maps; but in the nineteenth century the trade expanded and the process was used in the production of more elaborate work such as invitations, trade cards, music covers and billheads, where the lettering was combined with some kind of decoration or illustration. Trade engravers were skilled craftsmen in metal rather than artists – capable copyists who could interpret the sketchy lines of the artist and render their design into clearly defined lines ready for printing. Engraving dominated Birmingham's printing industry: through the eighteenth century 213 engravers traded in the town, a number which by the mid-nineteenth century had increased to 939. This far exceeded the numbers in other towns and made Birmingham the main centre of engraving outside London.[51] Engraving necessitated a different sort of press from that used by the general printers: rather than a wooden hand press, the engravers' copper plates required to be printed on rolling presses operated by copperplate printers. By the second half of the eighteenth century there were 37 such printers in the town, which rose to 715 in the nineteenth century.[52]

Birmingham was also the centre of transfer printing in Britain, and from the end of the nineteenth century it supplied a large proportion of the home market. This was a process that overcame the difficulty of duplicating documents and in 1788 James Watt (1736–1819) took out a patent for a method of copying letters by writing with special ink that could be partially transferred to a sheet of moist paper under pressure.[53] Ralph Wedgwood (1766–1837), a member of the Wedgwood family of potters, invented an early form of carbon paper in 1800, a method of duplicating writing which he called 'stylographic writing' or 'noctograph'.[54] The ceramics

A beautifully engraved trade card from the family firm of W. & T. Radclyffe, printers, engravers, etchers and lithographers, which traded from various addresses in Birmingham from around 1814 to 1849. The elaborate, rococo-inspired design was particularly popular at the turn of the century.
By permission of the Library of Birmingham, Birmingham Trade Card Collection, Box 11/718

An engraved trade card for Evans' paper manufacturers, which traded from various premises on Moor Street between 1820 and 1850. The business was just one of 262 paper merchants in Birmingham between 1700 and 1851. The card displays a wide variety of letterforms typical of the nineteenth century, and a representation of Evans' manufactory set in a romantically rural idyll.
By permission of the Library of Birmingham, Birmingham Trade Card Collection, Box 10/652

industry was a pioneer in the use of transfer printing as the primary method of decorating enamels or pottery, using an engraved copper or steel plate from which a monochrome print on paper was taken and transferred by pressing it on to the ceramic piece. It remains the most common method in the decoration of ceramics. For the nineteenth-century printing industry, lithography became the chief medium for transfer printing and to support this trade there were 82 lithographic printers in Birmingham during this period.[55]

In the nineteenth century Birmingham's printers increasingly specialized in the kinds of work undertaken. Birmingham developed a market for trade cards, the primary tools of publicity, which marked the start of a range of commercial printed material, including stationery and general promotional literature. Early cards contained much information about the trade they advertised in addition to details about location and terms of business, and were produced by general printers using letterpress machines and metal type. With the advent of Birmingham's specialist commercial engraving trade, the cards were given unlimited pictorial and decorative treatments including coats-of-arms or classical figures; others simply depicted the factory façade, or images of the items for sale; many of the designs were not pictorial, but presented the message in symmetrically arranged flourished letters; and while the majority of the cards were printed in monochrome, a few appeared in colour. Over time, the decorative customs of the engravers became standardized and images were frequently reused not only on competitors' trade cards, but also on other documents such as letterheads, billheads and receipts. The engravers' craft was revealed to good effect in *A Poetic Survey* (1800), published by James Bisset (c.1762–1832) and printed by Swinney and Hawkins; it was intended for visitors to the town and included engraved images of local views and manufactories and was a publicity tool used in the campaign to promote the town.[56] Bisset may, in part, have intended his publication to supplement trade cards, but he also aimed to find

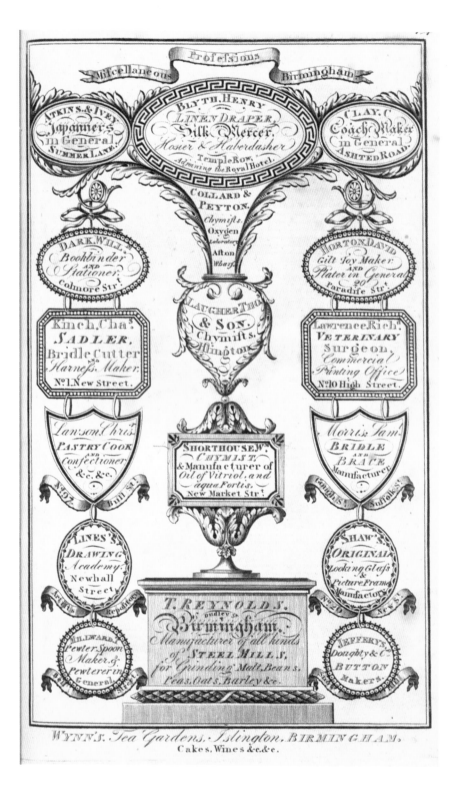

An engraving representing the 'Miscellaneous Professions, Birmingham' from Bisset's *Magnificent Directory* of 1808. The *Directory* was a novel attempt to 'sell' the city and its manufacturers by entertaining readers with visual delights. It also endeavoured to find new ways to display trade cards, and to preserve them in a manner that served to advertise businesses.

By permission of the Library of Birmingham, 47154

a new way to display trade cards and to preserve them in a manner that served to advertise the businesses involved. By editing the collection and admitting only tasteful examples, readers were entertained and had their senses pleased by this portfolio of the engravers' and printers' skill.

One significant development in nineteenth-century printing was the ability to produce colour printing economically, which became widespread by the mid-nineteenth century. The printing firm of James Upton, which operated from the euphoniously named 'Baskerville Works' on Centenary Square, specialized in colour printing. Its imprint appeared on numerous theatre posters produced nationwide which incorporated multi-coloured pictorial images with extravagant letter forms. Upton's continued its capabilities as a colour printer and its associations with the world of entertainment into the mid-twentieth century when it specialized in the printing of record sleeves.

During the twentieth century Birmingham became one of the largest and most versatile concentrations of printing activity in the country, and its firms printed for customers throughout the UK and beyond.[57] Businesses specialized either in serving a particular trade – for instance, Bradshaws of Birmingham catered for laundry needs – or concentrating on the manufacturing aspects of print. Kalamazoo Ltd (Redditch, c.1908–present) employed some 1,200 workers producing loose-leaf systems and business forms, and Kenrick & Jefferson Ltd (West Bromwich, c.1830–1993) employed over 1,300 workers and earned an international reputation for forms and systems as well as for general printing needs. Cornish Brothers and Hudson & Sons, both firms that had been established in the nineteenth century, continued to trade into the last quarter of the twentieth century as book printers. Transfer printing continued to be a specialism of the Birmingham trade, but slowly small firms were absorbed by larger ones, and in 1960 there were just three firms working in Birmingham in this field, the largest of which was Eagle Transfers Ltd (c.1920–79). Process engraving also continued to flourish and firms which were known beyond the city included Birmingham Engravers Ltd, W.I. Rodway & Company, V. Siviter Smith & Company, and Tone Engraving Company. If the specialist firms produced for markets far beyond their own city, there were also a number of general houses that attracted orders to Birmingham, many of which had London offices and sales representatives in other provincial cities. Among the best known were Buckler & Webb Ltd, James Conde Ltd, Drew & Hopwood Ltd, Silk & Terry Ltd, James Upton Ltd and the Weather Oak Press.[58] In addition, several of Birmingham's large enterprises had their own in-house printing plants; many of these, such as Cadbury's, were confined to servicing the needs of the parent company, but others also produced distinguished work for external organizations. The Kynoch Press, Witton (1876–1981), in-house printer to ICI, was one of the most influential printers in Britain during the twentieth century, a press with an international reputation that also produced work for discerning local businesses such as Hope's Metal Windows, Best & Lloyd and Barrow's Department Store in Corporation Street.[59]

An engraving from *The Buildings of Birmingham Past and Present* (1865), published by Thomas Underwood. It shows the shop of Charles Cornish, bookseller, printer, publisher and stationer, of 37 New Street; next door is Underhill, a papermaker and paper merchant who traded in Birmingham between 1811 and 1817, but abandoned the paper trade in favour of tea dealing.
Private Collection

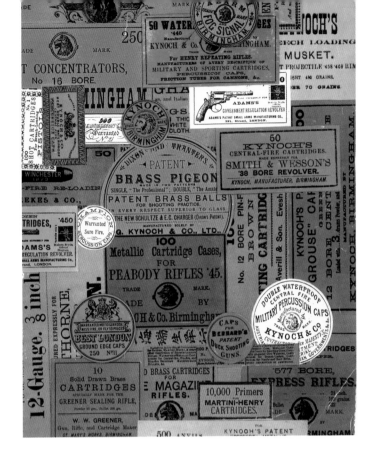

The Kynoch Press started life in 1876 as the in-house printer for Kynoch Ltd, a manufacturer of percussion caps and cartridges for which the early press produced a vast range of packaging material. This selection of labels illustrates the eclectic range of typefaces in use at the press at the turn of the century.
By permission of Caroline Archer-Parré

A Hope's Metal Windows trade catalogue printed as a limited edition by the Kynoch Press in the early 1920s and vibrantly illustrated by 'Mrs Barraclough'. It was a delightful and consciously collectable example of early twentieth-century industrial publishing.
By permission of Caroline Archer-Parré

A "HOPE" METAL CASEMENT

The ideal window for comfort in a Country House.

2

FEW people who have not lived in a house fitted with Hope's Casements can appreciate the comfort which they provide. "Casements" to the general public too often signify leakage and draught—not to mention the constant inconvenience caused by a contrivance which can only be set open at fixed points, at rather wide intervals. A Hope Metal Casement is designed and built to exclude rain and wind, to open and close without effort and to provide ventilation in all weathers. A little air is provided in the simplest manner by Hope's patent handle, which sets the casement open about 1 in. without rattling, while their non-projecting sliding stay, by the simple action of a thumb screw, sets the casement open rigidly at any other angle desired, and is an effectual safeguard against breakage in a gale. The illustration on the opposite page shows a side-hung casement of best quality, in a mullioned window, glazed with leaded glass and provided with the handle and stay described above. This class of casement is recommended for dwelling-houses and similar buildings where weather-tight and everlasting windows are desired. They are made to open inwards or outwards, with suitable fittings for all conditions.

3

For five centuries the printing industry relied upon the apprenticeship system for training, and printers and compositors acquired their skills 'on the job' under the guidance of a master printer. By the turn of the twentieth century, as a result of increasing specialization and the sub-division of the many trades involved in printing, apprentices were unable to obtain the same experience as their predecessors. Therefore schools of printing opened, offering apprentices formal training in parallel to their workshop experience.

The Birmingham School of Printing, established in 1914, had an influence and importance within the city commensurate with Birmingham printing's national position, and no other school in the provinces had to deal with the scale of work encountered in Birmingham.[60] Leonard Jay, head of the Birmingham School of Printing, was a teacher *par excellence* who transformed the outlook of a generation of typographers, thereby making a significant contribution to British typographic education in the first half of the twentieth century. Jay not only made the Birmingham School without equal in Britain – or possibly any other country – he also exercised a worldwide influence on printing education.[61]

When Jay began he was the only full-time teacher on the staff and there were only two half-day classes a week: at his retirement, 537 students attended the school and there were over 74 classes per week. Between 1925 and 1953, under Jay's guidance, the students of the school produced many examples of exemplary book printing. The first book designed, typeset, illustrated and printed by the boys in the school was

Photograph of pre-apprentice printers inside Vittoria Street Junior School of Art and Crafts c.1938. Behind the boys can be seen a display of printed exercises produced by the pre-apprentices at the school under the direction of its Head, Leonard Jay.
By permission of Caroline Archer-Parré

ON WENLOCK EDGE

WENLOCK EDGE

the wood's in trouble;
His forest fleece the Wrekin heaves;
The gale, it plies the saplings double,
And thick on Severn snow the leaves.

'Twould blow like this through holt and hanger
When Uricon the city stood:
'Tis the old wind in the old anger,
But then it threshed another wood.

Then, 'twas before my time, the Roman
At yonder heaving hill would stare:
The blood that warms an English yeoman,
The thoughts that hurt him, they were there.

There, like the wind through woods in riot,
Through him the gale of life blew high;
The tree of man was never quiet:
Then 'twas the Roman, now 'tis I.

The gale, it plies the saplings double,
It blows so hard, 'twill soon be gone:
To-day the Roman and his trouble
Are ashes under Uricon.

7

PRINTER OF THE
Mainz Psalter of the
year fourteen hundred
and fifty-seven in the
action which Johann

[36-point Granjon]

'On Wenlock Edge' is the opening spread of *Six Poems,* a selection of verses from *A Shropshire Lad* and *Last Poems* by A.E. Houseman. Designed, composed and printed by pre-apprentices at the Birmingham Junior School of Art and Crafts in 1937, it also demonstrates excellent examples of hand lettering.
By permission of Caroline Archer-Parré

The *Mainz Psalter* is a fine example of book production from the Birmingham School of Printing. The school always ensured work was produced using the most up-to-date equipment and contemporary typefaces; this was composed in the newly released Linotype Granjon.
Bt permission of Caroline Archer-Parré

a passage from the Book of Ecclesiasticus, 'Let us now praise famous men' (1926), which was followed by over 150 publications, the last of which was the *Collects and Gospels from the Book of Common Prayer* (1953). Aware of Birmingham's typographic heritage, Jay did much to perpetuate the name of John Baskerville, and produced six items related to the eminent Birmingham printer.[62] *The Torch* (1933–50), an innovative vehicle for displaying the work of the school, was a substantial occasional publication, which contained sample pages and illustrations of the books published by the school,[63] for which it won praise throughout the world for the quality of its design and production, its use of a wide range of contemporary Monotype and Linotype typefaces,[64] and its subtle use of colour. Among the typographically cognizant, the work of the Birmingham School was regarded as unequalled and the specimens were 'tantalizingly flawless from the technical side'.[65]

Leonard Jay made a major contribution to the development of typographic education. His combination of idealism and practicality transformed not only the work of the Birmingham School but, in due course, the prevailing landscape of printing in one of the largest and most important centres in Britain and Europe.

Viewed across three centuries, the pattern of Birmingham's printing industry is remarkably like that of the country as whole in its evolution and diversity. There are aspects of the town's printing trade, however, which are of interest far beyond its boundaries and which have made Birmingham a pioneer nationally and internationally. Thanks to the work of pioneer printers such as John Baskerville and the Kynoch Press, to new developments in the fields of engraving and transfer printing and the innovative work of Leonard Jay and the School of Printing, Birmingham occupies a high place in the history of global as well as national printing.

Notes

1   A type founder is one engaged in the design and production of metal type including the cutting, casting and dressing of letters.

2   An engraver cuts or incises lines or design in metal, wood and other surfaces by manual use of tools. Often, but improperly applied to etching.

3   British Printing Industry Federation, *UK Printing: The Facts and Figures* (2014), www.britishprint.com (accessed 9 November 2015).

4   Birmingham's early booksellers, with trading dates: Thomas Simmons (1652–?), George Calvert (1673–?), Hieron Gregory (1673–1705), William Parkes (1687–1728), Michael Johnson (1687–1731), Andrew Johnson (1694–1702), Matthew Unwin (1712–43), J. Osborne (1716–?), Andrew Buckley (1717–?) and Thomas Hide (1721–?). University of Oxford, *British Book Trade Index* (2015), http://bbti.bodleian.ox.ac.uk (accessed 1 November 2015).

5   D. Daniell, 'Rogers, John (c.1500–1555)', *Oxford Dictionary of National Biography* (hereafter *ODNB*) (Oxford, 2004), online edn, http://www.oxforddnb.com/view/article/23980 (accessed 14 November 2015).

6   J. Hill, *Bookmakers of Old Birmingham* (Birmingham, 1907).

7   E.A. Malone, 'Barton, John (c.1605–1675)', *ODNB*, online edn, http://www.oxforddnb.com/view/article/74234 (accessed 14 November 2015).

8   N. Keene, 'Roberts, Francis (1609–1675)', *ODNB*, online edn, http://www.oxforddnb.com/view/article/23748 (accessed 14 November 2015).

9   C.D. Gilbert, 'Hall, Thomas (1610–1665)', *ODNB*, online edn, http://www.oxforddnb.com/view/article/11990 (accessed 14 November 2015).

10 In 1662 Charles II passed the Printing or Licensing Act, which prohibited printing in provincial England and restricted the trade to a limited number of presses in London, Oxford, Cambridge and York; type founders too were tightly regulated and restricted to the capital. The controls on English printing remained in place until 1693, after which printers and type founders were free to establish themselves in towns across the country, but it was not until the beginning of the eighteenth century that provincial printing began to prosper.

11 Probably written by the Revd John Bridgeman, in Hill, *Bookmakers of Old Birmingham*, 36.

12 H.R. Plomer et al., *A Dictionary of the Printers and Booksellers who were at work in England, Scotland and Ireland from 1726 to 1775* (London, 1932).

13 S. Morison, *Four Centuries of Fine Printing* (London, 1949), 40.

14 M. Twyman, *Printing, 1770–1970* (London, 1998), 8.

15 J. Pendred, *The London and country printers, booksellers and stationers* (London, 1785), ed. G. Pollard (London: Bibliographical Society, 1955).

16 J. Hinks and M. Bell, 'The English provincial book trade: an evaluation of the evidence from the British Book Trade Index', in M. Suarez and M. Turner (eds), *The Cambridge History of the Book in Britain, vol. V (1695–1830)* (Cambridge, 2009), 335–51.

17 Twyman, *Printing, 1770–1970*, 15.

18 University of Oxford, *British Book Trade Index*.

19 University of Oxford, *British Book Trade Index*.

20 J. Horden, 'Freeth, John (1731–1808)', rev., *ODNB*, online edn, http://www.oxforddnb.com/view/article/37433 (accessed 14 November 2015).

21 Birmingham's leading ballad printers, with trading dates: Theophilus Bloomer (1817–27), Joseph Russell (1811–39), William Pratt (c.1840–60), William Wright (1820–55), Thomas Watts (1834–50) and William Jackson (c.1840–55). University of Oxford, *British Book Trade Index*.

22 R. Palmer, 'Birmingham broadsides and oral traditions', in D. Atkinson and S. Roud (eds), *Street Ballards in Nineteenth Century Britain, Ireland, and North America* (Aldershot, 2014), 37.

23 R. Palmer, *Birmingham Ballad Printers* (2010), www.mustrad.org.uk/articles/birming1.htm (accessed 1 November 2015).

24 Palmer, *Birmingham Ballad Printers*.

25 University of Oxford, *British Book Trade Index*.

26 Hill, *Bookmakers of Old Birmingham*.

27 University of Oxford, *British Book Trade Index*.

28 In type founding a punch is an original die of the letter or character to be cast. The letter is cut on the end of a small bar of soft steel, which is afterwards hardened and becomes the punch. This punch is used to drive an impression into a bar of copper, which in turn becomes a matrix used for casting type.

29 J. Mosley, 'The early career of William Caslon', *Journal of the Printing Historical Society*, Old Series No. 3 (London, 1967), 66–81; J. Mosley, 'Caslon, William, the elder (1692–1766)', *ODNB*, online edn, http://www.oxforddnb.com/view/article/4857 (accessed 5 December 2015).

30 In nineteenth-century Birmingham, like London, the town's jewellery, gun and printers quarters bordered one other in an area between Hockley, Steelhouse Lane, Shadwell Street and Loveday Street.

31 C. Clare, *A History of Printing in Britain* (London, 1965), 190.

32 C. Archer-Parré and M. Dick (eds), *John Baskerville: Art, Industry and Technology in the Enlightenment* (Liverpool, forthcoming 2017); W. Bennett, *John Baskerville: The Birmingham Printer, his Press, Relations and Friends* (Birmingham, 1937); J.H. Benton, *John Baskerville: Typefounder and Printer, 1706–75* (Boston, 1914); H.H. Bockwitz, *Baskerville in the Judgement of German Contemporaries* (Birmingham, 1937); T. Cave, *John Baskerville: The Printer 1706–75, his Ancestry* (Birmingham, 1936); F.E. Pardoe, *John Baskerville of Birmingham, Letter-founder and Printer* (London, 1975); R. Straus and R. Dent. *John Baskerville: A Memoir* (London, 1907).

33 T.B. Reed, *A History of the Old English Letter Founders* (London, 1952), 341.

34 J. Mosley, 'Baskerville, John (1706–1775)', *ODNB*, online

edn, http://www.oxforddnb.com/view/article/1624 (accessed 14 November 2015); W. Hutton, 'An account of John Baskerville, printer', in *The Edinburgh Magazine or literary miscellany* (Edinburgh, 1785), vol. II, 375; Straus and Dent, *John Baskerville*, 4.

35 Y. Jones, *Japanned Papier Mâché and Tinware c.1740–1940* (Woodbridge, 2012), 115–18.

36 A platen is a flat surface made of brass and is the part of the printing press on which the sheet of paper that takes the impression is placed.

37 T.B. Macaulay, *The History of England from the Accession of James II* (Cambridge, 2011), 343.

38 J. Baskerville, 'Preface', in *Paradise Lost* (London, 1758).

39 Baskerville, 'Preface.'

40 P. Gaskell, *John Baskerville: A Bibliography* (Cambridge, 1959).

41 J.E. Tierney, 'Dodsley, Robert (1704–1764)', *ODNB*, online edn, http://www.oxforddnb.com/view/article/7755 (accessed 14 November 2015).

42 Morison, *Four Centuries of Fine Printing*.

43 C. Perfect, G. Rookledge and P. Baines, *Rookledge's Classic International Typefinder* (London, 2005), 272.

44 University of Oxford, *British Book Trade Index*.

45 Reed, *A History of the Old English Letter Founders*, 361.

46 A compositor assembles metal printing characters into words, lines and paragraphs of text for reproduction by printing.

47 C. Upton, *A History of Birmingham* (Stroud, 2011), 45–6.

48 'Let's take a look at Birmingham as a printing centre', *The British Printer* 73.9 (London, September 1960), 74–82.

49 An accomptant was a manual for instructing merchants, gentlemen of estates and others in maintaining their account books.

50 Twyman, *Printing, 1770–1970*, 6.

51 Total number of engravers between 1700 and 1849: Birmingham (1,158), Manchester (441), Liverpool (374), Sheffield (202), Bristol (114). University of Oxford, *British Book Trade Index*.

52 University of Oxford, *British Book Trade Index*.

53 Twyman, *Printing, 1770–1970*, 35.

54 Twyman, *Printing, 1770–1970*, 35.

55 Lithography is a method of printing from a flat stone. The image to be printed is drawn on a stone with a specially prepared ink, which clings to and dries on the surface. The surface is then subjected to the action of a weak acid that hardens the ink and slightly etches the unprotected parts. The process of printing first requires moistening the surface with water, which is absorbed by the blank parts and repelled by the hard, greasy lines of the design. Printing ink is then rolled over the stone and is, in turn, repelled by the wet parts but adheres to the ink-drawn image. The stone is then ready to make an impression on the sheet.

56 *A Poetic Survey round Birmingham with a brief description of the different curiosities and manufactures of the place, accompanied with a magnificent directory, with names and professions, &c., superbly engraved in emblematic plates* (1800).

57 D.C. Norman in *The British Printer* (London, September 1960), 77.

58 'Let's take a look at Birmingham as a printing centre', 74–82.

59 C. Archer, *The Kynoch Press: The Anatomy of a Printing House 1876–1981* (London, 2000).

60 Cadbury Research Library (CRL), University of Birmingham, XLJ, John Johnson (Printer to the University at Oxford) to Leonard Jay, 1938.

61 L. Wallis, *Leonard Jay: Master Printer-craftsman, First Head of the Birmingham School of Printing 1925–53* (London, 1963).

62 Bennett, *John Baskerville*; Benton, *John Baskerville*; Cave, *John Baskerville*; L. Jay, *Letters of the Famous Eighteenth-century Printer John Baskerville of Birmingham* (Birmingham, 1932); Straus and Dent, *John Baskerville*; Benjamin Walker, *The Resting Places of the Remains of John Baskerville* (Birmingham, 1944).

63 For a complete list of books produced at the Birmingham School of Printing, see Wallis, *Leonard Jay*.

64 CRL, University of Birmingham, XLJ, William Maxwell (R + R Clark, Edinburgh) to Leonard Jay, 18 November 1938.

65 CRL, University of Birmingham, XLJ, D.R. King, Secretary (Birmingham District Master Printers & Allied Trades Association) to Leonard Jay, 1938.

CHAPTER ELEVEN

The Transformation of Post-War Birmingham

MATT COLE

I found the city exciting. The modern buildings reflect its position as the nation's industrial powerhouse. You feel as if you've been projected into the twenty-first century.

Telly Savalas Looks at Birmingham (Harold Baim, 1981)

When I came to Birmingham twenty years ago now, I arrived at a city at a real turning point. The last twenty years has really seen a massive change. Heart and soul, it's really coming back.

Forward: a film for Birmingham (Blue Monday, 2015)

Birmingham's post-war life is a game of two halves, divided by a low point of economic challenge to which the city responded with its renowned resilience and reinvention. The half-hour promotional cinema film for the city presented by the Oscar-nominated star of *Kojak* looks ironic now not only for its production values, but also because the city was, as Savalas spoke, enduring the early stages of a decline in its historical manufacturing base. This was accompanied by changes in the national political environment which would extinguish much of Birmingham's post-war optimism. A generation later, however, the online video made by a Birmingham production company to mark the opening of the Grand Central shopping centre over the rebuilt New Street railway station recognized the achievements that had subsequently been made in reviving and redeveloping the city's economy, its physical environment, and its public facilities. The story of post-war Birmingham is one of trial, some error, and ultimately of transformation.

The redevelopment of Birmingham's city centre has been a continuous process since the Second World War, but it can be simplified into two periods guided by distinctive objectives: the first sought to rebuild following the damage caused by aerial bombardment in the war and to capitalize upon the motor industry as the cornerstone of Birmingham's economy; the second responded to the decline in that industry and in manufacturing more generally by reconfiguring the city physically and economically to meet new commercial and citizen demands.

The first of these two phases was dominated by Herbert Manzoni, Birmingham's city surveyor from 1935 onwards. Anticipating the damage that would be done to the city centre by German air attacks, Manzoni established four council panels, and after the war secured a cross-party consensus supporting his plans for the wholesale reconstruction of central Birmingham's roads and public buildings. 'It is difficult,' wrote Kenneth Newton in 1976, 'to overestimate Manzoni's influence at the height of his power.'[1] Although shortages of labour and materials, as well as central government hesitation, delayed the project immediately after 1945, Digbeth had been remodelled within ten years of the peace. In 1960 the first stages of the inner ring road – Britain's first one-way system – were opened by the Transport Secretary and the completed project was opened eleven years later by Queen Elizabeth. In between subsequently familiar landmarks appeared on the skyline, including the Rotunda (1964), a new concrete shopping centre with 200 outlets imposed on the Bull Ring between 1962 and 1967, and the Central Reference Library (1974), opened, in Chris Upton's words, 'as a remarkable sign of the '70s City Council's continuity with the Civic Gospel of the Victorians'.[2]

Birmingham's city-centre redevelopment in the 1960s prompted first curiosity and later some ridicule for its mixture of brutalism and utopianism. Initially its ultra-modern appearance attracted interest and managers of older shops complained that they were being driven out of business by the Bull Ring. Moreover, the inner ring road swept away historic sites and buildings: Great Charles Street was transformed, while the old reference library, the 1856 Birmingham and Midland Institute and the Bishop's Palace by Pugin were all demolished. Pugin's St Chad's Cathedral – described by Andy Foster as 'a major work in the Gothic revival' – survived by just one vote in a council ballot.[3]

It quickly became clear, however, that long-standing assets of the city had been lost in an over-reaction to the destruction of the city centre in the Blitz, together with Manzoni's assumption that 'the car is king'. One Birmingham town planner said: 'had Manzoni listened to more people and looked at the social issues at the time, he would probably have acted differently and the city could have been very different'.[4] Commentators came to regard Manzoni's vision of Birmingham as a 'Godless, concrete hell',[5] a 'non-place bounded by motorways'.[6] Within two decades of its completion, the Bull Ring's decline symbolized that of the city centre as a whole, as Stirling Prize winner Will Alsop remarked: 'I remember Birmingham being the epitome of modernity … Birmingham was the

Smallbrook Street, photographed in 1960, one of the first stages of Birmingham's new inner ring road that formed part of the major post-war rebuilding of the city centre. The ring road was designed to serve the needs of motor transport.
© University of Birmingham, photograph by Phyllis Nicklin, 1960

The Rotunda has become a familiar landmark on the skyline of Birmingham. Phyllis Nicklin's photograph of Holloway Circus and Smallbrook Street was taken in 1966, on the site of the old route to Edgbaston along Holloway Head.
© University of Birmingham, photograph by Phyllis Nicklin, 1966

The post-war Bull Ring with the old market hall in the background. The photograph was taken on the last day of street trading in September 1959.
© University of Birmingham, photograph by Phyllis Nicklin, 1959

future – in a sense it has been the future, but that bit of the future is worn out now and we need a new one.'[7]

In response to that decline, Birmingham's civic leaders coordinated the search for a new future, in partnership with private commercial interests and with the European Union. Following symposia at Joseph Chamberlain's home in 1988 and 1989, they developed the 'Highbury Initiative' to re-establish Birmingham's national and international profile. Since then the centre of Birmingham has been redeveloped in an ongoing process to promote the city's trade and profile nationally and internationally. Regeneration projects created Brindleyplace, the National Indoor Arena and the International Convention Centre (1991), and a pedestrianized Bullring Centre featuring the striking contrast between St Martin's and the new Selfridge's building (2003). In 2008 and 2010 Council Leader Mike Whitby unveiled the Birmingham

The building of Brindleyplace and the National Indoor Arena were two regeneration projects in late twentieth-century Birmingham which also extended opportunities for leisure and recreation in the city.
Courtesy of Marketing Birmingham

The Library of Birmingham
was opened in 2014. It
provided a new home for the
city's world-class archives
and rare books as well as
a space for learning and
research.
Photograph by Bs0u10e01,
Wikimedia Commons

City Centre Masterplan setting out the council's vision for the next three decades.[8] This aims to expand the city core by 25 per cent, to establish a public performance space called the 'Golden Square', and to draw investment into six economic zones spread around the city. This was followed by the opening in 2013 of an award-winning new home for the Library of Birmingham at a cost of £188 million, which Chris Upton had regarded twenty years earlier as 'probably inconceivable';[9] and the rebuilding of New Street station and the development of Eastside in readiness for the planned arrival of HS2 with its new terminus at Birmingham's first railway station, Curzon Street (1838).

Assessments of the new developments have been mixed. In 1994 Gordon Cherry wrote that Birmingham's townscape remained 'a matter of "bits and pieces"': 'the public image is improving' but 'Birmingham is on the edge, still poised to secure the premier position more than a thousand years of history have promised'.[10] Ten years later, Liam Kennedy noted the city's tendency towards 'creative destruction' and warned that it 'needs to learn from the errors of past generations, not simply seek to erase them through rebuilding or image makeovers';[11] while in 2003 Carl Chinn voiced concern that the investment in the new Bullring Centre had not benefited market traders and working-class shoppers on low incomes.[12]

Five years later, this view was supported by Austin Barber and Stephen Hall. They acknowledged the macro-economic and cultural benefits of redevelopment, but doubted whether all Birmingham people had benefited equally: 'The re-making of central urban space for new economic activities has been accompanied by much acclaim and boosterist hype, while proving highly influential on other cities as well. At the same time, the socio-spatial impact of economic restructuring and the resulting policy response has been extremely uneven.'[13] Despite such criticism, Cherry has emphasized a consistent theme in municipal activity for over one hundred years:

> A powerful local authority has proved adept in using development powers to boost its own civic image. Joseph Chamberlain's Corporation Street, Manzoni's inner ring road, the National Exhibition Centre, the Airport and the successive civic centre schemes which ultimately led to the International Convention Centre and Centenary Square, all share the same lineage.[14]

From slum clearance to urban renewal: the challenge of housing

Manzoni was again the moving force behind the changes in housing after the war in Birmingham. The city had a history of slum housing originating in the Victorian era which left it with 50,000 unfit homes. This housing problem was exacerbated by the destruction of over 12,000 Birmingham homes in the Second World War and the influx of war workers to the city. By 1948 the waiting list for council houses in Birmingham had 65,000 names. Like the modernization of the city centre, Manzoni's housing policy matched faith in planning with a disdain for the past which produced mixed results, and to which later civic authorities had to return.[15]

Birmingham had the advantages of a history of municipal interest in public housing and a good deal of preparation and planning both by national and local

The demolition of houses in Anderton Street, Ladywood, in 1968 with children playing. Ladywood was one of five designated redevelopment areas which provided council homes and flats for tenants of nineteenth-century terraces, back-to-backs and court dwellings.
© University of Birmingham, photograph by Phyllis Nicklin, 1968

Tower blocks in Tangmere
Drive, Castle Vale, in 1968, on
the site of the former Castle
Bromwich aerodrome.
© University of Birmingham,
photograph by Phyllis Nicklin, 1968

authorities as well as by voluntary bodies such as the Bournville Village Trust.[16] The shared sense of the urgency of the provision of improved housing was reflected in the formation of Birmingham's cross-party Joint Housing Committee in 1949 and the Housing Management Department in 1951, and also in the council's policy of receiving housing applications only from Birmingham residents of five years' standing.[17]

The 1940s saw limited progress, with less than 1,000 new homes built each year and most investment in the 'soling and heeling' of existing back-to-back properties. From 1950 the council began to implement Manzoni's plans, which identified five redevelopment areas in which slum and back-to-back housing would be replaced by new homes. The first of these, Nechells, was cleared by 1953, and Newtown, Ladywood, Highgate and Lee Bank followed in projects stretching out to 1972 and embracing over 1,600 acres of land. Half of Birmingham's slum properties were replaced, and in the sixteen years from 1951 the proportion of Birmingham homes sharing a toilet fell from one in five to one in ten, while the proportion without a fixed bath dropped from nearly half to a quarter. Cherry acknowledges that 'it was a scale of activity unparalleled in any British city'. Even place names were redesignated by the council, symbolizing the way 'the social geography and the very appearance of the city were transformed'.[18] Sir Frank Price, chairman of the Public Works Committee, who regarded his upbringing in the back-to-backs as 'my university campus', was proud to demolish them in 'the greatest slum clearance and redevelopment programme in the country'.[19]

Like those in other cities, however, Manzoni's projects had their critics, who grew in number as the years passed. In 1952 Professor Charles Madge from Birmingham University proposed that the council establish a study of the sociological effects of redevelopment; and thirteen years later Canon Norman Power from Ladywood wrote that he 'saw a living community torn apart by the bulldozers'.[20] Grievances about the failure of housing policy were largely responsible for the Labour Party's loss of its councillors in Newtown and the parliamentary seat of Ladywood to community campaigning by the Liberals in the 1960s.[21]

The use of 400 tower blocks – some 32 storeys high – to replace streets which were the templates of communities generations old broke social ties; some residents rehoused in new districts found themselves at a distance from family and work; and there remained a hard core of properties – including a majority of those in the central wards in the late 1960s – without hot water or a fixed bath or their own toilet. Inevitably, hindsight gave greater credence to critics, and the critics themselves argued both that too much and too little had been done. The legacy of the redevelopment plans is easy to understate: 'Few now would defend high-rise flats as ideal homes,' Chinn concluded, but 'there is little romantic in burning bugs from the attic ceiling before bed-time'.[22]

Moreover, the challenge of housing was a moving target: despite having the largest housing stock of any council in Europe, Birmingham struggled to keep pace with demographic change, including the nationwide declining average size of households and the growing population of the city in the post-war years. Some of this pressure was relieved by organized or voluntary relocation to new towns, and by the expansion of the city council's territory in 1966 to allow new developments in Wythall, Northfield and Frankley, which grew to a population of 12,000. In the 1970s council house building slowed and in the 1980s stock was cut by over a quarter by the introduction of compulsory council house sales. In 2002 the Labour-led council, faced with the need for a £1 billion investment in its 90,000 properties, proposed to transfer all its housing stock to a Registered Social Landlord; this was resisted by tenants' groups and trade unions, who argued that rents would rise and homes would be demolished without residents' agreement. In a ballot of tenants with a 65 per cent turnout the proposal was rejected by two to one.[23]

The council from the 1970s adopted a new strategy based on the rehabilitation of existing properties under the title Urban Renewal. This most often affected privately owned 'tunnel-back' housing in the middle ring of the city, which had been respectable late Victorian properties but which had fallen into transitory use or were occupied by residents unable to afford modernization or basic repairs. By the end of 1972 the council had established 68 General Renewal Areas in total, where grants were made available to pay for most of the costs of renovation after visits from council officers. The environment around properties benefiting from grants also often received council investment in an approach labelled 'enveloping', tackling for example waste land, pedestrianization and play areas.[24]

By 1993 over 53,000 grants had been disbursed for home improvements across the city. Critics made the self-evident observation that 'the policy switch from clearance to improvement did not resolve the problems faced by those in housing need'.[25] Indeed, it was the inaccessibility of resources and powers to clear areas or build anew as in the past which was partly the genesis of Urban Renewal. However, in forging links with established voluntary organizations and spawning new ones, tackling vandalism, lending house tools and recommending contractors, Birmingham Urban Renewal has been the pathfinder for imitators in other cities and is in Chinn's assessment 'the most active and progressive organisation of its kind in Britain'.[26]

From manufacturing to service: the transformation of Birmingham's economy

Reviewing the first quarter-century of Birmingham's post-war economic history, Sutcliffe and Smith confirmed the truism that 'Birmingham's ethos and character have been determined to a very large extent by its industrial structure'.[27] As familiar as this claim was, it included the assumption that the city's work was industrial, and while work may have remained at the heart of Birmingham's character, the nature of the work was transformed, and not always painlessly, on the journey to the twenty-first century. Birmingham's economic structure after the Second World War was both simple and paradoxical: it was very clearly an overwhelmingly industrial city; yet, though dominated by the motor industry, it could nonetheless still lay claim to its title as 'the city of a thousand trades' because of the variety of established traditional manufacturers employing large numbers of workers.

Across the whole of the British economy, the service sector had employed more workers than manufacturing industry since 1881, and by the 1950s it claimed almost half the workforce while industry struggled to maintain one in three. In Birmingham, however, industry still ruled. The 1951 census showed that 64 per cent of Birmingham workers were in manufacturing, nearly twice as many as in all service jobs. The split remained 60–40 in industry's favour in 1961, and at the start of the 1970s 55 per cent of Birmingham workers were still manufacturing, while the national figure had fallen below a third.[28]

Motor manufacturing was the lion in the industrial jungle of Birmingham, with the production of cars and accessories employing 16 per cent of the city's workforce at the start of the 1950s; the total number was still over 12 per cent in 1966. There was, however, a diversity of other animals in the jungle, and Sutcliffe and Smith noted that, while their numbers were small compared to both the car factories and the past, the brass, hollow-ware and jewellery trades in Birmingham had dispro-portionate shares of the workforce compared to the rest of the country. Indeed, one study of the jewellery trade remarked that Birmingham industry was 'more broadly based than that of any city of comparable size in the world'.[29]

While the continued dominance of industry was a reassuring reflection of

Birmingham's past, the marginal decline of that dominance was the warning of the future, which saw a sudden acceleration in the contraction, merger and closure of once-familiar plants during Britain's economic trials in the 1970s and 1980s. The local unemployment rate had never been above 2 per cent before 1966, but thereafter the decline in manufacturing was for Birmingham a more damaging pattern than for other cities, and by 1984 four out of five jobs lost were in manufacturing. International, national and technological factors all played a part in reducing the Birmingham workforce so that by 1976 the city's unemployment rate was above the national average for the first time since the war. By 1983 relative earnings in the West Midlands were at the bottom of the national league table, having been at the top in 1970, and the economic difficulties of the Thatcher era saw the unemployment rate for Birmingham reach nearly 20 per cent.[30] In five adjoining city centre wards the jobless rate was over a third of the population.[31]

The Gravelly Hill interchange from the south-east. Better known as 'Spaghetti Junction', it opened in May 1972 to ease the convergence of road and motorway traffic to the north of Birmingham. This huge engineering project cemented Birmingham's reputation as Britain's 'motor city'. Ironically, it was built over the confluence of the rivers Tame and Rea and Hockley Brook, and canals and railway lines also bisected the site.
Photograph by the Highways Agency, Wikimedia Commons

Birmingham's identity as Britain's 'motor city' was at the heart of its boom, its rebuilding and its decline, for it was the industry at Longbridge that provided the confidence for investment and the redevelopment of the 1960s. The former Austin motor company became BMC in 1952, and in 1968 was amalgamated into British Leyland, which became principally state-owned in 1975. Despite successive cuts in staff and the introduction of 'lean' production, the industrial and market decline and, in 2005, closure of the car plant both caused and symbolized the need for new jobs and a different approach. Some commentators see this as an inevitable, even characteristic change. Robert Gwynne concluded that 'regional specialisation has been reduced in the 1980s and 1990s as both other manufacturing and service sectors have been developed. The emphasis of employment growth in the West Midlands has returned to the region's traditional source of strength – the small adaptable firm.'[32]

The redevelopment of the city centre consciously ran alongside significant shifts in the economy of Birmingham by opening up the infrastructure to facilitate and attract employment in the services. However, this did not take immediate effect on the city, as John B. Smith found:

The lowest point of the city's economic fortunes came in 1993 at which stage Birmingham compared to 1971 had lost 30 per cent of total employment with manufacturing jobs down 66 per cent … In the mid-1990s the rate at which jobs were being gained through the expanding service sector finally exceeded the corresponding rate of loss in manufacturing.[33]

Since then the regular meetings and media events at the ICC and NIA – Birmingham attracts 40 per cent of the UK's conference trade, and the Broad Street complex of venues has hosted party political conferences, Cabinet meetings, a G8 summit and the TV show *Gladiators* – nourished the development of Broad Street's hotels, clubs and restaurants. The new office and residential accommodation built around the Gas Street canal basin was filled with a growing complement of professionals in law, banking and accountancy: Birmingham has the two largest sets of barristers' chambers in the country and a Law Society 4,500 strong; its financial and insurance services sector is the fourth biggest in the UK and, with banking, employs over 111,500 people, while 62 per cent of the private-sector jobs in Birmingham city centre are in knowledge-intensive business services.[34] Professional employment in education has also grown with the expansion of the city's five universities – which now have nearly 80,000 students – and further education colleges; and in healthcare, the Queen Elizabeth Hospital at Edgbaston opened in 2010 with a staff of 8,000.

Most obvious in the city centre's development has been the profile of retail outlets, with the sequence of the Pallasades (opened with New Street station in 1971), Pavilions (1988), Mailbox (2000) and Bullring (2003) developments. Access to these facilities has also required the engagement and investment of the civic authorities, whether in the construction of Spaghetti Junction, the expansion of Birmingham International Airport or the railway stations there and at Moor Street, Snow Hill and New Street.

Manufacturing industry now employs only one worker in ten in Birmingham and generates less than 10 per cent of the city's wealth,[35] though niche industries continue to thrive, for instance in the Jewellery Quarter. Here, with the city council and working with a range of local agencies, the Quarter's Urban Village Regeneration Partnership was formed to support the hundreds of businesses in the

The Mailbox was a reinvention of the city's Royal Mail main sorting office. Opened in 2008, it provided retail outlets, restaurants and a home for the BBC and a walkway to the canal network at Gas Street basin.
Courtesy of Marketing Birmingham

district.[36] Elsewhere, Brandauer, the firm established for the making of steel pen nibs in Newtown in 1862, continues to prosper after a history of making parts for fighter aircraft, record players, computers and even the Large Hadron Collider at CERN, which praised Brandauer as 'one of very few high-precision presswork specialists in Europe with the necessary skills and technical capability to produce components that meet our extremely demanding specifications'.[37] Acme whistles, started in a back-to-back in St Mark's Street in the 1860s and now in Hockley, still sells its signature product to 119 countries for organizations ranging from the Metropolitan Police to the UN, the Rugby World Cup and the NFL.[38] Importantly, thousands of Birmingham workers carry on vehicle manufacture at the Jaguar Land Rover plants in Castle Bromwich into the twenty-first century.[39]

Newer businesses were also established following immigration from South Asia and the Caribbean in the post-war period. East End foods moved from Wolverhampton to Highgate in Birmingham in the 1970s to meet the demands of the city's growing number of Indian restaurants. The largest importer of ethnic foods in the UK, in 2011 the company spent £10 million in transforming the former HP site at Aston Cross into one of the largest trade-only cash and carry stores in the country.[40] Nearby in Nechells is the headquarters of Wing Yip, widely recognized as the UK's leading Oriental grocer. The family's first shop was opened in Digbeth in 1970, but by 2015 the company's turnover had reached almost £100 million.[41] Similarly, the African Caribbean Business Forum has promoted the enterprise of its own community in a growing diversity of fields.[42]

Circumstances have not favoured those charged with protecting the fortunes of a city with great expectations and a great legacy in the post-war period. There has been a loss of powers from local government, global threats and economic downturns, and demographic and social change placing new burdens on an established system. Some of their efforts have foundered or misfired. Some recent glamorous city-centre redevelopment has come under fire for giving little benefit to some parts of the population.[43] Yet the city of Birmingham has – whether by trial and error or by long-term planning – found the opportunities to reshape the economy and remodel the urban landscape. Since the first market charter in 1166, Birmingham has faced remaking and reinvention. Innovation has shaped a city's history where the conflict between tradition and change are in constant creative tension.

Notes

1 K. Newton, *Second City Politics* (Oxford, 1976), 20. For a biography of Manzoni, see T. Caulcott, 'Manzoni, Sir Herbert John Baptiste (1899–1972)', *Oxford Dictionary of National Biography* (Oxford, 2004), online edn, http://www.oxforddnb.com/index/65/101065625/ (accessed 20 May 2016).

2 C. Upton, *A History of Birmingham* (Chichester, 1993), 206.

3 A. Foster, *Pevsner Architectural Guides: Birmingham* (New Haven, CT, 2005), 47

4 'The history behind Birmingham's St Chad's and Queensway tunnels', BBC News 20 July 2013, http://www.bbc.co.uk/news/uk-england-birmingham-23319775 (accessed 28 August 2015). The planner quoted is Nick Corbett, author of *Transforming Cities: Revival in the Square* (London, 2004).

5 S. Bayley, 'It's all change in the second city … again', *The Observer*, 29 June 2008.

6 J. Chatwin, 'Viewpoint: Brindleyplace implementation', *Urban Design Quarterly*, 62 (1997), 12.

7 Interviewed by L. Kennedy, *Remaking Birmingham: The Visual Culture of Urban Regeneration* (Abingdon, 2004), 45.

8 http://bigcityplan.birmingham.gov.uk/birmingham-development-plan/ (accessed 26 August 2015).

9 Upton, *History of Birmingham*, 206.

10 G. Cherry, *Birmingham: A Study in Geography, History and Planning* (Chichester, 1994), 235–6

11 Kennedy, *Remaking Birmingham*, 10.

12 'Historian says Bull Ring lacks heart', BBC News, 4 September 2003, http://news.bbc.co.uk/1/hi/england/west-midlands/3078514.stm (accessed 19 August 2016).

13 A. Barber and S. Hall, 'Birmingham: whose urban renaissance? Regeneration as a response to economic restructuring', *Policy Studies*, 29.3 (2008), 281–92.

14 Cherry, *Birmingham*, 236.

15 C. Chinn, *Homes for People: Council Housing and Urban Renewal in Birmingham 1849–1999* (Studley, 1999).

16 Bournville Village Trust, *When We Build Again* (1941).

17 Cherry, *Birmingham*, 77–125

18 Ibid., 170.

19 F. Price, *Being There* (Upfront Publishing, 2002), 135, 137.

20 N.S. Power, *The Forgotten People* (Arthur James, 1965), 14.

21 The winner of the parliamentary by-election was the Liberal council group leader Wallace Lawler. See his entry in D. Brack et al., *Dictionary of Liberal Biography* (London, 1998), 216–17

22 Chinn, *Homes for People*, 108.

23 'Tenants vote to stay with Birmingham City Council', *Local Government Chronicle*, 8 April 2002.

24 Chinn, *Homes for People*, 127–55.

25 Cherry, *Birmingham*, 189.

26 Chinn, *Homes for People*, 155.

27 A. Sutcliffe and R. Smith, *Birmingham 1939–70* (Oxford, 1974), 154.

28 Ibid., 156–61. Comparative national figures are from the Office for National Statistics.

29 M.J. Wise, 'On the evolution of the jewellery and gun quarters in Birmingham', *Institute of British Geographers, Transactions and Papers*, 15 (1951), 66.

30 Cherry, *Birmingham*.

31 BCC Development Department, *Developing Birmingham 1889 to 1989: 100 Years of City Planning* (1989), 131.

32 R.N. Gwynne, 'From craft to lean: technological change and the motor-vehicle industry in the West Midlands', in A. Gerrard and T.R. Slater (eds), *Making a Conurbation: Birmingham and its Region* (Studley, 1996), 185.

33 J.B. Smith, 'The economic history of Birmingham', in C. Chinn (ed.), *Birmingham: Bibliography of a City* (Birmingham, 2003), 162.

34 Birmingham Law Society; Nomis, official labour market statistics (Office for National Statistics); E. Clarke, P. Swinney and D. Sivaev, *Beyond the High Street: Birmingham Analysis* (Centre for Cities, 2013).

35 Nomis, official labour market statistics; Office for National Statistics, Regional Gross Value Added data, December 2014.

36 *Jewellery Quarter: Unlocking the Industrial Middle* (Prince's Trust, 2012).

37 http://www.brandauer.co.uk/ (accessed 20 May 2016).

38 http://www.acmewhistles.co.uk/ (accessed 20 May 2016).

39 'Jaguar Land Rover to retain three UK factories', BBC News, 15 October 2010, http://www.bbc.co.uk/news/uk-england-11549823 (accessed 19 August 2016).

40 See M. Ram, T. Jones, T. Abbas and B. Sanghera, 'Ethnic minority enterprise in its urban context: South Asian restaurants in Birmingham', *International Journal of Urban and Regional Research*, 26.1 (2002), 24–40.

41 'Rich List 2015: No. 35 – Woon Wing Yip', *Birmingham Post*, 23 January 2014.

42 'Quartet from Birmingham's ethnic business community chase African Caribbean Business Federation awards', *Birmingham Mail*, 15 October 2009.

43 'Ethnic minorities and poor "left behind" by Birmingham businesses', *Birmingham Post*, 4 September 2008.

FORWARD

CHAPTER TWELVE

Birmingham: Forward into the Future

CARL CHINN

Birmingham is dynamic, exciting and innovative. Inclusive, with its fascinating fusion of lifestyles, ethnicities and beliefs, it is yet expansive, reaching out to the world with its youthful and growing population.[1] Refreshingly different to most other British cities in both the diversity of its people and its multiform economy, Birmingham is a many faceted place that intrigues and attracts visitors, for, as Sindy Chan of the *China Daily* recognized in 2013, it is a city full of adventures.[2] Those adventures began in 1166 when the lord of the manor gained the right to hold a market. Then and since, Birmingham has confidently looked forward to the future, thanks to the entrepreneurship, skilfulness, adaptability, vitality and ingenuity of its people.

In the admiring words of the French observer Faujas de Sant Fond, who visited Birmingham in 1784, the town was one of the most curious in England, boasting as it did numerous and varied industries which were supported by the genius of invention and by mechanical skill of every kind.[3] This awareness of the essentiality of work to the emergence, rise and ongoing development of Birmingham was also recognized by Charles Dickens in 1837, when he pronounced that it was 'the great working town' in his novel *The Pickwick Papers*.[4] Nine years later, that defining feature was as obvious to the celebrated composer Felix Mendelssohn when he came to Birmingham for the first performance of his *Elijah*. During his stay, he drew a pen and ink sketch that showed a passenger train passing before a host of factory chimneys and workshops that were crowding around the Town Hall – all of which were framed within the imposing arch of a viaduct.[5]

In that drawing, Mendelssohn identified another characteristic of Birmingham: a vigorous bond between manufacturing and the arts – for embedded as it was within an industrial landscape, yet was the Town Hall the cultural centre of the town and the setting for his great oratorio. This bond was emphasized publicly in 1885 when the inscription stone of the Public Art Gallery was laid, which pronounced: 'By the gains of industry we promote art'. Eight years later, that powerful link was officially proclaimed in Birmingham's arms which were granted after it gained the status of a city and which were supported by two figures. On the right and representing Industry was a smith holding in his right hand a hammer resting on an anvil; and on the left and representing Art was a woman holding in her right hand a book resting on the shield and in her left hand a painter's palette with two brushes.[6]

The intimate relationship between culture and the making of things was articulated energetically by another renowned composer, the Czech Antonín Dvořák, who premiered his new work *Requiem* at the Town Hall in 1891. In a letter, he declared that 'I'm here in this immense industrial city where they make excellent knives, scissors, springs, files and goodness knows what else, and, besides these, music too. And how well! It's terrifying how much the people here manage to achieve.'[7]

Dvořák's performance came in the midst of a period when Birmingham's people were displaying to the full their ability to adapt swiftly to changing economic circumstances. Many older trades were badly affected by shifts in fashion and went into decline. As G.C. Allen emphasized, demand moved to products designed with simplicity and away from ornate domestic fittings in japanned ware, brass foundry and bedsteads and also from elaborate personal items such as heavy watch chains, expensive gold watches and 'voluminous garments requiring a multitude of buttons and heavy fastenings, and mother of pearl decorations'.[8] Changing tastes in fashion were exacerbated by other market forces. By placing taxes on foreign goods, the McKinley Tariff of 1890 dealt a massive blow to Birmingham's pearl button makers,

The Town Hall, built for public meetings as well as musical events, has been at the heart of Birmingham's civic and cultural life since it opened in the early nineteenth century.
Courtesy of Marketing Birmingham

'By the gains of industry we promote art.' Local manufacturers were instrumental in founding Birmingham's Museum & Art Gallery where art and industry combined in the Industrial Galleries.
Courtesy of Marketing Birmingham

who had previously exported half of their output to the United States of America. Their misfortunes were deepened by cheaper imports from Austria and later Japan, so that by 1914 the number of pearl button makers had dropped drastically from 2,500 to around 500. Sporting gun manufacturers were as badly affected by the loss of exports to America as well as by competition from Belgium.[9]

Their production was workshop-based; by contrast that of military armaments was concentrated at the Birmingham Small Arms (BSA) factory in Small Heath. This also faced problems, but during a downturn in trade in 1880, the company realized that its works and machinery was particularly suited to the manufacture of bicycles. By the early twentieth century, thanks to the flexibility and foresight of the company and the skills and versatility of its workers, BSA had become a major force in the trade. So too were other Birmingham firms and by 1914 the city was the chief centre of bicycle making, employing almost 10,000 people.[10] By then BSA was also manufacturing motorbikes, another industry which went on to boom in Birmingham – as did the production of cars.[11]

It was from his expanding works at Longbridge that in 1922 Herbert Austin brought out the small-sized Austin Seven. This 'motor for the million' democratized car ownership and had a profound effect internationally. A left-hand-drive version was made under licence in Germany and became BMW's first car; a French version was produced at the Peugeot factory; and a Japanese firm that was later taken over by Nissan used the Austin Seven as the model for its Datsun. It was also at Longbridge that Sir Alec Issigonis designed the Mini, one of the icons of the twentieth century.[12] The rapid progress of the car industry in Birmingham was the catalyst for the growth of a host of smaller firms supplying components, and several bigger concerns. Among them were Dunlop, the tyre company, and Lucas, which became the largest supplier of electrical equipment to British-made vehicles.[13] Eric Hopkins also drew attention to the rise of other businesses in the electrical field, such as the General Electric Company, and to the transformation of the engineering industry in the early twentieth century. Perceptively, he emphasized that the expansion of these new sectors was accompanied by that of services.[14]

This latter sphere would continue to grow and take on increasing importance as a result of the recession that devastated manufacturing nationally in the 1980s. As the country's major industrial centre, Birmingham was hit especially hard and between 1978 and 1989 local employers laid off 107,205 workers. Unemployment ravaged many areas of the city. In 1966 less than 2 per cent of Birmingham's workforce had been registered as out of work, but by 1981 this proportion had soared to 21 per cent. This global statistic failed to emphasize the concentration of unemployment in certain parts of the city. By the end of the 1980s the Small Heath inner-city parliamentary constituency had a depressing unemployment rate of 30.1 per cent, while on the Cockhill council estate in Rubery it reached a dismal 70 per cent. Widespread job losses were associated with a fall in wages and in the two years from 1979 to 1981 average incomes in the West Midlands plunged from second place in the national league table to the bottom position.[15]

The effects of the recession continue to affect the city. In 2010, according to the

Department for Communities and Local Government Index of Multiple Deprivation, 40 per cent of Birmingham's population lived in areas described as being in the most deprived 10 per cent in England, while the city was ranked as the most deprived on both income and employment deprivation levels, although these latter statistics were largely influenced by the size of the authority compared to other major cities.[16] Such deprivation obviously presented serious challenges regarding community cohesion, challenges which are ongoing and which the council recognizes and has sought to address positively since the 1980s. In particular, councillors quickly realized that in that decade, and for the first time in its history, no new manufacturing sectors were emerging to replace those that were disappearing. Previously, Birmingham's people had been able to respond proactively to economic decline but now the council had to take the lead in helping to create jobs.

Based on a political consensus, a three-pronged strategy was adopted: to encourage inward investment, to work with employers and to provide the environment and facilities to draw in those with spending power. This proactive approach attracted favourable comments, and in 1991 Paul Cheeseright of the *Financial Times* stressed the municipal activism of the council.[17] Since then, and under different political leaderships, the council's enterprise has facilitated the development of landmark buildings and the radical reshaping of the city centre to encourage inward investment and to promote Birmingham nationally and internationally to visitors. It has done so successfully, so much so that in 2015 Christine Monin of *Le Parisien* asserted that 'Birmingham has made a spectacular recovery' and that 'the city with a population of one million people holds its head up high'.[18]

The provision of modern facilities began in the early 1990s with the expansion of Birmingham Airport and the National Exhibition Centre (NEC) on the outskirts of Birmingham. These were accompanied in the city centre by the opening of the National Indoor Arena, the International Convention Centre and Symphony Hall, which, on its twenty-first anniversary in 2012, was declared to be the United Kingdom's best hall for orchestral music by Tom Service of the *Guardian*.[19] These high-profile developments were soon followed by the completion of the Water's Edge, a canalside scheme of shops, restaurants and bars. This was the first part of the ambitious Brindleyplace project which now includes three public squares, leisure facilities such as the National Sea Life Centre, and business buildings, the most recent of which opened in 2009.[20] Three of these buildings are occupied by Royal Bank of Scotland, while in 2014 another became a new centre of excellence for Deutsche Bank. Graeme Brown of the *Birmingham Post* emphasized that the German business 'had been ramping up its Birmingham operations in recent years – growing its team from fewer than 30 to more than 2,000 through largely back-office functions'. Henceforth, it would be 'servicing 500 clients previously handled by London across debt, listed derivatives and cash equities, with a 270-seat trading floor on the way'.[21] This expansion led Neil Rami, chief executive of Marketing Birmingham, to affirm in 2014 that 'Birmingham's business, financial and professional services sector is the largest of any UK city outside London, with more than 7,500 companies employing 100,000 people'.[22]

There is a synergy between the modern expansion of banking and Birmingham's past, for the city was at the forefront of the banking revolution that was so crucial to empowering the Industrial Revolution. Lloyd's Bank was founded by two prominent manufacturers as Taylor and Lloyd's Bank in Dale End in 1765, while the Midland Bank began as the Birmingham and Midland Bank in Union Street in 1826.[23] In 1992 the Midland became part of the HSBC Group in one of the biggest banking mergers of its time, but the close connection with Birmingham was re-established in March 2015 when HSBC announced its decision to create the head office of its ring-fenced HSBC UK bank in the city. Around 1,000 head office roles would be moved from London to Birmingham, where the company already employed 2,500 people. The relocation resulted in the largest property deal in the city for over a decade because of the bank's acquisition of '2 Arena Central on a 250-year lease, reflecting the company's long-term investment in the ring-fenced bank's head office'.[24] The relocation by HSBC is an important show of confidence in the 9.2-acre Arena Central development which aims to deliver 1.2 million square feet of mixed-use development within a landscaped public space fronting Broad Street and adjacent to Centenary Square.[25]

Symphony Hall and the International Convention Centre were important to the modernization of Birmingham in the 1990s. The arts gave a new sense of direction to the city with Centenary Square, redesigned by artist Tess Jaray, also providing a stage for many of the city's cultural events.
Photograph by Tony Hisgett, Wikimedia Commons

Other major companies within the business, professional and financial services sector have emerged directly from Birmingham's past. A prime example is DTZ, which merged with Cushman & Wakefield in 2015. Its founding predecessor firm was Chesshire Gibson, which started in the city in 1784, and its commitment to Birmingham was underlined in 2013 when it established in Colmore Square a new Financial Control European Centre of Excellence. This investment was made because of 'the depth of accountancy talent in the region, coupled with multi-lingual capabilities' which enabled the company to consolidate operations from across the UK, Germany, France and Poland.[26]

The importance of the business, professional and financial services sector in Birmingham is emphasized by the fact that it includes the four largest accounting firms in the world: Deloitte, PWC, Ernst and Young, and KPMG. Their presence has grown since the 1980s and provides Birmingham with significant credibility as a prime location for accountancy businesses.[27] The city is also a centre of legal

Central Square, part of the Brindleyplace project that revived the area around canal engineer James Brindley's Birmingham Canal Navigation. Business and leisure cluster side-by-side around around three public squares.

Colmore Row is at the heart of Birmingham's business, professional and financial services sector. The Colmore family opened up the area for development in the eighteenth century.
Courtesy of Marketing Birmingham

excellence and boasts global law firms such as DLA Piper, Eversheds and Gowling WLG, which emerged in 2016 from the merger of the Canadian practice Gowlings with Wragge and Co.[28] Headquartered at Two Snowhill in the Colmore Business District, Wragge and Co. had begun in 1834 with the partnership of Henry Wragge and Clement Ingelby.[29]

Birmingham's legal industry had been important for over a century, but in the early twenty-first century it expanded noticeably and to a greater extent than in other large cities outside London. An important factor in that advance was the association between many locally based firms and Birmingham's universities and law schools, which provide highly educated and professional legal graduates.[30] The University of

Birmingham's wider impact, in particular, was stressed in 2013 by a report by Oxford Economics. As the city's largest private sector employer, it had a highly skilled workforce, attracted students from across the world, and encouraged graduates to remain locally. Many of them worked in socially significant roles such as teachers, social workers and doctors. Through its provision of direct and indirect jobs and the spending of its students and visitors, the university 'generated a value-added contribution of over £460 million to Birmingham's economy in 2011/12'.[31]

The University of Birmingham is also a leading driver of investment in life sciences and in 2014 it opened a £6.8m biomedical hub offering incubation for fledgling firms through laboratory and office space. Nearby is the Life Sciences Campus, a bespoke facility promoting medical technology and healthcare companies where larger employers will have space to grow. The life sciences sector is one of the principal growth areas targeted by city leaders because it will create long-term and sustainable jobs in a high-value sector.[32] A most successful company in that field is Binding Site, which specializes in producing highly sensitive and specific antibodies used for the detection of certain cancers and serious disorders. In 2011 it moved its 600 UK-based employees into a new six-storey sustainable headquarters in the city centre. Binding Site's decision to remain in Birmingham arose not only from its strong academic links with the University of Birmingham but also because of its access both to a multicultural population mix and to excellent transport links.[33] These latter have been a key factor in driving forward Birmingham's growth. Richard McCarthy, the managing director of Deutsche Bank, Birmingham, made this clear when he pointed out that the new centre of excellence at Five Brindleyplace was an aspirational place in which to work and that its 'connection to the main transport hubs enables us to both attract and retain the very best talent'.[34]

Most importantly, the New Street Gateway has been crucial to creating better links between Birmingham and the rest of the UK. A £750 million project, it transformed Birmingham New Street station into one of the country's flagship railway stations and was opened in September 2015 after five years' work. The redevelopment included a new concourse benefiting from natural light that was five times the size of that at London's Euston station. Improved access to the station was facilitated by new escalators and public lifts and by better pedestrian links both to and through the station with its new entrances and public space.[35] Chris Moss of the *Telegraph* discerned, however, that the new building was more than merely functional, for 'railway stations are both symbolic and physical gateways into our cities' and 'they act as a symbol of civic pride and influence the overall impressions of visitors'. For him the success of the new structure was as a welcoming yet futuristic light-filled space through and around which travellers and shoppers move freely.[36]

Birmingham New Street station can handle 300,000 passengers each day and is the busiest station outside London, with a train leaving every 37 seconds.[37] The city's significance as a major hub of the British rail network will be enhanced by High Speed Rail (HS2), a major government-led investment project to develop a new railway line between London and Birmingham. Trains will operate at speeds up to 250 miles per hour, faster than any current operating speed in Europe, and the £40 billion project will reduce travel time between the two cities to 49 minutes. It is believed strongly that this rapid connectivity with the capital will accelerate Birmingham's economic growth potential, supercharge the city as a place to invest and locate, create up to 26,000 jobs (including in Solihull), and increase annual economic output by £4 billion in the Greater Birmingham region.[38]

In February 2016 HS2 Ltd opened its national headquarters at Snow Hill in Birmingham, with offices for 1,000 members of staff from engineers to procurement specialists, while the National College for High Speed Rail will be located at the Birmingham Science Park Aston in the city's Learning Quarter. This will provide thousands of young people with vocational learning and training in rail careers and engineering and also in high-tech manufacturing roles.[39] The HS2 line will be served by two local stations. Birmingham Interchange will give access to the NEC, Birmingham International station and Birmingham Airport and will be 38 minutes from London and less than an hour from Heathrow, while Birmingham Curzon will be the terminus station in the city centre. It will be the stimulus for the Birmingham Curzon Masterplan. Approved in 2015 by the city council, this will massively regenerate parts of Digbeth and Eastside and is expected to create 136,000 jobs, boost the city economy by £1.4 billion per year, and lead to the building of 4,000 homes.[40]

Movement within Birmingham city centre has been improved by the Metro extension from Snow Hill to New Street station, while the city can now fully reach out to the world because of Birmingham Airport's £40 million runway extension.[41] Opened in 2014, it added 40 metres to the existing 3,003 metres of runway, thereby allowing airlines to offer direct long-haul passenger services. China Southern was the first airline to take advantage of the extended runway with a 248-seat Airbus A330-200 that arrived from Beijing on 22 July of that year, while in March 2016 on a flight from Dubai, the world's largest aeroplane, the Airbus A380, landed at Birmingham Airport for the first time.[42] Fifty airlines now operate 143 direct routes from Birmingham, including daily flights to New York, Istanbul, Dubai and major European cities, while a further 280 global connections are available via hub airports including Delhi, Dubai, Istanbul, Frankfurt, Amsterdam and Paris.[43]

These connections have driven forward strong growth in international tourism, and in 2014 the Office for National Statistics revealed that a record 944,000 international visitors had come to Birmingham and that they spent £300 million.[44] But as Emma Birchley of Sky News recognized in October 2015, the city was also drawing in other people. She praised it as 'a thriving economic hub, and the fastest-growing regional tourism destination in Britain, Birmingham is undergoing a transformation'.[45] Named in November 2015 as the most popular destination outside London for corporate conferences and events, Birmingham also attracted higher numbers of leisure tourists that year with total arrivals to the city 'expected to reach 38.1 million, and tourism revenue hitting an all-time high of £6.2 billion'.[46] The city's burgeoning popularity was fired by a variety of attractions from the large-scale annual Frankfurt Christmas Market with its millions of visitors to the smaller high-quality restaurants for which the city has gained a high reputation.[47] Indeed Jamie Doward of the *Observer* pronounced in the autumn of 2015 that Birmingham 'finds itself at the

The New Street Gateway, opened in 2015, enhanced rail connections between Birmingham and the rest of the UK. This is the third New Street station on the site. Photograph by Bs0u10e01, Wikimedia Commons

epicentre of the nation's culinary map' and that it had 'more Michelin-starred restaurants than any city outside London, pushing Edinburgh, with four, into third place. Manchester has none.'[48]

Two years previously, in a short but insightful appraisal of Birmingham for the *New York Magazine*, Julie Earle-Levine also drew attention to the city's food scene, including 'the famed Balti Triangle, packed with over 50 South Asian restaurants'; but she also identified other reasons why 'Londoners, as well as the rest of the world, are starting to reconsider the Brums'. These included Birmingham's 'cultural offerings which can keep pace with the capital's,' such as 'the world-renowned Birmingham Royal Ballet, Birmingham Repertory Theatre Company, and the City of Birmingham Symphony Orchestra, plus a rock scene that launched Ozzy Osbourne and Duran Duran'. To these could be added the famed Cadbury chocolate factory; one of the UK's biggest and oldest jewellery quarters; the Custard Factory, where young artists, actors and musicians convene; and the new Library of Birmingham with its Shakespeare Memorial Room and impressive collection of Shakespeareana.[49] Built at a cost of £189 million and opened in 2013, in the following year the Library of Birmingham welcomed almost 2,500,000 visitors and was the only venue outside London to be included in a top ten of the UK's most-visited tourist attractions compiled by the Association of Leading Visitor Attractions.[50]

The ongoing importance of cultural attractions is matched by the growing appeal of Birmingham as a shopping destination, a recent phenomenon as made clear by Gerard Seenan of the *Guardian* in 2004:

> Think retail glamour and Birmingham may not spring to mind, but the Midlands city was yesterday named the third best place to shop in Britain – a jump of 10 places in a year. Birmingham's new £500m Bullring shopping centre has propelled it into the top three shopping destinations, in a list compiled by Experian, behind the West End of London and Glasgow. After struggling for years to attract big-name shops to Birmingham's centre, investment in the Bullring has finally brought in the retail giants.

Seenan stressed that 'in jumping so far up the shopping league so quickly, Birmingham has leapfrogged northern cities such as Leeds and Manchester, which have become famed for their shopping in recent years'. That it had done so was thanks to the reinvention of the Bull Ring through visionary new investment as well as 'the bizarrely futuristic Selfridges store. Inspired, appropriately enough, by a Paco Rabanne dress, the store is covered by 15,000 aluminium discs.'[51]

Since its sudden rise, Birmingham has consolidated its reputation as a world-class shopping centre, so much so that in 2015 Gemma Bowes of the *Guardian* asserted that 'Brum is a great city to head to for the January sales, with a huge number of shops to trawl. Add into the mix fun and varied restaurants and nightlife, plus

The Custard Factory, where young artists, actors and musicians convene, is located on the site of the former Bird's Custard manufactory in Digbeth.
Courtesy of Marketing Birmingham

The interior of Selfridges, opened as part of the redeveloped Bullring complex in 2003, added to the appeal of Birmingham as a shopping destination.
Courtesy of Marketing Birmingham

a decent arts scene, and this unfairly maligned city ticks all the boxes for an indulgent quick break, as well as being widely accessible for a large proportion of the population.' She highlighted modern developments such as The Mailbox, 'an old Royal Mail sorting office turned designer mall, featuring Harvey Nichols, Hugo Boss and Emporio Armani', as well as the Great Western Arcade, 'a restored Victorian gem with a wide variety of retailers – everything from designer shops to cigar and whisky parlours'.[52]

In September 2015, with the opening of Grand Central shopping centre above the revamped New Street station, Birmingham became the only location outside London to boast a John Lewis, a Selfridges and a Harvey Nichols department store. John Murray Brown of the *Financial Times* emphasized that Birmingham City Council had played a vital role in this development through having bought the Pallasades, the previous shopping centre above the old New Street station. It did so to facilitate Grand Central, which it envisioned as the retail link between the more mass market Bullring Centre and the high-end Mailbox and also as a means to regenerate the south side of the city centre. To achieve these aims the council worked hard to secure John Lewis as the anchor of the new development.[53]

After a long period of job losses and a depressing economic outlook, and also a deeper recession in 2008/09 than almost any other British city, in September 2015 Andy Bounds of the *Financial Times* pronounced that Birmingham was not only growing again but was 'bouncing back more strongly too'. Billions in property investment and the prospect of HS2 had 'recast a manufacturing powerhouse into a hub for professional services and retail with jobs growth fastest in the remodelled city centre'. Yet Bounds was also aware that 'advanced manufacturing industry remains the bedrock of the economy'.[54] Indeed in 2010, SEMTA, the Sector Skills Council for Science, Engineering and Manufacturing Technologies, identified Birmingham as the English local authority with the largest number of firms involved in 'leading edge technology sectors' – electronics, marine, aerospace and other engineering activities. It was also the foremost area of employment for mature engineering.[55]

Tufnol Composites Ltd of Perry Barr exemplifies the concept of advanced manufacturing. Formed in the mid-1920s, it manufactures laminates and other composite materials for electrical insulation and general engineering purposes and it works with leading companies such as GKN Aerospace, BAE Systems, Rolls Royce and Airbus UK. It was one of the first firms in Birmingham to sign up to the SC21 Supply Chain programme, which aims to increase the competitiveness of the aerospace and defence industry in the UK, while in 2015 it manufactured a unique cotton fabric reinforced laminate that was specified and installed by architectural engineers working on the redevelopment of New Street station.[56] This particular laminate was specified for 'its combined properties of excellent mechanical strength, rigidity, toughness, machinability and low friction. It provided a simple and cost effective method to [counter] natural corrosion in steelwork by isolating dissimilar metals and preventing destructive, corrosion-inducing electrical currents from flowing.'[57]

By far the biggest employer in the manufacturing sector in Birmingham is Jaguar Land Rover. A British multinational automotive company, it is a wholly owned subsidiary of India's Tata Motors and develops and manufactures the iconic Jaguar and Land Rover vehicles. Employing 32,000 people globally, the company supports more than 210,000 jobs in the UK through its supply chain, dealer network and wider economy.[58] In Birmingham it has an advanced manufacturing plant at Castle Bromwich. Over 3,000 people were employed there in 2013 and it boasts body shops, paint and final assembly lines for all models, and a press shop that operates 24 hours a day. It is also equipped with advanced aluminium body construction facilities and almost 340 body construction robots.[59] Jaguar Land Rover made a significant investment of £200 million in the plant to prepare for the launch of the all-new Jaguar F-Type Coupe range in 2014. A year later the announcement was made that the company was investing 'more than £450 million in Castle Bromwich – including the most significant boost to the plant in a generation' to turn it into a world-class hub for aluminium cars, building the next generation XF.[60]

The importance of advanced manufacturing is emphasized by the development of the Advanced Manufacturing Hub (AMH) in Aston, close to Jaguar Land Rover and with ready access to the motorway network. A joint venture of Birmingham City Council with the Homes and Communities Agency, it is one of six economic zones promoted by the council to fast-track economic development. Made possible with a £1 million investment through the Greater Birmingham and Solihull Local Enterprise Partnership (GBSLEP) City Deal, it is expected to create up to 3,000 jobs after reclamation works are completed.[61] HydraForce Hydraulics, with its headquarters in the USA, was the first company to commit to the Hub and in 2015 its 220 workers moved into a 120,000 square foot purpose-built facility. The maker of electrohydraulic controls then announced plans to almost double its workforce to 500 in the next three years.[62] It will be joined from 2017 by German-owned Guhring, which is investing £12 million to become the second foreign company to locate to the Advanced Manufacturing Hub. A precision engineering firm, it supplies companies such as BMW, Ford, JLR, Nissan, Airbus and BAE Systems and its move will create 50 new jobs as well as safeguarding a further 75. Importantly Guhring's factory will accommodate both research and development as well as full manufacturing processes.[63]

Extraenergy, a German power supplier, is another recent investor in Birmingham. It has 500,000 customers and is moving its 400 staff to bigger offices in Birmingham.[64] There is no doubt that foreign companies such as this are increasingly attracted to a city that is changing positively. Yet for all this optimism, the city continues to face serious challenges from the closure of large factories and the loss of mass employment in manufacturing in the 1980s, as Bounds also recognized in his *Financial Times* article. At 21 per cent, the city had 'a greater proportion of working age residents with no qualifications than the average for England of 15 per cent'. Moreover, even though the city's gross value added – its contribution to economic growth – rose to 4.2 per cent in 2013, 'at £22,033 per head, it remains below the national average of £23,755. That is because only 62 per cent of the working age population is employed.'[65] David Bailey, professor of industrial strategy at Aston Business School, agrees that a shortage of skills is a cause for concern for the West Midlands auto industry in particular but asserts that so too is a lack of land.[66]

There is a real need to act decisively with regard to training in skills across a variety of sectors because it is those without skills who are most likely to suffer unemployment. That problem disproportionately affects people from black, minority and ethnic (BME) communities and younger citizens, as was made obvious in a study by brap, an equalities think tank. At the end of March 2012, 19.2 per cent of economically active BME people in Birmingham were unemployed compared to

10.2 per cent of white people. As for youth unemployment, it was particularly high in Birmingham, standing at 31.1 per cent in March 2012 compared to 21.1 per cent across the whole of England.[67] These discouraging figures emphasize the urgent need for economic growth to extend more quickly and strongly from the city centre and to the deprived neighbourhoods of Birmingham.

Congestion is another problem, and will be addressed by the new West Midlands Combined Authority which will have the power to take decisions on the regional economy and transportation infrastructure at the appropriate scale. This body will also provide an opportunity for the devolution of powers and budgets to a local level and allow strategic planning, including satisfying housing need in a more coherent fashion. Moreover, the Combined Authority will have the means to encourage employment opportunities in sectors of economic growth such as digital media, the creative industries, ICT, and financial and legal services.

An ability to attract international companies like HydraForce Hydraulics will be crucial to the success of the Combined Authority as much as to Birmingham, because such firms create highly skilled jobs in high-value sectors of the economy. Fortunately the city has begun to reap economic rewards from this strategy. As John Murray Brown of the *Financial Times* stressed in September 2015, figures show that 'it is growing faster than any other large UK city, with greater levels of foreign investment, and a better export performance'.[68] Roger Wood, director of Midven, a venture capital firm based in Birmingham, highlighted another important factor in Birmingham's recovery in a revealing article in the *Guardian*. In 2013 the city 'topped the new startup list with more companies (16,281) being launched here than in any other UK city outside of London'. Crucially, technology start-ups, especially, were thriving and 'a flourishing tech community exists at the Innovation Birmingham Campus, where 38,000 square feet of open work space promotes mobile working for startups'.[69]

Wood drew further attention to 'a generation of young entrepreneurs, such as Nick Holzherr (of The Apprentice fame), who are leading a bow-wave of pioneering digital enterprises like Birmingham-based Whisk, a successful grocery shopping list app integrated into the online delivery operations of Tesco and Waitrose'.[70] His optimism that Birmingham and the West Midlands 'has a growing momentum and feels like an exciting and innovative place to be' was shared by Francesca Steele, who claimed of Birmingham that 'it's hip and affordable and young professionals are moving there'.[71]

The importance of encouraging entrepreneurs and enhancing Birmingham's strength in key sectors such as professional and financial services, digital media, ICT and the creative industries is a key motivator for the City Centre Enterprise Zone. This includes the Birmingham Science Park Aston (BSPA), founded as Aston Science Park in 1982 and the UK's third oldest science park; the new Beorma Quarter in Digbeth with its plans for the city's tallest building; Birmingham Smithfield, which will transform the wholesale markets site into a world-class family zone; and 'Paradise', the £500 million regeneration of Paradise Circus, which was begun in 2015 and is scheduled for completion in 2026.[72] The latter is a huge and imaginative scheme that involves the demolition of the old Central Library and Paradise Forum shopping centre to be replaced with new office blocks, a cycle hub, landscaping and a highway system.[73]

When Paradise is finished Birmingham's city centre will have been transformed. Indeed change has been a constant in the city's history and that awareness of the need to embrace change is encapsulated in the city's motto of 'Forward', which was adopted in 1838. A second constant is the verve of Birmingham's people, something that captivated William Hutton, Birmingham's first historian when he first visited in 1741.[74] In 2012 Mark Vanhoenacker of the *New York Times* was similarly impressed: 'With an only-in-Britain tapestry of vividly multiethnic neighborhoods, a post-industrial urbanity that's gentrifying before your eyes and a food scene that can't be ignored, Birmingham is no longer simply flyover country. Welcome to England's heartland metropolis: big-shouldered, friendly and fun.'[75]

'Come Forward into the Light'. Change and transformation are encapsulated in Birmingham's motto, 'Forward'. The motto and the city's arms, supported by art and industry, are represented in a stained glass window at Birmingham Museum & Art Gallery.
Photograph by Avatarthugee, Wikimedia Commons

Notes

1   The Office for National Statistics (ONS) estimated that Birmingham's resident population was 1,092,330 in 2013, an increase of 107,700 (10.9 per cent) since 2001. Analysis of the statistics showed that there were fewer people in the older age groups than in the younger, emphasizing that Birmingham has a youthful age profile. 'Mid-2013 Mid-year Population Estimates BDB2015/02', Birmingham Demographic Briefing, 2014, 1–2.

2   Sindy Chan, 'A thousand trades, a thousand tales', *China Daily*, 5 October 2013.

3   B. Faujas de St-Fond, *A Journey through England and Scotland to the Hebrides in 1784. Volume Two* (Cambridge, 2007 [1799]), 346.

4   C. Dickens, *The Pickwick Papers* (Wordsworth Classics edn, Hertfordshire, 2000 [1837]), 655.

5   A. Duggan, *A Sense of Occasion. Mendelssohn in Birmingham 1846* (Studley, 1998), 1.

6   Charles A. Vince, *History of the Corporation of Birmingham, Volume 3* (Birmingham, 1902), 382.

7   O. Šourek, *Antonín Dvořák: Letters and Reminiscences* (Prague, 1954), 95.

8   G.C. Allen, *The Industrial Development of Birmingham and the Black Country 1860–1927* (rev. edn, New York, 1966 [1929]), 247.

9   Ibid., 265–6.

10 C. Chinn, *Birmingham. The Great Working City* (Birmingham, 1994), 60; and E. Hopkins, *Birmingham. The Making of the Second City 1850–1939* (Stroud, 2001), 38.

11 Chinn, *Birmingham*, 58–9; Hopkins, *Birmingham*, 39.

12 C. Chinn and S. Dyson, *'We Ain't Going Away!' The Battle for Longbridge* (Studley, 2000), 11–12, 16.

13 Hopkins, *Birmingham*, 38; Chinn, *Birmingham*, 56–7, 61–2.

14 Hopkins, *Birmingham*, 38, 42.

15 Chinn, *Birmingham*, 110–11.

16 'Areas of Deprivation – Birmingham City Council', www.birmingham.gov.uk (accessed 31 March 2016).

17 P. Cheeseright, 'The inheritors of Chamberlain', *Financial Times*, 18 October 1991.

18 C. Monin, 'Royaume-Uni: le nouveau souffle de Birmingham', *Le Parisien*, 30 April 2015.

19 T. Service, 'The country's best hall for orchestral music? No contest: Birmingham's Symphony Hall', *The Guardian*, 12 January 2012; see also T. Grimley, *Symphony Hall – A Dream Realised* (Birmingham, 2014).

20 'The History of Brindleyplace', http://www.brindleyplace.com/ (accessed 31 March 2015).

21 G. Brown, 'Eyes of banking world on Birmingham as Deutsche Bank expands', *Birmingham Post*, 3 July 2014.

22 Ibid.

23 The Midland Bank name was replaced in 1999.

24 G. Brown, 'Work starts on new HSBC home in Birmingham', *Birmingham Post*, 8 September 2015.

25 T. Jones, 'Arena Central's first phase poised to get green light', *Birmingham Post*, 5 August 2014.

26 *Greater Birmingham. Making Business Happen* (Birmingham, 2014), 13.

27 *Profile of Birmingham's Business and Professional Services Sector* (Birmingham, 2011), 8.

28 Ibid., 5.

29 T. Jones, 'New chapter for Wragge Lawrence Graham & Co.', *Birmingham Post*, 22 February 2016; Chinn, *Birmingham*, 118.

30 *Profile of Birmingham's Business*, 5.

31 Oxford Economics, *The Impact of the University of Birmingham* (Oxford, 2013), 3–4.

32 G. Brown, 'International interest in city life science push', *Birmingham Post*, 23 November 2013.

33 *Greater Birmingham*.

34 Ibid., 12.

35 'Birmingham New Street Station opens to passengers', http://www.networkrailmediacentre.co.uk/news/ (accessed 7 April 2015).

36 C. Moss, 'Refurb in review: Birmingham New Street redevelopment', *Daily Telegraph*, 28 October 2015.

37 'Birmingham New Street Station'.

38 J. Walker, 'HS2 high speed rail's national headquarters opens in Birmingham', *Birmingham Mail*, 4 February 2016; 'HS2 Proposals and Benefits', http://www.birmingham.gov.uk/ (accessed 7 April 2015).

39 T. Jones, 'Go ahead for new National College for High Speed Rail', *Birmingham Post*, 5 February 2016.

40 N. Elkes, 'Curzon Street HS2 Masterplan set for green light', *Birmingham Post*, 21 July 2015.

41 T. Jones, 'Midland Metro extension will complete in 2016', *Birmingham Post*, 10 November 2015.

42 G. Smith, 'Birmingham Airport runway extension ready next week', *Business Traveller*, 23 April 2014; A. Richards, 'Airbus A380 arrives at Birmingham Airport for first historic passenger flight', *Birmingham Mail*, 27 March 2016.

43 https://birminghamairport.co.uk/about-us/doing-business-with-us/airlines/ (accessed 7 April 2016).

44 B. Hurst, 'Birmingham booming as international tourists flock to city', *Birmingham Mail*, 21 May 2015.

45 E. Birchley, 'Investment helps drive recovery outside London', 27 October 2015, http://news.sky.com/video/1577202/birmingham-boost-to-economy (accessed 7 April 2016).

46 'Birmingham named top city for business events', November 2015, http://www.bqlive.co.uk/2015/11/30/birmingham-named-top-city-for-business-events/ (accessed 7 April 2016); http://centreofenterprise.com/2015/12/08/birminghams-visitor-economy-to-hit-all-time-high-in-2015/ (accessed 7 April 2016).

47 D. Bentley, 'Millions of visitors expected at Birmingham's German Christmas Market', *Birmingham Mail*, 31 October 2015.

48 J. Doward, 'Michelin stars are icing on the cake for the Yummy Brummies', *The Observer*, 4 October 2015.

49 J. Earle-Levine, 'Birmingham instead of London', *New York Magazine*, 25 October 2013.

50 B. Gibbons and G. Brown, 'Library of Birmingham named one of 10 most popular attractions in country', *Birmingham Mail*, 16 March 2015.

51 G. Seenan, 'Birmingham soars up the shopping list', *The Guardian*, 3 March 2004.

52 G. Bowes, 'Let's go to … Birmingham', *The Guardian*, 6 January 2015.

53 J.M. Brown, 'Regeneration and quality woo savvy shoppers to Birmingham', *Financial Times*, 28 September 2015.

54 A. Bounds, 'Reversing industrial decline has been a priority in Birmingham', *Financial Times*, 28 September 2015.

55 SEMTA, *England Report Sector Skills Assessment for Science, Engineering and Manufacturing Technologies* (2010), 19–20.

56 Birmingham City Council and Business Birmingham, *Profile of Birmingham's Advanced Manufacturing Sector* (Birmingham, 2010), 8.

57 'Birmingham New St. redevelopment utilises Tufnol components', http://www.tufnol.com/press.aspx (accessed 8 April 2016).

58 http://www.jaguarlandrover.com/gl/en/about-us/ (accessed 7 April 2015).

59 http://www.jaguarlandrover.com/gl/en/about-us/news/2013/11/28/jaguar-f-type-coupe-bursts-out-of-castle-bromwich-plant/ (accessed 7 April 2015).

60 G. Brown, 'Jaguar Land Rover to invest £450m in Castle Bromwich factory to build new XF', *Birmingham Mail*, 24 March 2015.

61 T. Jones, 'Advanced Manufacturing Hub ready for development', *Birmingham Post*, 21 January 2015.

62 G. Brown, 'Recruitment drive as HydraForce moves into new Birmingham plant', *Birmingham Post*, 12 August 2015.

63 G. Brown, 'Guhring to invest £12m in Advanced Manufacturing Hub base', *Birmingham Post*, 29 July 2015.

64 Bounds, 'Reversing industrial decline'

65 Ibid.

66 A. Sharman, 'Skills and land shortages hold back West Midlands car industry', *Financial Times*, 25 September 2015.

67 brap, 'Birmingham economy and jobs overview and scrutiny committee inquiry: closing the skills gap', August, 2012, www.brap.org.uk/component/docman/.../81-bhamskillsgapbrapresponse (accessed 16 April 2016).

68 Brown, 'Regeneration and quality woo savvy shoppers'.

69 'Make it the Midlands: why the UK's centre is ripe for startups', http://www.theguardian.com/media-network/media-network-blog/2014/apr/04/midlands-uk-startups-london-birmingham (accessed 8 April 2015).

70 Ibid.

71 F. Steele, 'Birmingham finds a new hip identity', *The Times*, 5 December 2014.

72 http://www.ukspa.org.uk/members/bspa (accessed 8 April 2016); N. Elkes, 'Beorma Quarter building work to start early next year', *Birmingham Post*, 11 December 2015; and G. Brown, 'Replay: Birmingham Smithfield plans for world-class family zone in the city centre', *Birmingham Mail*, 16 March 2016.

73 T. Jones, 'Road to "Paradise" mapped out as 11 years of building begins', *Birmingham Post*, 18 December 2014.

74 W. Hutton, *An History of Birmingham* (Birmingham, 1783), 60.

75 M. Vanhoenacker, '36 Hours: Birmingham, England', *New York Times*, 26 January 2012.

Birmingham Timeline

Early and medieval period

c.500,000–4000 BC	Existence of flint tools provides archaeological evidence for the first people – hunters and gatherers – in the Birmingham area
c.1500–1000 BC	The survival of burnt mounds confirms the presence of human settlement in the local area
c.300 BC	Radiocarbon dating of grains has revealed evidence for arable farming
late 40s–50s AD	Building of Roman fort at Metchley
c.600–700	Likely arrival of the first Anglo-Saxons in the Birmingham area
1066	Norman Conquest
1086	Domesday Book: first mention of Birmingham in a written document
1166	Birmingham's first market charter granted
1263	First documentation for Birmingham's parish church: St Martin's in the Bull Ring, though there was probably a church on the site beforehand
1296	Borough Rental provides detailed information on Birmingham's inhabitants
1344–45	A second Borough Rental provides additional information on Birmingham's population
1379	The poll tax return of that year provides the first evidence of metalworking in the town

1500–1800

1538	John Leland describes Birmingham as an industrial town of 'smiths and cutlers'
1552	Foundation of King Edward VI's Free Grammar School.

1643	Battle of Birmingham during the Civil War. Birmingham is sacked and burned by the Royalists under Prince Rupert
1656	The first known pictorial representation of Birmingham is included in William Dugdale's *Antiquities of Warwickshire*
1686	Date of the first Settlement Certificates for Birmingham, which are important for understanding migration to the town until 1726
1715	Consecration of St Philip's Anglican church
1742	Birmingham's first newspaper, *Aris's Birmingham Gazette*, published
1765	Opening of Matthew Boulton's Soho Manufactory in Handsworth and the general hospital in Birmingham. Formation of Lloyd's Bank
1766	Probable first meeting of the Lunar Society
1769	Opening of Birmingham's first canal
1773	Establishment of Birmingham's Assay Office by Act of Parliament to maintain the quality of local silverware
1782	First edition of William Hutton's *An History of Birmingham* published
1783	Formation of Birmingham Commercial Committee, the forerunner of the Chamber of Commerce
1791	'Church and King' or Priestley riots
1793	The beginning of a lengthy war with France which retards the growth of the local economy

1800–49

1800	First edition of Bisset's *Magnificent Directory* of Birmingham
1813	Creation of Birmingham's Gun-Barrel Proof House to test the quality of guns made locally
1819	Opening of Hazelwood School by Matthew and Rowland Hill
1820s–50s	Beginnings of substantial Irish immigration to Birmingham
1825	The Female Society for the Relief of British Negro Slaves is created to campaign against slavery
1829	Birmingham Society of Artists (later Royal Birmingham Society of Artists) founded
1831–32	Newhall Hill rallies organized by the Birmingham Political Union, led by the banker Thomas Attwood, to campaign for parliamentary reform
1832	Election of Birmingham's first MPs: Thomas Attwood and Joshua Scholefield
1834	Opening of Birmingham Town Hall

1838	Opening of London to Birmingham Railway and Curzon Street station
1838	Birmingham secures its Charter of Incorporation, which leads to the formation of its first town council
1839	The 'Bull Ring' or Chartist riots
1841	Opening of Queen's Hospital, Birmingham's first purpose-built teaching hospital
1849	Birmingham's Industrial Exhibition held in Bingley Hall, a precursor of the Great Exhibition

1850–99

1851	The Great Exhibition at the Crystal Palace in London's Hyde Park is a showcase for Birmingham's manufacturing industry
1852	St Chad's Roman Catholic Cathedral consecrated, the first Roman Catholic cathedral consecrated in England since the Reformation. Opening of Snow Hill station
1854	Opening of New Street station
1856	Singers Hill synagogue built
1857	Founding of the *Birmingham Post*
1861	Creation of the Birmingham Small Arms Company in Small Heath to consolidate gun manufacturing under one roof
1866	Publication of Samuel Timmins, *The Resources, Products and Industrial History of Birmingham*
1869	Creation of the National Education League to campaign for universal, free and unsectarian education
1870	Founding of the *Birmingham Mail*
1871	Opening of Birmingham's Women's Hospital
1873	Joseph Chamberlain becomes mayor of Birmingham,
1874	Aston Villa Football Club formed
1875	Beginning of Birmingham City Football Club
1876	Establishment of Edgbaston High School, the first secondary school for girls in Birmingham. Joseph Chamberlain becomes a Birmingham MP
1879	Richard and George Cadbury's chocolate factory opened in Bournville
1880s–90s	Emergence of Birmingham's Italian and Jewish quarters
1885	Opening of Birmingham Museum and Art Gallery. Creation of Birmingham Municipal School of Art
1889	Birmingham granted city status by Queen Victoria
1891	Opening of the Victoria Law Courts
1890s	Decline of older industries such as button making and japanned ware

1900	Establishment of the University of Birmingham
1904	Completion of Elan Valley scheme which brought fresh water from Wales to Birmingham
1905	Establishment of Austin Motor Company at Longbridge
1909	Height of suffragette agitation in the city
1914	The beginning of the First World War stimulates munitions production. During the war Birmingham becomes a major centre for trauma surgery. Death of Joseph Chamberlain
1916	Creation of Birmingham's Municipal Savings Bank
1919–21	Austen Chamberlain, eldest son of Joseph Chamberlain, serves as Chancellor of the Exchequer
1919–39	Growth of companies making cars, motorbikes, bicycles and electrical engineering products
1920	Beginning of City of Birmingham Symphony Orchestra
1922	Herbert Austin brings out the Austin Seven
1924–29	Austen Chamberlain serves as Foreign Secretary
1925	Opening of the Hall of Memory
1926	General Strike
1937–40	Neville Chamberlain, youngest son of Joseph Chamberlain and former Lord Mayor of Birmingham, serves as Prime Minister
1935	Appointment of Herbert Manzoni as city surveyor. He leads clearance and redevelopment schemes in much of Birmingham over the next three decades
1939	Opening of the Medical School and Queen Elizabeth Hospital in Edgbaston. The beginning of the Second World War stimulates production of aircraft and other war industries
1940–41	Birmingham experiences heavy German bombing which inflicts severe casualties and damage to homes and industries

1950s	Expansion of motor vehicle manufacturing and related production
1950s–60s	Clearance of Victorian back-to-back houses and redevelopment of Birmingham's central districts
1950s–60s	Large-scale migration to Birmingham from Ireland, the West Indies, India, Pakistan and what would become Bangladesh
1959	Launch of the Mini, designed by Alex Issigonis at Longbridge
1964	Bull Ring Centre, the culmination of Manzoni's plans for remodelling the city, opened

1967	Opening of the rebuilt New Street station
1972	Gravelly Hill interchange or 'Spaghetti Junction' opened
1974	Opening of the Central Library
1977	National Exhibition Centre opened
1980s	Recession: decline of manufacturing and rise in unemployment
1980s	Arrival of Vietnamese refugees
1982	Birmingham Central Mosque opened
1990s	Growth of the service sector and expansion of Birmingham Airport
1991	Opening of the National Indoor Arena, International Convention Centre and Symphony Hall
1993	Beginning of the Brindleyplace development

2000–

2000s	Development of manufacturing industries based on new technologies
1990s and 2000s	Migration of refugees from Bosnia, Iraq, Iran and several African states and migrants from new European Union member countries in Eastern Europe
2003	Opening of the new Bullring
2013	Opening of the new Library of Birmingham
2015	Opening of Grand Central, the replacement for New Street station
2016	Demolition of Paradise Forum and the Central Library

Birmingham Population Figures

Before 1801, the size of Birmingham's population can only be estimated. After that, returns from the national Census, which was held every ten years except for 1941, provide systematically collected demographic evidence. These figures, however, are not totally reliable and probably underestimate certain groups of people such as young men and migrants.

Date	Population
1066	Less than 100
1300	1,000
1538	1,300
1650	5,472
1700	15,032
1731	23,286
1778	42,250
1785	52,250
1801	73,670
1811	85,753
1821	106,722
1831	146,986
1841	182,922
1851	232,638
1861	296,076
1871	343,787
1881	400,774
1891	478,113
1901	522,204
1911	525,833
1921	919,444
1931	1,002,603
1939	995,039 (estimate)
1951	1,112,685
1961	1,107,187
1971	1,014,670
1981	1,006,527
1991	961,041
2001	977,087
2011	1,074,300

Further Reading

The extensive endnotes for each chapter provide references to further reading, so the list of texts below is simply a guide to general books on the history of Birmingham. Carl Chinn (ed.), *Birmingham: Bibliography of a City* (Birmingham, 2003), contains detailed themed chapters which list sources published before 2003. *Midland History* (formerly the *University of Birmingham Historical Journal*) is the main academic journal for articles on local history.

Two websites, www.revolutionaryplayers.org.uk and www.historywm.com, contain articles, films and podcasts relating to the history of Birmingham. The *Oxford Dictionary of National Biography* is an excellent online biographical resource. British History Online: http://www.british-history.ac.uk/, founded by the Institute of Historical Research and History of Parliament Trust, is a digital library of printed primary and secondary sources. Much recent research is contained in PhD theses which can be accessed via the British Library's EThOS service: http://ethos.bl.uk/.

The Library of Birmingham is the main location for publications, archives, photographs, films and oral histories which illuminate the history of the city. A substantial collection of local archival material is also held at the University of Birmingham's Cadbury Research Library. The various Birmingham museums display aspects of the history of the locality and hold many collections of artefacts, images and oral histories. 'Birmingham: its people and its history', a permanent exhibition in the Museum and Art Gallery, is the best visual introduction to the history of Birmingham from earliest times to the present.

General texts

A, Briggs, *History of Birmingham vol. II, Borough and City, 1865–1938* (London and New York, 1952). For many years the standard text for late nineteenth- and early twentieth-century political history, but its findings have been modified by later research.

G.E. Cherry, *Birmingham: A Study in Geography, History and Planning* (Chichester, 1994). A general guide to the changing local landscape and the forces that shaped it.

C. Chinn, *Birmingham: The Great Working City* (Birmingham, 2002). A readable and informative overview of aspects of local economic life.

R.K. Dent, *Old and New Birmingham* (Birmingham, 1880). This substantial nineteenth-century history is still a point of reference for those interested in local history. Its approach to interpreting the history of the town has strongly influenced contemporary perceptions of the nature of Birmingham's past.

M. Dick, *Birmingham: A History of the City and its People* (Birmingham, 2005). A short, well-illustrated introduction for the newcomer to Birmingham's history.

A. Foster, *Pevsner Architectural Guides: Birmingham* (New Haven, CT, and London, 2005). A well-illustrated guide to the architecture and history of local buildings.

C. Gill, *History of Birmingham vol. I, Manor and Borough to 1865* (London and New York, 1952). A standard text for many years on the early political and administrative history of the town, but like Briggs's monograph, its findings have been modified by subsequent investigation.

M. Hodder, *Birmingham: The Hidden History* (Stroud, 2004). A survey of how archaeological evidence is important for understanding local history.

E. Hopkins, *The Rise of the Manufacturing Town: Birmingham and the Industrial Revolution* (Stroud, 2nd edn, 1998). A thoroughly researched economic and social history of the eighteenth and early nineteenth centuries.

E. Hopkins, *The Making of the Second City 1850–1939* (Stroud, 2001). A thoroughly researched economic and social history of the late nineteenth and early twentieth centuries.

W. Hutton, *An History of Birmingham* (Birmingham, 1783 and thereafter). The first history of Birmingham and a useful guide to the eighteenth-century town: there are various editions and it has been republished in the twentieth century and is also available online.

P.M. Jones, *Industrial Enlightenment: Science, Technology and Culture in Birmingham and the West Midlands, 1760–1820* (Manchester, 2008). An important academic study of Birmingham during the Industrial Revolution.

W.B. Stephens (ed.), *A History of the County of Warwick. Volume VII: The City of Birmingham*, Victoria County History (London, 1964). A useful source for detailed and well-referenced information on various aspects of local history.

A Sutcliffe and R. Smith, *History of Birmingham vol. III, Birmingham 1939–1970* (Oxford, 1974). A study of Birmingham in the mid-twentieth century.

J. Uglow, *The Lunar Men: The Friends who Made the Future, 1730–1810* (London, 2002). A detailed and readable collective biography of Birmingham's most famous group of intellectuals, inventors and industrialists.

C. Upton, *A History of Birmingham* (Chichester, 1993). A detailed, readable and illuminating account of the history of the town.

R. Ward, *City-State and Nation. Birmingham's Political History 1830–1940* (Chichester, 2005). A thoroughly researched political history of the nineteenth and early twentieth centuries.

Notes on Contributors

Caroline Archer-Parré is Professor of Typography and Director of the Typographic Hub at the Birmingham Institute of Art & Design, Birmingham City University, where she works to promote the history, theory and practice of typography (see www.typographichub.org). She is the author of *The Kynoch Press: The Anatomy of a Printing House* (British Library Publishing, 2000), *Tart Cards: London's Illicit Advertising Art* (Mark Batty, 2003) and *Paris Underground* (Mark Batty, 2005). She is co-editing a forthcoming book on John Baskerville. She is a frequent contributor to the trade and academic press.

Dr Steven Bassett was a Senior Lecturer in the University of Birmingham's Department of History until 2011. He specializes in the Anglo-Saxon and later medieval history and landscape development of the West Midlands. His publications include articles in *Midland History* entitled 'Anglo-Saxon Birmingham' (2000) and 'Birmingham before the Bull Ring' (2001).

Carl Chinn, MBE, PhD, is Professor of Community History at the University of Birmingham and history advisor for the schools of Perry Beeches The Academy. He is a social historian with a national profile, a newspaper columnist, public speaker, writer and charity fundraiser. Professor Chinn is the author of 31 books, including studies of working-class housing, urban working-class life, working-class women's lives, manufacturing, Birmingham, the Black Country and ethnic minorities.

Dr Matt Cole is a Teaching Fellow at the University of Birmingham and Deputy Convenor of the university's MA in West Midlands History. He is a Visiting Fellow of the Hansard Society, the author of *Democracy in Britain* (Edinburgh University Press, 2006), *Richard Wainwright, the Liberals and Liberal Democrats* (Manchester University Press, 2011) and *Political Parties in Britain* (Edinburgh University Press, 2012), and the Political Analyst for BBC Radio West Midlands.

Richard Cust is Professor of Early Modern History at the University of Birmingham. He is a specialist in Tudor and Stuart England, and has published a number of books and articles, the latest of which is *Charles I and the Aristocracy, 1625–1642* (Cambridge University Press, 2013). He is particularly interested in the local history of the midlands and is editor of the journal *Midland History*.

Dr Malcolm Dick is Director of the Centre for West Midlands History at the University of Birmingham and Editor-in-Chief of History West Midlands project (www.historywm.com). He managed the Revolutionary Players project, which created a website on the history of the West Midlands during the Industrial Revolution (www.revolutionaryplayers.org), and has written a history of refugees for Refugee Action and of Birmingham for Birmingham City Council. He has edited a book on Joseph Priestley and two on Matthew Boulton. Forthcoming publications are devoted to John Baskerville and James Watt.

Dr Sally Hoban is a design, antiques and art consultant, lecturer and writer with an interest in art, design and architecture in the West Midlands. She is the author of *Miller's Collecting Modern Design* (2001) and completed a PhD at the University of Birmingham on women in the Arts and Crafts Movement. Sally has contributed to the local, national and international press and has written arts reviews for *The Lancet*. She has broadcast on television, worked as Research Editor (Film) for *History West Midlands* (www.historywm.com) and is an accredited lecturer for the National Association of Decorative and Fine Arts Societies. She is working on a history of Birmingham Law Society.

Dr Mike Hodder was formerly Birmingham City Council's Planning Archaeologist and is Honorary Lecturer in Archaeology at the University of Birmingham. He has been involved in the investigation and management of sites and landscapes ranging from the prehistoric to post-medieval periods in Birmingham and its surroundings for over thirty years, including research into Bronze Age burnt mounds, excavations of prehistoric and Roman sites along the M6 Toll motorway, and the excavation and display of Metchley Roman fort. He has written two books and many articles and contributed to the West Midlands Archaeological Research Framework.

Richard Holt has been Professor of Medieval History at the University of Tromsø, Norway, since 2001. He was previously employed at the University of Birmingham. He has published extensively on English and Norwegian urban history and on technological change in the Middle Ages. He is currently working on *The Urban Transformation in England, 900–1200* (Ashgate).

Ann Hughes is Senior Research Fellow and Professor Emerita at Keele University, where she was Professor of Early Modern History. She is the author of *Politics, Society and Civil War in Warwickshire* (Cambridge University Press, 1987) and of many other articles and essays on the midlands in the seventeenth century. In recent years she has worked on religious debate and polemic, print culture, gender and radicalism with publications including *Gender and the English Revolution* (Routledge, 2011) and, edited with Thomas Corns and David Loewenstein, *The Complete Works of Gerrard Winstanley* (Oxford University Press, 2009).

Jonathan Reinarz is Professor of the History of Medicine at the University of Birmingham. He has published on the history of hospitals and medical education. His publications include *Health Care in Birmingham* (Boydell & Brewer, 2009), edited with C. Bonfield and T. Huguet-Termes, *Hospitals and Communities, 1100–1960* (Peter Lang, 2013) and edited with L. Schwarz, *Medicine and the Workhouse* (Rochester University Press, 2013). He is working on a history of medical education in provincial England, which focuses on five schools, including Birmingham.

Roger Ward is Visiting Professor of History at Birmingham City University. He completed a postgraduate thesis on tariff reform in Birmingham, 1877–1906, in 1971 at London University and was formerly Principal Lecturer in the Social Science Faculty at the University of Central England, where he was also course director of the largest part-time politics programme in the country. Among his publications are several articles in a variety of journals and magazines and *City-State and Nation: Birmingham's Political History c. 1830–1940* (Phillimore, 2005). He is working on a study of Joseph, Austen and Neville Chamberlain.

Ruth Watts is Professor Emerita of History of Education at the University of Birmingham. Her books include *Gender, Power and the Unitarians in England, 1760–1860* (Longman, 1997) and *Women in Science: A Social and Cultural History* (Routledge, 2007), for which she won the History of Education Society Book Prize in 2010. She has also written extensively on the history of education and of women in Birmingham, including co-writing 'Schooling and education in Birmingham' with Ian Grosvenor in Carl Chinn (ed.), *Birmingham: Bibliography of a City*. She is ex-President of the British History of Education Society.

Index

References to figures are given in italics